MARRIAGE AND THE FAMILY

MARRIAGE
AND
THE
FAMILY

A CRITICAL ANALYSIS
AND PROPOSALS FOR CHANGE
EDITED BY CAROLYN C. PERRUCCI
AND DENA B. TARG PURDUE UNIVERSITY

DAVID McKAY COMPANY, INC.
NEW YORK

MARRIAGE AND THE FAMILY
A Critical Analysis and Proposals for Change

Copyright © 1974 by David McKay Company, Inc.

International Standard Book Number: 0-679-30248-4
Library of Congress Catalog Card Number: 73-93038
Manufactured in the United States of America
Designed by Angela Foote

Acknowledgments

"The Contemporary Women's Movement: The Family and Social Change" by Dena B. Targ. Copyright © 1974 by Dena B. Targ.

"A Conflict Theory of Sexual Stratification" by Randall Collins is reprinted from *Social Problems* 19, no. 1 (Summer 1971) by permission of the author and *Social Problems*, copyright © 1971 by The Society for the Study of Social Problems.

"The Origin of the Family" by Kathleen Gough is reprinted from *Journal of Marriage and the Family* 33, no. 4 (November 1971) by permission of the author and *Journal of Marriage and the Family*, copyright © 1971 by National Council on Family Relations.

"Black Women 1970" by Nathan Hare and Julia Hare is reprinted from *Trans-action* 8, nos. 1 and 2 (November–December 1970) by permission of the author and *Trans-action*, copyright © 1970 by Trans-action, Inc.

"Welfare Is a Women's Issue" by Johnnie Tillmon is reprinted from *Ms.* 1, no. 1 (Spring 1972) by permission of the author and *Ms.*, copyright © 1972 by Majority Enterprises, Inc.

"To My White Working-class Sisters" by Debby D'Amico is reprinted from *Up From Under* 1, no. 2 (August/September 1970) by permission of the author and *Up From Under, A magazine by, for and about women*, 339 Lafayette St., New York, N.Y. 10012, copyright © 1970 by Deborah D'Amico.

"Is She or Isn't She? Is Jackie Oppressed?" by Bobbie Goldstone (now known as Bobbie Spalter-Roth) is reprinted from *off our backs* 1, no. 20 (April 15, 1971) by permission of the author and *off our backs*, copyright © 1971 by Bobbie Goldstone.

"On Sisterhood" by Dana Densmore is reprinted from *No More Fun and Games: A Journal of Female Liberation*, issue 2 (published February 1969; written December 1968) by permission of the author, copyright © 1968 by Dana Densmore.

To Alissa and Rebecca

Preface

The purpose of this collection of articles is to combine feminist values with a sociological perspective of marriage and the family in the present-day United States. The idea for this book grew out of the disjunction between our attitudes and experiences as relatively liberated women, wives and mothers, on the one hand, and some aspects of our training and experiences as sociologists of marriage and the family, on the other hand. We note that for some time feminist writers have been offering scholarly and imaginative critiques of women's situation in the family and the various constraints on their liberation. Until quite recently, however, many sociologists of marriage and the family, especially textbook authors, have tended to work under the influence of more traditional domain assumptions; to inaccurately and/or incompletely describe and analyze current marriage and family phenomena from a male perspective; and to search for limits in family form and sex roles in opposition to experimentation and innovation therein.

The functions that are now fulfilled typically by the nuclear family result primarily from women's enactment of the prescribed roles of wife and mother. In important respects, however, it is precisely these prescribed roles that limit women's freedom. As Juliet Mitchell forcefully argues, no matter how subordinate the situation of women may be within the occupational world, it is within the family—with the development of the feminine psyche and in the enactment of the roles of housewife and mother—that women experience the oppression that is theirs alone. The institutions of marriage and the family, moreover, are difficult spheres within which to effect social change. In discussing the phenomenon of inequality, Alice Rossi distinguishes forms and types of inequality. Forms of inequality range from explicit legal statute to social pressure. Types of inequality refer to the area of life, public or private, in which the inequality occurs. Creating change is increasingly more difficult as the form of inequality varies from legal statute to social pressure, and as the type of inequality varies from the public to the private sector. As Rossi indicates, therefore, it is less difficult to change laws that discriminate against women as workers, students, or citizens than it is to bring about social changes within the areas of marriage and the family.

In the spirit of Alvin Gouldner's call for a reflexive sociology, this book takes an explicitly partisan approach in the presentation and discussion of materials regarding marriage and the family. We hope that this collection will serve to acquaint the reader with feminist critiques of and alternatives to various aspects of marriage and the family and do so in such a way as to reveal the suffering of women as underdogs in our society and their active opposition to barriers to sex equality. The contrast between feminist material in this book and the traditional approach to this aspect of the discipline may further the definition, discussion, debate of, and research on, issues in the field, as well as encourage the growth and development of a family sociology that will relate more meaningfully to the private lives of current and future classes of college students.

Some articles in this book are empirically based; all exemplify a sociological imagination. We have featured alternatives to the existing inequality of sex roles and to the structure and functions of the ideal-typical nuclear family which would probably result in more positive consequences for women in society. Although the focus of the book, like the Women's Liberation Movement in general, is mainly a middle-class one, we have tried to include variations in the perspectives of modern women that are based on racial and social-class distinctions.

The collection is organized into four parts. The general Introduction discusses women's socialization, sexual and reproduction roles within marriage and the family as well as women's extrafamilial economic role. A feminist analysis of these four elements of woman's condition provides the framework around which the collection is organized. Part 1 discusses the family in societal context, including variation historically in the interrelation of sex roles and family structure and variation by race and social class in feminist perspectives on marriage and the family. Part 2 concerns the preparation of girls for adult roles, both traditional and otherwise, and considers sex-role socialization from birth to adulthood; attitudes toward sex expression; and birth control. In part 3, marital roles and some feminist alternatives are treated. The fourth part focuses on the functions typically performed by the family and some structural alternatives to the nuclear family for their fulfillment. It considers the perils and prospects at middle age of women who fill traditional as opposed to more innovative adult roles.

We would like to thank our parents, Kathleen M. and the late Clarence L. Cummings and Sylvia S. and Peter H. Epstein, for their support and encouragement. We are indebted to Robert Perrucci and Harry Targ for their helpfully innovative definitions of their colleague and husband roles, not only during the preparation of this collection, but generally. We could not possibly put into words the intellectual and personal contribution they have made to our lives. We express special thanks to Robert Perrucci for his counsel on many publishing matters and for making available to us a considerable amount of secretarial time. We are especially grateful to Jeanne Plumb for her excellent and efficient secretarial and editorial assistance during the past year. We are also indebted to Enid Satariano for her competent secretarial and editorial contributions during earlier stages of this project. We would like to thank Dr. Leonard Breen as head of the Purdue Department of Sociology and Anthropology for the resources made available to us in connection with the project. Finally, at David McKay, we express our appreciation for the interest and patience of Edward Artinian and the continuous support and assistance of Claudia Bepko.

Carolyn C. Perrucci
Dena B. Targ

Purdue University
West Lafayette, Indiana
January 1974

CONTENTS

B. Prospects for Middle Age 427

MARRIAGE AND THE FAMILY

A Feminist Critique
of Marriage and the Family:

An Introduction
During the course of history in the United States, structural differentiation has taken place whereby certain functions formerly carried out by the family were taken over by other specialized units in society, leaving the family with fewer functions and its adult members with altered roles. Although definitions of the family as well as characterizations of its current functions vary considerably among sociologists, the ideal-typical form of the family is nuclear, including parents and offspring; and the functions that urban middle-class families most commonly perform are generally posited as including socialization, sexual regulation, reproduction, and economic cooperation. It is also generally maintained that in a family of procreation the adult male is involved primarily in the economic sphere, while the adult female plays a more important role in the family itself. The middle-class wife-mother, then, has major responsibility for socializing children; is more "regulated" than her husband in terms of a norm of sexual exclusivity; bears a larger part of the reproductive burden; and is usually less involved than her husband in paid employment outside the home.

Woman's condition can be adequately understood and improved only through awareness and careful analysis of the complex interrelationships among the four elements of socialization, sexuality, reproduction, and production.[1] A feminist analy-

1. Juliet Mitchell, *Woman's Estate* (New York: Pantheon Books, 1971), pp. 99–151. Our analysis parallels that of Mitchell. The elements treated in two of the four parts, namely, those concerning women's sexuality and work, are comparable to two of the elements of women's condition as delineated by Mitchell. Two parts, however, deviate somewhat from her delineation. The first part, labeled Sexism, Socialization, and Family Roles, deals with the socialization function, but more broadly than Mitchell. The third part, Marriage and the Family, deals with several elements of woman's condition.

sis of these elements within the context of marriage and family life constitutes the substance of this reader and provides the organizing framework for this general introduction. The remainder of this introduction consists of four parts, each of which critically analyzes at least one element of woman's condition in the present-day United States. The elements are considered here in the order of their treatment in the reader, beginning with a discussion of sexism and its perpetuation through traditional sex-role socialization in our society. Female sexuality is the second element of woman's condition to be treated. The third section, Marriage and the Family, deals with many aspects of the roles of housewife and mother, including the sexual, reproductive, and socialization functions of women. Finally, the extrafamilial or work situation of women is considered.

Sexism, Socialization, and Family Roles

Sexism is the ideology of male supremacy. The concept is clearly analogous to that of "racism" and indicates the inferior status assigned by one sex to the other.[2] Sexism divides a society and keeps it divided along sex lines. Even in ideologically egalitarian societies, a belief in male supremacy is often disguised as the myth of "separate but equal"; that is, each sex has a different set of roles—with no hierarchy or stratification implied. According to this doctrine, the "natural" qualities of men fit them specially for pursuits in the economic world while women are assumed to have qualities best suited for expression in the family. Another common explanation for the sexual division of labor in modern societies is that the ascriptive differentiation of roles is the most efficient method of role allocation. According to this argument, even if it can be demonstrated that men and women are in all important respects equally capable of performing instrumental and expressive roles, it is simply more efficient to continue the present pattern.

This is a plausible argument from a short-term societal

---

2. Ibid., p. 64.

perspective. To reeducate both men and women so that both would and could participate in the occupational and familial sectors would be an expensive undertaking. Women, moreover, are often unemployed or underemployed within the present system, and even their full participation in the occupational sector would not immediately offset the short-run costs of resocialization and the decrease in male participation in the occupational sector. In the long run, however, national productivity might be drastically increased by the full employment of women as well as by the industrialization of domestic services.

The above arguments are probably irrelevant to individual families because they usually do not judge their efficiency in societal terms. Rather they consider the merits and negative aspects of various work and home time allocations according to the needs and desires of their individual family. Given the present social structure there can be little doubt that the "efficient" choice within most families would be for the male to assume the economic responsibilities and the female, the domestic responsibilities.[3]

Many groups in modern society are questioning the primacy of efficiency both as a personal and as a societal value. Today's college generation especially holds beliefs that may contradict or at least supersede economic efficiency. The first of these is a belief in personal growth which emphasizes individuality and self-fulfillment; the second is a belief in interpersonal relationships which emphasizes openness, honesty, and equality in all human relationships.[4]

Relegating women to a separate but equal sphere at best limits female horizons and stifles their personal growth. Channeling women into the housewife-mother role turns biology into destiny, and denies humanness to a large extent because it is the ability to reach beyond biology that constitutes humanness. Within the

---

3. Harriet Holter, *Sex Roles and Social Structure* (Oslo, Norway: Universitetsforlaget, 1970), pp. 28–32.

4. Sandra L. Bem and Daryl J. Bem, "Training the Woman to Know Her Place: The Power of a Non-conscious Ideology," *Women: A Journal of Liberation* 1, no. 1 (Fall 1969): 9. This article also appears as "Case Study of a Non-conscious Ideology: Training the Woman to Know Her Place," in *Beliefs, Attitudes, and Human Affairs*, ed. Daryl J. Bem (Belmont, Calif.: Brooks/Cole, 1970), pp. 89–99.

middle class especially, differentiation of roles by sex means that at birth the future of a female baby will be determined by her sex—she will be a wife and mother—while the primary occupation of a male baby will be determined more by his aptitudes and interests.

It would be unjust if women were simply channeled into separate but equal spheres. The real situation is worse, however, since separate usually is unequal and inferior; and the differentiation of roles is not exceptional in this respect. Women are considered inferior and consider themselves inferior in all aspects of their lives. When a woman leaves the "masculine" economic sector to assume the feminine role of housewife, for example, she devalues her self-concept—no matter how low the status of her former occupation. Jessie Bernard aptly describes the inferior evaluation of the housewife role compared to that of other occupations:

> from being a secretary, sales girl, teacher or nurse in her own right she becomes a housekeeper, an occupation that is classified in the labor market and in her own mind as menial and of low status. The apologetic "I'm just a housewife" that she tenders in reply to what she does illustrates how low her self-evaluation of her occupation is, no matter how loudly and defensively she proclaims her pleasure in it.[5]

Not only their primary occupation, but also the ability of women compared to men is judged as inferior. When a group of women college students evaluated a series of articles, for example, they rated identical articles lower when their authors were assumed to be female than when their authors were assumed to be male. This differential rating applied in all areas of expertise, including such traditionally female areas as home economics.[6]

That men are considered to be more valuable than women is suggested by the observation that when large numbers of women enter an occupation formerly the province of men, the average

---

5. Jessie Bernard, "The Paradox of the Happy Marriage," in *Woman in Sexist Society: Studies in Power and Powerlessness*, eds. Vivian Gornick and Barbara K. Moran (New York: Signet Books, 1972), p. 154.

6. Philip Goldberg, "Are Women Prejudiced Against Women?" *Trans-action* 5, no. 5 (April 1968): 28–30.

pay for that occupation decreases.[7] Further, men are often paid more than women for the same as well as different jobs which require comparable levels of effort, skill, and education.[8] Finally, when women have achieved excellence, even in nonfeminine roles, the achievement is sometimes not regarded positively. One study, for example, reports an overwhelmingly negative response on the part of college women to the description of a woman medical student whose grades placed her at the top of her class.[9]

Individually, as well as collectively, women are considered to be inferior by themselves as well as by men. Young women drop out of school to support their husbands—so that the husbands can complete their educations. Young women, irrespective of their own abilities, are more likely to put their husbands through graduate, medical, or law school than to obtain an advanced education themselves. Young women become nurses while their brothers become doctors; public school teachers while their brothers become college professors.

When women do achieve levels of education equal to that of their husbands, as is sometimes the case in dual-profession families, the accepted description is that the man has the major career, the wife has a subordinate occupation and responsibility for the house and children. When one family member must curtail other activities because of domestic demands, moreover, it is usually the wife.[10] Sex-role socialization thus effectively limits the options of women to the feminine role which is subordinate to the masculine role and consists primarily of "occupation: housewife." This process begins unsurprisingly in infancy, if not sooner. The stereotyping of babies by sex begins before birth: folk wisdom says that while in the womb boys kick their mothers

7. Dean D. Knudsen, "The Declining Status of Women: Popular Myths and the Failure of Functionalist Thought," *Social Forces* 48, no. 2 (December 1969): 188.

8. See in this volume the article by Carolyn Perrucci. See, in addition, Caroline Bird with Sara Welles Briller, *Born Female: The High Cost of Keeping Women Down* (New York: Pocket Books, 1969), pp. 62–64.

9. Matina Horner, "Fail: Bright Women," *Psychology Today* 3, no. 6 (November 1969): 36–38, 62. See also in this volume the summary of the Horner study by Joy D. Osofsky and Howard J. Osofsky, in their article "Androgyny as a Life Style."

10. See, for example, Margaret M. Poloma and T. Neal Garland, "The Married Professional Woman: A Study in the Tolerance of Domestication," *Journal of Marriage and the Family* 33, no. 3 (August 1971): 533–36.

more than girls. Certainly from the time of birth, children are treated differently according to their sex.[11] Boys are dressed in blue, girls in pink. Boys are tossed up in the air more; girls are talked to more. The examples are endless.

Girls are restricted not only in practice, but also by example. Cultural stereotypes are carried over into the fantasy world of picture books: boys are presented as active and girls are presented as passive figures. Similarly, girls are depicted indoors (with the implication that they are too timid to venture forth) performing domestic activities. "Picture books imply that women cannot exist without men. The role of most of the girls is defined in relation to that of the boys and men in their lives." [12] Adult women do not fare much better, for in most stories they are portrayed only as wives and mothers and even within these roles their activities are quite restricted.

When children leave picture books behind, what do they learn in school? The same old story. Elementary school reading books present little girls as the second sex:

> Girls often depend on boys when they are quite capable of handling the situation themselves. . . . Almost without exception females in the readers are subordinate to males.[13]

as self-sacrificing:

> Altruism is admirable. Everybody knows that. Yet in the readers, the altruism of girls is always tinged with self-abnegation. Girls' frequent efforts to help others are motivated by very generous and noble impulses, but such efforts always require a personal sacrifice which is presented as a normal thing. . . .
>
> Boys, when *they're* good, give up some time and energy for others but there is no sense of sacrifice. They are creating something new and not taking something away from themselves. They are *civic*-minded. . . .[14]

---

11. See, for example, the various discussions of early childhood sex-role socialization in part 3 in this volume.

12. See in this volume the article by Lenore Weitzman et al.

13. Phyllis Alroy et al., *Dick and Jane as Victims: Sex Stereotyping in Children's Readers* (Princeton, N.J.: Women on Words and Images, 1972), p. 13.

14. Ibid., pp. 17–18.

---

as destined for a future only with domestic chores:

> Girls in the readers rehearse their domestic chores
> continuously. . . . The reader mother is a limited, colorless,
> mindless creature. . . . Not only does she wash, cook, clean,
> nurse and find mittens; *these chores constitute her only happiness.*[15]

Books are only one of the pieces of the educational puzzle that fit together to present the picture of the sexist school system in which teachers expect girls to conform to the quiet, dependent feminine stereotype.[16] Girls begin school with abilities more advanced than those of boys and many retain this advantage until junior high school when several factors may cause a decrease in female academic competence. First, girls begin school with superior verbal abilities while boys tend to excel in spatial and analytic skills which are more relevant to mathematics and science. It is the verbal skills which are emphasized in elementary school and which contribute to increased male competence therein while the spatial and analytic skills are all but ignored. One possible explanation for the fact that sex differences in verbal skills decrease with age is that males benefit from extensive verbal training. In contrast, females do not receive comparable training in the skills relevant to mathematics and science.[17] At the junior high level, the focus of the curriculum begins to change subtly toward mathematics and science, subjects in which girls have lesser ability and in which they are not expected to achieve excellence. Further sex tracking occurs blatantly in such courses as home economics and shop. Finally, the emphasis on male competencies and the blatant sex tracking of courses is reinforced by the beginning of the dating game. All girls, and especially those who have resisted or avoided the feminine stereotype, are expected by their peers as well as by adults to relinquish their individuality and turn into models of femininity. And most do.

---

15. Ibid., p. 26; italics ours.

16. See in this volume the article by Alice Rossi, "Equality Between the Sexes."

17. Julia A. Sherman, "Socializing for Maximal Female Competence" (Paper delivered at the Meetings of the American Association for the Advancement of Science, Washington, D.C., December 29, 1972), p. 9.

As discussed above, even college-educated women and women with professional degrees consider their careers to be subordinate to their husbands' and accept ultimate responsibility for house and child care. Until recently women have been "written out of" history courses, assigned only the expressive role in sociology courses, and admonished that biology is destiny in psychology courses. Sex-role socialization is continuous from birth through adulthood and is, therefore, effective in masking alternatives. Little girls who are taught by their families, by their teachers, and by their peers, grow up into wives and mothers who in turn teach their little girls . . .

Thus far we have been examining just one side of the coin. If girls are expected to be the second sex, dependent, incompetent, and afraid, boys are expected to be the first, independent, capable, and brave. If girls are channeled into the nurturant, expressive role of housewife-mother, boys are channeled into the rat race to succeed. What does this do to the American male?

> The socialization of the American male has closed off certain options for him, too. Men are discouraged from developing certain desirable traits such as tenderness and sensitivity just as surely as women are discouraged from being assertive and, alas, "too bright." Young boys are encouraged to be incompetent at cooking and child care just as surely as young girls are urged to be incompetent at mathematics and science.[18]

Thus, sex-role stereotyping stifles the male. In addition, unless the rigid definition of the male role is changed, it is unlikely that women can reach liberation. As long as it is expected that husbands are to assume the male provider role and that their wives and children are to be economically dependent on them, there is neither hope for change in the differential evaluation of the sexes nor hope for change in sex-typed personality traits.[19] If men continue to consider themselves as dominant, they will continue to need an object to dominate. They will continue to

18. Bem and Bem, "Training the Woman to Know Her Place," p. 12.
19. Erik Grønseth, "The Husband Provider Role and Its Dysfunctional Consequences," *Sociological Focus* 5, no. 2 (Winter 1971–72): 11.

bolster a system of hierarchy by turning their anger not against socially structured injustice or inequality, but against an individual female scapegoat. "For every man there is always someone lower on the social scale on whom he can take out his aggressions. And that is any woman alive." [20]

The traditional sex-role channeling of both men and women is detrimental to men, women, and society. In order for the female role to become a human role, the male role must also become a human role.

> This implies that neither sex should be limited by role stereotypes that define "appropriate" behavior. The present models of neither men nor women furnish adequate opportunities for human development. That one half of the human race should be dominant and the other half submissive is incompatible with a notion of freedom. Freedom requires that there not be dominance and submission, but that all individuals be free to determine their own lives.[21]

What can be done toward creating a world of cooperation instead of dominance and submission, a world of equality instead of superiority and inferiority, a world of choice and fulfillment instead of channeling and disappointment? At first glance the problem seems overwhelming. Rossi, however, sees the goal as attainable through a step-by-step process:

> Equality between the sexes cannot be achieved by proclamation or decree but only through a multitude of concrete steps, each of which may seem insignificant by itself, but all of which add up to the social blueprint for attaining the general goal.[22]

---

20. Susan Griffin, "The Politics of Rape," *Ramparts* 10, no. 3 (September 1971): 34.

21. Jack Sawyer, "The Male Liberation Movement" (Paper delivered at Women's Liberation Teach-In, Northwestern University, March 8, 1970), p. 2.

22. See in this volume the article by Alice Rossi, "Equality Between the Sexes." For a detailed discussion of alternatives to current sex-role socialization practices, see part 2 in this volume.

Sexuality and Family Roles

All known societies have some regulation of sexual expression, whether formal or informal in nature. In our own society there is the ever-present threat of government interference in one's sexual and reproductive life by virtue of the existence of laws that allow such practices as involuntary sterilization or punitive, conditional sterilization; restriction of birth-control techniques, including abortion;[23] and arrest and imprisonment for adultery, sodomy, and fornication, among other sexual activities.[24] These laws are part of an essentially male culture and are selectively enforced, generally on the relatively poor, the racial minorities, homosexuals, and women.

In addition to these legal constraints on women's (and men's) sexual lives, there is informal regulation from the typical process of psychosexual development. According to Simon and Gagnon, sexual behavior is not so much the expression of a primordial drive as it is scripted or learned behavior, which varies by sex.[25] A basic distinction between the developmental process of males and females is that males move from "privatized personal sexuality" (i.e., masturbation) to sociosexuality; whereas females do the reverse (that is, those who masturbate do so only after having experienced orgasm in some situation involving others). For all adolescent males, there is little training in how to handle emotional relations with girls. Females in all classes, in contrast to men, are relatively inactive sexually; whereas, they are well trained in the language and actions of romantic love. During dating, courtship, and later married and unmarried life, then, each sex must teach the other what it wants and expects in terms of sexual expression, and the exchanges are not always smooth or equitable.[26]

The lesser sexual activity on the part of females in comparison with males is in part a function of ignorance—of not learning as early as males how to be sexual—as well as fear of consequences

---

23. See in this volume the chapter on birth control.

24. Gloria Steinem, "Sexual Politics," *Newsweek* 80, no. 2 (July 1972): 32–33.

25. William Simon and John Gagnon, "Psychosexual Development," *Trans-action* 6, no. 5 (March 1969): 9–17.

26. See in this volume the article by Randall Collins.

of heterosexual activity. In general, females in our society have not been encouraged to be sexual. Historically, it was commonly assumed that women had weaker sexual needs and drives than men and that they indulged in sexual relations, not for personal satisfaction, but in order to meet their husbands' sexual needs and in order to reproduce the species.[27] Although men wanted to marry a woman of such description, they wanted for their own satisfaction other women who were sexually available. The latter, which included prostitutes, were labeled "bad" women. The former category, the "good" women, was composed of those women who were premaritally chaste and maritally restricted in their sexual interest. Women were (and often still are) considered by men as personal property, and only those in the "good" category could expect to become and to remain married.

The inhibition of women's sexuality was not limited to the process of psychosexual development prior to marriage. The prevailing values often removed female sexual satisfaction from the marriage relationship as well, for any personal sexual satisfaction therein could result in guilt feelings for women, and, if communicated, to suspicion by her husband that she really was not "good."

Somewhat more recently, women have learned that they can expect pleasure from sex but are sexually inferior to men, their pleasure being dependent on men via sexual intercourse. From this viewpoint, women who do not achieve a "transfer" of erotic sensation from clitoris to vagina are considered to be simply immature, neurotic, and masculine.[28]

In contrast to teachings about female sexuality in the past, however, recent work by sex researchers such as Masters and Johnson has clear implications for female sexual liberation.[29] Their clinical studies indicate, for example, that clitoral and vaginal orgasm are experienced the same physiologically; that

27. Robert R. Bell, *Marriage and Family Interaction* (rev. ed.; Homewood, Ill.: Dorsey Press, 1967).

28. For excellent discussions and critiques of psychoanalytic thinking about women's sexuality, see Susan Lydon, "Understanding Orgasm," *Ramparts* 7, no. 9 (December 1968): 59–63; and Mary Jane Sherfey, *The Nature and Evolution of Female Sexuality* (New York: Random House, 1972).

29. William H. Masters and Virginia E. Johnson, *Human Sexual Response* (Boston: Little, Brown, 1966).

women are multiorgasmic; and that the most intense orgasms experienced are by manual stimulation rather than by intercourse. This work is potentially liberating, then, for it discredits the notion of inferiority of clitoral orgasm and points generally toward great variety in female sexual response. At the same time it leaves unanswered many questions regarding the subjective, psychological nature of sexuality and has not basically affected equality of sexual relations among most men and women.

Who, then, is affected—and how—by the so-called sexual revolution? As indicated in the section on sexual expression, the "revolution" is in reality an evolution, more of attitudes and values than of behavior. This evolution beyond the norms regulating sexual intercourse, to rejection of the general taboo against sex and a positive affirmation of the goodness of nonprocreative sex, still has a long way yet to go toward attaining sexual equality for women. As some feminists put it, "the sexual revolution wasn't our war." [30] Their point is that the evolution away from Victorian morality leaves women of all social classes unprotected from masculine pressure to engage in sexual intercourse yet bound by all the consequences of sexual availability. To the older practices of selling themselves for money (prostitution) and for security in the suburbs (marriage), women now "sell" themselves in exchange for approval and affection, presumably love. True love it rarely can be, however, because love is based on two-way communication and respect between equals, and many structured inequalities between the sexes persist.

Despite a wish by many women to challenge the double standard by their premarital sexual behavior, the risk of undesirable consequences (e.g., illegitimate birth) remains a deterrent.[31] One precondition to sexual equality is, therefore, the disassociation of sexual relations from reproduction.[32] As Pope and Knudsen note in the section on sexual expression, we are approaching such disassociation slowly through the development and dissemination of effective contraceptive techniques and the

---

30. Anselma Dell'Olio, "The Sexual Revolution Wasn't Our War," *Ms.* 1, no. 1 (Spring 1972): 104–6, 109–10. In this volume see the article by Randall Collins for a discussion of the function of romantic love for women under varying social conditions.

31. See in this volume the article by Pope and Knudsen.

32. Mitchell, *Woman's Estate.*

availability of legalized abortion.[33] It is apparent, though, that we must await ultimately the development of something like "test-tube babies" [34] in order to realize sexual equality fully.

Within marriage, moreover, some evidence exists that, for the majority of women, sexuality is not very satisfying.[35] According to Ramey, extramarital sexuality in the form of swinging, on the other hand, may foster an increased sense of self-worth among wives because their capacity for prolonged sexual involvement exceeds that of their husbands. Despite the possibility of this benefit for some women once swinging is underway, however, entrance into, as well as departure from, swinging still depend more on male than female initiative. In contrast to swinging, other sexual life styles for pair-bonded couples involve commitment (i.e., dialogue, trust, and responsibility) and may be successful alternatives to more traditional kin, neighbor, and friend relationships among highly mobile, isolated nuclear-family members. The extent to which such alternatives to monogamous marriage (e.g., intimate friendships, evolutionary communes, and group marriage) are now practiced is not known, but they are believed to be limited largely to the geographically mobile upper middle class, and within this group to only some of those pair-bonded couples in which there is equality between the sexes.[36]

During the years of their lives when women may be able to overcome some of the sexual inhibition of their youth, they start being disqualified as sexually attractive persons.[37] There is a double standard of aging whereby women lose their sexual candidacy at a much younger age than men. The loss of youthful appearance among women and concurrent depreciation of their value as sexual property occurs sooner for the poor than for the advantaged, although the latter may experience psychological pain over this eventuality more commonly and more acutely.

33. See in this volume the chapter on birth control.
34. See in this volume the article by Edward Grossman.
35. John F. Cuber and Peggy B. Harroff, *Sex and the Significant Americans* (Baltimore, Md.: Penguin Books, 1968); William H. Masters and Virginia E. Johnson, *Human Sexual Inadequacy* (Boston: Little, Brown, 1970).
36. See in this volume the article by James Ramey.
37. Susan Sontag, "The Double Standard of Aging," *Saturday Review: The Society* 55, no. 39 (October 1972): 29–38.

The social judgment of aging and consequent sexual ineligibility of a woman may not be related to any real event in a woman's life, such as menopause. In fact, there is no cut-off time in women's lives to which it could be related. Research indicates, rather, that despite a gradual weakening which may take place with chronological aging, women's sex needs, interests, and abilities continue well past menopause, indeed indefinitely, especially among those who experience regular sexual stimulation (regardless of what manner of sexual expression is employed).[38]

Nevertheless, older husbands' desire progressively lessens or they may turn to younger women, and the older woman's opportunities for extramarital relations are slim. Aging widows, divorcees, and single women face even greater problems than married women in expressing their sexuality freely. Masturbation is one available sexual activity, of course, but it is not considered a valid outlet by some and leads to feelings of guilt among many aged practitioners. Our culture does not recognize the normality of sex expression for older persons generally[39] but, as Sontag maintains, "The revulsion against aging in women is the cutting edge of a whole set of oppressive structures (often masked by gallantries) that keep women in their place."[40]

Heterosexual activity may be feared and shunned by some women of all ages because it is clear that it serves (men's) power and status—as well as sexual—needs.[41] This point is well made by Ellen Willis:

> The sexual emancipation of the "new-woman" is . . .
> illusory. . . . True, the cruder aspects of the double
> standard are in disrepute. But real sexual freedom implies
> that each sex cares equally about the physical and
> emotional needs of the other. In our sexist society, this is far
> from the case. Women are brought up to be sensitive to a
> man's needs, to put him first. Men accept this sensitivity as

38. Isadore Rubin, "The Sexless Older Years—A Socially Harmful Stereotype," *Annals of the American Academy of Political and Social Science* 376 (March 1968): 86–95.

39. Simone de Beauvoir, "Joie de Vivre," *Harper's* 244, no. 1460 (January 1972): 33–40.

40. Sontag, "Double Standard," p. 38.

41. See in this volume the article by Ti-Grace Atkinson.

their due and rarely reciprocate. Rather they tend to see women as objects, as pretty or ugly, easy to get or a challenge, a good catch or a last resort.[42]

It is premature, then, to talk of sexual equality in the presence of other structured inequalities between the sexes.

Marriage and the Family

Once married, once having achieved the pinnacle of success, the achievement toward which their socialization has been directing them, women are invariably disappointed and often unhappy. As Jessie Bernard succinctly puts it, the realities of marriage are a "shock." She points out that no matter what indices of mental health are employed, married women suffer in comparison with unmarried women. Unmarried women present the positive traits expected of an integrated, autonomous adult in our society; whereas married women present a more negative profile.[43] The skeptical reader may ask whether this comparison suggests a flaw in the present institution of marriage or simply reflects the fact that more dependent and incompetent women marry. One study which questioned the same women both before and after marriage points to the conclusion that the adjustment to the wife role has a negative effect on women. Of the academically talented college women studied, those who married before completing their college education showed a change from the positive attributes they had exhibited as freshmen: "after marriage they showed less independence, reduced impulse expression and greater submissiveness and conservatism." [44]

A portion of the attitude change required of a housewife is described by Lopata as a shift in space placement. The typical American bride is still involved in school or work activities. She, therefore, sees her primary location as outside the home. Slowly the wife's focus shifts to inside the home. Her work increasingly is

---

42. Ellen Willis, "Whatever Happened to Women? Nothing—That's the Trouble," *Mademoiselle* 69, no. 5 (September 1969): 150, 206–9.

43. Bernard, "The Paradox of the Happy Marriage," pp. 145–62.

44. Alice S. Rossi, "Barriers to the Career Choice of Engineering, Medicine, or Science among American Women," in *Women and the Scientific Professions*, eds. Jacquelyn A. Mattfeld and Carol G. Van Aken (Cambridge, Mass.: MIT Press, 1965), p. 78.

seen instrumentally as a means to obtain purchases for the home. The shift of focus is complete when the woman becomes pregnant and outside employment or schooling fade out completely.[45]

Although the attitudinal transition required in the wife role is difficult, it is increasingly the housewife-mother role that presents the greater problems.[46] Many contemporary marriages assume a veneer of equality while the wife works to put the husband through school or to save the downpayment on a house. It is, then, with the birth of the first child that most women experience their greatest break with the past. Abruptly new attitudes and new tasks are demanded. Shulman, for example, points out that she and her husband had a happy and uncomplicated domestic life until their children were born. It was then that they assumed the traditional sex roles: man as breadwinner, woman as housewife-mother. It was then, too, that Alix Shulman began to feel cut off from part of her life.[47]

Postpartum depression may be as much the result of the total dependence of the infant upon the mother, the necessity that she be constantly at its beck and call, her break with the outside world and other identities, as it is the result of biological changes. Lopata aptly describes the situation of the new mother thusly:

> Because of the utter dependence of newborn infants upon
> practically 24-hour care by an adult, the number of
> activities such care necessitates, and the society's preference
> for its being undertaken by the biological mother, the young
> housewife suddenly finds herself confined to her house,
> carrying on a variety of housekeeping tasks; often inexpertly
> and alone.[48]

45. Helena Znaniecki Lopata, "The Life Cycle of the Social Role of Housewife," *Sociology and Social Research* 51, no. 1 (October 1966): 8–9. For extensive treatments of the social role of housewife see ibid., pp. 5–23, and Helena Znaniecki Lopata, *Occupation: Housewife* (London: Oxford University Press, 1971).

46. Alice S. Rossi, "Transition to Parenthood," *Journal of Marriage and the Family* 30, no. 1 (February 1968): 31. In order to avoid the personal difficulties and ecological consequences of parenthood, many young couples have decided to remain childless. For a discussion of the phenomenon of voluntary nonparenthood, see Ellen Peck, *The Baby Trap* (New York: Pantheon Books, 1971).

47. See in this volume the article by Alix Shulman.

48. Lopata, "Life Cycle of the Social Role of Housewife," p. 9.

Society's expectation that the mother will be constantly available to her children, the "fire-department ideology of child-rearing," [49] does not stop when children are no longer infants; and the mother's depression does not necessarily stop when her children outgrow infancy. Friedan, interviewing women in 1968 before they could have been influenced by the current wave of the women's movement, found that many mothers were experiencing "the problem that has no name," a general dissatisfaction with their housewife-mother role.[50]

One problem with the housewife-mother role at present is the full-time but not fulfilling definition of the role, both on a day-to-day and on a lifetime basis. On a day-to-day basis, as Gordon states picturesquely, their role in the nuclear family "deprives women of the company of adults (which is enough to turn an adult mind into mush—if you're not a mother and don't believe it, try spending just 48 hours with children only)." [51] A man assuming the role of househusband, a man who had already achieved a certain measure of success and status in the academic world, also uses the mind-mush analogy. After trying to read and write while taking care of three children, he found himself angry with his children most of the time.

> I soon reached the conclusion that if I was going to keep
> house and take care of the children, I might as well give up
> doing anything else at the same time if I hoped to maintain
> any equilibrium at all. . . . In half a day I could feel my
> mind turning into oatmeal, cold oatmeal, and it took the
> other half to get it bubbling again, and by then it was
> bedtime.[52]

The marriage relationship and especially the family relationship also promote the economic dependence of the female. The role of wife-mother takes the woman out of "equal" economic

49. This term was coined by Peter Rossi as reported by Alice S. Rossi. See in this volume "A Good Woman Is Hard to Find."

50. Betty Friedan, *The Feminine Mystique* (New York: Dell, 1963), pp. 11–27. For evidence that dissatisfaction with the housewife-mother role is not limited to college-educated women, see ibid., pp. 22–23, and Mirra Komarovsky, *Blue-Collar Marriage* (New York: Random House, 1962), pp. 59–60.

51. Linda Gordon, *Families* (Cambridge, Mass.: Bread and Roses, 1970), p. 3.

52. Joel Roache, "Men: Confessions of a Househusband," *Ms.* 1, no. 5 (November 1972): 25.

competition and often out of any economic competence, thereby leaving her without any independent means of support or any skills to attain support should divorce, widowhood, or economic reversals require her participation in the labor force.

Due to the lifetime definition of the housewife-mother role, many women fail to recognize the possible consequences and invest themselves wholly in children, husband, and home. They often come to see themselves primarily as mothers, and secondarily as wives. Rossi suggests that suburban housewives are so alike in age that most of these young women do not directly confront the "empty nest" stage of the housewife-mother role until it is too late for all of them.[53] Thus, inadequately prepared for the termination of the role of mother, middle-aged women are apt to suffer great difficulty especially if they have no alternate sources of involvement.[54] As Lopata asserts, the longer a woman has focused her life into the role of mother, "inside the home," the less likely she is to be able to take advantage of such alternatives as returning to work or school.[55]

Given current life-expectancy differences between men and women, moreover, the wife can expect to be a widow for about eleven years, on the average. In old age, then, many women must face alone the very serious task of finding satisfaction as useful people as well as coping with the continued problems of physical aging and death. Their troubles are often confounded by economic constraints because most husbands retire (and/or die) with inadequate retirement plans.[56]

If the present institutions of marriage and the family are as dismal as portrayed, why do women enter into and remain in the roles of wife and mother? Gordon explains that ". . . the family

---

53. Alice S. Rossi, "Equality Between the Sexes: An Immodest Proposal," in *The Woman in America*, ed. Robert J. Lifton (Boston: Houghton Mifflin, 1964), p. 126.

54. See in this volume the article by Jules Henry. See, in addition, Pauline Bart, "Mother Portnoy's Complaints," *Trans-action* 8, nos. 1 and 2 (November/December 1970): 69–74.

55. Lopata, "Life Cycle of the Social Role of Housewife," p. 12. It should be also noted that ecological considerations are important both for the creation of alternative modes of family and work life and for the integration of women into the existing social structure. Middle-class migration to the suburbs has the effect of accentuating the isolation of women from urban economic and cultural centers. Difficulties of employment or matriculation in school are intensified when commuting is necessitated.

56. Harold L. Sheppard, "The Poverty of Aging," in *Poverty as a Public Issue*, ed. Ben B. Seligman (New York: Free Press, 1965), pp. 98–99.

system has sometimes given women responsibilities to beloved husbands and children, and has usually provided a form of economic and emotional security that cannot just be shrugged off." [57] Epstein, furthermore, asserts that for the middle-class housewife there are compensations which mask her objective condition. First, while still married, she shares her husband's paycheck supposedly in exchange for household and child-care services. Although her actual legal status "demands" only minimal support, this is revealed only in extreme cases or in divorce court. In addition to economic rewards, there are many secondary rewards such as attainment of the social status of her husband regardless of her own achievements, and public recognition because of her husband's achievements. Also, the woman who can afford domestic help has a great deal of leisure time. Finally, women are not expected to work outside the home or to achieve high standards at such work and they are expected to revoke their decision to work at most any time.[58]

Although there are negative consequences of the feminine sex role as discussed above, this role may seem to have positive consequences for the middle-class woman insofar as she is provided with a style of life that she probably could not achieve alone, given current sex discrimination. This may give her a vested interest in the status quo momentarily. By the time a woman feels trapped it is usually too late to change her life pattern and she holds on even tighter to the conventional ideal.

Many women (and men) see beyond the apparent advantages of the housewife-mother role. At present there appears to be a great deal of experimentation with both the form of the family and the definition of sex roles within the family. These experiments involve many different alternatives to the present ideal of the nuclear family with husband as a breadwinner, wife as housewife-mother, and children as investment and product of the family. Three commonly discussed alternatives are communes, the dual-career family, and the society-wide redefinition of sex roles currently being undertaken in Sweden.

57. Gordon, *Families*, p. 2.
58. Cynthia Fuchs Epstein, *Woman's Place: Options and Limits in Professional Careers* (Berkeley: University of California Press, 1971), pp. 129–32.

Communes, the alternative involving changes in the form of the family, are the intentional experiments receiving the widest press. The first communes of the 1960s were products of the counterculture, whose members were reacting to many different aspects of contemporary technological society, including the Protestant work ethic, Victorian sex norms, the present state of industrial capitalism, monogamy, and the privatization of the nuclear family. All these aspects of our society obviously impinge upon women's lives. It should be understood, however, that communes do not necessarily include equality for women in their conceptualization or practice. In fact, it is almost as easy for women and men to assume traditional sex roles in a communal family as in a nuclear family.[59] As a new family form, nevertheless, communes could be a definite source of greater sex equality because their creators are questioning society in general and because they offer a greater availability of "manpower."

Within the context of the nuclear family, important contemporary attempts to change sex roles include (1) the egalitarian family, most often the dual-career family; and (2) the society-wide program for sex equality proposed by the government of Sweden. Although it is not a new form, the dual-career family seems to be gaining in popularity and is getting more serious attention from social science researchers.[60] The dual-career family is a type of household in which both adults pursue jobs that require a high degree of commitment and involve a continuous developmental character and in which both adults as parents maintain a family life together with children. There is a definite emphasis on sex equality although when one person must

59. See, for example, Vivian Estellachild, "Hippie Communes," *Women: A Journal of Liberation* 2, no. 2 (Winter 1971): 40–43; and Kit Leder, "Women in Communes," *Women: A Journal of Liberation* 1, no. 1 (Fall 1969): 34–35. For an example of sex-role innovation within a small commune, see Vicki Cohn Pollard and Jean Munley, "The Five of Us," *Women: A Journal of Liberation* 2, no. 2 (Winter 1971): 28–32.

60. See, for example, Rhona Rapoport and Robert N. Rapoport, *Dual-Career Families* (Baltimore, Md.: Penguin Books, 1971); idem., "The Dual-Career Family: A Variant Pattern and Social Change," *Human Relations* 22, no. 1 (February 1969): 3–30; Michael P. Fogarty, Rhona Rapoport, and Robert N. Rapoport, *Sex, Career and Family* (Beverly Hills, Calif.: Sage Publications, 1971); Lynda Lytle Holmstrom, *The Two-Career Family* (Cambridge, Mass.: Schenkman, 1972); and Margaret M. Poloma and T. Neal Garland, "The Married Professional Woman: A Study in the Tolerance of Domestication," *Journal of Marriage and the Family* 33, no. 2 (August 1971): 531–40.

curtail activities, travel less, or lessen ambitions, it is usually the woman who does so. Although family strains occur when the wife and mother has a career, they can be outweighed by the benefits for the woman. Rapoport and Rapoport summarize the gains that accrue to such women thusly:

> All the women in this sample have as part of their personal identities a sub-identity associated with a professional work role. Many indicated that if the satisfactions from work were to be removed, they would experience a major loss . . . in every case they are realizing in major degrees what they really want to do and feel is worth doing as human beings, making full use of their capacities.[61]

It is still extremely difficult, however, for individual couples to create an island of change within the larger society. Innovative families must battle continuously with scheduling problems and child-care dilemmas as well as the disapproval of friends and acquaintances, neighbors, relatives, and the surrounding community. Despite problems, many marital partners are trying to give equal consideration to the occupational and family roles of wife and husband. As the experience of these couples becomes more publicized, it is likely that other couples may consciously adopt an egalitarian pattern.

A rather complete proposal for elevating the status of women within the nuclear family has been presented by the Swedish government, and this public program has a distinct advantage over isolated couples in its attempt to equalize sex roles.[62] Whereas individual families must try to innovate within the context of an existing system, a government can endeavor to create society-wide change. The Swedish proposal includes wide-ranging changes in domestic, child-care, and occupational arrangements, in familial and economic responsibilities and rewards, while it gives full emphasis to the educational and psychological dimensions of socialization. Finally, drafters of the proposal recognize the important fact that the status of women can be altered only by changing the roles of both men and women.

---

61. Rapoport and Rapoport, *Dual-Career Families*, p. 299.
62. Maj-Britt Sandlund, *The Status of Women in Sweden: Report to the United Nations*, 1968 (Stockholm: The Swedish Institute, 1968).

> Eventually to achieve complete equality . . . a radical
> change in deep-rooted traditions and attitudes must be
> brought about among both women and men to encourage a
> change in the roles played by both.[63]

Economics and Family Roles

At present the use of women who work outside the home as a "secondary" labor supply, as well as a more marked sexual division of productive labor wherein many women simply do not work outside the home, is viewed by many sociologists and lay people alike as functional for our industrial economy. Discussions of the "fit" between the nuclear family form and industrialization maintain, for example, that the family unit with a home-bound wife-mother serves well the economic system's demand for men who are free to work at persistently high levels of efficiency and creativity.[64] Such a family, moreover, is believed to be especially well suited for our economy insofar as the wife-mother's "expressive" role provides support against the emotional stress created for the husband by the industrial system (e.g., stress resulting from job allocation and work evaluation on the basis of achievement and universalism).[65] The relative isolation of nuclear family units, finally, is conducive to the acquisition of durable consumer goods and the inferior status of women makes them especially suitable (exploitable) as consumers.[66]

Along with such evidence of "fit," however, the lack of fit between home work and our industrialized economy for women in particular also is being recognized.[67] Housework and child care are the responsibilities of women, even those who also work outside the home. Although this housework constitutes a large amount of socially necessary production, it is private production

---

63. Ibid., p. 5.

64. Alice S. Rossi, "Sexual Equality: The Beginnings of Ideology," *Humanist* 29, no. 5 (September–October 1969): 3–6, 16.

65. William J. Goode, *World Revolution and Family Patterns* (New York: Free Press of Glencoe, 1963).

66. See in this volume the article by Jules Henry.

67. See, especially, Goode, *World Revolution*, and Arlene and Jerome Skolnick, eds., *Family in Transition* (Boston: Little, Brown, 1971).

and there is a definite tendency to view as unimportant those services for which a wage or salary is not paid. The material basis for the inferior status of women, then, is their definition as a group who work outside our money economy.[68] As long as housework and child care are matters of private production and the responsibilities of women only, most women who are also gainfully employed outside the home will perform double work duty[69]—all for about 60 percent of the salary of men. Thus, the industrialization of housework and socialization of child care—as well as equal access to equal work among jobs currently available—are both economic preconditions for equality between the sexes.

There have been wide variations historically in the kind, amount, and relative status of the work performed by the respective sexes, but male-female economic participation has never been strictly comparable.[70] Historically, a sexual division of labor wherein women were subordinate to men may have been largely a matter of survival of the species. Gough maintains, for example, that the exigencies of primitive technology—the prevalence of heavy work for which many women were less capable than men—as well as the necessarily prolonged period of childbearing and nursing for which women only were capable, formed the predominant basis for systems of sexual inequality prior to the agricultural revolution and for several thousands of years afterward.

The important effects of technological developments on women's economic participation during the industrial revolution are also well documented.[71] In preindustrial times women had two major roles of doing economically productive work and

---

68. Margaret Benston, "The Political Economy of Women's Liberation," *Monthly Review* 21, no. 4 (September 1969): 13–27.

69. Some women among the relatively advantaged can delegate housework and child care to paid "help" (i.e., achieve individual freedom via exploitation of lower-class women); but this option becomes less feasible as the occupational category of household worker decreases in size in all Western industrialized countries. Suggestions for solving the problems by upgrading domestic helper and child-care occupations are offered by Rapoport and Rapoport, *Dual-Career Families*.

70. See in this volume the article by Kathleen Gough.

71. Neil J. Smelser, *Social Change in the Industrial Revolution* (Chicago: University of Chicago Press, 1959).

raising a family which were fused into a single way of life at home. Women (and children) lost the opportunity to participate in productive work as it moved eventually outside the context of small-scale family enterprises to large-scale industries that employed individual workers. The effect of industrialization was uneven across social classes, with working-class women being the first to be brought into paid jobs. The evils of the early factory system—including the physical hardships of employment; the lack of safety precautions and health regulations; long hours of work, beginning at very early ages; and cruelty to working children—led often to physical exhaustion and neglect of children and homes. Such was the context in which women's concentration on homemaking came to be regarded clearly as an improvement in their standard of living over employment outside their homes.[72]

As the middle classes grew in size and prosperity, moreover, another ideal quite different from that of the hard-working housewife grew in importance. This ideal is that of the leisured lady whose appearance and social entertaining testify to her husband's wealth. Together these two ideals circumscribe the place of women's role enactment to the home.

In our modern-day industrialized society, automation and cybernation remove most of the hard physical work. As Perrucci demonstrates, nevertheless, sex status continues to be an important influence upon occupational placement, even in high-status professional occupations.[73] Although there is some variation by specific occupation and work place in the relative integration of the sexes into the world of work, many occupations are clearly sex typed, resulting generally in the continuation of either male or female predominance among the practitioners therein. Consistent with the minority status of women, female-dominated professions tend to be of lower status than those dominated by men. When sexual integration of traditionally female-dominated professions does occur, moreover, it appears to involve a form of intraprofessional stratification whereby men assume the supervisory or otherwise more prestigious forms of the occupation or, in

72. Alva Myrdal and Viola Klein, *Women's Two Roles* (London: Routledge & Kegan Paul, 1968).

73. See in this volume the article by Carolyn C. Perrucci.

effect, take control of the occupation. Similarly, women who work in traditionally male-dominated professions are overrepresented in the lower-prestige specialities within the profession and are more likely than not to serve only minority-status clients. Judging, then, from the persistence of sex typing of jobs together with trends in unemployment, education, and income differentials, women's status (relative to men) has been declining instead of improving over the past quarter century[74] despite automation and cybernation.

It is evident, then, that the economic preconditions for sex equality are as yet unmet in their entirety in any country in the world. Since Marxism forms an important ideological basis for theorists of women's liberation, however, a significant group within the movement is critically examining the experience of Soviet socialism for guidance and for the testing of ideas. In the USSR, one presumed precondition for the liberation of women exists in that social ownership and planned production have replaced private ownership and production for profit via the market. An examination of the current situation of Soviet women indicates that it differs from that of women in Western Europe and America in that many current demands of the movement have been met. For example, full legal equality between the sexes is written explicitly into the Soviet Constitution; women (55 percent of the population) constituted 54 percent of the civilian labor force as early as 1959; contraceptives and advice on their use, including abortion on demand, are available to all women; divorce is easily accessible to childless couples; and an extensive network of child-care institutions are provided. In other respects, however, the situation of Soviet women does not differ much from that of women in the West as evidenced by the problems that still remain in connection with educational opportunities, job opportunities, earnings, sexual freedom, and men's attitudes generally.[75] Full explanation of these failures of Soviet society to advance as fast or as far as hoped by some members of the

---

74. Knudsen, "Declining Status of Women," pp. 183–93; Abbott L. Ferriss, *Indicators of Trends in the Status of American Women* (New York: Russell Sage Foundation, 1971).

75. G. R. Barker, "Women's Liberation and Socialism: Feminism's 'Second Wave' and Soviet Society" (Paper delivered at the Twelfth International Seminar on Family Research, Moscow, April 17–23, 1972).

women's movement awaits much needed research, and the extent to which the Soviet (or any other socialist) society will eventually meet all the requirements for sex equality simply remains to be seen.

Despite doubts about whether our own capitalist economy can expand enough to put most women to work as part of the normally employed labor force, it is hoped especially by radical women that women's full integration into paid work will not only occur but also will give them more than the same rather limited freedom now given most men. It is desired that more meaningful work which provides greater chances for personality development be a more central part of the lives of both women and men, and that responsibility for housework and child care be shared more equally as well.[76]

Less revolutionary, perhaps, is the feminist goal of economic security for both sexes. Limitations of the rights to support of women and children, as well as inadequacies in enforcement of such rights, are increasingly recognized. Some feminist proposals for change include the provision of unemployment insurance and social security to housewives and organized support for state ratification of the Equal Rights Amendment.[77] Opponents notwithstanding, no evidence exists that the Amendment would

---

76. One possibility along these lines worthy of examination is the small-scale semiofficial family-policy measure underway in Norway whereby there is a conjugal work-sharing family pattern (i.e., both the wife-mother and husband-father work only half-time with their work hours synchronized so that one spouse would be off work while the other was at work). See Erik Grønseth, "Work Sharing Families" (Paper delivered at the Twelfth International Seminar on Family Research, Moscow, April 17–23, 1972).

77. See, respectively, Joanna Clark, "Motherhood," in *The Black Women*, ed. Toni Cade (New York: Signet Books, 1970), pp. 63–72; and discussion of the Swedish system of social insurance in Sandlund, *Status of Women in Sweden.*

The Equal Rights Amendment to the U.S. Constitution reads: "Equality of rights under the law shall not be denied or abridged by the United States or by any state on account of sex." It was passed by Congress on March 22, 1972, and must be ratified (by thirty-eight states) within seven years to become law. As of March 1, 1974, thirty-three states had ratified the amendment. For a supportive statement on ERA, see Bernice Sandler, Statement Before the Senate Judiciary Committee Subcommittee on Constitutional Amendments, May 6, 1970, Re: S.J. Res 61 (Equal Rights Amendment).

There is some opposition to the Equal Rights Amendment from working-class women because they believe that it would nullify a good deal of "protective" legislation for women workers. See Joan Jordan, "Comment: Working Women and the Equal Rights Amendment," *Trans-action* 8, nos. 1 and 2 (November–December 1970): 16, 18, 20, 22.

deprive women of any enforceable rights of support or weaken the father's obligation to support the family. It is more likely to be used in a positive fashion to require spouses in divided families to contribute equally within their means to the support of child care so that the spouse with custody does not bear a larger share of the responsibility for support than the other spouse.[78]

Economic security for women is also being approached through current structures (e.g., the U.S. Equal Pay Act of 1963, Title VII of the 1964 Civil Rights Act, Executive Order 11246 amended by 11375, which prohibits sex discrimination by all holders of federal contracts; and fair employment practices laws in some states) which facilitate feminist goals of equal opportunity for formal education and for in-service training; equal opportunity to be hired and promoted for equal work; to receive equal pay for equal work; and to benefit equally from unionization of work.[79]

It is recognized that in addition to the structured economic inequalities discussed above, the sex role socialization process, in which adult women themselves (as wives-mothers and counselors) as well as men play an important part, is also problematic for sex equality because it results in women's generally inadequate vocational preparation and work motivation and their reliance on marriage as a means of financial security.[80] It is believed, nevertheless, that the necessary resocialization will be more meaningful and easy once the structural inequalities are eliminated.

In conclusion, all aspects of women's biographies are deeply affected by, as well as themselves affect, marriage and the family—present and future, real and imaginary. If the negative and often destructive elements of women's lives are to be eliminated, a thorough critique of contemporary marriage and the family as well as a discussion and implementation of alternatives will be required. It is toward an analysis of the past and present conditions as well as proposals for the future that we now turn.

78. Catherine East, "The Equal Rights Amendment and Alimony and Child Support Laws," Citizens' Advisory Council on the Status of Women Item No. 23-N, January 1972.

79. Joan Jordan, *The Place of American Women: Economic Exploitation of Women* (Detroit, Mich.: Radical Education Project, n.d.).

80. Knudsen, "Declining Status of Women," pp. 183–93.

PART ONE

THE
FAMILY
AND
SOCIETY

A
Sex Roles and Family Structure: Stability and Change

B
Racial and Social-class Perspectives on Marriage and the Family

A
Sex Roles and Family Structure:
Stability and Change The contemporary

women's movement was formed to foster change in the present
situation of women. There is agreement among its members that
the status of women is subordinate to that of men. However, there
are as many ideologies or analyses of the causes and solutions as
there are small women's groups around the country. To some
extent each ideology posits the cause of women's secondary
status, formulates strategies for bringing about equality, and to a
limited degree presents a vision of an egalitarian future. Targ
synthesizes these various ideologies into a framework consisting
of three models of equality.

The first, an assimilation model, posits very little change in the
family. Seeing the cause of women's equality in the economic
sector, members of such groups as NOW (National Organization
for Women) propose to redress their grievances through legal
actions leading to women's assimilation into the present structure
of society. Both the radical political analysis and the cultural
feminist analysis seek a thoroughgoing change in the family as
well as in the structure of society. The political feminists see the
capitalist system as dependent upon women's oppression within
the family and believe that ultimately only in a socialist society can
all humans be not only equal but liberated as well. They are
working first, however, to remove from the home some of the
functions that women perform for the family; for example, child
care.

The cultural feminists, on the contrary, see the male-female
role system as the primary cause of women's inferior status. They
are concerned with abolishing all manifestations of that role
system—especially the nuclear family. Cultural feminists tend to
stress the importance of the form of the family and to emphasize

and work within alternative forms such as women's communes. They also envision a future in which all humans—men, women, and children—are equal and liberated.

While few would argue with the statement that the contemporary situation of women is determined by their ultimate definition as housewives and mothers, not all would agree with a negative interpretation of this statement. Many would argue for the positive aspects of the division of labor between the sexes; for example, that this division of labor is functional for the society and efficient for the family. Even among those who present a negative evaluation of the contemporary situation of women, the debate continues over the historical basis for sexual stratification and the sexual division of labor within the family. We shall consider the importance of historical interpretation especially in its implications for the possibility of change.

According to Randall Collins, the basis of the sexual stratification system is conflict. Combining Freud's proposition that human beings universally exhibit strong sexual and aggressive drives with Weber's proposition that humans strive to achieve as much dominance as their resources allow, leads to the conclusion that women will be the sexual prizes for men, since men are physically larger and stronger than women.

The basis of the sexual stratification system is, therefore, woman as prize or woman as property. Although the phenomenon of woman as property may be seen more clearly in other societies, Collins points out that in modern societies, women are still considered to be the sexual property of their husbands; for example, the legal definition of rape does not include sexual assault within a marriage.[1]

Historical variations in sexual stratification are the result of interdependent changes within a society of the location of important resources: force and economic power. Each variation is, of course, supported by a changing ideology. As a consequence of this conflict theory we would expect that when economic resources and force are equalized between men and women within society, sexual conflict and marital bargaining will be individualized rather than divided across sex lines. Viewed from a

1. See in this volume the article by Verna Tomasson for an elaboration of this theme.

historical perspective, the contemporary situation has seen a slight increase in the economic resources of women. While recognizing fully the inequities of the present occupational structure, Collins points out that many women can now earn their own living even if it is not a luxurious one. Therefore, women have a measure of independence from men and the ability to make demands on the marital bargain. As Collins concludes, however, the primacy of males as a group in controlling economic institutions will tend to perpetuate the existing pattern of sexual inequality.

Economic factors are often mentioned in connection with the secondary status of modern women. Force, on the contrary, is not often considered as a factor in maintaining the contemporary system of sexual stratification. Collins refers to the use of male physical power particularly in dating and marital situations. In addition, the more general use and threat of force, especially rape, should be considered as a means of social control integral to the perpetuation of the current form of male-female stratification.

We do not usually think of rape as a form of social control because we are accustomed to thinking of rape as an individual crime with a solitary victim. When we think of rape in societal terms, it is ordinarily to ask questions concerning which features of society coincide with an increased or decreased incidence of the crime. Nevertheless, women are beginning to view the threat of rape and the differential punishment of rape as means to keep women in their place.[2]

The attitudes of the legal authorities and the operation of the judicial system illuminate the social function of rape. In the case of alleged rape, *the victim must prove her innocence.* Defense attorneys often attempt to discredit the witness's morals to prove that she consented to the rape. As a result, if the victim has not entirely conducted herself according to society's prescriptions, she is told that it was her fault that she was raped—she is both the cause and the victim of the crime. And the message is clear to all women: If you are not chaste, if you go out alone, if you in any

2. See, for example, Janice McKenna Reynolds, "Rape as Social Control" (Paper delivered at the Meetings of the Michigan Sociological Association, Detroit, Michigan, September 1971); Susan Griffin, "The Politics of Rape," *Ramparts* 10, no. 3 (September 1971): 26–35; Terri Schultz, "Rape, Fear and the Law," *Chicago Guide* 21, no. 11 (November 1972): 56–62.

way behave as if you are free, you may get raped and you will deserve your fate!

In view of Collins' analysis, it is not surprising that contemporary discussions of rape often are concerned with methods for counteracting rape and thus equalizing force. Suggestions for women are usually on the individual level: use of weapons, knowledge of physical defense, and screaming for help. Increased ability in the area of self-defense should ameliorate sexual inequality, but again it must be remembered that organized force—the police and the military as well as the legal system—is still controlled by males.

In contrast to Collins, Gough stresses the cooperative aspects of the development of the institution of the family. She defines the family as a husband and wife or other related individuals, most of whom share a common dwelling, and cooperate both economically and in the socialization of children. In addition, she presents the following as universal characteristics of the family: (1) some type of incest taboo, (2) marriage between identifiable individuals, (3) a division of labor based upon sex, and (4) a status differential between men and women.

Using evidence from primate societies, human evolution, and contemporary hunting and gathering societies, Gough asserts that the characteristics of the family are *not* instinctual, but at each stage of development are a result of necessary adaptation to the environment, ecological change, or species change. The evidence related to sexual division of labor and male dominance is of particular interest here. First, among nonhuman primates, male dominance is most pronounced in those that live largely on the ground and therefore have to be more concerned with defense than tree dwellers. Second, as hunters had to roam farther for food and as infants required more care, the sexual division of labor developed. Finally, even in egalitarian hunting and gathering societies, there is a division of labor characterized by the secondary status of women. That status varies somewhat; the evaluation of women is highest in those societies where they make an important contribution to food gathering. Although Gough stresses cooperation rather than conflict as the basis for hierarchy and dominance, she implies general agreement with

Collins in citing the central role of force (monopoly of heavy weapons)[3] and economic factors (the particular division of labor) in the stratification system of the hunting societies.

Gough concludes by arguing that the necessity for the sexual division of labor disappears in industrial (and certainly in postindustrial) society. Scientific development of alternative means of reproduction and cooperative child care would allow men to share responsibility for children while changes in the physical capabilities required in production would allow women to assume an equal share in economic responsibilities. Not only has the necessity for women to be defined in reproductive terms disappeared but also the restriction of women to subordinate roles in the family and, as a result, at work is detrimental to women as individuals and to the general development of human potential. Gough states that we do not know what form social relations will take in the future, but we need not fear the demise of the family as defined by the past.

The sexual division of labor may have originated from necessary cooperation between the sexes. The original meaning has been lost, however. As Gough herself points out, with the emergence of private property and the state, male domination dramatically increased. In addition a complex ideology arose to support that domination. We agree that the history of the family should not limit its future. But the possibility of equality does not ensure its probability.

---

3. In a recent critique of Collins' paper, Stoll seriously questions the emphasis of sex drive on human behavior and stresses instead the importance of political struggles among men. See Clarice Stasz Stoll, "On Sexual Stratification," *Social Problems* 20, no. 3 (Winter 1973): 392–95.

1

THE CONTEMPORARY WOMEN'S MOVEMENT: THE FAMILY AND SOCIAL CHANGE

DENA B. TARG

"What do these women want?" has been the standard question since the beginning of the contemporary women's movement. "Equality" is the standard reply. Equality would seem to be a cherished American ideal, yet everyone attaches a different meaning to the word. Alice Rossi has outlined three models of equality which may be considered by any society which hopes to include sex equality as a goal and a reality.[1] These models, which have been used in the past to discuss ethnic and racial equality, are: (1) the pluralist model; (2) the assimilation model; and (3) the hybrid model. The pluralist model is best described as the "separate but equal" model. It is a conservative model calling for maintenance of the status quo, with roles assigned according to biology. This model is inconsistent with the current women's movement wherein women are no longer willing to have their potential as actors in the world determined by their biological status. Furthermore, this model would never create equality on a society-wide basis, since, as Rossi points out, "separate but equal" inevitably leads to "separate but less."

The second model, believed by some to lead ultimately to equality between two groups, is the assimilation model. It is a liberal model; that is, one in which no fundamental changes in society are expected. According to this model, there is no flaw—or little flaw—in the existing society except that the minority group has not been integrated into it. The minority group simply wants an equal amount of power, an equal share of the pie, or a seat in the front of the bus. The assimilation model tends to ignore other major problems of the society.

The third model is the hybrid model. This is a "melting pot" model in which changes in both sex groups are deemed necessary. It is a radical model because it envisions a change in the structure of society. Inequality is the problem but equality in the existing order is not the

---

1. Alice Rossi, "Sex Equality: The Beginnings of Ideology," *Humanist* 29, no. 5 (September–October 1969): 3–6, 16.

answer. As Herbert Marcuse has stated, "Equality should not mean that women partake equally as exploiters and oppressors; that is, that women become equally efficient as competitors in business, for example."[2] Critical of contemporary society, this model questions power relationships at home, work, and in government; the technological society which has as its goal, efficiency rather than human fulfillment; the bureaucracy which serves itself rather than the public; the values of competition, consumption, and conformity; a sexual ethic which restrains rather than frees.

Rossi defines the hybrid model as a model for liberation:

> With . . . the hybrid model of equality one envisages a future in which family, community, and play are valued on a par with politics and work for both sexes, for all the races, and for all social classes and nations which comprise the human family.[3]

Both the assimilation model and the hybrid model have proponents within the contemporary women's movement. The hybrid model is proposed from two differing viewpoints—that of the political feminists and that of the cultural feminists.

While recognizing that the movement is composed of a multiplicity of groups, we will analyze the ideology of equality which characterizes it in terms of these three models.

The Assimilation Model

The major analysis of the assimilation position, *The Feminine Mystique*,[4] preceded the emergence of the current movement. Its author, Betty Friedan, became the first president of the reform organization, NOW (National Organization for Women). According to Friedan, the feminine mystique states that a woman will find fulfillment only if she exhibits certain natural qualities. To be feminine and to find happiness in a commitment to that femininity is to be sexually passive, submissive

---

2. Herbert Marcuse as told to Robert Allen, "Marcuse on Students, Women," *Guardian* 21, no. 8 (23 November 1968): 11.

3. Rossi, "Sex Equality: The Beginnings of Ideology," p. 16.

4. Betty Friedan, *The Feminine Mystique* (New York: Dell, 1963).

to male domination, and to provide nurturing maternal love. Since World War II this mystique has been translated for American women into "Occupation: Housewife." American women were informed by the media, by leading educators and intellectuals, by all available proponents, that they should seek fulfillment only in the home, through husband and children, with any deviation from this course resulting in personal maladjustment, in a loss of femininity. Women were faced with what Friedan calls "the mistaken choice" or with the absence of choice. Either they choose femininity and love, children, home and warmth, or they choose a career; either they choose to be natural or unnatural.

Women in the 1950s tried to live up (or down) to the mystique. They tried to be "happy housewife homemakers," baking bread, sewing their own clothes, decorating and redecorating their homes, and having more and more children. But still many found that their myriad of household chores, even when volunteer work was added, did not fill their lives. Something was missing. As a consequence of living life through their families rather than creating an identity of their own, women became objects. In Friedan's words,

> It is my thesis that the core of the problem for women today is . . . a problem of identity—a stunting or evasion of growth that is perpetuated by the feminine mystique . . . our culture does not permit women to accept or gratify their basic need to grow and fulfill their potentialities as human beings, a need which is not solely defined by their sexual role.[5]

To change this situation, women must demand more of themselves. They must combine marriage and motherhood with a career. Education is the only way for a woman to remove herself from this deadening trap—education combined with a new life plan, a commitment to do fulfilling work. The new prevailing condition will then find women equal to men in being able to grow to their full human potential.

This solution reflects the fact that *The Feminine Mystique* is basically an analysis of a certain segment of the society of women. This segment is composed of intelligent, creative women who typically have been to college. These women are now financially comfortable suburban

---

5. Ibid., p. 69.

housewives. To complete the description, their husbands are college educated and are engaged in fulfilling occupations or professions.

These were the women who, when they did commit themselves to life careers, encountered discrimination against working wives and mothers as to hiring, firing, and all the more "subtle" practices in-between. These were the women who, in their forties, returning to work after a long absence or finding a first job, felt the contradiction between their treatment as a middle-class wife and a woman worker. It was in order to combat inequities in the working world of relatively advantaged women that NOW was formed. The NOW Statement of Purpose[6] details the secondary occupational status of American women: (1) their concentration in low-prestige jobs; (2) the ever-increasing wage gap between males and females; (3) the small percentage of women going on to higher education; (4) the token number of women professionals; and, finally (5) the replacement of women by men in what were formerly women's professions.

In order to combat this inequality, NOW relies heavily on legislation —the introduction of new legislation, the enforcement of current legislation, or the repeal of unfair past legislation. NOW proposes to change American society through existing channels:

> We believe that the power of American law, and the
> protection guaranteed by the United States Constitution to
> the civil rights of all individuals, must be effectively applied
> and enforced to isolate and remove patterns of sex
> discrimination.[7]

NOW also proposes to use a tactic of the suffragists: supporting those political candidates who support their cause and striving to "ensure that no party, candidate . . . or any public official who betrays or ignores the principle of full equality between the sexes is elected or appointed to office." [8]

The change which NOW proposes to legislate is equality for women within the existing framework of American society. The references to civil rights within the Statement of Purpose underscore the parallel that is often drawn between the NAACP and NOW—in both cases the

---

6. National Organization for Women, "Statement of Purpose (1966)," in *Up from the Pedestal: Selected Writings in the History of American Feminism*, ed. Aileen S. Kraditor (Chicago: Quadrangle Books, 1968), pp. 363–69.

7. Ibid., p. 366.

8. Ibid., p. 369.

"underdog" is asking for equality; in both cases it is the middle class within each group which stands to gain the most. The following passage from the Statement illustrates the stress on integration rather than on changing the structure of society: "N.O.W. is dedicated to the proposition that women, first and foremost are human beings, who, like all other people in our society, must have the chance to develop their fullest human potential." [9]

Further, the primary area of integration is the economic sphere. The changes NOW promotes are directed toward elevating women to equality with men in the occupational realm. As Alice Rossi states: "The range of women's problems that N.O.W. is concerned with has broadened greatly since 1966, but the core continues to be equal treatment in hiring and promotion." [10] Thus education to full human potential is not an end in itself but a means to integration into the economic system.

> We believe that it is essential for every girl to be educated to her full potential of human ability as it is for every boy—with the knowledge that such education is the key to effective participation in today's economy. . . .[11]

Critique

The assimilation position assumes that all men are equal now. It indicates that all men are equal in being able to realize their full human potential. The purpose of change then becomes the elimination of sex typing of contemporary roles. Yet one of the basic problems facing our contemporary society is that most men are engaged in work which enslaves them rather than liberates them. The reform attitude ignores the men who perform repetitive clock-punching jobs, let alone the men who work in paint and plastic factories inhaling dangerous fumes. It would seem that if women were equal to men, they would have an unlimited opportunity to grow. If women were equal to men in today's society, more women would have better pay, more women would have creative, satisfying jobs, but the majority of workers would still not be rewarded adequately nor realize their fullest capacity as human beings.

---

9. Ibid., pp. 363–64.

10. Alice S. Rossi, "Women—Terms of Liberation," *Dissent* 17, no. 6 (November–December 1970): 534.

11. National Organization for Women, "Statement of Purpose (1966)," p. 367.

The First Hybrid Model—Radical
Political Viewpoint

While the assimilation position argues for an equal place in the economic system, the radical position sees the economic system as the basis of women's secondary status. According to the radical political position, the financial dependence of wives and children helps to perpetuate the capitalist system in many ways. First, because the husband only is provider, it is difficult for either the husband or wife to contemplate change. Due to his total responsibility for his family's support, he cannot consider any alternative to a standard nine-to-five job or eleven-to-seven shift; he is pressured to succeed so he can provide for his wife and family. The wife's dependence leads her, too, to be conservative, fearful, and supportive of the status quo. Men are able to participate fully in the production sector of the economy only because their wives are providing essential services in the home. They take care of all or most domestic details so their husbands are free to immerse themselves in their work. Even more important, perhaps, the home provides an emotional haven from the harsh realities of the marketplace.

In addition to ensuring that her husband continues as an active member of the work force, the housewife supports the capitalist system through her role as consumer. The nuclear family itself can be seen as a small, wasteful unit of consumption. Each separate household requires its own furnishings, housewares, and large appliances. Buying the correct items in the latest style indicates that a woman is carrying out her role as wife and mother and expresses her concern for the family. In addition, because housewives lack an identity of their own, they are motivated to buy, redecorate, and buy again to express themselves through material ownership. Marlene Dixon describes the interaction between the capitalist system and the housewife in the following manner:

> The American system of capitalism depends for its survival
> on the consumption of vast amounts of socially wasteful
> goods, and a prime target for the unloading of this waste is
> the housewife. She is the purchasing agent for the family,
> but beyond that she is eager to buy because her own identity

---

depends on her ability to satisfy the wants of her husband and children.[12]

Yet the consumer role is deceiving, for despite the fact that women purchase vast amounts of consumer goods, both large and small, staples and perishables, they have no control over what is produced nor over the larger economy.

Even when women themselves enter the money economy, whether through force or choice, the ideology of the family keeps labor costs down. This occurs in part because many employers consider a woman's earnings supplementary—irrespective of her actual family situation— the female worker is discriminated against in terms of wages. Second, because men workers also see women as secondary labor, they are less likely to ally with them against management when fighting for wages, benefits, or better working conditions. This causes a split in the working class which helps only employers. Third, women alone are not as likely as men to organize because they believe the ideology that they "belong at home" ánd because they have been socialized generally to be more docile than men. Finally, the ever-present role of housewife allows the woman to fade in and out of the work force without causing the massive discontent and dislocation that unemployment engenders among men. As Margaret Benston states,

> The "cult of the home" makes its reappearance during times of labor surplus and is used to channel women out of the market economy. This is relatively easy since the pervading ideology ensures that no one, man or woman, takes women's participation in the labor force very seriously. Women's real work, we are taught, is in the home; this holds true whether or not they are married, single, or the heads of households.[13]

According to Benston, the structural preconditions to women achieving real equality are (1) equal access to jobs outside the home and (2) the industrialization of housework and child care or placing both into the public economy. The process is circular. Equality in jobs will not be achieved until the constraints of housework and child care

---

12. Marlene Dixon, "The Rise of Women's Liberation," *Ramparts* 8, no. 6 (December 1969): 60–61.

13. Margaret Benston, "The Political Economy of Women's Liberation," *Monthly Review* 21, no. 4 (September 1969): 21.

---

are lifted from women and housework and child care will not be industrialized until women are leaving the home for jobs. It must be realized that these two conditions are just preconditions. A belief in the inferior nature of women is deeply ingrained in most men and women in our society and the belief will not begin to change until the objective reality is changed.[14]

The segment of the movement that espouses the radical political position grew out of the New Left in America. These women had worked within the New Left in the civil rights movement, in the peace movement, in community organizing and in campus activism to try to eradicate the problems of racism, war, and poverty. They worked to erase the economic and power inequities inherent in the capitalist system; they worked for the "liberation of the human being from a subservient role in the present social machinery to a self-determining position where the individual because he is free is neither master or slave." [15] But continuously they found that although they were working for equality for all men, movement women were relegated—as are women generally—to the tasks the men did not want. They began to see that they were not taken seriously by movement men. They began to see that they were considered not as individual human beings but as sexual objects. By now Stokely Carmichael's quote is legend: "The proper position for women in the movement is prone."

Radical women formed the Women's Liberation Movement and began to organize around women's issues. Although they themselves are from middle-class origins, the political feminists emphasize organizing working-class women toward the ultimate goal of achieving a classless socialist state. They recognize that socialism does not automatically include women's liberation. However, since woman's cheap, if not free, labor and her role in the nuclear family is required by contemporary capitalism, liberation is impossible under capitalism. With changes in women's functions for the family and with the subsequent elimination of the ideology of the nuclear family, women's liberation is at least possible under socialism.

The political feminists propose to organize working-class women around the concrete problems which stem from their subordinate status in the nuclear family. Among the most often raised demands are: (1) community or parent-controlled day-care centers so that both parents

14. Ibid., pp. 21–22.
15. Lauri Hunt and Nancy Brand, "Women's Liberation," *Bauls* 2, no. 1 (2 February 1969): 4.

can be free to work or have time for personal projects; (2) shortened workweeks or four-hour days so that both fathers and mothers can work and engage in growth experiences with children; (3) access to equal work and at the most limited level, the same pay for the same work; (4) equal access to education; and (5) free society-wide dissemination of birth-control information and devices, including abortion counseling and services so that biology is no longer destiny.

The major concern here is with changing the content of the family lives of women, especially for women who have no measure of independence, rather than trying to argue against the nuclear family form. Telling poor women with several children that they shouldn't have gotten themselves into such a mess is no news and no help at all. As McAfee and Wood so aptly state,

> Organizing against the family cannot be the basis of a program. An uneducated working class wife with five kids is perfectly capable of understanding that marriage has destroyed most of her potential as a human being—probably she already understands this—but she is hardly in a position to repudiate her source of livelihood and free herself of those children. If we expect that of her, we will never build a movement.[16]

Juliet Mitchell argues further for organizing to change the division of labor among women and men without explicitly aiming at a change in the form of the family. According to Mitchell, it is important to challenge women's inequality in the areas of production, reproduction, sexuality, and the socialization of children. Once sex roles are equal in relation to the functions only women now play in each of these areas, the family as we know it will disappear.[17]

Radical women see a future in which technology will free humans to work only at those tasks that will contribute to human development and his or her own self-actualization. Before this cybernetic age arrives, pleasant and unpleasant work alike should be shared so that no race, sex, or class carries the burden of others. In order to reduce or eliminate unnecessary work and wasteful consumption, the primary requirement

---

16. Kathy McAfee and Myrna Wood, "Bread and Roses," *Leviathan* 1, no. 3 (June 1969): 44.

17. Juliet Mitchell, *Woman's Estate* (New York: Pantheon Books, 1971), pp. 99–122, 144–51.

is a socialist economic structure. Only when no one is forced to work for the enrichment of others will work be intrinsically interesting and rewarding. At that time, for example, advertisers will have no reason to convince consumers to buy new cars each year, to see cigarettes as essential to a positive "image," and to deodorize everything from head to toe as well as from kitchen to bathroom.

It is more difficult to fill in the outlines of the future. In discussing marriage and the family, for example, Mitchell rails against the emphasis on only one form—the nuclear family. We have been bound normatively to one pattern of intersexual and intergenerational relationships. While the society of the future will undoubtedly have patterned, institutionalized ways to recognize personal relationships, the legitimate ways will be various and not limited. As examples Mitchell offers the following:

> Couples—of the same or of different sexes—living together or not living together, long-term unions with or without children, single parents—male or female—bringing up children, children socialized by conventional rather than biological parents, extended kin groups, etc.—all these could be encompassed in a range of institutions which match the free invention and variety of men and women.[18]

Critique

The political feminists are concerned with achieving some of the same goals as the members of assimilationist groups. Unlike assimilationists, however, they see goals such as equal pay for equal work and the general availability of day care as means to a final end and not only as ends in themselves. By organizing women toward changing the functions of the family, as a means to elevate their consciousness and thus enlist their aid in creating a new society, the political feminists face a danger. This is the danger that the attainment of discrete individual reforms will come to be seen as the ultimate goal of the movement.

The suffragists, for example, originally wanted the vote as an instrument to achieve changes in American society. They were concerned about poverty, working conditions, discrimination against women in all sectors of society. As the movement continued, getting the

18. Ibid., p. 151.

vote itself became the goal. Once the vote was won, the movement was considered successful, and most women ceased political activity, especially political activity directed toward change.

An analogous situation exists for the political feminists. By concentrating on short-term or immediate goals, they face the risk that success will be defined in terms of these goals rather than in terms of a less well-defined, more long-range change in society. For example, day-care centers are now seen as both a goal and as a means toward change. Some factories have already instituted day-care facilities within their buildings. They are owned, operated, and controlled by the owners of the factory. They are unlikely, however, to be much of a force toward radical change. The values taught therein, for example, are most likely to be those that benefit the current capitalist economic system: individualism, competition, the consumer ethic, and stability. There is no overall change in the quality of life for the mother, either as worker or housewife. Admittedly, the availability of such day-care centers probably eliminates some anxiety for the mothers involved and perhaps is of some financial benefit. Nevertheless, female workers who use factory-run day-care facilities are less likely than female workers who do not have the advantage of convenient day care to organize against their employers or the larger system. In this instance, a short-term goal has been reached; but its identity as part of the means to a more radical long-range goal has been lost.

The Second Hybrid Model—Cultural Feminist Viewpoint

The cultural feminists argue that the male-female role system was the first class system. Within this system, women as a class are defined by their ability to bear children. One-half of mankind took advantage of the burden placed upon women by childbirth and child care and defined the other half in terms of this reproductive function. As a result, the female role is characterized as inherently maternal, sacrificing, submissive, and weak. Thus limited by their biological nature, women are denied humanness, individuality, and creativity.

This first class system has always formed the basis for all other institutions. Therefore, contrary to the radical political analysis, women's inferior position does not serve primarily to reinforce the economic system. Rather, the purpose of the economic system is to reinforce the male-female role system. The primary nature of the latter system is illustrated by the fact that equality has not been achieved in such revolutionary socialist states as the Soviet Union and Cuba.

In order to destroy the sex class system, all other institutions that originate from it must also be eliminated because "(1) they are not only the expressions of this role system but perpetuate this system as well; (2) they are rigid and destroy individuality; (3) they divide (cause competition between) and isolate the oppressed." [19] Oppressive male-female institutions include love, sexual intercourse, and marriage, and especially the family. Love between equals can end the experience of isolation and loneliness which every individual feels, especially in modern societies. However, the unequal power distribution between men and women prevents men from committing themselves to a full relationship with women who are by definition inferior. Society measures women and they in turn measure themselves by their ability to acquire the love (and support) of a man. "Thus once more the phenomenon of love, good in itself, is distorted by a given political situation: women need love not only for healthy reasons but actually to validate their existence." [20] Although sexual intercourse would seem to be the most personal of acts, it is also political since it reflects the male-female role system. It is the means to procreation which binds women to their biological function and thereby strengthens the ideology that the maternal role is women's natural, inherent role. In addition, the biological family is a basic institution for promulgating and preserving unequal roles. However, even more basic is the one difference that was originally the cause of women's dependence on the male—women's ability to bear children. Measures such as contraception and abortion only begin to make women equal to men. What technology can do to eradicate the biological basis of women's unequal position is to develop ways of creating new humans outside of the uterus.

The above analysis indicates that although the cultural feminists are not unaware of the larger political and economic system, they emphasize the sex-role system and the psychology of power. The

19. The Feminists, "The Feminists: A Political Organization to Annihilate Sex Roles," in *Notes From the Second Year*, ed. Shulamith Firestone (New York: Radical Feminism, 1970), p. 117.

20. Shulamith Firestone, "Love," in Firestone, *Notes From the Second Year*, p. 21.

cultural feminists begin with education and life style, expecting to change the larger system through converting individuals. The major form of education is in small, tightly knit consciousness-raising groups. By sharing their experiences and analyzing their larger significance, women can become aware of their oppression and then change their life style to indicate an unwillingness to participate in the male-female role system.

It was the question of life style that caused Ti-Grace Atkinson to break away from the National Organization for Women and form The October 17th Movement (which eventually became The Feminists). If women are trying to eradicate power and hierarchy in the larger society, she reasoned, then their organizations should reflect this new equality rather than mirroring the faults of the male society. Therefore, cultural feminist groups are organized to be small, egalitarian, and leaderless. All women assume all roles—no matter what their experience or the status of the job.

The women who subscribe to the cultural feminist perspective are well informed and thoroughly inculcated with the idea that alternate life styles must begin immediately rather than changing piecemeal or evolving slowly. They evidence alternative life styles in egalitarian communes, often women's communes, and are often lesbians who are unwilling to live in a subordinate personal relationship with any male.

The future envisioned by the cultural feminists is predicated upon a society in which all individuals have equal responsibilities and privileges. From this premise, Shulamith Firestone[21] has posited in general terms one possible alternative future. This future is a technological utopia, a socialist cybernetic state. Under socialism, work would be distributed equally, and as advances are made in technology, work as drudgery would disappear completely. Without work as drudgery, all individuals, not just the elite, would be able to follow their own interests. Everyone would take different educations to develop their own interests just as craftsmen used to be apprentices before they became members of a guild. All education and creative work would take place in new cities which would be combinations of public and private areas similar to college campuses.

Within this society, Firestone has three suggestions for forms to

---

21. Shulamith Firestone, *The Dialectic of Sex: The Case for Feminist Revolution* (New York: William Morrow, 1970), pp. 257–74.

replace the male-female role system. First, she suggests that single professions such as astronaut and stewardess be expanded. Second, she suggests the society-wide acceptability of "living together" in its various forms. Finally, she delineates a form called the "household" for raising children. The household would consist of about ten adults who contracted to stay together for an extended period in order to raise a child or children. The household would carry with it none of the negative connotations of the biological family: biological reproduction, sexual division of labor, power and hierarchy.

Critique

A central criticism of the cultural feminists as a force for change concerns the effectiveness of the consciousness-raising group. The small group is seen by the cultural feminists as an ideal environment to provide support and encouragement for women as they first admit to personal troubles and ultimately as a secure working environment for women when they recognize later the public and political nature of their troubles. Mitchell describes consciousness-raising as "the process of transforming the hidden, individual fears of women into a shared awareness of the meaning of them as social problems, the release of anger, anxiety, the struggle of proclaiming the painful and transforming it into the political." [22]

However, critics assert that consciousness-raising serves too often the same purpose as debased psychotherapy, or encounter groups in which inhibited individuals change into uninhibited *individuals*. In the same manner, the effect of women's groups can become circular not linear: individual women leave home, come to understand their problems through the group, and return home, thus strengthening instead of working to weaken the current social fabric. In contrast, according to Mitchell, revolutionary politics is linear—it must move from the individual, to the small group, to the whole society." [23]

Conclusion

In conclusion, we should like to consider the possibility that at this time in history the assimilation and hybrid models can be complemen-

---

22. Mitchell, *Woman's Estate*, p. 61.
23. Ibid., p. 23.

tary. The radical's disdain for the egalitarian ethic leads to a search for actions and goals commensurate with a new vision of society, with a liberation ethic. This disdain in turn often leads either to inaction or to concern with other societal problems to the exclusion of the problems of women specifically. Despite the danger described above, that working for reformist goals may lead to a strengthening of the current system, inaction precludes the possibility of change. And concern with economic stratification or alienated work usually takes on a male perspective.

Freeman asserts that both ethics are important:

> Separately they speak to limited interests; together they speak to all humanity. Separately they are but superficial solutions; together they recognize that while sexism oppresses women, it also limits the potentiality of men. . . . Separately these two ethics do not lead to the liberation of women; together they also lead to the liberation of men.[24]

24. Jo Freeman, "The Women's Liberation Movement: Its Origins, Structures and Ideas," in *Recent Sociology No. 4*, ed. Hans Peter Dreitzel (New York: Macmillan, 1972), p. 206.

2

A CONFLICT THEORY OF SEXUAL STRATIFICATION

RANDALL COLLINS

In recent years, we have been sharply reminded that there is a system of stratification by sex. This paper[1] presents a sociological theory of sexual stratification, constructed from the perspectives of Freud and

1. I am indebted to Joseph R. Gusfield and Stanford Lyman for critical comments on an earlier version of this paper.

Weber. Freud's work has been interpreted as a general theory of individual psychological functioning. Sociological and historical perspectives have been introduced primarily in criticism of Freud's psychology, especially to argue that sexual repression and its related family constellations are not universal, but only characteristic of Victorian Europe. But what may be a limitation on a psychological theory can prove fruitful in historical sociology. Freud's major discoveries—the biologically universal drives of sexuality and aggression, and the historically specific repression of these drives through an idealized moralism—thus become the keys to unlock the history of sexual stratification.

Weber provides a sociological perspective in which to interpret these insights. He presents a conflict model of stratification: that persons struggle for as much dominance as their resources permit; that changes in resources lead to changes in the structure of domination; and that ideals are used as weapons in these struggles, both to unify status communities and to justify power interests. From a combination of these perspectives, we may derive a theory to explain both the general fact of sexual stratification and the conditions for variations in it throughout human history.

Sexual Discrimination in Employment

Employment discrimination on the basis of sex is widespread. Women are concentrated in the lowest ranking positions of the work force. . . .

Two common explanations of the low occupational rank of women are (1) lack of training, and (2) low commitment to jobs due to marriage and child rearing. The first explanation is contrary to the facts. A comparison of the educational attainment of workers with the skill requirement of their jobs indicates that women are currently overtrained for their present jobs.[2] The second explanation is a self-fulfilling prophecy. If women are given opportunities only for menial jobs, they might well view home and children as preferable employment. To argue that someone must take care of the house and

---

2. Ivar Berg, *Education and Jobs: The Great Training Robbery* (New York: Praeger, 1970), pp. 38–60.

children does not settle the point; it is conceivable that men could take over or share these tasks, or that less emphasis could be placed on having a house and children. If women are given the opportunity for satisfying careers, they appear to pursue them no less consistently than men: the percentage of law degree holders who are in practice is similar among women and among men, and figures for male and female doctors also are similar.[3]

A more plausible explanation is that women are the subordinate class in a system of sexual stratification. That is, there is a system of stratification by sex which is different from familiar forms of stratification by economic, political, or status group position, although it interacts with these other stratification systems. The principle of this system is that women take orders from men but do not give orders to them; hence only men can give orders to other men, and women can give orders only to other women. This principle is modified primarily when sexual stratification interacts with economic or other stratification (for example, when upper-class women give orders to male servants).

Women managers are found almost exclusively in organizations hiring many women. . . .

In the professions women are concentrated in specialities where they deal principally with children or other women, rarely with men of high status.[4]

Women's subordinate position at work may be viewed as a continuation of their subordinate position in the home. Although twentieth-century American society has changed a good deal from the traditional husbandly dictatorship, the female role in the home continues to center around that of domestic servant. The married woman has primary responsibility for cooking, dishwashing, laundering, housecleaning, and child care—occupational roles that are classified as low-prestige service positions when listed in the labor force. The modern American male is more likely to help voluntarily with some of these tasks than his ancestors or his non-Western counterparts,[5] but the responsibility for these tasks still rests generally with the woman, even if she has an outside job. The basic pattern is male dominance in practical activities

---

3. Cynthia Fuchs Epstein, *Woman's Place* (Berkeley: University of California Press, 1970), p. 73.

4. Ibid., pp. 163–64.

5. William J. Goode, *World Revolution and Family Patterns* (New York: Free Press, 1963), pp. 66–70.

both at home and at work, although there is some weakening of this pattern in some highly modern societies.

Basic Propositions

What is the basis of this form of stratification? We may begin with two propositions: (1) that human beings have strong sexual and aggressive drives; and (2) that males are physically dominant over females, since they are generally bigger, and females are further made physically vulnerable by bearing and caring for children.[6] The combination of these propositions means that men will generally be the sexual aggressors, and women will be sexual prizes for men.

Evidence for this is widespread. Rape is defined as a crime only as committed by males, and cases of sexual assault by women are virtually unknown;[7] men are the sexual aggressors in free courtship systems; men are much more motivated by sexual interests as a reason for marriage, whereas women emphasize romantic love, intimacy, and affection more highly than men;[8] exclusively male culture has a heavy component of sexual jokes, bragging of sexual conquests, pinups, and pornography, which have little or no equivalent among women;[9] prostitution occurs almost exclusively among women, and male prostitutes are sex objects for male homosexuals, not for women;[10] men are much more likely to masturbate, experience sexual arousal earlier in life, and are generally more active sexually than women.[11] Men act as the sexual aggressors in modern society, as in virtually all other societies.

---

6. Liebow gives modern examples of how in the relatively open sexual warfare of the urban black lower-class men can exploit a woman's vulnerability through her children. See Elliot Liebow, *Tally's Corner* (Boston: Little, Brown, 1967), pp. 95–96.

7. Leo Kanowitz, *Women and the Law* (Albuquerque: University of New Mexico Press, 1969), p. 18.

8. Ernest W. Burgess and Paul Wallin, *Engagement and Marriage* (Chicago: Lippincott, 1953), p. 699; and Ernest W. Burgess, Harvey Locke, and Mary Thomas, *The Family* (New York: American Book, 1963), p. 368.

9. Ned Polsky, *Hustlers, Beats and Others* (Chicago: Aldine, 1967), p. 197.

10. Kanowitz, *Women and the Law*, pp. 15–18. Gigolos are an exception. However, it appears that they cater exclusively to wealthy, elderly, unmarried women (spinsters and widows), and the role occurs only in societies in which women are relatively emancipated from male control; thus the stereotype of the wealthy American widow and the young man from Latin America or other relatively poor society.

11. Alfred Kinsey and Paul Gebhard, *Sexual Behavior in the Human Female* (Philadelphia: Saunders, 1953), pp. 422–27.

It is not necessary to assume a lesser sexual drive on the part of the human female to explain this pattern. There is reason to believe that female sexual drives are comparable to those of males,[12] and that women are simply more deeply and pervasively repressed sexually than men. The sources of varying restraints on female sexuality will be discussed below, but the basic explanation can be derived from men's physical dominance. Human beings have relatively strong sexual preoccupations compared to most other animals, but even so, no one person is sexually arousable all the time. Since members of the bigger sex can force themselves on the smaller sex, the former can satisfy their sexual drives at will, whereas the latter have sex forced upon them at times they may not want it. Unattractive males can force themselves on attractive females, but unattractive females can rarely do the reverse. Males thus become the sexual aggressors, and females generally adopt a defensive posture. The element of coercion is thus potentially present in every sexual encounter, and this shapes the fundamental features of the woman's role. As we shall see, sexual repression is a basic female tactic in this situation of struggle among unequals in physical strength.

Basic Pattern: Male Sexual Property

The basic feature of sexual stratification is the institution of sexual property: the relatively permanent claim to exclusive sexual rights over a particular person. With male dominance, the principal form of sexual property is male ownership of females; bilateral sexual property is a modern variant which arises with an independent bargaining position of women.

Lévi-Strauss[13] has made the most sweeping use of the notion of sexual property, to explain the basic structure of kinship systems. Men taking permanent sexual possession of particular women constitutes the biological family; children are part of the family because they belong to the woman and hence to the owner of the woman. Within the family, we may note, the incest taboos reflect the facts of sexual property;

12. Clelland S. Ford and Frank A. Beach, *Patterns of Sexual Behavior* (New York: Harper, 1953).

13. Claude Lévi-Strauss, *Les Structures Elementaires de la Parente* (Paris: Presses Universitaires de France, 1949).

indeed, they are the negative side of sexual property rights. The most serious kind of incest is mother-son incest, for this is a violation of the father's primary sexual property by his most immediate rival. Sibling incest violates the father's rights to dispose of the sexual property of his daughters as he sees fit. The father-daughter incest prohibition is hardest to explain in this fashion, although rules of sexual exchange can perhaps account for it.[14]

As Lévi-Strauss argues, if sons cannot get women in their own families, they must get them elsewhere, and that means from those men who have women to spare—the fathers, brothers, or husbands who can give away their daughters, sisters, or wives. Lévi-Strauss applies Marcel Mauss' model of gift-exchange systems to marriage customs: they are sets of rules which guarantee that if a man gives away some of his women, he can get others back from other families. In this way kinship networks develop as opposed to the biological family. Beneath variations in rules of descent, household locality, and marriage choice, kinship systems can be seen as based on sexual property and its related rules of sexual prohibition and exchange.

In modern societies, the pattern is overlaid with a complex set of moral injunctions backed up by church and state, but beneath the ideological surface similar forces operate. Marriage is fundamentally a socially enforced contract of sexual property, as indicated by the facts that marriage is usually not legal until sexually consummated, sexual assault within a marriage is not legally a rape, and the major traditional ground for divorce was sexual infidelity.[15] That the basis of sexual property rights is male violence is still demonstrated by the generally acknowledged dispensation of fathers and brothers to kill rapists of their daughters and sisters. . . .

Once women have been acquired for sexual purposes, they may also be used as menial servants. In primitive societies, women are generally the agricultural and handicrafts workers, while men are the armed fighters and hunters. One may say generally that sexual stratification is the sole basis of social stratification in societies with a very low technological level. In a situation of social instability, women are often

14. Father-daughter incest is by far the most common form of incest, especially if the mother is dead or absent. See S. K. Weinberg, *Incest Behavior* (New York: Citadel Press, 1955).

15. Kanowitz, *Women and the Law.*

regarded as booty in war,[16] and it is likely that the institution of slavery began with women and was later extended to men.[17]

Variations in Sexual Stratification

Male sexual property in women is the basic pattern of sexual stratification. Variations result from two factors: forms of social organization affecting the use of force, and those affecting the market positions of men and women. These two factors operate interdependently. Where force operates freely, the distribution of power among males determines the nature of sexual stratification quite straightforwardly, and women have no bargaining power of their own. In such a context, any market of sexual exchanges operates only as part of the system of bargaining among heads of families and is based on family resources, not on the personal resources of individual men and women. A market for personal sexual qualities and other personal resources can emerge only where the private use of force is limited by the state. Thus, the emergence of a personal sexual market, like that of an economic market, depends fundamentally on the emergence of a particular form of the organization of power. Hence, social structures determining the distribution of force and those producing individual resources for use on a sexual market must be treated as interrelated structural complexes.

Table 2.1 presents in summary form hypotheses about the effects of four main types of social structure on sexual stratification. It states the male and female resources made available in each situation, the resulting system of sexual roles, and the dominant sexual ideology. *Low-technology tribal societies* are those in which the degree of economic productivity allows little stratification. *Fortified households in stratified society* refers to the typical preindustrial organization based on independent households; it corresponds to Weber's patriarchal and patrimonial forms of organization. *Private households in market economy* refers to the typical domestic organization in a society dominated by the bureaucratic state, where the work place is separated from the home. *Advanced market economy* refers to the development of the preceding type

---

16. The *Iliad* gives a readily accessible example; the whole Trojan War is fought over possession of a woman, and Homer's poem begins with a quarrel between Achilles and Agamemnon over women captives.

17. E. A. Thompson, "Slavery in Early Germany," in *Slavery in Classical Antiquity*, ed. Moses I. Finley (Cambridge: W. Heffer & Sons, 1960), pp. 196–98.

Table 2.1. Types of Social Structure, Sexual Stratification, and Dominant Ideologies

Social Structure	Male and Female Resources	Sexual Roles	Dominant Ideology
1. Low-technology tribal society	Male: personal force, personal attractiveness. Female: personal attractiveness.	Limited male sexual property; limited female exploitation.	Incest taboos.
2. Fortified households in stratified society	Male: organized force; control of property. Female: upper-class women head lineage during interregnum of male line.	Strongly enforced male sexual property; high female exploitation; women as exchange property in family alliances.	Male honor in controlling female chastity.
3. Private households in market economy, protected by centralized state	Male: control of income and property. Female: personal attractiveness; domestic service; emotional support.	Sexual market of individual bargaining; bilateral sexual property in marriage.	Romantic love ideal in courtship; idealized marriage bond.
4. Advanced market economy	Male: income and property; personal attractiveness; emotional support. Female: income and property; personal attractiveness; emotional support.	Multidimensional sexual market of individual bargaining.	Multiple ideologies.

into a society of a high level of affluence and widespread nonmanual employment. The four types of social structure are ideal types; combinations of these yield intermediate forms of stratification, combining elements from adjacent systems of sexual stratification.

1. *Low-technology Tribal Societies.* Societies in which the technology produces little or no economic surplus beyond that necessary to keep

each producer alive, have little economic, political, or status stratification.[18] Accordingly, sexual stratification can exist only in a mild form.
Superior male force can be used to enforce sexual property rights
(marriage, incest taboos), but women cannot be forced to do a
disproportionate amount of the work, since all members of society must
work to survive. Insofar as work is divided and leisure is possible,
women appear to work longer and at the more menial tasks. Since there
is little surplus and little economic and political stratification, which
intermarriages occur makes little difference to affect families; where the
economic system does not permit substantial brideprices or dowries and
no families are powerful enough to be highly preferred for political
alliances, there is little reason for daughters to be strongly controlled,
since they are not used as property in a bargaining system. Thus it is in
low-technology tribal societies that most known norms favoring premarital sexual permissiveness are found.[19] The greater the economic surplus
in such 'societies, the greater the tendency for male control over
daughters to be asserted [20] and for women to do a larger proportion of
the menial labor.

2. *Fortified Households in Stratified Society.* In most historical preindustrial
societies, the basic social unit is the fortified household.[21] The use of
force is not monopolized by the state; economic and political organization usually coincides with the family community. Thus, the owner of a
farm, workshop, business, or political office not only makes his place of
work or his official seat in his home; his own family helps in his work, as
do family servants. All work subordinates are treated as servants (of
higher or lower level) and are supported from the household economy.
The family occurs in an intact form only around the heads of such
establishments; servants generally do not have an active family of their
own so much as they are attached to their master's family. In the
absence of police or other peacekeeping forces, the household is an

18. Gerhard Lenski, *Power and Privilege* (New York: McGraw-Hill, 1966), pp. 94–141.

19. This may be established from the data in Murdock which deal almost exclusively
with tribal societies and show widespread norms of sexual permissiveness, and in Goode
which show strong restraints on sexual permissiveness in stratified agrarian societies,
somewhat modified with industrialization. See George Peter Murdock, *Social Structure*
(New York: Macmillan, 1949), pp. 260–83; and Goode, *World Revolution.*

20. Morris Zelditch, Jr., "Family, Marriage and Kinship," in *Handbook of Modern
Sociology,* ed. R. E. L. Faris (Chicago: Rand McNally, 1964), p. 687.

21. Max Weber, *Economy and Society* (New York: Bedminster Press, 1968), pp. 356–84
and 1006–69.

armed unit; its head is also its military commander. Such households may vary considerably in size, wealth, and power, from the court of a king or great lord, through the households of substantial merchants and financiers, knightly manors, down to households of minor artisans and peasants. Stratified below the heads of even the smallest units, however, are nonhouseholders—propertyless workmen, laborers, and servants.

In this form of social organization, male sexual dominance is maximized. The concentration of force and of economic resources in the hands of household heads gives them virtually unopposable control. Where sharp inequality among households permits, an upper class may practice polygamy or concubinage, monopolizing more than their share of females. Correspondingly, men of the servant and laborer classes are sexually deprived, and may never be permitted to marry. Women are most exploited in such societies; they are likely to make up a considerable proportion of the slave class if there is one, as in ancient Greek and Roman society or in Arab society. Wives and daughters as well do most of the menial work, while men concentrate on military pursuits or leisure.[22]

Male rights in sexual property are asserted most strongly in this type of society. Intrahousehold alliances carry much weight in a situation of general distrust and sporadic warfare; the giving of women in marriage is virtually the only gift-exchange system which can produce such ties regularly, and substantial dowries or brideprices usually add weight to the bargain. Women are thus important among the householding classes as exchange property, and hence are closely guarded so as not to lose their market value; the institutions of the harem, the veil, the duenna, and the chaperone are employed here.

On the ideological side, sexual property is regarded as a form of male honor. The honored man is he who is dominant over others, who protects and controls his own property, and who can conquer others' property. In highly warlike societies like that of the Bedouin Arabs, the result is an overriding concern for adultery and the institution of extreme controls over women. The ideal of female chastity (including premarital virginity) is an aspect of male property rights and is regarded as enforceable only by males; women are commonly regarded as sexually amoral, unclean, and lacking in honor, and hence are to be

22. Goode, *World Revolution*, pp. 90 and 141.

controlled by force.[23] The practice of clitoridectomy among the Bedouin in order to reduce women's sexual drives is an extreme reflection of this belief.[24]

The ideological pattern is based on the fact that women are used as sexual objects for the men who properly own them; they are to act as sexual creatures, although within the confines of a male property system. Total asceticism by women is not allowed. Hence women have low status in the religious systems of societies of this type. In Brahminism, Islam, Jainism, Confucianism, and the official Roman cults, women are usually regarded as incapable of detaching themselves from the mundane world, and high religious status is reserved for men.[25]

Women can achieve power of their own in this system only as adjuncts to dominant men. Thus the wife of a household head may derive some power over men servants in the household; in the case of a noblewoman, this can produce considerable deference. In the extreme case, a woman may exercise absolute authority as head of a household lineage during an interregnum in the male line. That this is an exceptional circumstance is proved by the fact that the general status of women does not improve during the reign of a queen; queens like Elizabeth I of England or Catherine the Great of Russia may combine a severe personal autocracy with the enforcement of traditional status of women in society.

In the lower ranks of fortified households, neither men nor women have much honor. Sexual permissiveness here is possible where opportunity permits, although women at the more attractive ages are likely to be monopolized (perhaps sub rosa) by their masters or masters' sons.[26] In general, only the upper-class women will have the leisure and wealth to make themselves sexually attractive; there may also be some genetic selection for attractiveness among upper-class women, as dominant males may select attractive women from the lower orders as

---

23. The literature of medieval Arab culture shows an obsession with maintaining sexual property in the harems; the unabridged *Arabian Nights* consists largely of variations on the plot of men whose wives are unfaithful, usually with male slaves.

24. Goode, *World Revolution*, pp. 147 and 211.

25. Christianity is a partial exception, for reasons discussed below. Buddhism in practice tends to give low status to women although not in theory. Some of the heterodox Hindu and Buddhist-Taoist cults did explicitly include women as full members. See Weber, *Economy and Society*, pp. 488–90.

26. Steven Marcus, *The Other Victorians* (New York: Basic Books, 1964).

mates. What is left is a true sexual underground, with neither stable opportunities for marriage, ideological restraints in the form of notions of sexual honor, nor physical attractiveness and personal leisure. Sexual activity among the underclasses of traditional society must have had much of the elements of the grotesque. This circumstance may have helped the growth of Puritanism among the lower middle class during the breakdown of traditional society.

3. *Private Households in a Market Economy.* The basic structure of home life changes with the rise of the centralized bureaucratic state claiming a monopoly on the legitimate use of violence. A complex of interrelated changes occur: the grand household declines with the diminution of private armaments.[27] The centralized state usually fosters expansion of commerce and industry, hence a proliferation of (a) small shops and crafts enterprises; and (b) large industrial establishments separated from the household. The bureaucratic agencies of the state provide further workplaces separate from the household.[28] The result is that households become smaller and more private, consisting more exclusively of a single family. With the expansion of a market economy, more persons can afford households of their own; a private family-oriented middle class appears.[29]

In this situation, sexual roles also change. The use of force by men to control women diminishes as household armaments disappear and the state monopolizes violence, especially with setting up of a police force to which appeal can be made in violent domestic disputes. Men remain heads of household and control its property; they monopolize all desirable occupations in state and economy as well. Women become at least potentially free to negotiate their own sexual relationships, but since their main resource is their sexuality, the emerging free marriage market is organized around male trades of economic and status resources for possession of a woman. In petty bourgeois families lacking servants, women serve not only as sexual objects but as domestic labor as well. Where the crowded setting of a large household is replaced by the comparative solitude of a small one, the woman also can become an important source of companionship and emotional support. The

27. Lawrence Stone, *The Crisis of the Aristocracy, 1558–1641* (New York: Oxford University Press, 1967).

28. Weber, *Economy and Society*, pp. 375–81 and 956–1003.

29. Phillipe Aries, *Centuries of Childhood* (New York: Random House, 1962), pp. 365–404.

woman's capacity to provide these things are her resources on the sexual market. In wealthier families, the woman's resources may also include her family's wealth and social status, although the general importance of interfamily alliances based on marriage diminishes as political and economic aid can be acquired from nonfamily organizations.

The ideology arising from this situation is that of romantic love, including a strong element of sexual repression. The most favorable female strategy, in a situation where men control the economic world, is to maximize her bargaining power by appearing both as attractive and as inaccessible as possible. Thus develops the ideal of femininity, in which sexuality is idealized and only indirectly hinted as an ultimate source of attraction, since sexuality must be reserved as a bargaining resource for the male wealth and income that can only be stably acquired through a marriage contract. An element of sexual repression is thus built into the situation in which men and women bargain with unequal goods.

In contrast to the male-supported female chastity norm of traditionalistic societies, the romantic sexual repression is upheld principally by the interests of women. A hierarchy of moral evaluation emerges among women, in which women who sell their favors for short-run rewards (prostitutes, "loose women") are dishonored; this moral code reflects female interests in confining sexuality to use as a bargaining resource only for marriage.[30]

Within marriage itself, women can use their improved bargaining position to demand the extension of sexual property norms to the husband. Adultery becomes tabooed not only for women but for men. The strategy for the improvement of women's position both before and after marriage is the same: the idealization of sexuality, made possible by women's newly freed bargaining position and greater protection from violence. Sexual bargaining now takes place by idealized gestures and symbolization rather than the frank negotiations of traditional parents or marriage brokers. The attractive (and the wealthy) women, in particular, can demand much deference during courtship, including an outright ban on direct sexual advances and discussions. Sexuality is referred to only under its idealized aspect of spiritual devotion and

---

30. Compare with David Riesman, "Introduction," in *Crestwood Heights*, ed. John R. Seeley, R. Alexander Sim and Elizabeth W. Loosley (New York: Basic Books, 1955), pp. 5–15.

aesthetic beauty, i.e., the romantic love ideal. Male sexual motives operate beneath the surface of polite manners, but they are forced out of official consciousness. It is in these social situations that sexuality becomes repressed in the sense that Freud observed it.

The romantic love idea is thus a key weapon in the attempt of women to raise their subordinate position by taking advantage of a free market structure. Used in courtship, it creates male deference; after marriage, it expresses and reinforces women's attempt to control the sexual aggressiveness of their husbands toward themselves and toward other women. The idealized view of the marriage bond as a tie of mutual fidelity and devotion calls for absolute restriction of sexuality to marriage, thereby reinforcing the sexual bargaining power of the wife, since she is the only available sex object. Idealization further has the effect of reducing female subordination within marriage by sublimating aggressive male drives into mutual tenderness.

Goode[31] has emphasized that this romantic love norm reflects increased needs for personal emotional support in a society of relatively isolated nuclear households. Both historical shifts from the large households of traditional society,[32] and current shifts from the crowded, public living conditions of modern working-class life to a more affluent private homelife[33] show an increase in the ideal and in mutual emotional support of spouses. This shift to greater interpersonal reliance is undoubtedly one source of the romantic love ideal; however, its classical features, notably the repression and idealization of sexuality, appear to derive only from the struggle over sexual domination. In this perspective, the needs of men for psychological support become important primarily as an additional bargaining point for women in attempting to improve their power position within the family. As the stratification theory predicts, women are a good deal more attached to the romantic ideal than are men.[34]

The first approximation to the private household market economy structure appeared in the cities of the Roman Empire, and it is here that the first major love ideal is found as well, contained within

31. William J. Goode, "The Theoretical Importance of Love," *American Sociological Review* 24, no. 1 (February 1959): 38–47.

32. Goode, *World Revolution*; and Aries, *Centuries of Childhood.*

33. Lee Rainwater, "Sexual Life and Interpersonal Intimacy: Class Patterns," *Journal of Marriage and the Family* 26, no. 4 (November 1964): 457–66.

34. Burgess et al., *The Family*, p. 368.

Christianity. Christianity had its origins among the small independent craftsmen, merchants, degraded landowners, and other petty bourgeois of this flourishing international economy.[35] Its major innovations were: (a) it established a community independent of family or ethnic ties; (b) it admitted women to full and equal membership. The first feature Christianity shares with the other great world religions: Buddhism, Islam, and (to a lesser degree) Confucianism; the latter feature was developed nowhere else to a similar degree. Indeed, the appeal to women was a key in Christianity's rapid spread and eventual success over its rivals.[36] The Christian community was united among its members by spiritual love and shared norms of asceticism; in a Durkheimian interpretation, the theological doctrine of mutual love between Christ and his followers reflects and sanctions this community bond. Christianity in this regard appears to be an adaptation of Oriental asceticism and spiritualism to an urban lower-middle-class community which could not escape into mystical contemplation in a tropical countryside.

The process by which Christianity arose cannot be reconstructed precisely. There is clearly an affinity of interests between the lower-middle-class women who were acquiring a sexual bargaining position during the shift from a society of armed households to the comparatively peaceful and highly commercial society of the Roman Empire, and the Christian priests attempting to spread an ascetic spiritual movement by acquiring new converts. A corollary of Christian church membership was the confining of sexuality to Christian marriage, with its idealized and desexualized view of the marriage bond. It is possible that the changed position of women in the Roman lower middle class had an important effect in shaping Christianity; it is also conceivable that the rise of the religion was important in raising women's status by giving them strong allies in the church. Probably influences operated in both directions.[37]

---

35. Weber, *Economy and Society*, pp. 481–84.

36. Ibid., pp. 488–90.

37. In general, women's greater religious attachment and religious conservatism (in Christian countries at least) reflects the continuing alliance between the interests of priests in promoting spiritualism and asceticism, and women in protecting themselves against subordination to male sexual aggression. See Joseph H. Fichter, "The Profile of Catholic Religious Life," *American Journal of Sociology* 58, no. 2 (September 1952): 145–49; and Charles Y. Glock, Benjamin B. Ringer, and Earl R. Babbie, *To Comfort and to Challenge* (Berkeley: University of California Press, 1967), pp. 41–59.

Until the modern industrial era, religious organizations have been virtually the only specialized culture-transmitting institution; hence all ideologies tended to take religious form, including the ideologies of sexual interest groups. The early Christian expression of the romantic love ideal has been obscured historically because of the decline of urban Rome and the reruralization of European society until approximately the fifteenth century A.D. The fortified household reappeared as the principal social structure; women's position reverted to traditional subordination. When private middle-class households do reemerge with the bureaucratic European state of the sixteenth and seventeenth centuries, the romantic love ideal, the idealized family ties, and the repression of male sexuality develop with it.[38] The Victorian ethic of extreme prudery and sentimental idealization does not originate in the nineteenth century; it is an ideal of middle-class families, and especially of middle-class women, found as far back as the early stages of emancipation of middle-class households from the great households of patrimonial society. Its original ideological form was Christian, although the rise of secular culture (through the mass reading market and public education) has given it other cultural bases. Where the private middle-class household spreads throughout the modernizing world, the romantic/puritanical love ideal seems likely to spread.

The romantic ideal has one major weakness as a strategy for improving the position of women. It is based on the relative inaccessibility of women as sexual objects; it is a strategy of "hard-to-get," of demanding idealized devotion (and firm economic contracts) in return for sexual access. This strategy maintains the cultural barrier between men and women; the very idealization of women, where it is most successful, keeps them confined in a fantasy world of aesthetic symbols, to be protected from the actualities of political conflict, economic activity, and aggressive sexual desire. Thus, male control of the economic world is reinforced because women with the greatest resources idealize themselves out of it; the all-male "backstage"[39] culture of sexual jokes and discussions has served as a tangible social barrier against the employment of women in male-dominated occupations. Moreover, women must rely on men to protect their inaccessibility from

38. Stone, *The Crisis*, pp. 269–302; see also Denis de Rougemont, *Love in the Western World* (New York: Pantheon, 1956), pp. 49–139.

39. Erving Goffman, *The Presentation of Self in Everyday Life* (New York: Doubleday, 1959).

sexual assault; the "helpless female" ideal, the woman as object to be protected, is simultaneously a way of exacting deference from men and of being trapped in a female role.[40]

4. *Advanced Market Economy.* A further shift in bargaining resources occurs with the attainment of a high level of affluence and the rise of widespread employment opportunities for women. Women become freed from parental homes to go to school and to work. This not only makes the sexual market freer, by reducing parental controls, but also gives women additional bargaining resources. To the extent that women have their own incomes, they are free to strike their bargains without economic compulsion; and their incomes may become a bargaining resource of their own.

Women's occupational position even in advanced industrial society does not match that of men. Hence the older sexual market in which female attractiveness tends to be traded for male economic prospects continues to operate.[41] In the working class, however, a woman's earning capacity may be an important resource in establishing sexual relationships (although it may be balanced off by a freer use of male force.)[42] In the educated middle class, women with qualifications for professional jobs can double a family income, and hence represent considerable bargaining power. In general, the higher the relative income of a wife compared to her husband, the greater her power within the family;[43] this circumstance, no doubt, gives a woman some bargaining power before marriage as well. Although women are far from economically equal with men, it is now possible for a number of different things to be bargained: income resources as well as sexual

40. Women's propensity to political conservatism may be explained by their special reliance on the state to control private violence. See Seymour Martin Lipset, *Political Man* (New York: Doubleday, 1960), p. 260. "Law and order," for women, appears to have a special sexual meaning, as rhetoric about "crime in the streets" abundantly implies. The appearance of this conservatism, following the successful late-Victorian campaign for women's suffrage, is no anomaly, considering the nature of the battle for sexual liberation in that period. That the women's suffrage movement should overlap substantially with the temperance movement is in keeping with the conflict theory here presented; the prohibition of alcohol was an effort to eliminate a substance that made men uninhibited, as well as to destroy a masculine sanctuary, the saloon. See Joseph R. Gusfield, *Symbolic Crusade* (Urbana: University of Illinois Press, 1963), pp. 88–91.

41. Glenn Elder, Jr., "Appearance and Education in Marriage Mobility," *American Sociological Review* 34, no. 4 (August 1969): 519–33; and Willard Waller, "The Rating and Dating Complex," *American Sociological Review* 2, no. 5 (October 1937): 727–34.

42. Liebow, *Tally's Corner*, pp. 137–60.

43. Zelditch, "Family, Marriage and Kinship," p. 707.

attractiveness, social status, personal compatibility, deference, and emotional support. The greater freedom of women from economic dependence on men means that sexual bargains can be less concerned with marriage; dating can go on as a form of short-run bargaining, in which both men and women trade on their own attractiveness or capacity to entertain in return for sexual favors and/or being entertained. Where women bring economic resources of their own, they may concentrate on bargaining for sexual attractiveness on the part of men. The result is the rise, especially in youth culture, of the ideal of male sexual attractiveness.[44] A pure market based on ranking in terms of sexuality, in the sense discussed by Zetterberg,[45] thus becomes more prominent for both men and women, but as only one of the many sexual markets in existence.

This is the situation in which the current ideology of women's liberation gains a following. As long as men controlled virtually all economic resources, women's primary strategy was to emphasize the feminine ideal, and with it to accept the compartmentalization of life which reinforced male economic dominance. Working-class women, who were in the least favorable position to use the feminine ideal, first cracked the job barrier on the manual level; lower-middle-class clerical workers provided a further opening, and the expansion of college attendance by middle-class girls (originally motivated primarily by status and husband-hunting considerations) has mobilized a large number of women with at least some work experience (usually clerical) and the capacity to articulate a new ideology, or at least to debunk previous ideologies of femininity.

Combined Patterns

We have been dealing with ideal types. Historical reality is usually a mixture of forms and processes; we may characterize different historical situations (and the situations of different social classes in each period) by a particular weighting of resources in the struggle over sexual dominance.

44. Elaine Walster, Vera Aronson, Darcy Abrahams and Leon Rotterman, "Importance of Physical Attractiveness in Dating Behavior," *Journal of Personality and Social Psychology* 4, no. 5 (November 1966): 508–16.

45. Hans L. Zetterberg, "The Secret Ranking," *Journal of Marriage and the Family* 27, no. 2 (May 1966): 134–42.

Thus, force is still available as a male resource even in the modern middle class. A 1954–55 survey of girls at a midwestern college found that slightly more than half of them experienced sexual attacks, with the average number of reported experiences being six times in the year.[46] (In another study, Kanin reported that 23 percent of a sample of Midwestern male undergraduates admitted attempting rape on dates.[47]) Paradoxically, the more serious the attack—attempted intercourse vs. petting below the waist vs. petting above the waist—the *less* likely was the girl to report it to the authorities or even to talk about it with her girl friends. The reason becomes clear when we find that the more severe assaults usually came from steady boy friends or fiancés. The closer to marriage, the more sex that is expected.[48]

Thus, a mild use of force is taken into account in the dating system; women generally allow themselves to be made subject to force only after a tentative bargain has been struck. The availability of male force simply adds another element to the bargaining situation, and generally requires women to take the role of the sexually pursued, and thus to attempt to enforce an ideal of some degree of sexual inaccessibility except under the idealized bond of romantic love.

As a general principle, the more male violence is available in a sexual market, the more puritanical and sentimental the female ideology. Thus, working-class women are more puritanical than middle-class women,[49] since male violence must be more continuously guarded against; it is among stably married working-class women that the distinction between respectable women and "loose" women is most strongly enunciated.

The casual use of force is most prevalent in societies organized around fortified households. As we have seen above, this type of social organization produces severe controls over female sexuality, but primarily as external restraints imposed by men. In the period of transition from the situation of patriarchal dominance to that of private

---

46. Clifford Kirkpatrick and Eugene Kanin, "Male Sex Aggression on a University Campus," *American Sociological Review* 22, no. 1 (February, 1957): 52–58.

47. Eugene Kanin, "Reference Groups and Sex Conduct Norm Violation," *Sociological Quarterly* 8, no. 4 (Autumn 1967): 495–504.

48. Conversely, rapes that are reported are almost always committed by strangers. See Kaare Svalastoga, "Rape and Social Structure," *Pacific Sociological Review* 5, no. 1 (Spring 1962): 48–53. We can surmise that many successful rapes are never mentioned, because they are committed by boy friends.

49. Rainwater, "Sexual Life," pp. 457–66.

households in a peaceful market economy, men's interests in controlling their women and women's interests in improving their position through an idealization of sexuality are likely to coincide in producing a maximal degree of puritanism. Idealization requires that women, although desired sexual objects on the courtship market, should be inaccessible to male assault; this allows women to exact deference and at least overt cooperation in idealizing themselves from prospective suitors. But in a situation where violence is still widespread, women must depend on men to protect them. Thus the initial effort at idealization leads women to reinforce patriarchal efforts at female sexual restraint; the improvement in women's power position comes only from extending this restraint to the men themselves—in effect, getting men to enforce sexual restraint on each other and hence on themselves.

The period of the greatest idealization and of sexual repression, then, is the transitional one in which the first great battle is fought by women to raise their status, using as resources both their new personal worth on a courtship market, and male ideologies and interests in female chastity surviving from traditional society. The heights of European sexual repressiveness, referred to popularly as Victorianism, were not confined to the nineteenth century; sexual puritanism developed as far back as the fifteenth century wherever the fortified household was giving way to the newer middle-class home. However, it was in the nineteenth century when the number of families first undergoing the transition was great enough to make sexual puritanism into a dominant public ideology.[50] As the new family structure came to prevail and the relatively peaceful middle-class social order became taken for granted, extreme sexual restraint disappears.

Freud's discoveries about sexual repression and idealization thus grew out of a particular historical era, as he treated the casualties of the first major battle in the struggle for women's liberation. The pattern emerges in other places, however, whenever the same combination of conditions occurs. Families undergoing change from traditional rural settings to urban middle-class settings are likely to be the most puritanical, for the patriarchal organization tends to prevail in the countryside (especially in more backwoods or frontier areas), and hence the initial battle for woman's liberation is still being fought. Societies

50. Compare with Marcus, *The Other Victorians*, pp. 77–160.

which attempt massive modernization, such as the Soviet Union or Communist China, thus generally undergo periods of sexual repressiveness during the transition.[51]

As the peaceful market system becomes fully established, the degree of sexual restraint relaxes, and the feminine ideal becomes more overtly sensual and less sentimentalized.[52] This does not foreshadow universal promiscuousness, however. Sexual attractiveness can still be used as a bargaining resource, although in a more complex market than previously; it remains a resource only to the extent that it is not simply given away. Hence, we find only a mild increase in the rate of premarital intercourse in mid-twentieth-century America, a society in which the advanced market situation has been most nearly approached.[53] Further shifts in sexual ideologies depend upon further equalization of the economic positions of women.[54] The cumulative advantage of males as a group monopolizing higher occupational positions would tend to reinforce existing emphases in the market of sexual relationships, and vice versa. Breakthroughs in one sphere of the struggle for sexual dominance thus would have repercussions in other spheres.

Conclusions

The area of sexual relations may thus be fruitfully analyzed in terms taken from the conflict theory of stratification begun by Marx and

---

51. Indeed, there may be an explicit alliance between radical politicians and women in bringing about a revolution both within the traditional male-dominated family and in the larger society; this has occurred most prominently in Communist China, and to a lesser degree in the Soviet Union.

52. The history of clothing styles could provide a further test of this hypothesis, as would changes in the sexual ideals depicted in literature.

53. Ira L. Reiss, *Premarital Sexual Standards in America* (New York: Free Press, 1960), pp. 228–34.

54. Even in a situation of full economic equality, domestic domination would not necessarily disappear in all cases. Domestic service and personal subservience are goods that could be offered on the market, and less attractive or economically productive persons could make an improved sexual bargain by offering them. Women are currently still household servants in conventional marriages because their economic disadvantage makes this part of the standard sexual contract. With greater economic equality, this might be part of the bargain by either sex in particular cases.

Weber. Sexual stratification is analytically separable from stratification based on power, material property, or ideal status, in that it involves yet another good, sexual attractiveness itself. On a higher level of abstraction, the processes and arrangements of resources that determine variations in sexual subordination and in sexual ideals are similar to those emphasized by Weber in analyzing stratification as it is more conventionally defined. In general, variations in the distribution of the means of violence, and within the context set by this organization of violence, variations in market resources, determine both sexual behavior and sexual ideology. The prospects are good that the conflict theory of stratification may be extended to include a general theory of the forms of family structure and behavior.

3

THE ORIGIN OF THE FAMILY

KATHLEEN GOUGH

The trouble with the origin of the family is that no one really knows. Since Engels wrote *The Origin of the Family, Private Property and the State* in 1884, a great deal of new evidence has come in. Yet the gaps are still enormous. It is not known *when* the family originated, although it was probably between 2 million and 100,000 years ago. It is not known whether it developed once or in separate times and places. It is not known whether some kind of embryonic family came before, with, or after the origin of language. Since language is the accepted criterion of humanness, this means that we do not even know whether our ancestors acquired the basics of family life before or after they were human. The chances are that language and the family developed together over a long period, but the evidence is sketchy.

Although the origin of the family is speculative, it is better to speculate with than without evidence. The evidence comes from three sources. One is the social and physical lives of nonhuman primates—especially the New and Old World monkeys and, still more, the great apes, humanity's closest relatives. The second source is the tools and home sites of prehistoric humans and protohumans. The third is the family lives of hunters and gatherers of wild provender who have been studied in modern times.

Each of these sources is imperfect: monkeys and apes, because they are *not* prehuman ancestors, although they are our cousins; fossil hominids, because they left so little vestige of their social life; hunters and gatherers, because none of them has, in historic times, possessed a technology and society as primitive as those of early humans. All show the results of long endeavor in specialized, marginal environments. But together, these sources give valuable clues.

Defining the Family

To discuss the origin of something we must first decide what it is. I shall define the family as "a married couple or other group of adult kinsfolk who cooperate economically and in the upbringing of children, and all or most of whom share a common dwelling."

This includes all forms of kin-based household. Some are extended families containing three generations of married brothers or sisters. Some are "grandfamilies" descended from a single pair of grandparents. Some are matrilineage households, in which brothers and sisters share a house with the sisters' children, and men merely visit their wives in other homes. Some are compound families, in which one man has several wives, or one woman, several husbands. Others are nuclear families composed of a father, mother, and children.

Some kind of family exists in all known human societies, although it is not found in every segment or class of all stratified, state societies. Greek and American slaves, for example, were prevented from forming legal families, and their social families were often disrupted by sale, forced labor, or sexual exploitation. Even so, the family was an ideal which all classes and most people attained when they could.

The family implies several other universals. (1) Rules forbid sexual relations and marriage between close relatives. Which relatives are forbidden varies, but all societies forbid mother-son mating, and most, father-daughter and brother-sister. Some societies allow sex relations, but forbid marriage, between certain degrees of kin. (2) The men and women of a family cooperate through a division of labor based on gender. Again, the sexual division of labor varies in rigidity and in the tasks performed. But in no human society to date is it wholly absent. Child care, household tasks, and crafts closely connected with the household tend to be done by women; war, hunting, and government, by men. (3) Marriage exists as a socially recognized, durable, although not necessarily lifelong relationship between individual men and women. From it springs social fatherhood, some kind of special bond between a man and the child of his wife, whether or not they are his own children physiologically. Even in polyandrous societies, where women have several husbands, or in matrilineal societies, where group membership and property pass through women, each child has one or more designated "fathers" with whom he has a special social, and often religious, relationship. This bond of *social* fatherhood is recognized among people who do not know about the male role in procreation, or where, for various reasons, it is not clear who the physiological father of a particular infant is. Social fatherhood seems to come from the division and interdependence of male and female tasks, especially in relation to children, rather than directly from physiological fatherhood, although in most societies, the social father of a child is usually presumed to be its physiological father as well. Contrary to the beliefs of some feminists, however, I think that in no human society do men, as a whole category, have *only* the role of insemination, and *no* other social or economic role, in relation to women and children. (4) Men in general have higher status and authority over the women of their families, although older women may have influence, even some authority, over junior men. The omnipresence of male authority, too, goes contrary to the belief of some feminists that in "matriarchal" societies, women were either completely equal to, or had paramount authority over, men, either in the home or in society at large.

It is true that in some matrilineal societies, such as the Hopi of Arizona or the Ashanti of Ghana, men exert little authority over their wives. In some, such as the Nayars of South India or the Minangkabau of Sumatra, men may even live separately from their wives and children, that is, in different families. In such societies, however, the fact is that women and children fall under greater or lesser authority from the women's kinsmen—their eldest brothers, mothers' brothers, or even their grown-up sons.

In matrilineal societies, where property, rank, office and group membership are inherited through the female line, it is true that women tend to have greater independence than in patrilineal societies. This is especially so in matrilineal tribal societies where the state has not yet developed, and especially in those tribal societies where residence is matrilocal—that is, men come to live in the homes or villages of their wives. Even so, in all matrilineal societies for which adequate descriptions are available, the ultimate headship of households, lineages, and local groups is usually with men.[1]

There is in fact no true "matriarchal," as distinct from "matrilineal," society in existence or known from literature, and the chances are that there never has been.[2] This does not mean that women and men have never had relations that were dignified and creative for both sexes, appropriate to the knowledge, skills, and technology of their times. Nor does it mean that the sexes cannot be equal in the future, or that the sexual division of labor cannot be abolished. I believe that it can and must be. But it is not necessary to believe myths of a feminist Golden Age in order to plan for parity in the future.

Primate Societies

Within the primate order, humans are most closely related to the anthropoid apes (the African chimpanzee and gorilla and the Southeast Asian orangutan and gibbon), and of these, to the chimpanzee and the

---

1. For common and variant features of matrilineal systems, see David M. Schneider and Kathleen Gough, eds., *Matrilineal Kinship* (Berkeley: University of California Press, 1961).

2. The Iroquois are often quoted as a "matriarchal" society, but in fact Morgan himself refers to "the absence of equality between the sexes" and notes that women were subordinate to men, ate after men, and that women (not men) were publicly whipped as punishment for adultery. Warleaders, tribal chiefs, and *sachems* (heads of matrilineal lineages) were men. Women did, however, have a large say in the government of the long house or home of the matrilocal extended family, and women figured as tribal counselors and religious officials, as well as arranging marriages. See Lewis H. Morgan, *The League of the Ho-de-ne Sau-nee or Iroquois* (New Haven: Human Relations Area Files, 1954).

gorilla. More distantly related are the Old, and then the New World, monkeys, and finally, the lemurs, tarsiers, and tree shrews.

All primates share characteristics without which the family could not have developed. The young are born relatively helpless. They suckle for several months or years and need prolonged care afterward. Childhood is longer, the closer the species is to humans. Most monkeys reach puberty at about four to five and mature socially between about five and ten. Chimpanzees, by contrast, suckle for up to three years. Females reach puberty at seven to ten; males enter mature social and sexual relations as late as thirteen. The long childhood and maternal care produce close relations between children of the same mother, who play together and help tend their juniors until they grow up.

Monkeys and apes, like humans, mate in all months of the year instead of in a rutting season. Unlike humans, however, female apes experience unusually strong sexual desire for a few days shortly before and during ovulation (the estrous period), and have intensive sexual relations at that time. The males are attracted to the females by their scent or by brightly colored swellings in the sexual region. Estrous mating appears to be especially pronounced in primate species more remote from humans. The apes and some monkeys carry on less intensive, month-round sexuality in addition to estrous mating, approaching human patterns more closely. In humans, sexual desires and relations are regulated less by hormonal changes and more by mental images, emotions, cultural rules, and individual preferences.

Year-round (if not always month-round) sexuality means that males and females socialize more continuously among primates than among most other mammals. All primates form bands or troops composed of both sexes plus children. The numbers and proportions of the sexes vary, and in some species an individual, a mother with her young, or a subsidiary troop of male juveniles may travel temporarily alone. But in general, males and females socialize continually through mutual grooming[3] and playing as well as through frequent sex relations. Keeping close to the females, primate males play with their children and tend to protect both females and young from predators. A "division of labor" based on gender is thus already found in primate society between a female role of prolonged child care and a male role of

_____
3. Combing the hair and removing parasites with hands or teeth.

defense. Males may also carry or take care of children briefly, and nonnursing females may fight. But a kind of generalized "fatherliness" appears in the protective role of adult males toward young, even in species where the sexes do not form long-term individual attachments.

Sexual Bonds among Primates

Some nonhuman primates do have enduring sexual bonds and restrictions, superficially similar to those in some human societies. Among gibbons a single male and female live together with their young. The male drives off other males and the female, other females. When a juvenile reaches puberty it is thought to leave or be expelled by the parent of the same sex, and he eventually finds a mate elsewhere. Similar de facto, rudimentary "incest prohibitions" may have been passed on to humans from their prehuman ancestors and later codified and elaborated through language, moral custom, and law. Whether this is so may become clearer when we know more about the mating patterns of the other great apes, especially of our closest relatives, the chimpanzees. Present evidence suggests that male chimpanzees do not mate with their mothers.

Orangutans live in small, tree-dwelling groups like gibbons, but their forms are less regular. One or two mothers may wander alone with their young, mating at intervals with a male, or a male-female pair, or several juvenile males, may travel together.

Among mountain gorillas of Uganda, South Indian langurs, and hamadryas baboons of Ethiopia, a single, fully mature male mates with several females, especially in their estrous periods. If younger adult males are present, the females may have occasional relations with them if the leader is tired or not looking.

Among East and South African baboons, rhesus macaques, and South American woolly monkeys, the troop is bigger, numbering up to two hundred. It contains a number of adult males and a much larger number of females. The males are strictly ranked in terms of dominance based on both physical strength and intelligence. The more dominant males copulate intensively with the females during the latters' estrous periods. Toward the end of estrus a female may briefly attach herself to a single dominant male. At other times she may have relations with any male of higher or lower rank provided that those of higher rank permit it.

Among some baboons and macaques the young males travel on the outskirts of the group and have little access to females. Some macaques expel from the troop a proportion of the young males, who then form "bachelor troops." Bachelors may later form new troops with young females.

Other primates are more thoroughly promiscuous, or rather indiscriminate, in mating. Chimpanzees, and also South American howler monkeys, live in loosely structured groups, again (as in most monkey and ape societies) with a preponderance of females. The mother-child unit is the only stable group. The sexes copulate almost at random, and most intensively and indiscriminately during estrus.

A number of well known anthropologists have argued that various attitudes and customs often found in human societies are instinctual rather than culturally learned, and come from our primate heritage. They include hierarchies of ranking among men, male political power over women, and the greater tendency of men to form friendships with one another, as opposed to women's tendencies to cling to a man.[4]

I cannot accept these conclusions and think that they stem from the male chauvinism of our own society. A "scientific" argument which states that all such features of female inferiority are instinctive is obviously a powerful weapon in maintaining the traditional family with male dominance. But in fact, these features are *not* universal among nonhuman primates, including some of those most closely related to humans. Chimpanzees have a low degree of male dominance and male hierarchy and are sexually virtually indiscriminate. Gibbons have a kind of fidelity for both sexes and almost no male dominance or hierarchy. Howler monkeys are sexually indiscriminate and lack male hierarchies or dominance.

The fact is that among nonhuman primates male dominance and male hierarchies seem to be adaptations to particular environments, some of which did become genetically established through natural selection. Among humans, however, these features are present in variable degrees and are almost certainly learned, not inherited at all. Among nonhuman primates there are fairly general differences between

---

4. See, for example, Desmond Morris, *The Naked Ape* (London: Jonathan Cape, 1967); and Robin Fox, *Kinship and Marriage* (London: Pelican Books, 1967).

those that live mainly in trees and those that live largely on the ground. The tree dwellers (for example, gibbons, orangutans, South American howler and woolly monkeys) tend to have to defend themselves less against predators than do the ground dwellers (such as baboons, macaques, or gorillas). Where defense is important, males are much larger and stronger than females, exert dominance over females, and are strictly hierarchized and organized in relation to one another. Where defense is less important, there is much less sexual dimorphism (difference in size between male and female), less or no male dominance, a less pronounced male hierarchy, and greater sexual indiscriminancy.

Comparatively speaking, humans have a rather small degree of sexual dimorphism, similar to chimpanzees. Chimpanzees live much in trees but also partly on the ground, in forest or semiforest habitats. They build individual nests to sleep in, sometimes on the ground but usually in trees. They flee into trees from danger. Chimpanzees go mainly on all fours, but sometimes on two feet, and can use and make simple tools. Males are dominant, but not very dominant, over females. The rank hierarchy among males is unstable, and males often move between groups, which vary in size from two to fifty individuals. Food is vegetarian, supplemented with worms, grubs, or occasional small animals. A mother and her young form the only stable unit. Sexual relations are largely indiscriminate, but nearby males defend young animals from danger. The chances are that our prehuman ancestors had a similar social life. Morgan and Engels were probably right in concluding that we came from a state of "original promiscuity" before we were fully human.

Human Evolution

Judging from the fossil record, apes ancestral to humans, gorillas, and chimpanzees roamed widely in Asia, Europe, and Africa some 12 to 28 million years ago. Toward the end of that period (the Miocene) one appears in North India and East Africa, Ramapithecus, who may be ancestral both to later hominids and to modern humans. His species were small like gibbons, walked upright on two feet, had human rather than ape corner teeth, and therefore probably used hands rather than teeth to tear their food. From that time evolution toward humanness must have proceeded through various phases until the emergence of modern *homo sapiens* about 70,000 years ago.

In the Miocene period before Ramapithecus appeared, there were several time spans in which, over large areas, the climate became drier and subtropical forests dwindled or disappeared. A standard reconstruction of events, which I accept, is that groups of apes, probably in Africa, had to come down from the trees and adapt to terrestrial life. Through natural selection, probably over millions of years, they developed specialized feet for walking. Thus freed, the hands came to be used not only (as among apes) for grasping and tearing, but for regular carrying of objects such as weapons (which had hitherto been sporadic) or of infants (which had hitherto clung to their mothers' body hair).

The spread of indigestible grasses on the open savannahs may have encouraged, if it did not compel, the early ground dwellers to become active hunters rather than simply to forage for small, sick, or dead animals that came their way. Collective hunting and tool use involved group cooperation and helped foster the growth of language out of the call systems of apes. Language meant the use of symbols to refer to events not present. It allowed greatly increased foresight, memory, planning, and division of tasks—in short, the capacity for human thought.

With the change to hunting, group territories became much larger. Apes range only a few thousand feet daily; hunters, several miles. But because their infants were helpless, nursing women could hunt only small game close to home. This then produced the sexual division of labor on which the human family has since been founded. Women elaborated upon ape methods of child care, and greatly expanded foraging, which in most areas remained the primary and most stable source of food. Men improved upon ape methods of fighting off other animals, and of group protection in general. They adapted these methods to hunting, using weapons which for millennia remained the same for the chase as for human warfare.

Out of the sexual division of labor came, for the first time, home life as well as group cooperation. Female apes nest with and provide foraged food for their infants. But adult apes do not cooperate in food getting or nest building. They build new nests each night wherever they may happen to be. With the development of a hunting-gathering complex, it became necessary to have a GHQ, or home. Men could bring meat to this place for several days' supply. Women and children could meet men there after the day's hunting, and could bring their vegetable produce for general consumption. Men, women, and children could build joint shelters, butcher meat, and treat skins for clothing.

Later, fire came into use for protection against wild animals, for lighting, and eventually for cooking. The hearth then provided the focus and symbol of home. With the development of cookery, some humans—chiefly women, and perhaps some children and old men—came to spend more time preparing nutrition so that all people need spend less time in chewing and tearing their food. Meals—already less frequent because of the change to a carnivorous diet—now became brief, periodic events instead of the long feeding sessions of apes.

The change to humanness brought two bodily changes that affected birth and child care. These were head size and width of the pelvis. Walking upright produced a narrower pelvis to hold the guts in position. Yet as language developed, brains and hence heads grew much bigger relative to body size. To compensate, humans are born at an earlier stage of growth than apes. They are helpless longer and require longer and more total care. This in turn caused early women to concentrate more on child care and less on defense than do female apes.

Language made possible not only a division and cooperation in labor but also all forms of tradition, rules, morality, and cultural learning. Rules banning sex relations among close kinfolk must have come very early. Precisely how or why they developed is unknown, but they had at least two useful functions. They helped to preserve order in the family as a cooperative unit, by outlawing competition for mates. They also created bonds *between* families, or even between separate bands, and so provided a basis for wider cooperation in the struggle for livelihood and the expansion of knowledge.

It is not clear when all these changes took place. Climatic change with increased drought began regionally up to 28 million years ago. The divergence between prehuman and gorilla-chimpanzee stems had occurred in both Africa and India at least 12 million years ago. The prehuman stem led to the Australopithecenes of East and South Africa, about 1,750,000 years ago. These were pygmylike, two-footed, upright hominids with larger than ape brains, who made tools and probably hunted in savannah regions. It is unlikely that they knew the use of fire.

The first known use of fire is that of cave-dwelling hominids (Sinanthropus, a branch of the Pithecanthropines) at Choukoutien near

Peking, some half a million years ago during the second ice age. Fire was used regularly in hearths, suggesting cookery, by the time of the Acheulean and Mousterian cultures of Neanderthal man in Europe, Africa, and Asia before, during, and after the third ice age, some 150,000 to 100,000 years ago. These people, too, were often cave dwellers, and buried their dead ceremonially in caves. Cave dwelling by night as well as by day was probably, in fact, not safe for humans until fire came into use to drive away predators.

Most anthropologists conclude that home life, the family, and language had developed by the time of Neanderthal man, who was closely similar and may have been ancestral to modern *homo sapiens*. At least two anthropologists, however, believe that the Australopithecenes already had language nearly 2 million years ago, while another thinks that language and incest prohibitions did not evolve until the time of *homo sapiens* some 70,000 to 50,000 years ago.[5] I am myself inclined to think that family life built around tool use, the use of language, cookery, and a sexual division of labor must have been established sometime between about 500,000 and 200,000 years ago.

Hunters and Gatherers

Most of the hunting and gathering societies studied in the eighteenth to twentieth centuries had technologies similar to those that were widespread in the Mesolithic period, which occurred about 15,000 to 10,000 years ago, after the ice ages ended but before cultivation was invented and animals domesticated.

Modern hunters live in marginal forest, mountain, arctic, or desert environments where cultivation is impracticable. Although by no means "primeval," the hunters of recent times do offer clues to the types of family found during that 99 percent of human history before the agricultural revolution. They include the Eskimo, many Canadian and South American Indian groups, the forest BaMbuti (pygmies) and the desert Bushmen of Southern Africa, the Kadar of South India, the Veddah of Ceylon, and the Andaman Islanders of the Indian Ocean.

5. For the former view, see Charles F. Hockett and Robert Asher, "The Human Revolution," in *Man in Adaptation: The Biosocial Background*, ed. Yehudi A. Cohen (Chicago: Aldine, 1968); for the latter, Frank B. Livingstone, "Genetics, Ecology and the Origin of Incest and Exogamy," *Current Anthropology* 10, no. 1 (February 1969): 45–61.

About 175 hunting and gathering cultures in Oceania, Asia, Africa, and America have been described in fair detail.

In spite of their varied environments, hunters share certain features of social life. They live in bands of about 20 to 200 people, the majority of bands having fewer than 50. Bands are divided into families, which may forage alone in some seasons. Hunters have simple but ingenious technologies. Bows and arrows, spears, needles, skin clothing, and temporary leaf or wood shelters are common. Most hunters do some fishing. The band forages and hunts in a large territory and usually moves camp often.

Social life is egalitarian. There is of course no state, no organized government. Apart from religious shamans or magicians, the division of labor is based only on sex and age. Resources are owned communally; tools and personal possessions are freely exchanged. Everyone works who can. Band leadership goes to whichever man has the intelligence, courage, and foresight to command the respect of his fellows. Intelligent older women are also looked up to.

The household is the main unit of economic cooperation, with the men, women, and children dividing the labor and pooling their produce. In 97 percent of the 175 societies classified by G. P. Murdock, hunting is confined to men; in the other 3 percent it is chiefly a male pursuit. Gathering of wild plants, fruits, and nuts is women's work. In 60 percent of societies, only women gather, while in another 32 percent gathering is mainly feminine. Fishing is solely or mainly men's work in 93 percent of the hunting societies where it occurs.

For the rest, men monopolize fighting, although interband warfare is rare. Women tend children and shelters and usually do most of the cooking, processing, and storage of food. Women tend also to be foremost in the early household crafts such as basketry, leather work, the making of skin or bark clothing, and in the more advanced hunting societies, pottery. (Considering that women probably *invented* all these crafts, in addition to cookery, food storage and preservation, agriculture, spinning, weaving, and perhaps even house construction, it is clear that women played quite as important roles as men in early cultural development.) Building dwellings and making tools and ornaments are variously divided between the sexes, while boat building is largely done by men. Girls help the women, and boys play at hunting or hunt small game until they reach puberty, when both take on the roles of adults. Where the environment makes it desirable, the men of a whole band or of some smaller cluster of households cooperate in hunting or fishing and divide their spoils. Women of nearby families often go gathering together.

Family composition varies among hunters as it does in other kinds of societies. About half or more of known hunting societies have nuclear families (father, mother, and children), with polygynous households (a man, two or more wives, and children) as occasional variants. Clearly, nuclear families are the most common among hunters, although hunters have a slightly higher proportion of polygynous families than do nonhunting societies.

About a third of hunting societies contain some "stem family" households—that is, older parents live together with one married child and grandchildren, while the other married children live in independent dwellings. A still smaller proportion live in large extended families containing several married brothers (or several married sisters), their spouses, and children.[6] Hunters have fewer extended and stem families than do nonhunting societies. These larger households become common with the rise of agriculture. They are especially found in large, preindustrial agrarian states such as ancient Greece, Rome, India, the Islamic empires, China, etc.

Hunting societies also have few households composed of a widow or divorcee and her children. This is understandable, for neither men nor women can survive long without the work and produce of the other sex, and marriage is the way to obtain them. That is why so often young men must show proof of hunting prowess, and girls of cooking, before they are allowed to marry.

The family, together with territorial grouping, provides the framework of society among hunters. Indeed, as Morgan and Engels clearly saw, kinship and territory are the foundations of all societies before the rise of the state. Not only hunting and gathering bands, but the larger and more complex tribes and chiefdoms of primitive cultivators and herders organize people through descent from common ancestors or through marriage ties between groups. Among hunters, things are

6. For exact figures, see George P. Murdock, "World Ethnographic Sample," *American Anthropologist*, 59, no. 4 (August 1957): 664–87; Allan D. Coult, *Cross Tabulations of Murdock's World Ethnographic Sample* (Columbia: University of Missouri, 1965); and George P. Murdock, *Ethnographic Atlas* (Pittsburgh: University of Pittsburgh, 1967). In the last-named survey, out of 175 hunting societies, 47 percent had nuclear family households, 38 percent had stem families, and 14 percent had extended families.

simple. There is only the family, and beyond it the band. With the domestication of plants and animals, the economy becomes more productive. More people can live together. Tribes form, containing several thousand people loosely organized into large kin groups such as clans and lineages, each composed of a number of related families. With still further development of the productive forces the society throws up a central political leadership, together with craft specialization and trade, and so the chiefdom emerges. But this, too, is structured through ranked allegiances and marriage ties between kin groups.

Only with the rise of the state does class, independently of kinship, provide the basis for relations of production, distribution, and power. Even then, kin groups remain large in the agrarian state and kinship persists as the prime organizing principle within each class until the rise of capitalism. The reduction in significance of the family that we see today is the outgrowth of a decline in the importance of "familism" relative to other institutions, that began with the rise of the state, but became speeded up with the development of capitalism and machine industry. In most modern socialist societies, the family is even less significant as an organizing principle. It is reasonable to suppose that in the future it will become minimal or may disappear at least as a legally constituted unit for exclusive forms of sexual and economic cooperation and of childcare.

Morgan and Engels (1942) thought that from a state of original promiscuity, early humans at first banned sex relations between the generations of parents and children, but continued to allow them indiscriminately between brothers, sisters, and all kinds of cousins within the band. They called this the "consanguineal family." They thought that later, all mating within the family or some larger kin group became forbidden, but that there was a stage (the "punaluan") in which a group of sisters or other close kinswomen from one band were married jointly to a group of brothers or other close kinsmen from another. They thought that only later still, and especially with the domestication of plants and animals, did the "pairing family" develop in which each man was married to one or two women individually.

These writers drew their conclusions not from evidence of actual group marriage among primitive peoples but from the kinship terms found today in certain tribal and chiefly societies. Some of these equate all kin of the same sex in the parents' generation, suggesting brother-sister marriage. Others equate the father's brothers with the father, and the mother's sisters with the mother, suggesting the marriage of a group of brothers with a group of sisters.

Modern evidence does not bear out these conclusions about early society. All known hunters and gatherers live in families, not in communal sexual arrangements. Most hunters even live in nuclear families rather than in large extended kin groups. Mating is individualized, although one man may occasionally have two wives, or (very rarely) a woman may have two husbands. Economic life is built primarily around the division of labor and partnership between individual men and women. The hearths, caves, and other remains of Upper Palaeolithic hunters suggest that this was probably an early arrangement. We cannot say that Engels' sequences are completely ruled out for very early hominids—the evidence is simply not available. But it is hard to see what economic arrangements among hunters would give rise to group, rather than individual or "pairing" marriage arrangements, and this Engels does not explain.

Soviet anthropologists continued to believe in Morgan and Engels' early "stages" longer than did anthropologists in the West. Today, most Russian anthropologists admit the lack of evidence for "consanguineal" and "punaluan" arrangements, but some still believe that a different kind of group marriage intervened between indiscriminate mating and the pairing family. Semyonov, for example, argues that in the stage of group marriage, mating was forbidden within the hunting band, but that the men of two neighboring bands had multiple, visiting sex relations with women of the opposite band.[7]

While such an arrangement cannot be ruled out, it seems unlikely because many of the customs which Semyonov regards as "survivals" of such group marriage (for example, visiting husbands, matrilineage dwelling groups, widespread clans, multiple spouses for both sexes, men's and women's communal houses, and prohibitions of sexual intercourse inside the huts of the village) are actually found not so much among hunters as among horticultural tribes, and even quite complex agricultural states. Whether or not such a stage of group marriage occurred in the earliest societies, there seems little doubt that pairing marriage (involving family households) came about with the

7. Y. I. Semyonov, "Group Marriage, Its Nature and Role in the Evolution of Marriage and Family Relations," in *Seventh Annual Congress of Anthropological and Ethnological Sciences, Vol. IV* (Moscow: Seventh Annual Congress of Anthropological and Ethnological Sciences, 1967).

development of elaborate methods of hunting, cooking, and the preparation of clothing and shelters—that is, with a fully-fledged division of labor.

Even so, there *are* some senses in which mating among hunters has more of a group character than in archaic agrarian states or in capitalist society. Murdock's sample shows that sex relations before marriage are strictly prohibited in only 26 percent of hunting societies. In the rest, marriage is either arranged so early that premarital sex is unlikely, or (more usually) sex relations are permitted more or less freely before marriage.

With marriage, monogamy is the normal *practice* at any given time for most hunters, but it is not the normal *rule*. Only 19 percent in Murdock's survey prohibit plural unions. Where polygyny is found (79 percent) the most common type is for a man to marry two sisters or other closely related women of the same kin group—for example, the daughters of two sisters or of two brothers. When a woman dies it is common for a sister to replace her in the marriage, and when a man dies, for a brother to replace him.

Similarly, many hunting societies hold that the wives of brothers or other close kinsmen are in some senses wives of the group. They can be called on in emergencies or if one of them is ill. Again, many hunting societies have special times for sexual license between men and women of a local group who are not married to each other, such as the "lights out" games of Eskimo sharing a communal snow house. In other situations, an Eskimo wife will spend the night with a chance guest of her husband's. All parties expect this as normal hospitality. Finally, adultery, although often punished, tends to be common in hunting societies, and few if any of them forbid divorce or the remarriage of divorcees and widows.

The reason for all this seems to be that marriage and sexual restrictions are practical arrangements among hunters designed mainly to serve economic and survival needs. In these societies, some kind of rather stable pairing best accomplishes the division of labor and cooperation of men and women and the care of children. Beyond the immediate family, either a larger family group or the whole band has other, less intensive but important, kinds of cooperative activities. Therefore, the husbands and wives of individuals within that group can be summoned to stand in for each other if need arises. In the case of Eskimo wife lending, the extreme climate and the need for lone wandering in search of game dictate high standards of hospitality. This evidently becomes extended to sexual sharing.

In the case of sororal polygyny or marriage to the dead wife's sister, it is natural that when two women fill the same role—either together or in sequence—they should be sisters, for sisters are more alike than other women. They are likely to care more for each others' children. The replacement of a dead spouse by a sister or a brother also preserves existing intergroup relations. For the rest, where the economic and survival bonds of marriage are not at stake, people can afford to be freely companionate and tolerant. Hence premarital sexual freedom, seasonal group license, and a pragmatic approach to adultery.

Marriages among hunters are usually arranged by elders when a young couple are ready for adult responsibilities. But the couple know each other and usually have some choice. If the first marriage does not work, the second mate will almost certainly be self-selected. Both sexual and companionate love between individual men and women are known and are deeply experienced. With comparative freedom of mating, love is less often separated from or opposed to marriage than in archaic states or even than in some modern nations.

The Position of Women

Even in hunting societies it seems that women are always in some sense the "second sex," with greater or less subordination to men. This varies. Eskimo and Australian aboriginal women are far more subordinate than women among the Kadar, the Andamanese or the Congo Pygmies—all forest people.

I suggest that women have greater power and independence among hunters when they are important food obtainers than when they are mainly processors of meat or other supplies provided by men. The former situation is likelier to exist in societies where hunting is small scale and intensive than where it is extensive over a large terrain, and in societies where gathering is important by comparison with hunting.

In general in hunting societies, however, women are less subordinated in certain crucial respects than they are in most, if not all, the archaic states, or even in some capitalist nations. These respects include men's ability to deny women sexuality or to force it upon them; to command or exploit their labor or to control their produce; to control or rob them of their children; to confine them physically and prevent their movement; to use them as objects in male transactions; to cramp their creativeness; or to withhold from them large areas of the society's knowledge and cultural attainments.

Especially lacking in hunting societies is the kind of male possessiveness and exclusiveness regarding women that leads to such institutions as savage punishments or death for female adultery, the jealous guarding of female chastity and virginity, the denial of divorce to women, or the ban on a woman's remarriage after her husband's death.

For these reasons, I do not think we can speak, as some writers do, of a class division between men and women in hunting societies. True, men are more mobile than women and they lead in public affairs. But class society requires that one class control the means of production, dictate its use by the other classes, and expropriate the surplus. These conditions do not exist among hunters. Land and other resources are held communally, although women may monopolize certain gathering areas, and men, their hunting grounds. There is rank difference, role difference, and some difference respecting degrees of authority between the sexes, but there is reciprocity rather than domination or exploitation.

As Engels saw, the power of men to exploit women systematically springs from the existence of surplus wealth, and more directly, from the state, social stratification, and the control of property by men. With the rise of the state, because of their monopoly over weapons, and because freedom from child care allows them to enter specialized economic and political roles, some men—especially ruling-class men—acquire power over other men and over women. Almost all men acquire it over women of their own or lower classes, especially within their own kinship groups. These kinds of male power are shadowy among hunters.

To the extent that men *have* power over women in hunting societies, this seems to spring from the male monopoly of heavy weapons, from the particular division of labor between the sexes, or from both. Although men seldom use weapons against women, they *possess* them (or possess superior weapons) in addition to their physical strength. This does give men an ultimate control of force. When old people or babies must be killed to ensure band or family survival, it is usually men who kill them. Infanticide—rather common among hunters, who must limit the mouths to feed—is more often female infanticide than male.

The hunting of men seems more often to require them to organize in groups than does the work of women. Perhaps because of this, about 60 percent of hunting societies have predominantly virilocal residence. That is, men choose which band to live in (often, their fathers'), and women move with their husbands. This gives a man advantages over his wife in terms of familiarity and loyalties, for the wife is often a stranger. Sixteen to 17 percent of hunting societies are, however, uxorilocal, with men moving to the households of their wives, while 15 to 17 percent are bilocal—that is, either sex may move in with the other on marriage.

Probably because of male cooperation in defense and hunting, men are more prominent in band councils and leadership, in medicine and magic, and in public rituals designed to increase game, to ward off sickness, or to initiate boys into manhood. Women do, however, often take part in band councils; they are not excluded from law and government as in many agrarian states. Some women are respected as wise leaders, storytellers, doctors, or magicians, or are feared as witches. Women have their own ceremonies of fertility, birth, and healing, from which men are often excluded.

In some societies, although men control the most sacred objects, women are believed to have discovered them. Among the Congo Pygmies, religion centers about a beneficent spirit, the Animal of the Forest. It is represented by wooden trumpets that are owned and played by men. Their possession and use are hidden from the women and they are played at night when hunting is bad, someone falls ill, or death occurs. During the playing men dance in the public campfire, which is sacred and is associated with the forest. Yet the men believe that women originally owned the trumpet and that it was a woman who stole fire from the chimpanzees or from the forest spirit. When a woman has failed to bear children for several years, a special ceremony is held. Women lead in the songs that usually accompany the trumpets, and an old woman kicks apart the campfire. Temporary female dominance seems to be thought necessary to restore fertility.

In some hunting societies women are exchanged between local groups, which are thus knit together through marriages. Sometimes, men of different bands directly exchange their sisters. More often there is a generalized exchange of women between two or more groups, or a one-way movement of women within a circle of groups. Sometimes the husband's family pays weapons, tools, or ornaments to the wife's in return for the wife's services and later, her children.

In such societies, although they may be well treated and their consent sought, women are clearly the movable partners in an arrangement controlled by men. Male anthropologists have seized on this as evidence of original male dominance and patrilocal residence. Fox and others, for example, have argued that until recently, *all* hunting societies formed out-marrying patrilocal bands, linked together politically by the exchange of women. The fact that fewer than two-thirds of hunting societies are patrilocal today, and only 41 percent have band exogamy, is explained in terms of modern conquest, economic change, and depopulation.

I cannot accept this formula. It is true that modern hunting societies have been severely changed, deculturated, and often depopulated by capitalist imperialism. I can see little evidence, however, that the ones that are patrilocal today have undergone less change than those that are not. It is hard to believe that in spite of enormous environmental diversity and the passage of thousands, perhaps millions, of years, hunting societies all had band exogamy with patrilocal residence until they were disturbed by Western imperialism. It is more likely that early band societies, like later agricultural tribes, developed variety in family life and the status of women as they spread over the earth.

There is also some likelihood that the earliest hunters had matrilocal rather than patrilocal families. Among apes and monkeys, it is almost always males who leave the troop or are driven out. Females stay closer to their mothers and their original site; males move about, attaching themselves to females where availability and competition permit. Removal of the wife to the husband's home or band may have been a relatively late development in societies where male cooperation in hunting assumed overwhelming importance.[8] Conversely, after the development of horticulture (which was probably invented and is mainly carried out by women), those tribes in which horticulture predominated over stock raising were most likely to be or to remain matrilocal and to develop matrilineal descent groups with a relatively

---

8. Upper Palaeolithic hunters produced female figurines that were obvious emblems of fertility. The cult continued through the Mesolithic and into the Neolithic period. Goddesses and spirits of fertility are found in some patrilineal as well as matrilineal societies, but they tend to be more prominent in the latter. It is thus possible that in many areas even late stone age hunters had matrilocal residence and perhaps matrilineal descent, and that in some regions this pattern continued through the age of horticulture and even—as in the case of the Nayars of Kerola and Minangkabau of Sumatra—into the age of plow agriculture, of writing, and of the small-scale state.

high status of women. But where extensive hunting of large animals, or later, the herding of large domesticates, predominated, patrilocal residence flourished and women were used to form alliances between male-centered groups. With the invention of metallurgy and of agriculture as distinct from horticulture after 4000 B.C., men came to control agriculture and many crafts, and most of the great agrarian states had patrilocal residence with patriarchal, male-dominant families.

Conclusions

The family is a human institution, not found in its totality in any prehuman species. It required language, planning, cooperation, self-control, foresight, and cultural learning, and probably developed along with these.

The family was made desirable by the early human combination of prolonged child care with the need for hunting with weapons over large terrains. The sexual division of labor on which it was based grew out of a rudimentary prehuman division between male defense and female child care. But among humans this sexual division of functions for the first time became crucial for food production and so laid the basis for future economic specialization and cooperation.

Morgan and Engels were probably right in thinking that the human family was preceded by sexual indiscriminacy. They were also right in seeing an egalitarian group quality about early economic and marriage arrangements. They were without evidence, however, in believing that the earliest mating and economic patterns were entirely group relations.

Together with tool use and language, the family was no doubt the most significant invention of the human revolution. All three required reflective thought, which above all accounts for the vast superiority in consciousness that separates humans from apes.

The family provided the framework for all prestate society and the fount of its creativeness. In groping for survival and for knowledge, human beings learned to control their sexual desires and to suppress their individual selfishness, aggression, and competition. The other side of this self-control was an increased capacity for love—not only the love of a mother for her child, which is seen among apes, but of male for female in enduring relationships, and of each sex for ever widening groups of humans. Civilization would have been impossible without this initial self-control, seen in incest prohibitions and in the generosity and moral orderliness of primitive family life.

From the start, women have been subordinate to men in certain key areas of status, mobility, and public leadership. But before the agricultural revolution, and even for several thousands of years thereafter, the inequality was based chiefly on the unalterable fact of long child care combined with the exigencies of primitive technology. The extent of inequality varied according to the ecology and the resulting sexual division of tasks. But in any case it was largely a matter of survival rather than of man-made cultural impositions. Hence the impressions we receive of dignity, freedom, and mutual respect between men and women in primitive hunting and horticultural societies. This is true whether these societies are patrilocal, bilocal, or matrilocal, although matrilocal societies, with matrilineal inheritance, offer greater freedom to women than do patrilocal and patrilineal societies of the same level of productivity and political development.

A distinct change occurred with the growth of individual and family property in herds, in durable craft objects and trade objects, and in stable, irrigated farm sites or other forms of heritable wealth. This crystallized in the rise of the state, about 4000 b.c. With the growth of class society and of male dominance in the ruling class of the state, women's subordination increased, and eventually reached its depths in the patriarchal families of the great agrarian states.

Knowledge of how the family arose is interesting to women because it tells us how we differ from prehumans, what our past has been, and what have been the biological and cultural limitations from which we are emerging. It shows us how generations of male scholars have distorted or overinterpreted the evidence to bolster beliefs in the inferiority of women's mental processes—for which there is no foundation in fact. Knowing about early families is also important to correct a reverse bias among some feminist writers, who hold that in "matriarchal" societies women were completely equal with or were even dominant over men. For this, too, there seems to be no basis in evidence.

(The past of the family does not limit its future. Although the family probably emerged with humanity, neither the family itself nor particular family forms are genetically determined. The sexual division of labor—until recently, universal—need not, and in my opinion should not, survive in industrial society. Prolonged child care ceases to be a basis for female subordination when artificial birth control, spaced births, small families, patent feeding, and communal nurseries allow it to be shared by men. Automation and cybernation remove most of the heavy work for which women are less well equipped than men. The exploitation of women that came with the rise of the state and of class society will presumably disappear in poststate, classless society—for which the technological and scientific basis already exists.

The family was essential to the dawn of civilization, allowing a vast qualitative leap forward in cooperation, purposive knowledge, love, and creativeness. But today, rather than enhancing them, the confinement of women in homes and small families—like their subordination in work—artificially limits these human capacities. It may be that the human gift for personal love will make some form of voluntary, long-term mating and of individual devotion between parents and children continue indefinitely, side by side with public responsibility for domestic tasks and for the care and upbringing of children. There is no need to legislate personal relations out of existence. But neither need we fear a social life in which the family is no more.

B
Racial and Social-Class Perspectives
on Marriage and the Family The Women's

Liberation Movement originated in the United States as a white
middle-class movement.[1] Numerous parallels between the
inequalities underlying the women's movement and the black
movement have been documented,[2] although critical differences
between them have been noted, too. It has been suggested, for
example, that because of certain unique characteristics of sex
inequality, support for the women's movement is more limited
than support for black liberation.[3] In particular the most intimate
of human relationships is defined normatively as the heterosexual
one of marriage. Mate selection, furthermore, is typically
endogamous with respect to numerous social factors, including
race and class. Support for the black movement, then, may unite a
husband and wife whereas (the wife's) support of women's
liberation may divide them.

Married women's presumed unwillingness to work for sex
equality is based on the assumption common to social
stratification studies that women influence their own position in
the class structure only when they are not attached to a man (e.g.,
not in the role of daughter or wife). On the one hand, this and

---

1. Jo Freeman, "The Origins of the Women's Liberation Movement," *American Journal of Sociology* 78, no. 4 (January 1973): 792–811. The predominantly middle-class composition of the women's movement is consistent with at least one theory of social movements wherein it is posited that leadership emerges from among those who are in a position of actually realizing gains, rather than among those in extreme deprivation. See, for example, Juliet Mitchell, *Woman's Estate* (New York: Pantheon Books, 1971).

2. For some early considerations of parallels between sex and racial inequality see Clifford Kirkpatrick, *The Family* (New York: Ronald Press, 1955), pp. 158–60; Gunnar Myrdal, *An American Dilemma* (New York: Harper & Row, 1944); and Helen Mayer Hacker, "Women as a Minority Group," *Social Forces* 30, no. 1 (October 1951): 60–69.

3. Alice S. Rossi, "Sex Equality: The Beginnings of Ideology," *Humanist* 29, no. 5 (September–October 1969): 3–6, 16.

---

related assumptions lack empirical support.[4] On the other hand, there is some evidence that women themselves are less likely to prefer to satisfy their achievement needs directly than vicariously (e.g., through the accomplishments of their husbands)[5] and such preference must surely affect behavior and orientation to the women's movement as indicated above.

Although the women's movement is generally characterized as white and middle class even today, there is growing support for movement goals—which were broadened consciously in the current wave of feminism in order to meet a wider range of needs—among both nonwhite and non-middle-class women. Black Americans, the largest single nonwhite segment of the population, respond variously to movement goals regarding marriage and the family, as detailed by Hare and Hare. Variation in nature and strength of support for equality between the sexes among blacks, as among whites, is based importantly on socioeconomic standing in society, as discussed below. Variation in average socioeconomic standing (and related life styles) between blacks and whites, on the other hand, can be traced significantly to the former's history of repression in this country, particularly the cycle of segregation, educational and occupational deprivation, low income and a poverty-family life style which was substituted for slavery.

In 1970 about 27 percent of all black families had incomes between $3,000 and $5,999 and another 21 percent had incomes under $3,000, despite the fact that in more than half of these units the head of the family was employed full-time.[6] Low levels of education and skill result in tenuous occupational positions for men in these social strata, which lead, in turn, to circumscribed and often marginal family roles. In contrast, greater employability of black women makes them less dependent upon black men for support and dominant within the family, even when the husband

---

4. See Walter B. Watson and Ernest A. Barth, "Questionable Assumptions in the Theory of Social Stratification," *Pacific Sociological Review* 7, no. 1 (Spring 1964): 10–16; and Joan Acker, "Women and Social Stratification: A Case of Intellectual Sexism," *American Journal of Sociology* 78, no. 4 (January 1973): 936–45.

5. Jean Lipman-Blumen, "How Ideology Shapes Women's Lives," *Scientific American* 226, no. 1 (January 1972): 34–42.

6. Dean D. Knudsen, "Black Family" (Purdue University, 1972). Mimeographed.

is present. Relatively poor black women, then, play strong family and extrafamily (work) roles, in contrast to the traditional definition of sex roles at this social level.

As Tillmon relates, female-headed families are typically poverty-level families (under $3,000), whether the mother is employed or on AFDC (Aid to Families with Dependent Children). Although the general public (and some sociologists) tends to place "blame" for poverty on what is called the women's lack of motivation to work and succeed, it is largely the result of structured inequalities between the sexes and between the social classes. The "undeserving poor" women head families in the first place primarily because of the social conditions described above, together with a low sex ratio which lowers probability of marriage in general. When trying desperately to work to support themselves and children, moreover, they are handicapped by the persistent sex typing of jobs in our society whereby women are concentrated in the relatively less rewarded positions and, even then, earn only about 60 percent of the income of men in similar work. Finally, women on welfare live not only with sole responsibility for household and child care but also with the possibility of being threatened again in the near future with a public policy by which they would be charged for child-care services that would be provided while they were literally forced to work for low wages away from home.

Despite the greater proportion of blacks than whites at the relatively lower income levels, it is important to note that blacks are found at all economic levels, with about half of all black families in 1969 having incomes of $6,000 and over.[7] Among blacks in the upper-half income category, as well as in the lower, sex-role definitions tend to emphasize "instrumental" economic activities for men and maternal activities for women. There is some evidence that middle-class black wives are more satisfied with their marital companionship than are white wives at the same or higher income levels and black women are less supportive on the whole than whites of the women's movement partly because of a dual problem.

Among black women, of course, there are individual

---

7. Ibid.

---

variations in the relative significance attached to sexism and racism.[8] It is clearly recognized, for example, that in the economic sphere, both sexism and racism prevail. Considering median annual earnings, in fact, one finds support for the position that sexism, not racism, is the most fundamental basis of discrimination.[9] Median annual earnings (1968) for four sex and race groups (year-round full-time civilian workers) fall in the following descending order: white males (highest); nonwhite males; white females; nonwhite females.[10] Also, contrary to the apparent wishes of black women, there has been an improvement (since 1963) in income of nonwhite women relative to nonwhite men and contrary to the wishes of white women there has been a decline (since 1956, if not earlier) in income of white women relative to white men.[11]

Variations in economic level are even greater among whites than among blacks. As Tillmon points out, about two-thirds of all poor families in this country are white. The realities of life for working-class women contrast markedly with those of the middle and upper classes. White feminists in the working class, such as D'Amico, are concerned both about the discrepancy between their own characteristics and middle-class standards of beauty by which all women are judged, and about the persistence of class inequities generally. There is explicit recognition that low self-esteem and a life of hard work cut across many ethnic and racial groups who must unite and organize in order to succeed in and to change the society that now defines them all as relatively unworthy.

At the other end of the economic scale are the upper-class women, exemplified by Jacqueline Onassis in the selection by Goldstone. Although women in the upper class have many advantages in life compared with men and women in lower

---

8. In recognition of the socially imposed disadvantages of being both black and female, the National Black Feminist Organization was founded in August 1973.

9. See, in particular, Shulamith Firestone, *The Dialectic of Sex* (New York: William Morrow, 1970).

10. Abbott L. Ferriss, *Indicators of Trends in the Status of American Women* (New York: Russell Sage Foundation, 1971).

11. Ibid.; and Dean D. Knudsen, "The Declining Status of Women: Popular Myths and the Failure of Functionalist Thought," *Social Forces* 48, no. 2 (December 1969): 183–93.

classes, within their class they, like all other women, are clearly subordinate to men. In the final analysis, according to Goldstone, they are merely supermothers and homemakers who share responsibility for socializing the next generation (their own children) so as to perpetuate existing sex and class inequities.

Whatever women's racial and social-class characteristics, then, they seldom escape the disadvantageous effects of a pervasive system of sexual stratification. The relatively few women who do grow up to be what Densmore calls a "functioning individual" as opposed to an "undifferentiated function," particularly well-educated career women, should be wary of some probable reactions to their own apparent success in assimilation (or cooptation) into the dominant power structures. In particular they should try to identify with rather than reject the many other women who through no special individual failings have been less able to overcome the many barriers to success which exist for all women.

4

BLACK WOMEN 1970

NATHAN HARE and JULIA HARE

Ever since she first stepped off the slave ship (at least one woman was among the earliest African slaves imported to Virginia around 1620), the black woman has occupied a peculiar position in American society. Not only did she play a leading part in helping her race survive slavery, she has had to be, under many circumstances and in many ways, both male and female in the socioeconomic arena. For her efforts to compensate for her predicament, she has been labeled "aggressive" or "matriarchal" by white scholars and "castrating female" by blacks.

Today, she experiences dual—in fact triple—exploitation (black, female and, in most cases, poor), and, as one black woman recently put it, she "must do more of everything for less of everything than any other sexual group." She lives largely isolated from whites except in her occupational life, and she is particularly subject to ambivalent relations with her mate. Before the black power movement, which had as a major goal the restoration of the supremacy of the black male at her expense, she played a salient role in the struggle for civil rights. Since then her role and position have been expressly subordinated, yet she almost unanimously shuns the Women's Liberation Movement.

Black Women/Black Men

What does the black woman think—and feel—about her general situation? What are her relationships and experiences with white women? What are her attitudes toward white men, toward black men, and why has she rejected collaboration in the Women's Liberation Movement?

Though many black women reject the white sociologist's label of "matriarch," they nonetheless possess a keen sense of themselves as the backbone and major source of strength in the black family unit. Many feel cast into two roles, male by day and female after five, required to play the feminine role as prescribed by social custom yet driven to a masculine role by white society's harsher rejection of the black man occupationally. Thus even the positive virtues of being a black woman —easier access to jobs and financial favors compared to black men—have negative consequences in that they deprecate the black male. The more she asserts herself, the more intense her conflict with him. Accordingly even as she may despise and regret being forced into a "matriarchal" role, she boasts of her "mother wit," which she sees as compensating for her lack of formal education or real socioeconomic power to fulfill the role thrust upon her.

"Being a black woman is like being put by society into a bag. Nobody likes it. They feel that they are kind of trapped individuals." None of the women we talked with could name anything to like about the ordeal of being a black woman in the United States.

Toward the black man many black women must be deceptive. On the one hand these women must hide their conviction that black men have failed as liberators of the race, while on the other hand they are well aware of the necessity of being the backbone of the family without seeming to be so. They have mixed feelings about black men and speak of "hurting" experiences with them. They believe that they have been torn apart by whites and can't understand why black men do not, in their view, appreciate the way in which they, black women, have "helped the black race to survive."

They generally must take pains to avoid the appearance of posing a threat to black men as leaders or whatever and thus feel compelled to express positive attitudes toward them. At the same time, however, they have internalized white society's low regard for black men, but they are troubled by their appraisals of black men and their performance.

> The way the system has crushed and dehumanized the black man I can never forgive them.

> The black man spends too much time trying to prove that he is the great lover that he is accused of being by the white man.

> I really dug a black man who loved me, and I was the one, but couldn't manage to find time to cut some of his screwing around, not all, just some. It was explained that 200 years of brainwashing forced him to prove he was "super dick."

Thus the burden of the family seems to fall upon the black woman, in her view, at the same time as she is told that the man should be superior and that she must "play second fiddle."

Still, many of her attitudes toward the black male merely echo the white feminist's attitudes toward white men.

> Black men tend to take everything for granted—that you'll cook when they are hungry and screw when they want it. A "fox" is a sex machine, and that "ugly girl" sure can burn [cook].

> They come home from work and have a beer while you finish dinner, then they sit down and watch the sports while you are washing the dinner dishes, fall asleep on the sofa while you get the children ready for bed and then turn around after you've done all this work and stick his mouth out as long as something else is sticking out—his privates—if

you don't feel like screwing. They say that the white man is
more affectionate. I don't know, but I do know that the
black man jumps right up after screwing or turns over and
snores. He never just holds you. I used to fret when he got
mad if I didn't give him any, but now I don't care. If I'm
tired, I'm tired.

In the case of the educated black woman, all too often she must
marry beneath her station in life because this society has kept the black
man in lowly occupations. Census data show that college-trained black
women such as schoolteachers are more likely to marry than white
women in that group yet are more subject to see their families broken
up, partly due to conflicts resulting from their marrying down the
socioeconomic scale. Too often the marriage of a black woman is
confined to anyone she can find within the proximity of her movements.

Black Women/White Men

Although she longs for the financial security offered by the white
male, she feels ethically obliged to reject his overtures on grounds of
loyalty to her race and its suffering at the white man's hands. Besides,
she is aware and resentful of the fact that the white man marries only
the more successful black woman whenever he does marry a black
woman. As one woman put it, "It is almost an impossibility for a black
woman who has not achieved some prominence or fame to attract a
white man outside of some dark alley."
Another told us, "White men dig us but are too timid or weak to
engage in an open affair. He wants the women of both races. His mouth
waters when he sees all the beautiful flowers growing in pastures."
The relationships between most black women and white men are
restricted and, usually, clandestine and sinister sexual arrangements or
abuses. Black women complain of day-to-day rebuffs (white men letting
doors slam or close in their faces after holding them open for white
women) and sometimes more forthright insults. Many tell of being fired
for failure to capitulate to white male overtures, but some see the
withholding of sexual favors from white men as a last-ditch stronghold
against white domination.

When I was 13, living in San Diego, a white man swerved
his car to miss a white woman and killed my only brother.

He said it was an accident, but he went all the way across the street, so I'll always believe he made some choice. They try to flirt with me sometimes now, but I shine them on because if the white woman is first in death she might as well be first—and last—in sex. They can kill my brother, but they can't screw me to boot.

However, some claim that their experiences with black men have been disastrous, though largely because of an alleged black male disrespect for black women and their inability to "stand up as a man." She regards their submission to the white man as in some ways excessive and regrets the all too prevalent compensatory projection of their failure on to the black woman. One woman commented, "Having been told by whites that the black women emasculated them, they tend to take out their frustration on black women, when in reality it was whites who emasculated them."

Black men are generally recognized by black women to have been on the rise in recent years, but many women also feel that black men believe they have failed their roles and need to be "helped along" toward full manhood. The black woman anticipates that her rejection of the traditional female role would be psychologically threatening to the black male. She must encourage him and lay as much groundwork for black liberation as he will let her. It is necessary to be patient with black men whenever they engage in symbolic assertions of manliness. She must not dominate but merely assist strongly.

At the same time, however, there are many black women who feel deeply that the black man must be urged to "be a man but not to rock the boat," as this may risk the loss of jobs or affluence for her family. He must stand up to the white man but be no Malcolm X.

The more militant women oppose the black man's new suppression of the black woman's role—in contrast to the historical record from Harriet Tubman and Sojourner Truth to Daisy Bates, Artherine Lucy, and Gloria Richardson. These women are viewed as having assumed leadership, not as against black men but to help blacks as a whole. Some black women today condemn black men for shunting them into the background, especially since they lack complete confidence that black men will produce the necessary revolutionary results.

Black Women/White Women

Probably the most painful part of being a black woman, as she views it, is the rape of the short male supply by white women. "White women are using everything in the book to catch our men," said one. Black women already sense a shortage of black men, and it hurts to have to share them with white women (who get a whack at men from both races and whose motives are generally not thought to be trustworthy or commendable). What is worse, black women take it as a personal insult, a denunciation of their own black beauty. They express contempt for "black men who embrace the blue-eyed devils," for the "pain when they waltz around the white woman" and "white chicks who want to play the easy lay." Invariably, black women feel, the union is rooted in pathology and/or white subterfuge. Either the white woman is relieving guilt or the black man is compensating for his historical rejection ("lynched for touching white women") and chasing after forbidden fruit. White women are thought to exploit the myth of their superiority and the appeal of forbidden fruit to "take in" the black man and to aggravate the conflicts between black men and black women to their own advantage. The black man is merely a source of sexual gratification to the white woman, who is incapable of relating in genuine love relationships or otherwise across racial boundaries.

In defense of black men, some black women claim that the men are largely victims, that white women court them, lured by the myth of the black male animal, in compensation for the sexual failure of the white man. And in defense of black women it is sometimes argued that black women generally have been made more passive by their mothers who train them to defend themselves against anticipated sexual exploitation and thus make the white woman seem more forward by contrast. To many it is intolerable to see a black man with a white woman, and they grow furious over the sight of it. Only a minority are able to take a nonchalant approach to a union of white women and black men. In such cases, they accept it only philosophically as a necessary ideal. Reflecting this view, one woman said, "Love should be free. It is pathetic that races have to be considered at all. If race is considered before one loves, the relationship becomes a mission to find someone in a particular race to love. This infringes on the freedom to love."

The black woman's contacts with white women have hardly been more satisfactory than those with the white man. White women who are

---

strangers, not personal friends, exhibit a "cool, indifferent attitude," as a black woman put it. Even when white women try to be friendly they may frequently be mistrusted: "They are so phony. As soon as they see you they say, 'Oh, let me make this little black woman my friend.' All the time they don't give a damn about you." Liberal or otherwise, the white woman is perceived by the black as finding "little nasty ways" to put her down. She says "you girls," or she assigns the black woman the dirty work on the job or in her kitchen. Many black women reserve a special contempt and resentment for those white women, often with rich husbands, who do volunteer work in community programs and then leapfrog over the paid (of necessity) black workers to high job positions. Some of these women belong to volunteer organizations such as the Junior League which, though not admitting blacks, may monopolize much of the work at a given institution. Then the white volunteer who rises to the highest paid and most powerful position will say: "I started as a volunteer."

The bitterness that black women often feel toward white stems also from the fact that the black woman is expected to compete with the white woman in the beauty parade but all too often cannot afford the frills, finery, and cosmetics. On top of this, for years all the cosmetics and skin preparations were geared to the white woman, even down to the hair dryers and the curlers. Even bell bottoms were made for white women. Many young black girls can get them on, but the black woman's hips typically grow too large with age, in contrast to the flatter-hipped norms of white women.

On another level, the black woman's resentment is sometimes triggered by being treated as a "mammy object" by white women. One black woman told us the following story:

> They [white women] expect support and a great deal of candid understanding of their sexual problems. I roomed with a white girl once for four months when I first got out of college. It turned out that I was a social cover so she could have black men coming to see her. White men did not seem interested in her. She became bizarre. I moved out, and it became clear to everybody that she was seeing black men. Suddenly white men, even the janitor, began to hit on her. A black psychiatrist pointed out the homosexual motivation of these white men who found her a desirable vehicle for indirectly sharing a bed with black men.

Black Women/Women's Lib

Many black women express the same notions of the Women's Lib Movement as are common in the population at large. The movement, in this view, is flooded with lesbians, and we have heard black women boast of offers from white lesbians to "take me out of the ghetto if I would be her lover." At the same time, however, one often hears a kind of scornful understanding of what white Women's Lib people are doing. White women are said to be sexually inhibited and relatively more chained to girdles and corsets and artificiality and Emily Post and less free even in the way they serve their meals. It is thought to be understandable that they, white women, should rebel, and there is some wonder as to why they did not do so sooner, why in the South, for instance, they knowingly kept silent on the extramarital affairs their husbands were having with black mistresses who then gave birth to mulatto children "looking more like their husbands in some instances than their own." Another black woman spoke in the same tone: "Black women have not had the tradition of being bound down and girdled up in clothes. That's why we're burning buildings, not bras."

Still, no black women could remain unaffected by the difference between her status as a woman and that of the white woman as a woman:

> White women think they are God's gift to the world. Car doors opened for you. Holding your elbow when you step off the curb. Now white women are saying that they don't want that.

> The white woman has been taught from the cradle that she is to receive special treatment.

> The white man places white women on a pedestal while seeking black women as objects of sexual release in order to prevent an alliance of black and white women.

Even those black women who share the goals of the Women's Liberation Movement are reluctant to participate, on the grounds that white women always dominate in coalitions and are always in charge. Most, however, do not feel that the movement as currently projected relates to their interests. On the contrary, it appears to some that white and black women are in a race to change places. The white woman is trying to escape the drudgery of the home for rewarding employment outside, while the black woman still longs to escape the labor force and to get into the home. Domestics, for instance, say that they would rather be at home doing their own dishes instead of out doing those of the white woman while she seeks liberation. There is agreement, however, that both white and black women need freedom from the white man since "he is the oppressor," but "let white women worry about their own sex hangups with white men."

Women in the growing black middle class just coming into a modicum of affluence and its household gadgetry such as blenders, washing machines, and dryers want now to enjoy these things for a while. The lower-class black woman lacks the educational background to move into male positions and therefore does not see that as an immediate possibility. In any case, it is hard for a black woman to imagine liberating herself from the household when she already has been forced out to work. In the past she has long tried against great odds to adhere to society's concept of the woman's role and so now stands perplexed when she is suddenly told that the old ideals of marital and family life are no longer desirable.

> The things white women are demanding liberation from are what we've never even experienced yet. How many black women stay home bored with kids while husband is off earning a lot of money? I'm sure many black women would love to stay home and be "housewives."

They mock white women who "like to feel that our problems as a woman are the same as theirs—you too have cramps, my husband loves his roast beef rare, and so does yours."

On a political level, the black woman is inclined to regard the Women's Liberation Movement as potentially divisive of black men and women, as "a lot of trivia to get blacks off the main issue of racism." Some go so far as to suggest that it is deliberately so conspired and instigated, probably by some white men, to undercut the current black thrust. A black female college professor in New York City pointed out the striking historical parallel of the suffragettes coming into the limelight during the time of Marcus Garvey, just as today the Women's Liberation Movement has blossomed in an era of rising black consciousness. Almost unanimously in the minds of black women, the Women's Liberation Movement poses the danger of injecting a wedge between black men and black women at a time when black unity seems of paramount importance. Even those who foresee that they may someday have to fight the black man in the same way the white woman is fighting the white man now nevertheless believe that this is "putting the cart before the horse" and "we can cross that bridge when we get to it."

Meanwhile, racism is more oppressive, they feel, than sexism, and there is no justification for collaborating with the white woman at this time. A domestic worker explained: "You enter this life with one role assigned to you, and that is to make life pleasant for white people. But enough is enough." Besides, they fear that if Women's Liberation does succeed in obtaining access to better jobs and wages for black women, without at the same time raising the black man's lot, the problem of male-female relations among blacks will be deepened.

In addition, white women are regarded as "just as racist as the white man." "The white Lib movement is racist. They want to equate their oppression to that of black people. When has a white woman been lynched? Many of them are anti-men, don't want to have babies when that is one of the few things a black woman could ever say was hers." In many ways the movement is regarded as one of "crass insensitivity" to the cause of black freedom. White women want equal footing with white men (even at the expense of the black man) while black women want black men on the same base with white men. "The black woman's struggle is the black struggle."

Many black women are convinced that, before giving up his own, the white man would take the black man's jobs and give them to white women, pushing the black man still farther down. To this extent, the goals of Women's Liberation and black liberation are viewed as contradictory.

As one woman put it, "the black woman must take her place not behind or in front of the black man but beside him, and together they must strive for the freedom of the black race."

In other words, there can be no liberation of black women until black men—all black people—are free.

5

WELFARE IS A WOMEN'S ISSUE

JOHNNIE TILLMON

I'm a woman. I'm a black woman. I'm a poor woman. I'm a fat woman. I'm a middle-aged woman. And I'm on welfare.

In this country, if you're any one of those things—poor, black, fat, female, middle-aged, on welfare—you count less as a human being. If you're *all* those things, you don't count at all. Except as a statistic.

I am a statistic.

I am forty-five years old. I have raised six children.

I grew up in Arkansas, and I worked there for fifteen years in a laundry, making about $20 or $30 a week, picking cotton on the side for carfare. I moved to California in 1959 and worked in a laundry there for nearly four years. In 1963, I got too sick to work anymore. My husband and I had split up. Friends helped me to go on welfare.

They didn't call it welfare. They called it AFDC—Aid to Families with Dependent Children. Each month I get $363 for my kids and me. I pay $128 a month rent; $30 for utilities, which include gas, electricity, and water; $120 for food and nonedible household essentials; $50 for school lunches for the three children in junior and senior high school who are not eligible for reduced-cost meal programs. This leaves exactly $5 per person per month for everything else—clothing, shoes, recreation, incidental personal expenses, and transportation. This check allows $1 a month for transportation for me but none for my children. That's how we live.

There are millions of statistics like me. Some on welfare. Some not. And some, really poor, who don't even know they're entitled to welfare. Not all of them are black. Not at all. In fact, the majority—about two-thirds—of all the poor families in the country are white.

Welfare's like a traffic accident. It can happen to anybody, but especially it happens to women.

And that's why welfare is a women's issue. For a lot of middle-class women in this country, Women's Liberation is a matter of concern. For women on welfare it's a matter of survival.

Survival. That's why we had to go on welfare. And that's why we can't get off welfare now. Not us women. Not until we do something about liberating poor women in this country.

Because up until now we've been raised to expect to work, all our lives, for nothing. Because we are the worst-educated, the least-skilled, and the lowest-paid people there are. Because we have to be almost totally responsible for our children. Because we are regarded by everybody as dependents. That's why we are on welfare. And that's why we stay on it.

Welfare is all about dependency.

Welfare is the most prejudiced institution in this country, even more than marriage, which it tries to imitate. Let me explain that a little.

Forty-four percent of all poor families are headed by women. That's bad enough. But the *families* on AFDC aren't really families. Because 99 percent of them are headed by women. That means there is no man around. In half the states there really can't be men around because AFDC says if there is an "able-bodied" man around, then you can't be on welfare. If the kids are going to eat, and the man can't get a job, then he's got to go. So his kids can eat.

The truth is that AFDC is like a supersexist marriage. You trade in *a* man for *the* man. But you can't divorce him if he treats you bad. He can divorce you, of course, cut you off anytime he wants. But in that case, *he* keeps the kids, not you.

The man runs everything. In ordinary marriage, sex is supposed to be for your husband. On AFDC, you're not supposed to have any sex at all. You give up control of your own body. It's a condition of aid. You may even have to agree to get your tubes tied so you can never have more children just to avoid being cut off welfare.

The man, the welfare system, controls your money. He tells you what to buy, what not to buy, where to buy it, and how much things cost. If things—rent, for instance—really cost more than he says they do, it's just too bad for you. He's always right. Everything is budgeted down to the last penny; and you've got to make your money stretch.

The man can break into your house anytime he wants to and poke into your things. You've got no right to protest. You've got no right to privacy when you go on welfare.

Like I said, welfare's a supersexist marriage.

In fact, welfare was invented mostly for women. It grew out of something called the Mother's Pension Laws. To be eligible, you had to be female, you had to be a mother, you had to be "worthy." "Worthy" meant were your kids "legitimate," was your home "suitable," were you "proper"?

In 1935, the Mother's Pension Laws became part of the Social Security system. And they changed the name of the program to Aid to Families with Dependent Children.

Of course now there are other welfare programs, other kinds of people on welfare—the blind, the disabled, the aged. (Many of them are women, too, especially the aged.) Those others make up just over a third of all the welfare caseloads. We AFDCs are two-thirds. But when the politicians talk about the "welfare cancer eating at our vitals," they're not talking about the aged, blind, and disabled. Nobody minds them. They're the "deserving poor." Politicians are talking about AFDC. Politicians are talking about us—the women who head up 99 percent of the AFDC families—and our kids. We're the "cancer," the "undeserving poor." Mothers and children.

In fact, welfare isn't even for mothers. It's for the children. It's like a bonus for reproducing the race. Some bonus—all of $720 a year or $60 a month for a family of four if you live in Mississippi. It's more in other places—up to $346 a month for a family of four in New Jersey. But nowhere, nohow, is it enough to live on.

In this country, we believe in something called the "work ethic." That means that your work is what gives you human worth. But the work ethic itself is a double standard. It applies to men, and to women on welfare. It doesn't apply to all women. If you're a society lady from Scarsdale and you spend all your time sitting on your prosperity paring your nails, well, that's okay. Women aren't supposed to work. They're supposed to be married.

But if you don't have a man to pay for everything, particularly if you have kids, then everything changes. You've "failed" as a woman, because you've failed to attract and keep a man. There's something wrong with you. It can't possibly be the man's fault, his lack of responsibility. It must be yours. That's why Governor Reagan can get away with slandering AFDC recipients, calling them "lazy parasites," "pigs at the trough," and such. We've been trained to believe that the only reason people are on welfare is because there's something wrong with their character. If people have "motivation," if people only *want* to work, they can, and they will be able to support themselves and their kids in decency.

If this were true, we wouldn't have the working poor. Right now, 66 percent of the "employable" mothers are already employed—many full time—but at such pitifully low wages that we still need, and are entitled to, public assistance to survive.

The truth is a job doesn't necessarily mean an adequate income. A woman with three kids—not twelve kids, mind you, just three kids—that woman, earning the full federal minimum wage of $1.60 an hour, is still stuck in poverty. She is below the government's own official poverty line. There are some 10 million jobs that now pay less than the minimum wage, and if you're a woman, you've got the best chance of getting one. Why would a forty-five-year-old woman work all day in a laundry ironing shirts at 90-some cents an hour? Because she knows there's some place lower she could be. She could be on welfare. Society needs women on welfare as "examples" to let every woman, factory workers and housewife workers alike, know what will happen if she lets up, if she's laid off, if she tries to go it alone without a man. So these ladies stay on their feet or on their knees all their lives instead of asking *why* they're only getting 90-some cents an hour, instead of daring to fight and complain.

And still, 33 percent of the employable mothers are looking for work.

We are this country's source of cheap labor. But we can't, some of us, get any jobs.

The President keeps repeating the "dignity of work" idea. What dignity? Wages are the measure of dignity that society puts on a job. Wages and nothing else. There is no dignity in starvation. Nobody denies, least of all poor women, that there is dignity and satisfaction in being able to support your kids through honest labor.

We wish we could do it.

The problem is that our country's economic policies deny the dignity and satisfaction of self-sufficiency to millions of people—the millions who suffer every day in underpaid dirty jobs—and still don't have enough to survive.

People still believe that old lie that AFDC mothers keep on having kids just to get a bigger welfare check. On the average, another baby means another $35 a month—barely enough for food and clothing. Having babies for profit is a lie that only men could make up, and only men could believe. Men, who never have to bear the babies or have to raise them and maybe send them to war.

There are a lot of other lies that male society tells about welfare

---

mothers: That AFDC mothers are immoral. That AFDC mothers are lazy, misuse their welfare checks, spend it all on booze, and are stupid and incompetent.

If people are willing to believe these lies, it's partly because they're just special versions of the lies that society tells about *all* women.

For instance, the notion that all AFDC mothers are lazy: that's just a negative version of the idea that women don't work and don't want to. It's a way of rationalizing the male policy of keeping women as domestic slaves.

The notion that AFDC mothers are immoral is another way of saying that all women are likely to become whores unless they're kept under control by men and marriage.

AFDC mothers misuse their welfare checks? That's simply a justification for harassment. It comes from the male theory that women have no head for money, that they're naturally frivolous. In fact, an AFDC mother's probably got a better head for money than Rockefeller. She has to. She has so little to begin with that she's got to make every penny count, if she and her kids are even going to survive.

AFDC mothers are stupid, incompetent? That allows welfare officials to feel good about being paternalistic and justifies their policy of preventing AFDC mothers from making decisions about their own lives. It even explains why people are on welfare in the first place: because they're dumb, because there's something wrong with them.

AFDC mothers are the cause of slums and high taxes? Well, what's that but a special version of the notion that Eve, and Eve only, brought sin into the world? Welfare isn't the cause of high taxes. War is. Plus a lot of other things that poor women would like to see changed.

Society can continue to believe these lies only so long as women themselves believe them, as long as women sit still for them.

Even many of my own sisters on welfare believe these things about themselves.

Many ladies on welfare never get over their shame. But those of us who get beyond it are some of the strongest, most liberated women in this country.

To understand how this can be, you've got to remember that women on welfare are subject to all the same phony "female" ideals as all other women. But at the same time they're denied any opportunity to live up to those ideals.

On TV, a woman learns that human worth means beauty and that beauty means being thin, white, young, and rich.

She learns that her body is really disgusting the way it is, and that she needs all kinds of expensive cosmetics to cover it up.

She learns that a "real woman" spends her time worrying about how her bathroom bowl smells; that being important means being middle class, having two cars, a house in the suburbs, and a minidress under your maxicoat. In other words, an AFDC mother learns that being a "real woman" means being all the things she isn't and having all the things she can't have.

Either it breaks you, and you start hating yourself, or you break it.

There's one good thing about welfare. It kills your illusions about yourself, and about where this society is really at. It's laid out for you straight. You have to learn to fight, to be aggressive, or you just don't make it. If you can survive being on welfare, you can survive anything. It gives you a kind of freedom, a sense of your own power and togetherness with other women.

Maybe it is we poor welfare women who will really liberate women in this country. We've already started on our own welfare plan.

Along with other welfare recipients, we have organized together so we can have some voice. Our group is called the National Welfare Rights Organization (NWRO). We put together our own welfare plan, called Guaranteed Adequate Income (GAI), which would eliminate sexism from welfare. There would be no "categories"—men, women, children, single, married, kids, no kids—just poor people who need aid. You'd get paid according to need and family size only—$6,500 for a family of four (which is the Department of Labor's estimate of what's adequate), and that would be upped as the cost of living goes up.

Of course, nobody in power—and that means rich, white men— wants anything to do with GAI. It's too "radical." The President has his own plan, the Family Assistance Plan (FAP), before Congress now.

The President says we've got a "welfare crisis" in this country and that FAP's going to solve it. What he really means is that he's got a political problem, and that FAP's going to solve *it*. Because that's what FAP is, really, politics.

The President calls FAP a reform. It's not. It's a nice intellectual-sounding principle of an "income floor," but it won't help poor people a bit. Under FAP, a family of four would get $2,400 a year. Right now, 45 states and the District of Columbia are paying AFDC recipients over $2,400 a year in benefits and food stamps, and food stamps would be eliminated under FAP. That means that nine out of ten of all AFDC recipients—women and their children—would be even worse off under FAP than they are now.

And that's not all.

First. There's a built-in "family maximum." If you've got seven kids you get $3,600 a year. If you've got ten kids, you still get $3,600 a year. If you have that eighth kid, by choice or by chance—maybe because you couldn't get birth-control devices from the public clinic or because there was no clinic—then it's just too bad. That kid's invisible, as far as the government is concerned.

Second. That $2,400 applies only to AFDC—to women and children. They've got a whole *different* schedule for the "deserving poor"—the aged, blind and disabled. A better schedule. For instance, an aged couple—just two people—will get almost exactly the same as an AFDC family of *four*.

Third. A single woman—not aged, not disabled, not a mother—gets nothing at all from FAP, no matter how hard up and desperate and unable to get work she is. If you don't have kids, you're not a person.

Fourth. If a mother refuses a job or job training recommended for her by the welfare officials, she can be cut off and payments due her children are made to a "third party," someone outside her own family, someone she doesn't even choose. This brings up the most important point about FAP: forced work.

Under FAP, a woman has to take any job offered her. She doesn't decide whether the job is suitable and pays a living wage. In fact, the job can pay as little as $1.20 an hour, or less, if "prevailing wages" are less. She doesn't decide whether child-care facilities are good enough. The welfare people make these decisions for her. If she doesn't go along, her check is cut off.

"We can only put people in jobs that exist," the FAP people say. We all know what kinds of jobs those are—maids get as low as $20 a week in Mississippi, living in five or six days, and only seeing their kids on weekends. And even these kinds of jobs, low as they are, are few and far between.

Child-care provisions in FAP don't make any sense either. They're just decorations to make it seem okay to force women with little children to work. In fact, the way it looks now, AFDC mothers may have to pay for all or part of their child care out of their own earnings, even though they only need child care because of the forced-work law.

There is an important point for women to remember when they fight for quality universal child care. Be careful that your enthusiasm doesn't get used to create a reservoir of cheap female labor. Because that's who's going to be working in those child-care centers—poor women. If we don't watch it, an AFDC mother can end up paying a child-care center, which in turn will pay her less than the minimum wage to watch her children—and your children, too. Institutionalized, partially self-employed Mammies—that's what can happen to us.

A woman should be able to *choose* whether to work outside her home or in it, to choose whether she wants to care for her own children all the time or part-time. And the people who work in child-care centers have to be paid decent wages or our kids won't get decent care.

The same thing goes for the birth-control and abortion movements. Nobody realizes more than poor women that all women should have the right to control their own reproduction. But we also know how easily the lobby for birth control can be perverted into a weapon against poor women. The word is choice. Birth control as a right, not an obligation. A personal decision, not the condition of a welfare check.

As far as I'm concerned, the ladies of NWRO are the front-line troops of women's freedom. Both because we have so few illusions and because our issues are so important to all women—the right to a living wage for women's work, the right to life itself.

If I were President, I would solve this so-called welfare crisis in a minute and go a long way toward liberating every woman. I'd just issue a proclamation that women's work is *real* work. In other words, I'd start paying women a living wage for doing the work we are already doing—child raising and housekeeping. And the welfare crisis would be over, just like that. Housewives would be getting wages, too—a legally determined percentage of their husband's salary—instead of having to ask for and account for money they've already earned.

For me, Women's Liberation is simple. No woman in this country can feel dignified, no woman can be liberated, until all women get off their knees. That's what NWRO is all about—women standing together, on their feet.

If you agree, there are a lot of things you can do to help.

First, be honest about where your own head is at. Do you put down other women for being on welfare? Is it always "those people"? Well it could be you, and soon.

Stop for a minute and think what would happen to you and your kids if you suddenly had no husband and no savings.

Do you believe the "welfare Cadillac" myth? Inform yourself. Who's on welfare, why—and why can't they get off? NWRO's got plenty of information out on the subject, and so do other groups. Write and get it.

Do you understand what FAP's about? Read the bill, or NWRO's analysis of it.

Do you know how your senator's going to vote on FAP?

How does your own women's group stand on welfare? Push them a little. If we don't see that we're all women, all suffering from sexism, we'll never get anywhere. We have to work together.

Does your own community have people on welfare? Is there a local NWRO group? Help it.

Do you know your own rights to welfare? Find out.

Could you make it on a welfare budget (say, nineteen cents a meal)? Try it for a while. Just one week. Many women have done this—even wives of congressmen—and they're shocked to see what even seven days is like. Do it in your community. Challenge people to a seven-day experiment to wake them up.

Inform yourself on welfare. You may have to live on it sooner or later.

Because you're a woman.

6

TO MY WHITE WORKING-CLASS SISTERS

DEBBY D'AMICO

We are the invisible women, the faceless women, the nameless women . . . the female half of the silent majority, the female half of the ugly Americans, the smallest part of the "little people." No one photographs us, no one writes about us, no one puts us on TV. No one says we are beautiful, no one says we are important, very few like to recognize that we are *here*. We are the poor and working-class white women of America, and we are cruelly and systematically ignored. All our lives we have been told, sometimes subtly, sometimes not so subtly, that we are not worth very much. This message has been put across to me, a white working-class woman, all my life. I think the time has come to speak out against these insults, and so I have decided to write about parts of my life and my ideas. I am doing this for all my sisters who have been made to feel that they are not worth writing about, and for all those people who have to be convinced of poor white existence, those same people who told us that because we are all white our lives are the same as those of the middle and upper classes.

When I was in the second grade, we were given a sample aptitude test to accustom us to the test-taking rut that would ultimately determine whether we would be programmed toward college or a dead-end job. After we had answered several multiple-choice questions, the teacher had us check our answers against the "right" ones. One of the questions pictured a man in a tuxedo, a man in a suit, and a man in overalls. The question read: "Which man is going to work?" The "correct" answer was: the man in the suit. I can still feel the shame that came with the realization that what went on in my home was marked "incorrect." I responded the way oppressed people often respond—by secretly hating myself and my family. I remember constantly begging my father to put on a suit—my father who worked an average of 65 to 80 hours a week driving trucks, checking out groceries in a super-market, and doing any of the other deadening jobs which came his way. My mother didn't escape my judgments either. The unreal Dick, Jane, and Sally world our school books presented as the "right" way of life, reinforced by TV and middle-class schoolmates' homes, made me viciously attack her grammar whenever she spoke and ask her questions like: "How come *you* never wear dresses or get your hair done?" The world of my home gave me concrete answers: at the time my mother had three kids in diapers and another on the way, hardly a life style that called for a well-dressed mannequin. But the middle-class world was bigger than my home and I was overcome by its judgments.

As I went on through school, I continued to be taught about an America that had little to do with me. The picture of American life drawn in history books was almost always a comfortable one, with exceptions like wars and the depression (hardships which the middle class participated in and thus wanted to talk about). Working-class sisters, wake up! Black people were not the only ones left out of history books. George Washington is no relative of yours; neither is Henry Ford, or Nixon and Agnew. While George Washington was relaxing at his Mt. Vernon estate, *your* ancestors may have been among the two-thirds majority of white settlers who served as indentured servants for Master George and others like him. They may have been servants who were kidnapped from the slums of England and Ireland and brought here in chains to be sold to the highest bidder. Your grandmother might have been one of the "huddled masses yearning to breathe free," who came to America and wound up in a tenement where free air never blew, working from can see to can't see, made to feel alien and ashamed of an Old World culture infinitely more alive and colorful than the drab, Puritan, "Mr. Clean" ways of America. I have listened to the old folks in my family talk about how they "came over," and how they survived, the first Italians in an all-Irish neighborhood. That is *my* history. While Mr. Pullman was amassing his fortune, our people were fighting and dying for the rights of working men and women, our people were being shot and beaten for what they believed. I was not taught this in school but learned it later on my own. In high school I continued to learn middle-class ways. I spent years learning to talk like them, eat like them, look like them. I learned a language that had little to do with the concrete terms of my life or the lives of my family and fellow workers.

At the same time that books were deluging me with middle-class culture, I began to feel the pinch of unworthiness in other ways. I attended a parochial high school for one year which was upper-middle-class dominated. If your family had no influential friends to take out $50 ads in the yearbook, you were punished—shame on you! they said, for your failure to measure up in America, shame on you because you haven't made it in the land of the free and the home of the brave.

During my high school years I entered the great rat race of women who were dedicated to snagging any and all men considered desirable. I was again led by middle-class values, and so I rejected the knit-shirted, "greasy"-haired, dark-skinned Italians I grew up with and made a mad dash for the Brylcreem man. All the while, of course, feeling I could never get him, because I wasn't the *girl* in the Brylcreem commercial. I read all the middle-class fashion and glamour magazines and tried to look like people who were able to look that way because of a life style that included a closet full of clothes I couldn't afford and a leisurely existence that allowed them to look cool and unruffled all the time. And there I was working in a luncheonette so shabby I never mentioned it to anyone for a lousy six dollars a Saturday that I immediately spent in vain efforts to make myself "acceptable" looking. During the day I gossiped condescendingly about the way people dressed, playing at being the glorious magazine girl, and at night I sulked off to the phone company to be bitten by cord lice and told all night that I was either very slow or innately stupid.

And people, in social and job situations, have been saying that ever since. In social situations it is said as I sit quietly by and watch well-dressed, slick, confident women of the upper classes, America's idea of beauty, steal the eyes, applause, and the image of woman from me. It is said in many ways on the job: at my last job I was mimeographer at a school, a "liberal progressive" school at that. I once spoke up at a staff meeting and the first remark to follow the stunned silence was, "Why doesn't someone put her on the faculty?" Yes, put me among the educated middle class because you absolutely can't deal with a worker who thinks and has ideas. After I mentioned this, I was told that it was a compliment and that I should be *grateful.* Grateful that they thought I was as good as them. At the same school I was once asked, "Are you the switchboard?" Naturally—since we are looked on as extensions of the machines we operate, not as human beings.

What all this has done to us is create a deep, deep sense of unworthiness, a sense so deep it dooms us. I have a thirteen-year-old friend who is well on the way to life either in prison or on heroin. We, *as a people,* have nothing that says to him, "You shouldn't ruin your life. You're a good, worthwhile person." If or when he does go to jail, there will be no Black Muslims to tell him he is a worthwhile person just because of what he is. No one will be there to give him the respect and support of an alternate culture that respects what he is. That is what the judgment of middle-class America has done to us.

Why has this happened to us? It has happened because we believed in the American dream, in the dream that *anyone* can be *anything* if he only tries, works hard, and if he doesn't make it it's only because something about *him* is rotten. Since we don't have much to begin with, we're made to feel we don't deserve much. And we believe it—even though the truth of our lives tells us that we have worked, and damned hard, but we still didn't have the kinds of lives we read about and saw on TV. And America has kept us out of magazines and off TV *because* our faces and voices are full of this truth. We have hated black people, but we have hated ourselves more. By believing black people are inferior, we have kept the truth about ourselves from each other—that the people who have the power and money in America never intend to raise our incomes or those of black people, not because we aren't worthy, but because it would cut into their profits to do so. We believed black people were so inferior that they weren't supposed to make it—we believed we were superior and could make it—but we never did and we blame ourselves. As white people who haven't made it, we are the living proof of the American lie and we hate ourselves for it.

What can we do about all this? As poor and working-class women, we can *start* asking what is wrong with America and *stop* asking what is wrong with ourselves. In a culture where women are often judged by beauty alone, the standard of beauty does not fit us. We, as *ourselves,* as we go to work or wash dishes, we, *in our daily lives,* are never called beautiful. Black women have told themselves that they are beautiful in their natural lives, and we need to do the same for ourselves. We must begin to see ourselves as beautiful in our ability to work, to endure, in our plain honest lives, and we must stop aspiring to a false eyelash existence that is not and never has been for us. We are not the women in *Vogue, Glamour,* or *As The World Turns,* nor should we want to be. We are the women who have dealt all our lives with the truths and tragedies of real life, because we never had the option of the armchair-beautiful-people existence. We are the people who have no maids or therapists to dump our troubles on. We know what it is to work hard and we are not guilty of wearing silks while others wear rags. We should never admire the women in *Vogue,* because there is something undeniably ugly about women who wear minks while others can't afford shoes—and no amount of $20-an-ounce makeup can hide that brand of ugliness. We must start learning that other people have been victims of this middle-class culture aping the rich. Black and Puerto Rican, Mexican and Indian, Chinese and Japanese people have had their true history concealed and their faces scorned by TV and magazines. We must see that those who share the hardships we share

are not the white middle and upper classes, but the black and brown people who work at our sides. As white working-class and poor people we must begin to be proud of ourselves, our histories, and each other; we must unite and support ourselves as a people. Once we respect ourselves, we will find it necessary to struggle with a society and with jobs which tell us we are worthless. In that struggle we will learn that the anger of black and brown people which we have feared for so long has the same direction as our anger, that their enemies are our enemies, and their fight our fight.

7

IS SHE OR ISN'T SHE? IS JACKIE OPPRESSED?

BOBBIE GOLDSTONE

I have what at least one of my sisters has labeled a morbid interest in socialites cum celebrites, jet-setters, beautiful people, and upper-class women in general. I read with avid interest Jackie stories in movie magazines; Suzy—the columnist of the beautiful people; articles about Carter and Amanda; biographies and autobiographies of wives of the powerful; old copies of *Status*—the now-defunct magazine for the middle classes about the upper classes; accounts of hunt breakfasts, charity balls, and radical chic; upper-class family histories and comedies of manners about the British aristocracy. I read all this at no small personal cost—even movie magazines are 50 cents these days. Where has this fascination gotten me? I'm not sure yet, but at this time I am prepared to offer two lists. These lists are reasons pro and con, a little cost-benefit analysis on the question: Are upper-class women oppressed? Jackie Kennedy Onassis is used as an ideal type in considering this question. List I lists the ways in which Jackie et al. don't seem oppressed. List II lists the ways in which Jackie et al. do seem oppressed.

List I

1. They Have Power

The kinds of power women like Jackie wield come closer to being influence and privilege than direct political power. Mary Barelli Gallagher, one of the legions of Kennedy ex-servants who tell all, writes, "Some women are born to be queen—or its equivalent, Jacqueline Bouvier Kennedy Onassis is such a woman. Born to cause excitement wherever she goes, to attract all eyes. Always at the very center—and yet aloof from it. Born to exact homage, to be a law unto herself, to be obeyed, sought after. Born to have power, to be envied, followed, copied, watched—and to be worshipped." Jackie is reputed to have said, "There are two kinds of power. Power of the world and power of the bed. I want power of the bed."

Invitations from Mrs. Simpson (before Edward abdicated and became the Duke of Windsor) were reported to come to rank as commands. The Churchill women affected English politics by exercising power behind the throne (Jennie Churchill is reported to have written many of Lord Randolph's best-known speeches). According to all sources, Jackie, like the Duchess of Windsor, is less interested in influencing affairs of the state than the privilege to command and be obeyed.

2. They Have Prestige

To have prestige is to be admired and esteemed for one's good qualities. Prestige is an ego gratification not commonly open to the oppressed who more frequently experience neglect and contempt.

In his book, *Jackie, the Exploitation of a First Lady*, Irving Shulman lists the qualities that made Jackie especially esteemed as First Lady. She was: (1) young and winsome; (2) beautiful; (3) poised and charming; (4) mother of at least two children; (5) modest of demeanor, but regal of presence; (6) well educated, but not bookish; (7) good linguist so as to enhance the prestige of the United States; (8) tasteful homemaker and setter of styles; (9) reasonable, athletic, but not excelling at anything except maybe horsemanship; (10) a lady, who also loves power.

In her salad days, millions of women regarded Jackie as the ideal model of a young matron, the pinnacle of good breeding and good taste.

3. They Have Money

I know that money can't buy happiness . . . but can you really consider somebody who spends $1.4 million in a year on clothes and jewelry and beauty treatments oppressed?

4. Other People Do Their Shitwork

On board the *Christina* Jackie is reported to have a hand buzzer system that she can press to summon servants on different parts of the yacht. Jackie and others like her have nannies to take the children when they become a bother. They have secretaries to see to it that those gracious thank-you notes are sent, to take care of the bills, to make those annoying phone calls, to screen you from demands and requests when you're not up to it. Maids to see that your clothes are in order, that freshly pressed sheets are on the bed when you want to take a nap. They have chefs to whip up little goodies and make eating a delight. Gardeners to see that you always have fresh flowers. In short you can have a reputation for being a thoughtful, gracious, and tasteful woman and homemaker without doing any of the drudgery. (Having all those shitworkers at your beck and call is a bit more of a problem to the younger slightly left of center rich, like the Carter Burdens, who have tried to solve some of this problem by having only white servants.)

5. They Can Develop as Persons

Upper-class women are your basic leisure class (this does not mean that they aren't busy). They have the leisure time, the economic wherewithal, and even a great many times the encouragement to "develop" themselves. Frequently devotees of Culture and aesthetics, they are educated in the arts and classics. Almost all develop skills at these pursuits. Jackie paints, Joan plays the piano, and Gloria makes her collages.

6. They Perpetuate Class Distinctions

Upper-class women are primarily responsible for running the family's social life. But it is in their role of socializers of the next generation of upper-class people that they do the most to perpetuate class distinctions. Children are socialized to the idea that they're different. This can be done by sending them to the right combination of the right schools, the right dancing classes, the right camps, the right clubs, the right hobbies, the right friends, so as to end up with the right marriage (Bouviers and Auchinclosses are known for marrying well) and starting the cycle all over.

Children can also be socialized to the idea of noblesse oblige—the idea that the upper classes are better than others and are therefore entitled to their high position. But as part of the duty of high position they must teach and guide and lead and help the common folk. The most liberal version of noblesse oblige is Ethel Kennedy, who according to a number of ladies' mags, teaches her children that because they have been given so much, they must give in return. Giving in return means "going into public service," like being an ambassador or a senator or a president, not, however, by becoming a garbage collector.

List II

1. High Cost of Their Power

For a woman to possess power behind the throne, or power of the bed, or the power to make people want to obey her commands on a grand scale, requires these days that she be mysterious, girlish, aloof, witty, exciting, changeable, sexually viable, charming, especially to men. According to Jackie's cousin, Jackie's father (Black Jack Bouvier) taught her how to remain aloof yet alluring to maximize her desirability to men.

The era of the dowdy society matron (like Mrs. Roosevelt) is dead, surviving only in Boston. Now, as Jackie's friend Jayne Wrightsman says, "a girl (in her forties) can't be too thin or too rich."

2. Their Prestige Comes from a Man

On the list of the most admired women in the United States are Mrs. Nixon, Mrs. Eisenhower, Mrs. Johnson, Mrs. Ethel Kennedy, Mrs. Rose Kennedy, and Mrs. Kennedy Onassis. The wives of the power elite. (Jackie, by the way, was able to pull Onassis into the Social Register.) According to some recent poll or other, many people claim to prefer Mrs. Nixon to Mrs. Kennedy as a first lady. Mrs. Nixon, it was emphasized, was a real lady, a wife and mother who kept her nose out of her husband's business.

Jackie has clearly lost prestige since her later widow days and her remarriage to Ari. She plunged from the ideal young matron to an international, almost bad girl. Mary Barelli Gallagher bleats, "I had never thought that Jackie would remarry. I fully believed that she would remain tied to the perpetuation of the President's name and the Kennedy Library and all the works of a cultural nature connected with it."

3. They're Used to Sell Products

Jackie, Babe, and Amanda are good for big business. They are celebrated by the garment, cosmetics, jewelry, home furnishing, beauty, service industries and the mass media who sell the products. They sell products to millions of women for whom the most available means of emulating Jackie or Amanda is to buy. (Remember the Jackie Look—we all had it in 1962.) In the last few years the fashion socialists have become less the setters of styles or trends than the legitimators of trends for middle America. Remember the rich hippie look that was in last year. This year it's the artsy-craftsy look. When Gloria Vanderbilt DeCicco Stokowski Lumet Cooper decorates her house with patchwork quilts hot from Appalachia (made by women who get $1.50 an hour) or Joan wears hot pants to entertain the Boston Symphony (Jackie is reported to have ordered several pair, one in leather) then Sears or the Genesco Corporation will sell millions of items.

4. They're Superhomemakers

For all those servants Jackie and Amanda and Babe and Gloria are still in the same old homemaker merry-go-round. Only they have been socialized to perfection, running a winter home and a summer home and a little pied-à-terre of eleven rooms and a yacht. Babe Paley reportedly never has a hair out of place (although younger socialites spend a lot of time looking windblown). Having memorable dinner parties. (Poor Mrs. Nixon reportedly keeps files of everyone she's had to dinner and what they got to eat so as not to duplicate.) Seeing to their husband's comforts. As Mrs. Roosevelt said of Mrs. Churchill, "She knew that in the first place she must make life as easy as possible for him [Winston] at home, with as much attention to detail as possible, to ensure that his life would be comfortable and lightened of any burdens she could remove." A woman, Mrs. Roosevelt concluded, can make a home a heaven or a hell.

5. They Are P.R. for the Power Elite

Jackie's beauty, charm, and her ability to excite and fascinate could be used to enhance and make more palatable her husband's political power. As icing on the cake, window dressing, human interest, doer of good deeds, and softener of brute power. Lady Bird Johnson in her diary tells us how unhappy and lonely Lyndon felt as he destroyed Vietnam. Clementine Churchill is reported to have disagreed often with her husband in private (interestingly over the women's suffrage issue) but always used her public speaking ability, her wit, and her charm to staunchly defend him in public. Jackie diverted the public with Mount Vernon parties and Pablo Cassals parties as her husband surrounded Cuba and sent American "advisers" to Vietnam. Rich women do good works; a lot of charity, a lot of fund raising for good causes, a lot of championing of culture and aesthetics. General Mark Clark's wife (the Mark Clark who headed our troops in Korea) had blanket campaigns for Korean children orphaned by the war, Nixon's wife brings supplies to Peruvian earthquake victims, Lady Bird Johnson planted flowers in voteless Washington, D.C., now that Carter Burden fancies himself the new Robert Kennedy, Amanda is working at Head Start in Harlem, and Jackie fought to save the Metropolitan Opera House, but not to tear down the hideous Kennedy Merchandise Mart in Chicago. It is, after all, a wife's duty to support her husband and present him in the best light. Jackie, by the way, is reported to have been somewhat uncooperative at being icing. JFK got much sympathy on this score.

6. They're Programmed

Jackie is reported to have been a rebel and an outlaw at school (as much of one as you could be going to Miss Chapin's). The dean told Mrs. Auchincloss that the only reason the school didn't throw Jackie out was that she had the "most inspiring mind we've ever had at the school." Her ambition in her yearbook from Mrs. Porter's School was "not to be a housewife." But even Jackie got the old programming—she got it from her mother who wondered out loud to Jackie's friends why she wasn't a nice little girl, why was she always so naughty. She got it from the Chapin School dean who told her that wild horses weren't any good to anybody, you had to break them in. She got it from her newspaper boss, who told her he didn't want to hire another little girl (Jackie) who would leave to get married. She got it from JFK who "kiddingly" told a wedding-night party that he was marrying Jackie to get her out of newspaper reporting because she might be dangerous to his career. I don't want to sound soap-operaish, but from rebel to obsessive consumer is pretty depressing.

Conclusion

Well, Is She or Isn't She? Only you can decide for sure. But remember though every girl can potentially grow up to be a Jackie (remember Bobo Rockefeller), many are called and few are chosen. And at what a cost.

8

ON SISTERHOOD

DANA DENSMORE

Do you see yourself stronger, more able to resist or reject conditioning, more real than other women? Are you better able to act in this society as an individual rather than relating solely to the stereotypes of feminine behavior and the woman's place?

It is because you were fortunate enough to have some countervailing influences that others didn't have to counteract all that propaganda to some degree.

You were, perhaps, more trusted by your parents in your youth and learned to trust yourself and your own instincts. Or you were taught straight out that certain things were vanity, or silly, or unworthy. You were taught that individual action was honorable when others were taught only that inaction, womanly passivity, was honorable.

Now you both carry out what you have learned, both doing what you were taught was the honorable thing, and you look down on the others and say you have no sympathy for their suffering or the slights they incur, because they "ask for it," they "like it."

There is nothing male society succeeds in so well as divide and conquer. We have all fallen for it, so there can be no pointing the finger, but it is a shameful thing nonetheless.

"You are different," they say, and how eagerly we agree.

We are not like those other women who sit at home all day reading magazines and gossiping. We are not like those silly bunnies using their bodies and the padding of torturedly sleek bunny costumes to get big tips from silly men.

We are not like those empty-headed girls who spend all their money on clothes and all their ingenuity on snagging men into marriage and get together to giggle over nothing for hours. We are not like those nagging possessive wives who have nothing to offer but sap the life out of their husbands. We are not like those bitter, dried-up women of whatever age who hate sex and are desperately afraid that someone somewhere may be having a good time.

"You are different," the men say, and justify the most vicious prejudice and discrimination and cruelty by inviting us into their select little club (or rather by giving us the false illusion that we are in).

They make us accomplices; eager for respect and acceptance, we insist that we too are prejudiced; we tom, we agree eagerly that women are contemptible indeed—most women, that is, the masses of women, not *me* of course, but most women.

This is a strange but very widespread schizophrenia which results among women who have been not entirely ruined by the womanhood conditioning. They see that men are free and respected and identify with them, rejecting their own sex in horror, pretending that it is some kind of moral failing, convincing themselves of it even, saying the women like it because they are lazy and selfish.

In fact only a low self-image could produce that kind of self-destructive conduct, a low self-image and general despair.

They have been taught that it is immoral and selfish to try to make something of yourself, to care about yourself, not to devote yourself to your family and home. But it isn't easy to devote yourself to your family and all their faults are but symptoms of their unhappiness.

The kind of "moral strength" it takes to stand up and fight the world for the right to be an authentic person, a functioning individual rather than an undifferentiated function (housekeeper, mother) comes only from training and encouragement. The ego can be hopelessly crippled and it is at a very young age in American Indians, blacks, and women.

So you pulled yourself up by your bootstraps, did you? Despite the disadvantage of being a woman, and tainted with the laziness and unreliability and stupidity of other women, and subject to the very natural prejudice against women, you succeeded. This proves that any woman with ambitions could succeed too if she works hard enough to prove that she's different. Men will be glad to accept her as an equal if she only proves that she's different. Or at least most men will.

But the bootstrap theory is false. Those women are where they are because that's what they've been conditioned for.

They have been taught that to do otherwise is wrong, and enormous pressures are immediately brought against them if they try. And suppose they aren't intelligent enough to get your glamorous jobs even with the healthiest egos in the world? Do you then write them off?

You have no sympathy for women who "like" playing the feminine role. They "enjoy" the discrimination, they "ask for it." But they've been conditioned, programmed, even traumatized to shun "unfeminine" behavior.

If they do enjoy the attention a good job of femininity brings them, you are cruel to feel contemptuous of them for enjoying the one pleasure they're allowed, the one honor in all that degradation. They're too ruined to assert themselves the way you do, demanding attention as an individual; that requires self-respect and they have none; they were taught to believe fully in their inferiority.

We are all one. All the same influences have acted on us. If you have somehow escaped the consequences of your conditioning you are lucky, not superior, not different. We are all sisters.

We all work within the same constraints. The prostitute, the married woman, the model, the bunny, and the career woman who makes herself glamorous are all using their bodies to get what they want or need from men. We all play the role to one extent or another and in one style or another and the career woman who plays lends honor to the system that oppresses her less-healthy, ambitious, talented, educated, intelligent sisters.

But their oppression oppresses her because she will never be a man, she will never be accepted as a man; her mind and talents are just being used; ultimately all men know she is a woman and will never completely accept her. She *is* a woman, and women, as she so eagerly agrees, are stupid, selfish, and lazy, not to be respected, clearly not the equals of men. She cannot be exempted just by imagining she is.

This ugly elitism is rampant among the only-partially-ruined women, the golden ones who were brought up to have a strong sense of self, the intelligent educated talented ones who have "succeeded."

There is a complete identification with the ruling class, coupled not only with a rejection of their own class, but with an insistence that the pressures, influences, and conditioning that forced the women into their oppressed situation did not exist. ("They never should have *had* so many children, they should have thought ahead. They knew that marriages break up. They deserve to be in that fix. I can't have any sympathy for women with ten kids.")

This is bad faith and bad sociology. It is worse. It is an incredible lack of compassion, explainable only as a defensive rejection to avoid identification.

They are identifying with the men. To have sympathy for women is by implication to condemn the circumstances that oppress them, and those circumstances are the male power structure. But the elitist women cannot afford to criticize the male power structure even by implication because they are so busy currying favor from men to maintain their own "success."

So they must maintain an attitude of moral superiority toward those who do not succeed, and avoid at any cost analysis of why they "chose" their oppression.

An appalling snobbishment is involved in the elitist golden career girls brushing off impatiently as irrelevant the plight of the masses of women who don't identify with the men, who have been convinced that they are, in fact, inferior, and who are just trying to do the best they can in a miserable situation.

We are all one. We are all sisters. We all work within the same constraints. If some of us are more successful and less oppressed, it is because we are less crippled, not because we are superior, not because we are different.

December 1968

PART TWO

PREPARATION FOR ADULTHOOD: MARRIAGE AND BEYOND

A
Sex-role Socialization:
Present and Future

B
Attitudes Toward Sex Expression

C
Birth Control

A
Sex-role Socialization:
Present and Future Throughout an individual's
life cycle, various agents of society—parents, teachers, the media
—interpret and communicate the expectations of that society.
Socialization is the process through which each individual learns
the expectations of his social surroundings. Socialization is
directed toward the internalization of general societal norms and
values as well as the acquiring of knowledge and skills related to
specific roles.

The general rules of the family and in turn of the larger
society are presented to infants and children as objective
reality—concrete and immutable. From earliest infancy, children
learn that females are naturally inferior to males and that females
only are "naturally" suited to service roles, especially those of wife
and mother. Those who currently advocate an androgynous
society—one in which there are no roles allocated solely on
sex—have begun to examine the present sex-role socialization
process as well as to posit possible alternative modes of
socialization at each stage of the life cycle. This chapter focuses on
childhood socialization from crib through college.

The first socializing agents of most children are the members
of the family. As noted in the general Introduction, sex-role
patterning begins at birth if not before. Girl infants and boy
infants are dressed differently and treated differently. If a baby's
clothes do not advertise its sex to a stranger or visitor, she (he) will
inquire almost immediately about its sex. Within the family, infant
girls are talked to, touched, and watched more than infant boys.
By the time a girl is thirteen months old, she is already more fearful
than a boy of leaving her mother's side.[1] As the Osofskys note,

---

1. Sandra L. Bem and Daryl J. Bem, "Training the Woman to Know Her Place: A
Non-conscious Ideology," *Women: A Journal of Liberation* 1, no. 1 (Fall 1969): 9.

much more research is needed in the area, but it is likely that nonsexist treatment of children by adults would result in fewer sex-typed behaviors by the new generation. In addition to differential treatment of children by their sex, there is differential responsibility for the care of young children by sex of parents. Again, although there is no clear empirical evidence, it is likely that shared responsibility for child care on the part of fathers and mothers (or males and females) in contrast to the typical situation in which the mother has primary responsibility would influence children to see child care as an activity pertinent to both sexes. In general a nonsexist home environment would provide children of both sexes with training for independence, mastery, and strength as well as compassion, nurturance, and verbal skills.

While family members serve as the first socializing agents of most children, picture books soon introduce them to the larger society. Weitzman et al. study systematically sex-role characterizations in recent prize-winning picture books and determine what they communicate about societal expectations for boys and girls as well as for men and women. It is not surprising that the first lesson picture books teach is that women are not important. In fact, they could be described as invisible! Males predominate in pictures, in titles, and as central characters; and in almost one-third of the recent prize-winning books studied, there are no females at all. Even when females do appear in the books, they are shown as unimportant; they play supportive roles only and never do anything exciting. This is true for all females depicted, young and old alike. While little boys are active, little girls are passive. Little girls remain indoors while boys play outdoors; little girls serve while little boys lead; little girls are rescued while little boys perform the rescue. Adult women fare no better in these books. They are presented mainly as wives and mothers or fantasy figures, such as fairies. Adult men, however, are shown in a wide range of interesting roles: storekeepers, house builders, gods, fighters, and fishermen, to name a few. Picture books, moreover, present women's lives as even more restricted than they are in real life; for example, Weitzman et al. note that "Motherhood is presented as a full-time, lifetime job, although for most women it is in reality a part-time 10-year commitment." We would conjecture that such characterization contributes to empirical reality wherein most little girls grow into women who perceive motherhood as a lifetime, full-time commitment and who, therefore, view alternative plans as contingency plans rather than as central parts of their future lives.

Weitzman et al. conclude by proposing that picture books should portray both males and females in less rigid roles. Stories should involve women in various activities which require physical, intellectual, and creative as well as emotional assets. When women are depicted at home, moreover, they should be portrayed as active participants rather than simply decorations that blend into the background. Men should be shown doing domestic chores and taking care of children, and characterized as emotional and supportive as well as intellectual and courageous. By presenting a more balanced view of adults and adult roles, picture books could contribute to a more flexible existence for both men and women.

Books can help children of all age levels to see the variety in the world rather than restrict their vision. As Letty Pogrebin suggests, adults can carefully help children select books that illustrate alternative life styles, that present both men and women in diverse activities, and that provide a view of history not limited to males and male perspectives.[2] Writers and publishers have begun to fill the void in nonsexist literature for children. Hopefully the time is not too distant when a wide array of such books will be in the stores and on library shelves. In the meantime, women have begun to compile bibliographies of acceptable books that are currently available.[3]

Toys as well as books reinforce early sex-role socialization.[4] A recent study concludes that adult toy buyers maintain a set of traditional definitions whereby certain toys are regarded as appropriate to each sex. These definitions parallel the social norms for each sex. By an analysis of various sources, this study

2. Letty Cottin Pogrebin, "Down With Sexist Upbringing," *Ms.* 1, no. 1 (Spring 1972): 20, 25–26.

3. See, for example, Feminists on Children's Media, *Little Miss Muffet Fights Back: Recommended Non-sexist Books About Girls for Young Readers* (New York: Feminists on Children's Media, 1971).

4. This discussion of toys is based on Nancy Lyon, "Toys: More Than Child's Play," *Ms.* 1, no. 6 (December 1972): 54–59, 98.

determines that there is a larger selection of masculine than feminine toys and that the former are more costly, intricate, active, and social than the latter which, of course, are simple, passive, and solitary. Although neutral toys are the most creative and educational, adults buy the more involved and difficult of these for boys. Children of both sexes, for example, are depicted on boxes of simple building blocks and Tinkertoys while boys only are shown on complex Erector-set toys.

The sex-role stereotypes that children learn at home from family, books, and toys are typically reinforced in school. Rossi asserts, however, that schools should strive to undermine rather than reinforce sex linking of occupational and family roles. Children should, therefore, be presented with illustrations of and the facts about the number and variety of existing occupations for adults in our society. Class excursions into the community represent one means to such a goal. In addition, Rossi suggests that schools should invite atypical members of occupations to speak; for example, female doctors and male nurses. Finally, she maintains that the schools should make a concerted effort to attract male teachers for the primary grades in an effort to show children that men can participate in child care.

In terms of family life education, boys and girls together should take shop and domestic science courses. As adults, then, men and women will have skills relevant to home repair and cooking and child care. They will be able, and thus more likely, to perform in equal roles.

As the Osofskys point out, school curricula are reinforced by counselors who traditionally advise girls to see marriage and career as mutually exclusive options and encourage the girls to choose the former, more "acceptable" outcome. Parallel to changes in curricula, all guidance situations should, of course, consider children as individuals.[5] Once boys and girls receive comparable educations and develop comparable views regarding the purpose of education, they will be more likely to base their

5. The demand for educational equality in relation to curricula, counseling, and extracurricular activities is echoed in the recommendation of the National Organization for Women, New York Chapter to the New York City Board of Education. See Anne Grant West, "What We Recommend," in National Organization for Women, New York Chapter, *Report on Sex Bias in the Public Schools* (New York: NOW, n.d.), pp. 7–9.

choices of adult roles on abilities and interests rather than on sex.

Currently, boys are socialized to decide on an occupation and life style and to marry someone who will fit in with those plans. In contrast, girls are socialized for a life of contingencies. A woman must remain more unsure of her identity, more malleable, so that within limits she can agree with a variety of value systems and live a variety of life styles. Although marriage is to be to an as yet unknown spouse, marriage is the key contingency in a woman's life. Young women, for example, generally do not think that work or a career are likely to be central features in their lives. Even college women prepare for work roles as a contingency by pursuing degrees with a practical outcome (i.e., a degree in elementary education). With such training they can work "just in case" they do not marry, or have to support a husband through school, or want to work before having children or after children are grown.

For various reasons, most women are likely to work during a large segment of their lives, but this reality is obscured in young women's eyes as marriage assumes a greater importance. From their high school days, if not earlier, girls are socialized to act passive and to accept traditional sex-role responsibilities. During the preteen years, both boys and girls consider occupational opportunities, but by the time of college matriculation, boys only are thinking about occupations while the girls are thinking about marriage. In her study of women college graduates, Angrist found that it is not until the probability of long-term single status or until the contingency of working while married becomes a reality that women face the problem of their inadequate preparation for work.

Angrist highlights the fact that women continue to phase in and out of the work force. Furthermore, they are returning at earlier ages since they are completing their families sooner. In other words, the roles of wife and mother are no longer likely to be full-time, long-term roles within contemporary society. It is unrealistic, then, to socialize women to see marriage as their solitary goal in life. It often leads, moreover, to a personally shattering experience for women as they reach middle age.[6]

---

6. For a detailed discussion of the crisis many women confront during middle age, see in this volume the article by Jules Henry.

Until recently, the content of college courses which young women (and men) took rarely questioned the docile and domestic stereotype of women. In fact, college courses were extensions of earlier public schooling in that they projected an inferior image of women. The critical examination of all facets of American society that eventually led to Women's Studies began in the early 1960s. Students who first worked off-campus within the civil rights movement returned to college, and together with other students and faculty mobilized not only against racism, but also poverty, imperialism, and the war in Vietnam. Women whose political consciousness had been heightened by these other movements began to see the parallel between domination of other groups and the domination of women by men. Women then began to write and to read critical analyses of the contemporary situation of women; to teach and to learn from courses—first only on the predicament of women, then on the predicament of men as well. Women at all levels of the university, strengthened and supported by the Women's Liberation Movement, joined together to establish Women's Studies courses and programs.

Women's Studies, according to Tobias, originated within the university and many programs remain focused and organized entirely within the academic community. In some places, however, women have organized programs around community projects, and have defined personal experience, personally evaluated, as the goal. While women are striving to create new standards and new institutions, the old ones still exist. Women are torn between striving for masculine goals and declaring these goals invalid.[7] These views are often incompatible within the classroom and cause problems for Women's Studies on many campuses. Finally, Tobias presents several issues regarding the place of Women's Studies in relation to the rest of the academic community and to the larger community of men and women.

In modern industrial societies, socialization is only one factor contributing to the maintenance of role allocation by sex. Sex differentiation is an integral part of all social organization and is thus easier to maintain than to abolish. This differentiation reflects a deeply imbedded historical tradition that is now supported by a

7. For a general discussion of the difficulties women face in rejecting the standards of the existing male-dominated society, see in this volume the article by Dana Densmore, "On Sisterhood."

stratification system within which males receive higher rewards than females. In addition, this sexual dimension of the stratification system is reinforced by male dominance, in the economic sphere, in political power, and in physical force.[8]

As a result of the interdependence between social organization and sex differentiation, a change from role allocation by sex to new principles of allocation would require changes in all areas of social structure. If childhood socialization for nonsexist role allocation is to have real and positive consequences in adulthood, basic changes would be required not only in the organization of the family but also in the present structure of the American economic system. Currently our economic system depends on women as consumers, women as unpaid domestic workers, women as low paid and underpaid members of the work force as well as on men as full-time workers. While this book emphasizes change within the organization of the family, it is clearly recognized that this change cannot occur without concomitant change within the economic structure.

---

8. For an exposition and analysis of the sexual stratification system, see in this volume the article by Randall Collins.

9

ANDROGYNY AS A LIFE STYLE[1]

JOY D. OSOFSKY and HOWARD J. OSOFSKY[2]

Androgyny, as a term, may be defined in several ways. Dictionary definitions frequently refer to the term as meaning "both male and

---

1. A portion of this paper has been published by the first author in the article, Joy D. Osofsky, "The Socialization and Education of American Females," in *What Is Happening to American Women*, ed. Ann Scott (Atlanta, Ga.: Southern Newspaper Publishers Association, 1970).

2. Joy D. Osofsky, Ph.D., is an assistant professor of psychology, Department of Psychology, Temple University; and Howard J. Osofsky, M.D., is professor of obstetrics and gynecology, Department of Obstetrics and Gynecology, Temple University, Philadelphia, Pennsylvania 19122.

female in one." However, the more common practical definition, and the one which will be used as the reference point for this presentation, is "a society with no sex-role differentiation"—that is, a society in which there are no stereotyped behavioral differences between the roles of males and females on the basis of their sex alone.

Society never remains static, but, rather, continually undergoes change stimulated by diverse sources. Present-day society is experiencing great disruption and change due to a combination of unusual and rapidly moving political, social, and technological factors interacting at once. Many alternate life styles have been presented as possible solutions to all, or at best part, of the present problems. Androgyny as a life style, while perhaps less dramatic than others, may offer the most viable option for change in the traditional structure of relationships in the near, and foreseeable, future.

Whenever a period of rapid or erratic change occurs, one turns to institutional aspects of the society for stability and comfort. The family has traditionally been such a stable refuge. Roles of individuals within the family have been clearly defined and accepted, and it has been assumed that one can depend upon such continuities for reassurance. However, in the 1970s, traditional notions about the family and sex roles are being questioned. Along with other previously accepted definitions, the role of the family is changing. It is no longer possible to define the family as a unit in which the father works outside of the home to provide financial support, and in which the mother works within the home, primarily to be a helpmate to her husband and to provide emotional support for her children.

Within the family more women are working. Some are employed to gain income for family support; however, others, in increasing numbers, are working for personal satisfaction. Further, overpopulation is becoming a serious concern in this country and in the world at large. With greater emphasis upon the need for serious population control, many individuals find themselves questioning the validity and morality of having one-half of the population devote their lives solely to family life, with their primary function being directed to the rearing of children. In fact, the emphasis upon having children, for both women and men, is changing, perhaps, in part, related to the conclusions of demographers that limitation of procreation is necessary for the very survival of our society.

With such changes, it is important to give serious consideration to individuals and their new roles within society. Life styles of individuals must be thought through, and roles must be redefined. Old answers must be questioned; where they cannot withstand the test of time, new answers must supplant them. The present paper, in dealing with the issue of androgynous relationships, will analyze some of the traditional practices of socialization and education of individuals in society and will consider some of the changes which are logical, and likely to be accomplished in these changing times.

Socialization of Sex Roles: Learning, Abilities, and Achievement

Children in society have been taught behaviors which have been defined as appropriate for individuals of their sex by parents, teachers, and other authoritative figures in their environment. The processes through which children incorporate these behaviors, attitudes, and values are reinforcement, modeling (adults displaying sex-typed behaviors), and identification.[3] Reinforcing or encouraging the occurrence of sex-typed behaviors is important early in development, while identification and modeling become increasingly important later in development. Children imitate sex-appropriate behaviors of their parents and other authority figures in their environment.

While reinforcement, modeling, and identification are important processes through which children learn sex-appropriate behaviors, certain events or practices comprise the medium through which these general processes occur. Parents have traditionally dressed their sons and daughters in different ways, have given them different toys, have encouraged certain behaviors for a child of one sex (which have been discouraged for a child of the opposite sex), and have participated in sex-specified activities themselves. Therefore, an important question that should be considered, and which is related to differential socialization and treatment of females and males in society, is whether there are

---

3. Paul H. Mussen, "Early Sex Role Development" in *Handbook of Socialization Theory and Research*, ed. David A. Goslin (Chicago: Rand McNally, 1969), pp. 707–31.

innate differences in ability which would warrant differential treatment, or whether differences in ability and resulting behavior have been learned through the acculturation processes with our society.

Psychology has provided an abundance of literature concerning sex differences in abilities. However, it would seem worthwhile to look at the overall findings, since it is possible to draw different conclusions. The interested reader is referred to Terman and Tyler, Maccoby, and Mischel for further information in this area.[4] Few differences in abilities and behaviors are present when children are young; however, differentiation by sex increases after acculturation has occurred with age. One important specific intellectual sex difference related to age is that of language proficiency. School achievement tests and reading tests have shown that young girls generally do better than young boys; at a later point, the males have tended to gradually catch up with the females. Also, more young boys than girls have tended to be stutterers.

In postulating reasons for these sex and age differences in language ability, several plausible explanations are possible. The most likely is that sex differences in abilities and behaviors are not innate, but, rather, that they are learned through the socialization processes within the society. Identification with the same sex parent or with a same-sex adult is important for the child's sex role development. In our present family and school structure, most of the models for children in the home and in school have been female. For boys, there have been few appropriate males with whom to identify; therefore, language learning may have a female or "sissy" connotation. Further, in elementary school, male children have not yet been strongly encouraged to concentrate on achievement for career goals. For young females, school performance and achievement have been encouraged at this time. The increase with age in male children's verbal proficiency would logically be expected with increased reinforcement for educational success as future career expectations are emphasized. Females have shown a leveling-off and thereafter a decline in the earlier verbal competence; this decrease is understandable with relatively less reinforcement given

4. Lewis M. Terman and Leona E. Tyler, "Psychological Sex Differences," in *Manual of Child Psychology*, ed. Leonard Carmichael (New York: Wiley, 1946), pp. 1064–1114; Eleanor Maccoby, ed., *The Development of Sex Differences* (Stanford, Calif.: Stanford University Press, 1966); and Walter Mischel, "Sex Typing and Socialization" in *Carmichael's Manual of Child Psychology*, ed. Paul H. Mussen (New York: Wiley, 1970), pp. 3–72.

for educational success. The presence of more male models for boys to emulate in the higher grades, and proportionately fewer female models for girls to identify with in other-than-wife-and-mother roles, along with other types of differential socialization may have contributed to the reversal in language proficiency. However, precise data in this area are not yet available.

As for achievement in science and related areas, studies have shown that in the preschool and primary years there is little difference in science achievement among girls and boys. However, during junior high school boys have done better in science and related subjects than girls and in high school this sex difference has markedly increased. In attempting to explain these discrepancies, it can be hypothesized that they may be due to differences in interests and *encouraged* interests, rather than in basic abilities. The reason for this explanation is that the differences have not appeared early in life, but rather have occurred at an age when science has become socially more appropriate for males and less so for females.

Sex differences in arithmetic achievement have been similar to those reported for science achievement. Among preschool children, there have been few differences in arithmetic achievement. In grade school, tests have shown slight superiority among boys in arithmetic reasoning and either no differences, or superiority, for girls in simple computation. In higher grades boys have begun to outdistance girls; the skills required at this time have tended to include more complex levels of arithmetic reasoning. Again, interests and encouraged interests may have a role. However, no systematic investigations have been done to clarify these issues.

Kagan has offered some explanations and interpretations for sex differences in children's general and age-related abilities.[5] He has noted that girls have lower motivation to do well in science and mathematics; they have been taught to believe that they are less competent in these areas. Cultural definitions of the female sex role have placed more emphasis upon the ability to attract and maintain a love relationship than upon academic skills. For males, however, academic excellence has been a necessary antecedent to vocational success, and vocational success has been essential for the culturally appropriate sex-role identity.

5. Jerome Kagan, "Acquisition and Significance of Sex Typing and Sex Role Identity," in *Review of Child Development Research*, ed. Martin L. Hoffman and Lois W. Hoffman (New York: Russell Sage Foundation, 1964), pp. 137–68.

Although slower maturational processes may conceivably play a role in males' development, the primary reason for boys' early difficulty and later success would seem to relate to the traditional thinking that intellectual achievement, at an early age, is considered "feminine," and at a later age, is considered "masculine." Conversely, for girls motivation toward mastery has decreased with age. Anxiety has been experienced over feeling and behaving more intellectually competent than boys; conflicts have arisen over being competitive with boys. Girls at puberty may have consciously or unconsciously inhibited intellectual performance; this inhibition has increased during adolescence and adulthood, except where females have overcome strong cultural pressures.

Thus, data on sex differences in abilities and behaviors, with the possible explanations which were offered, lend support to the suggestion that sex differences in these areas have been learned through the socialization process. It is possible to make the further assumption that changes in the traditional sex-role learning of females and males, which could logically be accomplished through altering the socialization practices of parents, schools, and other institutions in our society, would result in different patterns of sex-role development.

Femininity and Masculinity

Although definitions of femininity and masculinity have varied for different ages certain traits have seemed to emerge as culturally appropriate. The definitions mentioned in the following section are culture-bound and and they seem to be changing. Their usefulness may certainly be questioned; however, they have existed to the present time and have had influence.

In the domain of physical attributes, males, in order to appear masculine, should have seemed tall, have had a muscular physique, and have had facial and body hair. Females, in order to be feminine, should have had an attractive face and body, have been pretty and small, and have had little extraneous facial and body hair. Of course, as is ironically apparent, these physical attributes have been racially specific to Anglo-Saxons. However, they have remained standard norms on dimensions of masculinity and femininity.[6]

---

6. Terman and Tyler, "Psychological Sex Differences."

Turning to behavioral characteristics, research evidence has supported culturally defined conceptions of masculinity and femininity. Males have been encouraged to be verbally and physically aggressive, whereas females have been discouraged and sometimes even prohibited from showing these traits. In fact, the same behaviors which have been encouraged among males have often been labeled as aggressive among females and have been condemned and prohibited for them.

By our cultural standards it has not been desirable for females to manifest the competency required of males. At the same time, males have been encouraged to inhibit passivity, dependency, and conformity, all of which have been encouraged among females. Males have been taught to show interpersonal dominance with men and women, initiation of sexual behavior and conquests, and concern with acquisition of money and power. Females have been taught to be submissive with males, inhibit overt signs of sexual desire, and cultivate domestic skills. As is apparent in these definitions a double standard in sexual behavior has been present. With the recent availability of contraceptives and the apparent loosening of moral standards among younger people there has been an apparent change in the double standard in sex. It is likely that this change will further occur when there is less male-female role differentiation.

When an individual has deviated from the societally specified norms, problems have arisen both in his self-perceptions and in societal conscriptions and judgments. Thus, men have not been expected to demonstrate warm, nurturant behaviors and have not been encouraged to be dependent upon others, particularly females, for support. Women have been taught to be nurturant toward children and submissive toward other people; they have been encouraged to be dependent upon males—rather than independent as individuals—in order to be considered feminine and "real women" by societal standards. Interestingly, college men have scored high in femininity on the masculinity-femininity scale, and college women have scored high in masculinity. Clearly there have been contradictions between societal definitions of masculinity and femininity and those of more educated people.

Even "professional" games have shown girls in subordinate relationships to men (for example, being a nurse to the male doctor or secretary to the male executive). When asked to judge whether toys are masculine or feminine, schoolchildren have clearly considered knives, boats, planes, trucks, and cement mixers to be masculine and dolls, cribs, dishes, and nurses' equipment to be feminine. Of importance in light of previous comments, there is also evidence to show that children, at least at an early age, have considered books and other things associated with school to be feminine.[7]

Masculinity-femininity tests have measured the degree to which children have incorporated these culturally defined standards of masculinity and femininity. The IT test presents children with a figure which is ambiguous with respect to sex and a variety of toys and objects.[8] The child is asked to select the object or activity that the IT figure prefers. It is assumed that the child's choices will reflect his personal preferences. The findings have tended to reveal the following information: Boys have shown an increasing preference for sex appropriate games with age. As early as age three, boys have been aware of and have tended to favor activities and objects which our culture regards as masculine. Although awareness of female role has been present with behavior reflecting this comprehension preferences of girls have been more variable up to nine or ten years of age. Girls between three and ten have shown a strong preference for masculine games, activities, and objects whereas it has been unusual to find many boys who prefer feminine activities during this period.[9] It may be that masculine activities and toys have been considered more desirable by both boys and girls suggesting reality factors as well as societal preferences. In addition to the differences in game preferences, girls have frequently stated a desire to be a boy or a wish to be a daddy, rather than a mommy, when they grow up.[10] Boys have not demonstrated a similarly great cross-sex preference.

Of some note, because of the incorporation of these arbitrary, societally proscribed definitions of femininity and masculinity, women who have worked have faced a difficult dilemma. Not only may male

7. Maccoby, *The Development of Sex Differences*; and Richard L. Kellogg, "A Direct Approach to Sex Role Identification of School-Related Objects," *Psychological Reports* 24, no. 3 (June 1969): 839–41.

8. Daniel G. Brown, "Masculinity-Femininity Development in Children," *Journal of Consulting Psychology* 21, no. 3 (June 1957): 197–202.

9. Brown, "Masculinity-Femininity Development"; Willard W. Hartup and Elsie A. Zook, "Sex Role Preferences in Three- and Four-Year-Old Children," *Journal of Consulting Psychology* 24, no. 5 (October 1960): 420–26; Max R. Reed and Willotta Asbjornsen, "Experimental Alteration of the IT Scale in the Study of Sex Role Preference," *Perceptual and Motor Skills* 26, no. 1 (February 1968): 15–24.

10. Brown, "Masculinity-Femininity Development."

peers and employers have presented difficulties but also strong internal conflicts have seriously affected working females.

Erik Erikson has summarized the problem in a symposium devoted to women in the scientific professions.[11] He has described the ambivalence which has existed in women who have attempted to achieve in the outside world while fulfilling traditionally defined female functions as well:

> If, as has often been said, the lack of available women in some areas constitutes more of a problem than the lack of available jobs, I think that one reason is to be found in whatever the prejudices of men are against an expansion of women's role in these fields, prejudices, as I have said, that only reinforce what the women themselves feel. The fact is that there is always a historical lag between any emancipation and the inner adjustment of the emancipated. It takes a much longer time to emancipate what goes on deep down inside us—that is, whatever prejudices and inequalities have managed to become part of our impulse life and our identity formation—than the time it takes to redefine professed values and to change legalities. And any part of mankind that has had to accept its self-definition from a more dominant group is apt to define itself by what it is *not* supposed to be. Thus, it is easy to impress on the working women of some classes and pursuits and proposition that they should not be unfeminine, or unmaternal, or unladylike, all of which may well come in conflict with that identity element in many successfully intellectual women whose background decreed that, above all, they should not be unintelligent. It is, then, not enough, as has been said, to be "changing with the changing forces." One must become part of a force that guides change, and this with a reasonably good conscience.

Similarly, a recent study performed by Horner has demonstrated and pointed up some of these difficulties empirically.[12] Horner investigated

---

11. Erik H. Erikson, "Concluding Remarks," in *Women and the Scientific Professions*, ed. Jacqueline Mattfeld and Carol Van Aken (Cambridge, Mass.: MIT Press, 1965), pp. 232–45.

12. Matina Horner, "Fail: Bright Women," *Psychology Today* 3, no. 6 (November 1969): 36–38; 62.

achievement motivation in females and males. She became interested in this area because many of the traditional studies concerning achievement motivation had not included women in the sample stating that to include women would confuse the results. She administered the Thematic Apperception Test (TAT) to measure achievement motivation to 99 college females and 88 college males and also asked her subjects to tell stories which she later rated for achievement orientation or achievement avoidance. Her results indicated that female achievement incurs anxiety; this result had been demonstrated previously by other experimenters.[13] Horner reasoned that most women equate intellectual achievement with loss of femininity. Therefore, in achievement-orientation situations, women would worry not only about failure but also about success. According to Horner, "If she fails, she is not living up to her own standards of performance; if she succeeds, she is not living up to societal expectations about the female role." Horner's major hypothesis was that, for women, the desire to achieve is often very much in conflict with what she labeled the "motive to avoid success." She found that 65 percent of the girls in her study demonstrated attitudes which could be classified as desiring to avoid success; fewer than 10 percent of the boys showed evidence of such conflicts.

In a second part of the experiment she investigated the effect of competition upon the performance of males and females. She found that men tended to do much better when they were in competition than when they worked alone. However, the reverse was true for the women; fewer than one-third of the women, as compared to two-thirds of the men, did significantly better in competition. Horner concluded that most women attempt to realize their intellectual potential only when they do not need to compete and that they do worst when they are competing with men. In addition, she concluded that achievement motivation in women is a much more complex drive than it is in men and that it is complicated by many factors which may inhibit both the motivation and the performance. Horner's study illustrates that the socialization process through which a female learns appropriate sex-typed behavior influences her achievement motivation and abilities.

13. Maccoby, *The Development of Sex Differences*; and Seymour B. Sarason, Kenneth S. Davidson, Frederick F. Lighthall, Richard R. Waite, and Britton K. Ruebush, *Anxiety in Elementary School Children* (New York: Wiley, 1960).

Some Thoughts Concerning the Future

What are the changes that are currently taking place and what are the prospects for future change in the socialization and education of women and men in American society? Alterations in the usual patterns of female and male behavior are occurring. They are undoubtedly altering definitions of sex-role development; in the future their effects will be even more profound. Although traditional sex roles still represent the accepted norm many variations are evident. Different patterns of behavior seem to be functional and acceptable to many individuals. At present changes are occurring in societally accepted roles for women. There is greater acceptance of and in some quarters encouragement of women's participating in meaningful work. Especially among the young there is more sharing of traditional household responsibilities by husbands and wives. Alternative marital and child-rearing patterns are becoming more common. Some of the changes will certainly affect accepted definitions of sex-appropriate behavior and concepts concerning masculinity and femininity. The socialization process itself which influences female and male development will of necessity also change. Women and men will be encouraged to foresee and experience greater opportunities in role choice than are presently available. Hopefully, such an increase in opportunities will allow all individuals to find satisfaction in many more ways. As has previously been pointed out by the authors both men and women are likely to benefit from androgynous changes.[14] The benefits of personal fulfillment for females are logical. The potential benefits for males have been less widely appreciated but they are still present—an opportunity for greater individual freedom and a chance for more meaningful relationships with women.

Appropriate "adjustment" should depend upon both individual inclinations and the good of society. It should not, however, be arbitrarily determined as has unfortunately frequently been the case by one group of individuals for others. Definitions of "adjustment" must allow for much variation and freedom; the needs of society neither benefit from nor require arbitrary conformity. A well-adjusted male may enjoy being a responsible executive. He may also—or instead—like

---

14. Howard J. Osofsky and Robert Seidenberg, "Is Female Menopausal Depression Inevitable?" *Obstetrics and Gynecology* 36, no. 4 (October 1970): 611–15; and Joy D. Osofsky and Sheila Tobias, *The Evolution of Female Personality* (book in progress).

being nurturant and catering, doing the cooking and taking care of the children. A well-adjusted female may similarly enjoy working full-time in a responsible executive position; she may wish to share household responsibilities with her husband or allocate most of them to him. On the contrary, she, too, may prefer household responsibilities and child rearing. Options which include assertive, competitive, and independent behaviors should not be closed to women. Options which include dependent, passive, and nurturant behaviors should not be closed to men. Changing role definitions for women in society should occur concurrently with changes for men. Socialization patterns should be determined by individual inclinations and abilities rather than by the supposedly biological grounds of sex.

In achieving these goals many changes may be made and much research is needed. Obviously, because of the need for brevity not all can be included. However, a few necessary alterations in our present system of socialization and education of American females will be described (the interested reader is also referred to the 1964 paper by Alice Rossi who has explored this subject),[15] and some suggestions for research will be considered.

Beginning when the child is very young, patterns of socialization and education can be changed. For example, at birth the clear differentiation in treatment of infants by sex can be eliminated. Female babies need not be dressed only in pink, feminine clothes and male babies in blue, more masculine outfits. Patterns of dressing infants spread to treatment of them with expectations for males including aggressive behavior, and those for females including passive behavior. As has been demonstrated in an unpublished study by Sloan, adults react to infants in ways that encourage these expectations.[16] Considerably more research is needed in this area. However, it is likely that changes in adult behavior toward infants would result in fewer sex-typed behaviors specifically assigned to females and males.

To the present time the mother has had primary responsibility and involvement in the care of the young child. It has been traditionally assumed that she, because of her sex, is better able to care for children. Further, in most families in our culture mothers have been at home and fathers at work. As has been mentioned, this situation is likely to

---

15. Alice S. Rossi, "Equality Between the Sexes: An Immodest Proposal" in *The Woman in America*, ed. Robert J. Lifton (Boston: Beacon Press, 1964), pp. 98–143.

16. D. Sloan, unpublished manuscript, 1969.

undergo change. Both parents may take an increasingly active role in child rearing. Of interest, not only would this change allow the father more of the rewards which exist but it would expose the child more fully to its father, a male figure, who is nurturant and concerned about child rearing. Some critics have suggested that the father is not important for the early development of the child. Yet, in homes where no father is present if the child becomes delinquent these same critics have questioned whether father-absence has been deleterious for the child, or whether or not good one-parent families are sufficient. There is no clear empirical evidence to support hypotheses negating the importance of the father's role; rather, logic and available data suggest the contrary. Much exciting work could result from a reinvestigation of the role of the father in child rearing and from further consideration of the effects of alternate styles of maternal behavior. It is logical to expect that children would benefit from having both parents participating fully in child rearing with additional behaviors and styles present to be modeled.

When the child enters school, major changes in existing patterns could be made. Children at this age should be raised with full involvement of both parents. This is not to suggest that mother and father need to be home at all times, but, rather, that they each make an active commitment to the child. It is likely, and probably desirable, that children be exposed to male and female teachers at all levels in school. It is also logical that children should be taught through the use of textbooks which depict females and males participating in many positions in society and not only in traditionally proscribed roles which have usually been depicted in textbooks. For example, women have been shown almost solely as housewives, nurses, and secretaries, and men have been depicted as blue- and white-collar workers, profession-als, and executives. Both women and men will likely be shown participating in work, homemaking, and child-rearing activities. Inves-tigating the effects and meanings of such changes would represent important and innovative research. It is anticipated that such changes in child rearing and education would lead to children learning many different nonsex-typed life styles based primarily on abilities and interests.

A fourth area related to education which could be changed concerns the covert and overt counseling which has been offered to females and males. On almost all levels as school progresses females have been encouraged to be passive and sometimes achieving. Males have been encouraged to be independent and constantly achieving. It has been shown that many teachers prefer and differentially reinforce such behavior, since active achievement is viewed as more important for males than females. Most guidance counselors and teachers have encouraged girls to get married and to be good wives and mothers; careers have usually been presented as an alternative if marriage is not achieved or if families need the money. Guidance counselors traditionally have not encouraged girls to take their careers seriously and to pursue both family and career lines simultaneously. Rather, they have suggested that a choice must be made between marriage and career the assumption being that the latter is a less fortunate outcome. Although this description sounds harsh, it unfortunately has been borne out by numerous reports and communications. The same counselors have encouraged males to compete, behave aggressively, and pursue careers in order to gain esteem and support a family. Males have rarely been provided with alternative options to such achieving behaviors. In other words, males have been encouraged to have a career and to marry, and have neither been required, nor usually allowed, to make a choice between these options. Females have been encouraged to marry and possibly work but if they want a career it has usually been presented as an alternative. A clear differential has been made for females between a *job* and a *career*. A job has brought in needed money and has been consistent with the role of helpmate; a career has connoted dedication and, thus, has been seen as excluding, or at least being divisive to, the appropriate full-time roles of wife and mother. In addition, meaningful job and promotion opportunities have frequently been unavailable. Assessments of the effects of alternate forms of education, counseling, and opportunities upon sex-role development, anticipations, and achievement would be expected to yield fruitful findings. Many more people would be expected to develop life styles consistent with their abilities and desires rather than those patterned as appropriate for their sex.

In conclusion it can be anticipated that the proposed changes in patterns of socialization and education of females and males will lead to increased alternatives and benefits for individuals of both sexes. Children who are brought up with new patterns of socialization may develop alternative directions for individual growth having considered many more options at each choice point. Young boys may no longer regard either school or household and child-rearing activities as feminine. This may well lead both to boys having a diminished incidence of early learning problems in school and to their achieving more fulfilled and relaxed lives as adults. Females may come to develop skills in accordance with their abilities, and may come to see achievement as not excluding homemaking and child rearing. This may lead both to females achieving greater self-development during education and having less conflict and resentment related to marriage and children at a later point. Thus, there may come to be increased development of talents of all individuals, regardless of sex, and at the same time more satisfaction in the many other meaningful aspects of life. Such a result would be both a reflection of, and an indication of further changes in, the androgynous life style.

Society and the individuals within it are changing. Some people will undoubtedly choose to follow traditional sex-typed roles. However, others will not and they will have both the ability and encouragement to develop new patterns. It may be expected that the changes which are occurring will lead to fuller development of the potential of a greater number of individuals in the society. Hopefully, people, in varied roles can contribute to a healthful orientation and progressive growth. There is a great challenge of both an innovative and investigative nature ahead. If it can be successfully met the results in terms of human satisfaction and fulfillment are likely to be most exciting.

10

SEX-ROLE SOCIALIZATION IN PICTURE BOOKS FOR PRESCHOOL CHILDREN[1]

LENORE J. WEITZMAN, DEBORAH EIFLER, ELIZABETH HOKADA, and CATHERINE ROSS

Sex-role socialization constitutes one of the most important learning experiences for the young child. By the time the child enters kindergar-

1. We are indebted to William J. Goode, Kai Erikson, Alice Rossi, and Erving Goffman for their insightful comments on an earlier draft of this paper which was

ten, he or she is able to make sex-role distinctions and express sex-role preferences. Boys already identify with masculine roles, and girls with feminine roles.[2] They also learn the appropriate behavior for both boys and girls and men and women. Hartley reports that, by the time they are four, children realize that the primary feminine role is housekeeping, while the primary masculine role is wage earning.[3]

In addition to learning sex-role identification and sex-role expectations, boys and girls are socialized to accept society's definition of the relative worth of each of the sexes and to assume the personality characteristics that are "typical" of members of each sex. With regard to relative status, they learn that boys are more highly valued than girls. And, with regard to personality differences, they learn that boys are active and achieving while girls are passive and emotional. Eight-year-old boys describe girls as clean, neat, quiet, gentle, and fearful, while they describe adult women as unintelligent, ineffective, unadventurous, nasty, and exploitative.[4] Indeed, Maccoby finds that, although girls begin life as better achievers than boys, they gradually fall behind as they become socialized.[5]

In this paper we wish to concentrate on one aspect of sex-role socialization: the socialization of preschool children through picture books. Picture books play an important role in early sex-role socialization because they are a vehicle for the presentation of societal values to the young child. Through books, children learn about the world outside of their immediate environment: they learn about what other boys and girls do, say, and feel; they learn about what is right and wrong; and they learn what is expected of children their age. In addition, books provide children with role models—images of what they can and should be like when they grow up.

---

presented to the 1971 meeting of the American Sociological Association, Denver, Colorado.

2. Daniel G. Brown, "Sex Role Preference in Young Children," *Psychological Monograph* 70, no. 14 (Whole No. 421, 1956): 1–19.

3. Ruth E. Hartley, "Children's Concepts of Male and Female Roles," *Merrill-Palmer Quarterly* 6, no. 2 (January 1960): 83–91.

4. Idem, "Sex-Role Pressures and the Socialization of the Male Child," *Psychological Reports* 5, no. 3 (June 1959): 457–68.

5. Eleanor Maccoby, "Sex Differences in Intellectual Functioning," in *The Development of Sex Differences*, ed. Eleanor Maccoby (Stanford, Calif.: Stanford University Press, 1966), pp. 25–55.

Children's books reflect cultural values and are an important instrument for persuading children to accept those values. They also contain role prescriptions which encourage the child to conform to acceptable standards of behavior. The Child Study Association, aware of the socialization potential of books, states that a book's emotional and intellectual impact on a young reader must be considered. Therefore it recommends that children's books present positive ethical values.[6]

Because books for young children explicitly articulate the prevailing cultural values, they are an especially useful indicator of societal norms.[7] McClelland used children's books as indicators of achievement values in his cross-cultural study of economic development.[8] In the period prior to increased economic development he found a high incidence of achievement motivation reflected in the children's books. This indicated a strong positive relationship between achievement imagery in children's stories and subsequent economic growth. McClelland noted that the stories had provided children with clear "instructive" messages about normative behavior.[9] Margaret Mead also commented that "a culture has to get its values across to its children in such simple terms that even a behavioral scientist can understand them." [10]

Study Design

Our study focuses on picture books for the preschool child. These books are often read over and over again at a time when children are in

---

6. Child Study Association, *List of Recommended Books* (New York: Child Study Association, 1969).

7. Erving Goffman has questioned the direct relationship we have postulated between the themes in children's literature and societal values. He suggests that literary themes may provide alternative cultural norms or irrelevant fantasy outlets. Unfortunately we do not know of any research other than McClelland's supporting either our own formulation or Goffman's. See David C. McClelland, *The Achieving Society* (New York: Free Press, 1961).

8. Ibid.

9. Ibid., p. 71.

10. As quoted in McClelland, *The Achieving Society*, p. 71.

the process of developing their own sexual identities. Picture books are read to children when they are most impressionable, before other socialization influences (such as school, teachers, and peers) become more important at later stages in the child's development.

We have chosen to examine how sex roles are treated in those children's books identified as the "very best": the winners of the Caldecott Medal. The Caldecott Medal is given by the Children's Service Committee of the American Library Association for the most distinguished picture book of the year. The medal is the most coveted prize for preschool books. Books on the list of winners (and runners-up) are ordered by practically all children's libraries in the United States. Teachers and educators encourage children to read the Caldecotts, and conscientious parents skim the library shelves looking for those books that display the impressive gold seal which designates the winners. The Caldecott award often means sales of 60,000 books for the publisher, and others in the industry look to the winners for guidance in what to publish.[11]

Although we have computed a statistical analysis of all the Caldecott winners from the inception of the award in 1938, we have concentrated our intensive analysis on the winners and runners-up for the past five years. Most of the examples cited in this paper are taken from the eighteen books in this latter category.[12]

---

11. Alleen Pace Nilsen, "Women in Children's Literature" (Paper presented at the Workshop on Children's Literature, Modern Language Association Meeting, New York, 27 December 1970).

12. The Caldecott winners and runners-up for the past five years follow. The 1967 winner is Evaline Ness, *Sam, Bangs, and Moonshine* (New York: Holt, Rinehart and Winston, 1967); the 1967 runner-up is Barbara Emberly, *One Wide River to Cross* (Englewood Cliffs, N.J.: Prentice-Hall, 1967). The 1968 winner is Barbara Emberley, *Drummer Hoff* (Englewood Cliffs, N.J.: Prentice-Hall, 1967); the 1968 runners-up are Leo Lionni, *Frederick* (New York: Random House, 1967); Taro Yashimo, *Seashore Story* (New York: Viking, 1967); and Jane Yolen, *The Emperor and the Kite* (Cleveland: World, 1967). The 1969 winner is Arthur Ransome, *The Fool of the World and the Flying Ship* (New York: Farrar, Straus & Giroux, 1968); the 1969 runner-up is Elphinstone Dayrell, *Why the Sun and the Moon Live in the Sky* (Boston: Houghton Mifflin, 1968). The 1970 winner is William Steig, *Sylvester and the Magic Pebble* (New York: Simon & Schuster, 1969); the 1970 runners-up are Ezra Jack Keats, *Goggles!* (Toronto: Macmillan, 1969); Leo Lionni, *Alexander and the Wind-Up Mouse* (New York: Pantheon, 1969); Edna Mitchell Preston, *Pop Corn and Ma Goodness* (New York: Viking, 1969); Brinton Turkle, *Thy Friend, Obadiah* (New York: Viking, 1969); and Harve Zemach, *The Judge* (New York: Farrar, Straus & Giroux, 1969). The 1971 winner is Gale E. Haley, *A Story, a Story: An African Tale Retold* (New York:

In the course of our investigation we read several hundred picture books and feel that we can assert, with confidence, that our findings are applicable to the wide range of picture books. In fact, the Caldecott winners are clearly less stereotyped than the average book, and do not include the most blatant examples of sexism.

In order to assure ourselves of the representativeness of our study, we have also examined three other groups of childrens books: the Newbery Award winners, the Little Golden Books, and the "prescribed behavior" or etiquette books.

The Newbery Award is given by the American Library Association for the best book for school-age children. Newbery books are for children who can read, and are therefore directed to children in the third to sixth grades.

The Little Golden Books we have sampled are the best sellers in children's books, since we have taken only those Little Golden Books that sold over 3 million copies.[13] These books sell for 39 cents in grocery stores, Woolworth's, Grant's, and toy and game stores. Consequently, they reach a more broadly based audience than do the more expensive Caldecott winners.

The last type of book we studied is what we call the "prescribed behavior" or etiquette book. Whereas other books only imply sex-role prescriptions, these books are explicit about the proper behavior for boys and girls. They also portray adult models and advise children on future roles and occupations.[14]

If we may anticipate our later findings, we would like to note here that the findings from the latter three samples strongly parallel those from the Caldecott sample. Although the remainder of this paper will be devoted primarily to the Caldecott sample, we will use some of the other books for illustrative purposes.

Atheneum, 1970); the 1971 runners-up are William Sleator, *The Angry Moon* (Boston: Little, Brown, 1970); Arnold Lobel, *Frog and Toad Are Friends* (New York: Harper & Row, 1970); and Maurice Sendak, *In the Night Kitchen* (New York: Harper & Row, 1970).

13. We wish to thank Robert Garlock, product manager of Little Golden Books, for his help with this information and for furnishing many of the books themselves.

14. The Dr. Seuss books, although popular among preschool audiences, were not included as a supplementary sample because they represent only one author and one publisher rather than a more broadly based series. They do, however, conform to the general pattern of sex-role portrayal that we found among the Caldecott winners.

The Invisible Female

It would be impossible to discuss the image of females in children's books without first noting that, in fact, women are simply invisible. We found that females were underrepresented in the titles, central roles, pictures, and stories of every sample of books we examined. Most children's books are about boys, men, and male animals, and most deal exclusively with male adventures. Most pictures show men—singly or in groups. Even when women can be found in the books, they often play insignificant roles, remaining both inconspicuous and nameless.

A tabulation of the distribution of illustrations in the picture books is probably the single best indicator of the importance of men and women in these books. Because women comprise 51 percent of our population, if there were no bias in these books they should be presented in roughly half of the pictures. However, in our sample of 18 Caldecott winners and runners-up in the past five years we found 261 pictures of males compared with 23 pictures of females. This is a ratio of 11 pictures of males for every one picture of a female. If we include animals with obvious identities, the bias is even greater. The ratio of male to female animals is 95:1.[15]

Turning to the titles of the Caldecott Medal winners since the award's inception in 1938, we find that the ratio of titles featuring males to those featuring females is 8:3.[16] Despite the presence of the popular *Cinderella, Snow White, Hansel and Gretel,* and *Little Red Riding Hood* in the sample of Golden Books that have sold more than 3 million copies, we find close to a 3:1 male/female ratio in this sample.[17] The 49 books that have received the Newbery Award since 1922 depict more than three

15. The illustrations of Caldecott winners and runners-up since 1967 included 166 male people, 22 female people, and 57 pictures of both males and females together. The animal illustrations included 95 of male animals, 1 of a female animal, and 12 of both male and female animals together. Together, this resulted in a total male/female ratio of 11:1. There were also 14 illustrations of characters without a sex.

16. The statistics for titles of the Caldecott winners from the inception of the award in 1938 show 8 titles with male names, 3 with female names, 1 with both a male and a female name together, and 22 titles without names of either sex. This resulted in an 8:3 male/female ratio. The statistics for titles of recent Caldecott winners and runners-up (since 1967) show 8 titles with male names, 1 with a female name, 1 with both together, and 10 titles without names of either sex. This resulted in an 8:1 male/female ratio.

17. The statistics for the titles of the Little Golden Books selling over 3 million copies show 9 titles with male names, 4 with female names, 1 with both together, and 14 titles without the names of either sex. This resulted in a 9:4 male/female ratio.

males to every one female.[18]

Children scanning the list of titles of what have been designated as the very best children's books are bound to receive the impression that girls are not very important because no one has bothered to write books about them. The content of the books rarely dispels this impression.

In close to one-third of our sample of recent Caldecott books, there are no women at all. In these books, both the illustrations and the stories reflect a man's world. *Drummer Hoff* is about a group of army officers getting ready to fire a cannon; *Frog and Toad* relates the adventures of two male animal friends; *In the Night Kitchen* follows a boy's fantasy adventures through a kitchen that has three cooks, all of whom are male; *Frederick* is a creative male mouse who enables his brothers to survive the cold winter; and *Alexander* is a mouse who helps a friend transform himself.[19]

When there are female characters, they are usually insignificant or inconspicuous. The one girl in *Goggles* is shown playing quietly in a corner.[20] The wife in *Why the Sun and the Moon* helps by carrying wood but never speaks.[21] There are two women in *The Fool of the World:* the mother, who packs lunch for her sons and waves goodby, and the princess whose hand in marriage is the object of the Fool's adventures.[22] The princess is shown only twice: once peering out of the window of the castle, and the second time in the wedding scene in which the reader must strain to find her. She does not have anything to say throughout the adventure, and of course she is not consulted in the choice of her husband; on the last page, however, the narrator assures us that she soon "loved him to distraction." Loving, watching, and helping are among the few activities allowed to women in picture books.

It is easy to imagine that the little girl reading these books might be deprived of her ego and her sense of self. She may be made to feel that girls are vacuous creatures who are less worthy and do less exciting things than men. No wonder, then, that the child psychologists report that girls at every age are less likely to identify with the feminine role,

18. The statistics for the titles of Newbery winners since the inception of the award in 1922 show 20 titles with male names, 6 titles with female names, none with both, and 23 titles without the names of either sex. This resulted in a 10:3 male/female ratio.

19. Emberley, *Drummer Hoff*; Lobel, *Frog and Toad*; Sendak, *In the Night Kitchen*; and Lionni, *Frederick*.

20. Keats, *Goggles.*

21. Dayrell, *Why the Sun.*

22. Ronsome, *The Fool.*

while boys of every age are more likely to identify with the masculine role.[23]

Although there is much variation in plot among the picture books, a significant majority includes some form of male adventure. The fisherman in *Seashore Story* rides a turtle to a hidden world under the sea.[24] After an encounter with a lion, Sylvester is transformed into a rock in *Sylvester and the Magic Pebble*.[25] *Goggles* tells of the adventures of Peter and his friends escaping from the big boys.[26] In *Thy Friend, Obadiah*, Obadiah rescues a sea gull; the Spider Man outfoxes the gods in *A Story, a Story*.[27] A boy rescues his girl friend from the moon god in *The Angry Moon*.[28] The male central characters engage in many exciting and heroic adventures which emphasize their cleverness.

In our sample of the Caldecott winners and runners-up in the last five years, we found only 2 of the 18 books were stories about girls.[29] In one of these stories, *Sam, Bangs, and Moonshine,* the girl has a boy's name.[30] In the second, *The Emperor and the Kite,* the heroine is a foreign princess.[31]

Each of these girls does engage in an adventure. Sam's adventure takes place in her daydreams, while the adventure of the princess Djeow Seow occurs when her father's kingdom is seized by evil men. Like the male central characters who engage in rescues, Djeow Seow manages to save her father, but she accomplishes this task only by being

23. Brown, "Sex Role Preference," pp. 1–19.
24. Yashimo, *Seashore Story.*
25. Steig, *Sylvester.*
26. Keats, *Goggles.*
27. Turkle, *Thy Friend, Obadiah;* and Haley, *A Story, a Story.*
28. Sleator, *The Angry Moon.*
29. The statistics for central characters in the Caldecott winners since 1938 show 14 males, 10 females, 6 males and females together, and 4 central characters without a sex. This results in a 7:5 male/female ratio. It is important to note that the situation is becoming worse, not better. During the last five years the ratio of male to female central characters has increased. The statistics for central characters in Caldecott winners and runners-up during the last five years show a 7:2 male/female ratio in contrast to an 11:9 male/female ratio for the years prior to 1967. The statistics for central characters in the Newbery winners since 1922 show 31 males, 11 females, 4 males and females together, and 3 central characters with a sex. This results in a 3:1 male/female ratio. The statistics for central characters in the Little Golden Books selling over 3 million copies show an 8:3 ratio of male/female people, a 5:2 ratio of male/female animals, and a 5:3 ratio of all males and females together.
30. Ness, *Sam, Bangs, and Moonshine.*
31. Yolen, *The Emperor.*

so tiny and inconspicuous that the evil men do not notice her. Although Djeow Seow is one of the two women central characters, the message conveyed to readers seems to be that a girl can only triumph by playing the traditional feminine role. Women who succeed are those who are unobstrusive and work quietly behind the scenes. Women who succeed are little and inconspicuous—as are most women in picture books. Even heroines remain "invisible" females.

The Activities of Boys and Girls

We can summarize our first findings about differences in the activities of boys and girls by noting that in the world of picture books boys are active and girls are passive. Not only are boys presented in more exciting and adventuresome roles, but they engage in more varied pursuits and demand more independence. The more riotous activity is reserved for the boys. Mickey, the hero of *In the Night Kitchen*, is tossed through the air and skips from bread to dough, punching and pounding.[32] Then he makes an airplane and flies out into the night and dives, swims, and slides until he is home again. Similarly, Archie and Peter race, climb, and hide in the story of Goggles.[33] Obadiah travels to the wharf in the cold of Massachusetts winter, and Sylvester searches for rocks in the woods.[34]

In contrast, most of the girls in the picture books are passive and immobile. Some of them are restricted by their clothing—skirts and dresses are soiled easily and prohibit more adventuresome activities. In *The Fool of the World and the Flying Ship*,[35] the hero, the Fool, is dressed in a sensible manner, one which does not inhibit his movement in the tasks he has to accomplish. The princess, however, for whom all the exploits are waged, remains no more than her long gown allows her to be: a prize, an unrealistic passive creature symbolizing the reward for male adventuresomeness.

A second difference between the activities of boys and girls is that the girls are more often found indoors.[36] This places another limitation on

---

32. Sendak, *In the Night Kitchen*.
33. Keats, *Goggles*.
34. Turkle, *Thy Friend, Obadiah;* and Steig, *Sylvester*.
35. Ronsome, *The Fool*.
36. The statistics for activities of boys and girls in Caldecott winners since 1967 show 48 male characters indoors, 105 male characters outdoors, 15 females indoors, and 26

the activities and potential adventures of girls. Even Sam, in *Sam, Bangs, and Moonshine*,[37] stays inside as she directs the activity of the book. Sam constructs a fantasy world and sends Thomas, a little boy, on wild goose chases to play out her fantasies. It is Thomas who rides the bicycle and climbs the trees and rocks in response to Sam's fantasy. Sam, however, waits for Thomas at home, looking out the windows or sitting on the steps. Similarly, in *The Fool of the World*, the princess remains peering out the window of her castle, watching all the activities on her behalf.[38] While boys play in the real world outdoors, girls sit and watch them—cut off from that world by the window, porch, or fence around their homes. This distinction parallels Erik Erikson's conception of the masculine outer space and the feminine inner space.[39]

Our third observation deals with the service activities performed by the girls who remain at home. Even the youngest girls in the stories play traditional feminine roles, directed toward pleasing and helping their brothers and fathers. Obadiah's sisters cook in the kitchen as he sits at the table sipping hot chocolate after his adventures.[40] In *The Emperor and the Kite*, the emperor's daughters bring food to the emperor's table, but their brothers rule the kingdom.[41]

While girls serve, boys lead.[42] Drummer Hoff, although only a boy, plays the crucial role in the final firing of the cannon.[43] Lupin, the Indian boy in *The Angry Moon*,[44] directs the escape from the moon god. He leads Lapowinsa, a girl exactly his size and age, every step of the way. Even at the end of the story, after the danger of the Angry Moon is past, Lupin goes down the ladder first "so that he could catch Lapowinsa if she should slip."

Training for a dependent passive role may inhibit a girl's chances for intellectual or creative success. It is likely that the excessive dependency

---

females outdoors. This means that 32.6 percent of the males are shown indoors, while 36.5 percent of the females are shown indoors.

37. Ness, *Sam, Bangs, and Moonshine.*

38. Ronsome, *The Fool.*

39. Erik H. Erikson, "Inner and Outer Space: Reflections on Womanhood," in *The Woman in America*, ed. Robert Jay Lifton (Boston: Houghton Mifflin, 1964), pp. 1–26.

40. Turkle, *Thy Friend, Obadiah.*

41. Yolen, *The Emperor.*

42. The statistics for activities of boys and girls in Caldecott winners and runners-up since 1967 show a 0:3 ratio of males/females in service functions, and a 3:2 ratio of males/females in leadership functions.

43. Emberley, *Drummer Hoff.*

44. Sleator, *The Angry Moon.*

encouraged in girls contributes to the decline in their achievement which becomes apparent as they grow older. Maccoby has found that "For both sexes, there is a tendency for more passive-dependent children to perform poorly on a variety of intellectual tasks, and for independent children to excel." [45]

The rescues featured in many stories require independence and self-confidence. Once again, this is almost exclusively a male activity.[46] Little boys rescue girls or helpless animals. Lupin saves a crying Lapowinsa from the flames.[47] Obadiah saves the seagull from a rusty fishhook, and Alexander saves Willie, the windup mouse, from the fate of becoming a "tossed-out toy." [48] In *Frederick,* Frederick's creativeness helps to spare his companions from the worst conditions of winter.[49] In *Sam, Bangs, and Moonshine,*[50] Sam does not play the role of the rescuer although she is the central character. Rather, her father must step in and rescue Thomas and Bangs from drowning. In the end, Sam herself "must be" saved from the potential consequences of her fantasy.

Finally, we want to note the sense of camaraderie that is encouraged among boys through their adventures. For example, *The Fool of the World* depends upon the help and talents of his male companions.[51] In *Goggles,* the two male companions together outwit a gang of older boys.[52] Similarly, the bonds of masculine friendship are stressed by Alexander, Frederick, and Frog and Toad.[53]

In contrast, one rarely sees only girls working or playing together. Although in reality women spend much of their time with other women, picture books imply that women cannot exist without men. The role of most of the girls is defined primarily in relation to that of the boys and men in their lives.[54] It is interesting to note that Sam turns

45. Maccoby, "Sex Differences," p. 35.

46. The statistics for activities of boys and girls in Caldecott winners and runners-up since 1967 show a 5:1 ratio of males/females in rescue functions.

47. Sleator, *The Angry Moon.*

48. Turkle, *Thy Friend, Obadiah* and Lionni, *Alexander.*

49. Idem, *Frederick.*

50. Ness, *Sam, Bangs, and Moonshine.*

51. Ronsome, *The Fool.*

52. Keats, *Goggles.*

53. Lionni, *Alexander;* idem, *Frederick;* and Lobel, *Frog and Toad.*

54. This problem is not confined to children's books. As Virginia Woolf pointed out over forty years ago, women in literature are rarely represented as friends: "They are now and then mothers and daughters. But almost without exception they are shown in their relation to men. It was strange to think that all the great women of fiction were, until

to a boy, not a girl, to accomplish all of the activity of her fantasies. Her dreams would have no reality without Thomas.[55]

The sex differences we have noted are even more apparent in the prescriptive or etiquette books. An excellent example is found in a pair of matched books: *The Very Little Boy* and *The Very Little Girl*.[56] Both books are written by the same author, follow the same format, and teach the same lesson: that little children grow up to be big children. However, the maturation process differs sharply for the very little boy and the very little girl.[57]

As we open to the first pages of *The Very Little Boy*[58] we find the boy playing on the living room floor by the fireplace. He has already discarded a big rubber ball and is now making a racket by banging on a pan with a spoon. In contrast, the first page of *The Very Little Girl*[59] shows the little girl sitting quietly in a big chair. There is no activity in the picture: the little girl is doing nothing but sitting with her hands folded in her lap. This is our introduction to an angelic little girl and a boisterous little boy.

In the following pages the author compares the size of the children to the objects around them; we find that the boy is smaller than a cornstalk, his baseball bat, his sled, his father's workbench, and a lawnmower. In contrast, the little girl is smaller than the rosebush, a kitchen stool, and her mother's workbasket. We note that the boy will be interested in sports—in fact, both the basketball and sled are *his,* waiting there for him until he is old enough to use them. The girl has been given no comparable presents by her parents. She can only look forward to conquering the rosebush and the kitchen stool.

Even more important is the way in which each of them relates to these objects. The little boy is in constant motion, continuously

---

Jane Austen's day, . . . seen only in relation to the other sex. And how little can a man know even of that when he observes it through the black or rosy spectacles which sex puts upon his nose. Hence, perhaps the particular nature of women in fiction; the astonishing extremes of her beauty and horror." See Virginia Woolf, *A Room of One's Own* (New York: Harcourt, Brace & World, 1929), p. 86.

55. Ness, *Sam, Bangs, and Moonshine.*

56. Phyllis Krasilovsky, *The Very Little Boy* (New York: Doubleday, 1962); and idem, *The Very Little Girl* (New York: Doubleday, 1962).

57. We gratefully acknowledge Barbara Fried's imaginative analysis of these two books in her paper, "What Our Children Are Reading," written for Sociology 62a, Yale University, fall term, 1970.

58. Krasilovsky, *The Very Little Boy.*

59. Idem, *The Very Little Girl.*

interacting with the world around him. He is *jumping* up to touch the scarecrow next to the cornstalk, *unwrapping* his baseball bat (leaving the mess of paper, string, and box for someone else to clean up), *building* blocks on top of his sled, *reaching* up on tiptoe to touch his father's workbench, and *spraying* the lawn (and himself) with the garden hose. In contrast, the little girl relates to each of the objects around her merely by *looking* at them.

Similarly, when the author indicates what each child is too small to do, we find that the little boy is too small to engage in a series of adventures. The little girl, however, is too small to *see* things from the sidelines. Thus, we are told that the little boy is too small to *march* in the parade, to *feed* the elephant at the zoo, and to *touch* the pedals on his bike. But the little girl is too small to *see* over the garden fence and to *see* the face on the grandfather clock. Even when the little girl is trying to see something she appears to be posing, and thus looks more like a doll than a curious little girl.

The little girl's clothes indicate that she is not meant to be active. She wears frilly, starchy, pink dresses, and her hair is always neatly combed and tied with ribbons. She looks pretty—too pretty to ride a bike, play ball, or visit the zoo.

Little girls are often pictured as pretty dolls who are not meant to do anything but be admired and bring pleasure. Their constant smile teaches that women are meant to please, to make others smile, and be happy. This image may reflect parental values. In a study of the attitudes of middle-class fathers toward their children, Aberle and Naegele report that the parent satisfaction with their daughters seemed to focus on their daughters being nice, sweet, pretty, affectionate, and well liked.[60]

If we follow the little boy and little girl as they grow up, we can watch the development of the proper service role in a little woman. We are shown that the girl grows big enough to water the rosebush, stir the cake batter, set the table, play nurse, and help the doctor (who is, of course, a boy), pick fruit from the trees, take milk from the refrigerator, prepare a baby's formula, and feed her baby brother. Conveniently enough for their future husbands, girls in storybooks learn to wash, iron, hang up clothes to dry, cook, and set the table. Of course, when the boy

---

60. David F. Aberle and Kasper D. Naegele, "Middle-Class Fathers' Occupational Role and Attitudes Toward Children," in *A Modern Introduction to the Family,* ed. Norman W. Bell and Ezra F. Vogel (New York: Free Press, 1960), pp. 188–98.

grows up, he engages in more active pursuits: he catches butterflies, mows the lawn, marches in the parade, visits the zoo to feed the elephants, and hammers wood at the workbench.

One particularly striking contrast between the two children is illustrated by the pictures of both of them with their dogs. In discussing how both have matured, the author tells us that both have grown up to be bigger than their pets. The picture of the little girl, however, makes us seriously doubt any grown-up self-confidence and authority. She is shown being pulled by a very small dog, whom she obviously cannot control. The little boy, in contrast, is in firm command of a much bigger dog, and does not even need a leash to control him.

It is easy to see why many little girls prefer to identify with the male role.[61] The little girl who does find the male role more attractive is faced with a dilemma. If she follows her desires and behaves like a tomboy, she may be criticized by her parents and teachers. On the other hand, if she gives up her yearnings and identities with the traditional feminine role, she will feel stifled. Girls who wish to be more than placid and pretty are left without an acceptable role alternative. They must choose between alienation from their own sex of assignment, and alienation from their real behavioral and temperamental preferences.

The rigidity of sex-role stereotypes is not harmful only to little girls. Little boys may feel equally constrained by the necessity to be fearless, brave, and clever at all times. While girls are allowed a great deal of emotional expression, a boy who cries or expresses fear is unacceptable.[62] Just as the only girls who are heroines in picture books have boys' names or are foreign princesses, the only boys who cry in picture books are animals—frogs and toads and donkeys.

The price of the standardization and rigidity of sex roles is paid by children of both sexes. Eleanor Maccoby has reported that analytic thinking, creativity, and general intelligence are associated with cross-sex typing.[63] Thus, rigid sex-role definitions not only foster unhappiness in children but they also hamper the child's fullest intellectual and social development.

---

61. Willard W. Hartup, "Some Correlates of Parental Imitation in Young Children," *Child Development* 33: 85–96; and Brown, "Sex Role Preference."

62. But Hartley also discovered that as a corollary the boys felt extreme pressure as a result of the rigid masculine role prescriptions which they saw as demanding that they be strong, intelligent, and generally successful. The boys believed that adults liked girls better because the girls were cute and well behaved. See "Sex-Role Pressures."

63. Maccoby, "Sex Differences," p. 35.

Role Models: Adult Men and Women

Adult role models provide another crucial component of sex-role socialization. By observing adult men and women, boys and girls learn what will be expected of them when they grow older. They are likely to identify with adults of the same sex, and desire to be like them. Thus, role models not only present children with future images of themselves but they also influence a child's aspirations and goals.

We found the image of the adult woman to be stereotyped and limited. Once again, the females are passive while the males are active. Men predominate in the outside activities while more of the women are inside. In the house, the women perform almost exclusively service functions, taking care of the men and children in their families. When men lead, women follow. When men rescue others, women are the rescued.[64]

In most of the stories, the sole adult woman is identified only as a mother or a wife. Obadiah's mother cooks, feeds him hot chocolate, and goes to church.[65] The wife of the Sun God carries wood to help him build the house, but she never speaks.[66] Sylvester's mother is shown sweeping, packing a picnic lunch, knitting, and crying.[67] And Mrs. Noah, who had an important role in the biblical story of the flood, is completely omitted from the children's book version.

The remaining three roles that women play are also exclusively feminine roles: one is a fairy, the second a fairy godmother, and the third an underwater maiden. The fairy godmother is the only adult female who plays an active leadership role. The one nonstereotyped woman is clearly not a "normal" woman—she is a mythical creature.

In contrast to the limited range in women's roles, the roles that men play are varied and interesting. They are storekeepers, house builders, kings, spiders, storytellers, gods, monks, fighters, fishermen, policemen, soldiers, adventurers, fathers, cooks, preachers, judges, and farmers.

---

64. Among the Caldecott winners and runners-up for the past five years, we found that women were engaged in a much narrower range of activities than men. The ratio of male to female adults engaged in service activities was 1:7, while the ratio of male to female adults in leadership activities was 5:0, and the ratio of the male to female adults in rescue activities was 4:1. In addition, 40 percent of adult females, but only 31 percent of adult males, were pictured indoors.

65. Turkle, *Thy Friend, Obadiah.*

66. Dayrell, *Why the Sun.*

67. Steig, *Sylvester.*

Perhaps our most significant finding was that *not one* woman in the Caldecott sample had a job or profession. In a country where 40 percent of the women are in the labor force, and close to 30 million women work, it is absurd to find that women in picture books remain only mothers and wives.[68] In fact, 90 percent of the women in this country will be in the labor force at some time in their lives.

Motherhood is presented in picture books as a full-time, lifetime job, although for most women it is in reality a part-time ten-year commitment. The changing demographic patterns in this country indicate that the average woman has completed the main portion of her child rearing by her mid-thirties and has twenty-four productive years in the labor force if she returns to work once her children are in school. Today even the mothers of young children work. There are over 10 million of them currently in the labor force.[69]

As the average woman spends even less time as a mother in the future, it is unrealistic for picture books to present the role of mother as the only possible occupation for the young girl. Alice Rossi has noted that today the average girl may spend as many years with her dolls as the average mother spends with her children.[70]

The way in which the motherhood role is presented in children's books is also unrealistic. She is almost always confined to the house, although she is usually too well dressed for housework. Her duties are not portrayed as difficult or challenging—she is shown as a housebound servant who cares for her husband and children. She washes dishes, cooks, vacuums, yells at the children, cleans up, does the laundry, and takes care of babies. For example, a typical domestic scene in *Sylvester and the Magic Pebble* shows the father reading the paper, Sylvester playing with his rock collection, and the mother sweeping the floor.[71]

The picture books do not present a realistic picture of what real mothers do. Real mothers drive cars, read books, vote, take children on trips, balance checkbooks, engage in volunteer activities, ring doorbells canvassing, raise money for charity, work in the garden, fix things in

---

68. U.S. Department of Labor, *1969 Handbook on Women Workers* (Washington, D.C.: Government Printing Office, 1969).

69. Ibid., p. 39.

70. Alice Rossi, "Equality Between the Sexes," in *The Woman in America,* ed. Robert Jay Lifton (Boston: Houghton Mifflin, 1964), p. 105.

71. Steig, *Sylvester.*

the house, are active in local politics, belong to the League of Women Voters and the PTA, etc.[72]

Nor do these picture books provide a realistic image of fathers and husbands. Fathers never help in the mundane duties of child care. Nor do husbands share the dishwashing, cooking, cleaning, or shopping. From these stereotyped images in picture books, little boys may learn to expect their wives to do all the housework and to cater to their needs. These unreal expectations of marriage will inevitably bring disappointment and discontent to both the male and the female partners.

Lonnie Carton's two books, *Mommies* and *Daddies*,[73] are excellent examples of the contrasting lives to which boys and girls can look forward if they follow the role models provided by the adult characters in picture books. As the books begin, Mommy puts on her apron to prepare for a day of homemaking, while Daddy dashes out of the house with his briefcase on the way to work. The next two pages show the real differences between the woman's world and the man's world. Daddies are shown as carpenters, executives, house painters, mailmen, teachers, cooks, and storekeepers. They are also the bearers of knowledge.

> Daddies drive the trucks and cars,
> The buses, boats and trains.
> Daddies build the roads and bridges,
> Houses, stores and planes.
> Daddies work in factories and
> Daddies make the things grow.
> Daddies work to figure out
> The things we do not know.

On the corresponding two pages (in *Mommies*), we learn that, although the mother supposedly does "lots and lots," her tasks consist of washing dishes, scrubbing pots and walls, cooking, baking, tying shoes, catching balls, and answering questions (which seems to be her most "creative" role so far). Mommy does leave the house several times but only to shop for groceries or to take the children out to play. (She does drive a car in this book, however, which is unusual.)

In contrast, when Daddy comes home he not only plays in a more exciting way with the children but he provides their contact with the

72. Only one of the Caldecott winners presents the woman as an active equal to her husband. See Mitchell, *Pop Corn and Ma Goodness*.

73. Lonnie C. Carton, *Mommies* (New York: Random House, 1960); and idem, *Daddies* (New York: Random House, 1960).

outside world. While Mommies are restrictive, and "shout if you play near the street," Daddies take you on trips in cars, buses, and trains; Daddies take you to the circus, park, and zoo; buy you ice cream; and teach you to swim. Daddies also understand you better because they "know you're big enough and brave enough to do lots of things that Mommies think are much too hard for you." Mothers, however, are useful for taking care of you when you are sick, cleaning up after you, and telling you what to do. Mommies do smile, hug, comfort, and nurture, but they also scold and instruct in a not altogether pleasant manner. They tell you to be quiet, and to "Sit still and eat!" Ironically, this negative image of the nagging mother may be a result of an exclusive devotion to motherhood. As Alice Rossi has observed: "If a woman's adult efforts are concentrated exclusively on her children, she is likely more to stifle than broaden her children's perspective and preparation for adult life. . . . In myriad ways the mother binds the child to her, dampening his initiative, resenting his growing independence in adolescence, creating a subtle dependence which makes it difficult for the child to achieve full adult stature." [74]

In addition to having a negative effect on children, this preoccupation with motherhood may also be harmful to the mother herself. Pauline Bart has reported extreme depression among middle-aged women who have been overinvolved with and have overidentified with their children.[75]

We have already noted that there are no working women in the Caldecott sample. It is no disparagement of the housewife or mother to point out that alternative roles are available to, and chosen by, many women and that girls can be presented with alternative models so that they, like boys, may be able to think of a wide range of future options.

Because there are no female occupational role models in the Caldecott books, we will turn to the prescribed role books to examine the types of occupations that are encouraged for boys and girls. For this analysis we will compare a very popular pair of Hallmark matched books: *What Boys Can Be* and *What Girls Can Be*.[76] Both books follow the same format: each page shows a boy or a girl playing an occupational role. We are told that boys can be:

74. Rossi, "Equality," p. 113.
75. "Mother Portnoy's Complaints," *Trans-Action* 8, nos. 1 and 2 (November/December 1970): 72.
76. Dean Walley, *What Boys Can Be* (Kansas City: Hallmark, n.d.); idem, *What Girls Can Be* (Kansas City: Hallmark, n.d.).

a *fireman* who squirts water on the flames, and
a *baseball* player who wins lots of games.
a *bus driver* who helps people travel far, or
a *policeman* with a siren in his car.
a *cowboy* who goes on cattle drives, and
a *doctor* who helps to save people's lives.
a *sailor* on a ship that takes you everywhere, and
a *pilot* who goes flying through the air.
a *clown* with silly tricks to do, and
a pet tiger owner who *runs the zoo.*
a *farmer* who drives a big red tractor, and
on TV shows, if I become *an actor.*
an *astronaut* who lives in a space station, and
someday grow up to be *President* of the nation[77]

The second book tells us that girls can be:

a *nurse,* with white uniforms to wear, or
a *stewardess,* who flies everywhere.
a *ballerina,* who dances and twirls around, or
a *candy shop owner,* the best in town.
a *model,* who wears lots of pretty clothes,
a *big star* in the movies and on special TV shows.
a *secretary* who'll type without mistakes, or
an *artist,* painting trees and clouds and lakes.
a *teacher in nursery school* some day, or
a *singer* and make records people play.
a *designer of dresses* in the very latest style, or
a *bride,* who comes walking down the aisle.
a *housewife,* someday when I am grown, and
a *mother,* with some children of my own[78]

The two concluding pictures are the most significant; the ultimate goal for which little boys are to aim is nothing less than the President of the nation. For girls, the comparable pinnacle of achievement is motherhood!

Many of the differences in the occupations in these two books parallel the male/female differences we have already noted. One is the inside/outside distribution. Eleven of the female occupations are shown being

77. Walley, *What Boys Can Be,* emphasis added.
78. Idem, *What Girls Can Be,* emphasis added.

performed inside, while only three are outside. Indeed, none of the female occupations listed necessitates being performed outdoors. The ratio for the male occupations is exactly reversed: three are inside, eleven outside.

We already observed that little girls are encouraged to succeed by looking pretty and serving others. It should therefore not be surprising to find that the women are concentrated in glamorous and service occupations. The most prestigious feminine occupations are those in which a girl can succeed only if she is physically attractive. The glamour occupations of model and movie star are the two most highly rewarded among the female choices. Since few women can ever achieve high status in these glamorous professions, the real message in these books is that women's true function lies in service. Service occupations, such as nurse, secretary, housewife, mother, and stewardess, reinforce the traditional patterns to feminine success.

Although some of the male occupations also require physical attractiveness (actor) and service (bus driver), there is a much greater range of variation in the other skills they require: baseball players need athletic ability, policemen are supposed to be strong and brave, pilots and doctors need brains, astronauts need mechanical skills and great energy, clowns must be clever and funny, and presidents need political acumen.

If we compare the status level of the male and female occupations, it is apparent that men fill the most prestigious and highly paid positions. They are the doctors, pilots, astronauts, and presidents. Even when men and women are engaged in occupations in the same field, it is the men who hold the positions which demand the most skill and leadership. While men are doctors, women are nurses; while men are pilots, women are stewardesses. Only one of the women is engaged in a professional occupation: the teacher. It is important to note, however, that the authors carefully specified that she was a *nursery school teacher*.

Similarly, most of the occupations that require advanced education are occupied by men. Four of the males have apparently gone to college, compared with only one of the women.

It is clear that the book *What Boys Can Be* encourages a little boy's career ambitions. He is told that he has the potential for achieving any of the exciting and highly rewarded occupations in our society.

In contrast, the book *What Girls Can Be* tells the little girl that she can have ambitions if she is pretty. Her potential for achieving a prestigious and rewarding job is dependent on her physical attributes. If she is not attractive, she must be satisfied with a life of mundane service. No women are represented in traditional male occupations, such as doctor, lawyer, engineer, or scientist. With women comprising 7 percent of the country's physicians and 4 percent of its lawyers, surely it is more probable that a girl will achieve one of these professional statuses than it is that a boy will become President.

The occupational distribution presented in these books is even worse than the real inequitable distribution of employment in the professions. Picture books could inspire children to strive for personal and occupational goals that would take them beyond their everyday world. Instead, women are denied both the due recognition for their present achievements and the encouragement to aspire to more broadly defined possibilities in the future.

Conclusion

Preschool children invest their intellects and imaginations in picture books at a time when they are forming their self-images and future expectations. Our study has suggested that the girls and women depicted in these books are a dull and stereotyped lot. We have noted that little girls receive attention and praise for their attractiveness, while boys are admired for their achievements and cleverness. Most of the women in picture books have status by virtue of their relationships to specific men—they are the wives of the kings, judges, adventurers, and explorers, but they themselves are not the rulers, judges, adventurers, and explorers.

Through picture books, girls are taught to have low aspirations because there are so few opportunities portrayed as available to them. The world of picture books never tells little girls that as women they might find fulfillment outside of their homes or through intellectual pursuits. Women are excluded from the world of sports, politics, and science. Their future occupational world is presented as consisting primarily of glamour and service. Ironically, many of these books are written by prize-winning female authors whose own lives are probably unlike those they advertise.[79]

---

79. A tabulation of the percentage of female authors indicates that 41 percent of the Caldecott and 58 percent of the Newbery Medal winners were written by women.

It is clear that the storybook characters reinforce the traditional sex-role assumptions. Perhaps this is indicative of American preferences for creativeness and curiosity in boys and neatness and passivity in girls. Many parents want their sons to grow up to be brave and intelligent and their daughters to be pretty and compliant.

In the past, social theorists have assumed that such strongly differentiated sex roles would facilitate a child's identification with the parent of the same sex. For example, Talcott Parsons has commented that "if the boy is to identify with his father there must be discrimination in role terms between the two parents." [80] More recently, however, Philip Slater has argued that adult role models who exhibit stereotyped sex-role differentiation may impede, rather than facilitate, the child's sex-role identification.[81] Children find it easier to identify with less differentiated and less stereotyped parental role models. It is easier for them to internalize parental values when nurturance (the typically feminine role) and discipline (the typically masculine role) come from the same person.

Not only do narrow role definitions impede the child's identification with the same sex parent, but rigid sex-role distinctions may actually be harmful to the normal personality development of the child. In fact, Slater has postulated a negative relationship between the child's emotional adjustment and the degree of parental role differentiation.[82]

Some evidence, then, suggests these sex roles are rigid and possibly harmful. They discourage and restrict a woman's potential and offer her fulfillment only through the limited spheres of glamour and service. More flexible definitions of sex roles would seem to be more healthful in encouraging a greater variety of role possibilities. Stories could provide a more positive image of a woman's potential—of her physical, intellectual, creative, and emotional capabilities.

Picture books could also present a less stereotyped and less rigid definition of male roles by encouraging boys to express their emotions as

---

However, women authors appear to be more positive than their male counterparts. The pre-1967 Caldecotts, which had a larger percentage of female central characters, also have a larger percentage of female authors: 48 percent compared with 33 percent.

80. Talcott Parsons, "Family Structure and the Socialization of the Child," in *Family, Socialization and Interaction Process*, ed. Talcott Parsons and Robert F. Bales (New York: Free Press, 1955), p. 80.

81. Philip Slater, "Parental Role Identification," in *The Family: Its Structure and Functions*, ed. Rose L. Coser (New York: St. Martin's, 1964), pp. 350–70.

82. Ibid.

well as their intellect. Books might show little boys crying, playing with stuffed toys and dolls, and helping in the house. Stereotypes could be weakened by books showing boys being rewarded for being emotional and supportive, and girls being rewarded for being intelligent and adventuresome.

Although Zelditch[83] has noted the cross-cultural predominance of males in instrumental roles and females in expressive roles—like the patterns we found in children's books—Slater[84] suggests that the ability to alternate instrumental and expressive role performance rapidly—what he calls interpersonal flexibility—is coming to be more highly valued in our society.

This argues for less stereotyped adult roles. Fathers could take a more active role in housework and child care. And, similarly, the roles of adult women could be extended beyond the limited confines of the home, as in fact they are. When women are shown at home, they could be portrayed as the busy and creative people that many housewives are. For example, the woman in *Pop Corn and Ma Goodness*, the single exception to the Caldecott norm, equally shares diversified activities with her husband.[85]

If these books are to present real-life roles, they could give more attention to single parents and divorced families. Stories could present the real-life problems that children in these families face: visiting a divorced father, having two sets of parents, not having a father at school on father's day, or having a different name than one's mother.

The simplified and stereotyped images in these books present such a narrow view of reality that they must violate the child's own knowledge of a rich and complex world.[86] Perhaps these images are motivated by the same kind of impulse that makes parents lie to their children in order to "protect" them.[87] As a result, the child is given an idealized

---

83. Morris Zelditch, Jr., "Role Differentiation in the Nuclear Family," in *Family, Socialization, and Interaction Process*, ed. Talcott Parsons and Robert F. Bales (New York: Free Press, 1955), p. 341.

84. Slater, "Parental Role Differentiation."

85. Preston, *Pop Corn and Ma Goodness*.

86. We are indebted to William J. Goode for this insight.

87. This is not to deny the value of fantasy. As Margaret Fuller wrote in 1855: "Children need some childish talk, some childish play, some childish books. But they also need, and need more, difficulties to overcome, and a sense of the vast mysteries which the progress of their intelligence shall aide them to unravel. This sense is naturally their delight . . . and it must not be dulled by premature explanations or subterfuges of any kind." See "Children's Books," in John J. Jewett, *Women in the Nineteenth Century* (Boston, 1855). Alice Rossi brought this work to our attention.

version of the truth, rather than having his real and pressing questions answered. Not only are the child's legitimate questions ignored, but no effort is made to create a social awareness which encompasses the wider society. Picture books actually deny the existence of the discontented, the poor, the ethnic minorities, and the urban slum dwellers.

Stories have always been a means for perpetuating the fundamental cultural values and myths. Stories have also been a stimulus for fantasy, imagination and achievement. Books could develop this latter quality to encourage the imagination and creativity of all children. This would provide an important implementation of the growing demand for *both* girls and boys to have a real opportunity to fulfill their human potential.

11

EQUALITY BETWEEN THE SEXES: AN IMMODEST PROPOSAL

ALICE S. ROSSI

What happens when youngsters enter school? Instead of broadening the base on which they are forming their image of male and female roles, the school perpetuates the image children bring from home and their observations in the community. It has been mother who guided their preschool training; now in school it is almost exclusively women teachers who guide their first serious learning experiences. In the boy's first readers, men work at the same jobs with the same tools he has observed in his neighborhood—"T" for truck, "B" for bus, "W" for wagon. His teachers expect him to be rugged, physically strong, and aggressive. After a few years he moves into separate classes for gym, woodworking, and machine shop. For the girl, women are again the ones in charge of children. Her first readers portray women in aprons, brooms in their hands or babies in their arms. Teachers expect her to be quiet, dependent, with feminine interests in doll and house play and dressing up. In a few years she moves into separate classes for child care, cooking, and practical nursing. In excursions into the community, elementary school boys and girls visit airports, bus terminals, construction sites, factories, and farms.

What can the schools do to counteract these tendencies to either outmoded or traditional images of the roles of men and women? For one, class excursions into the community are no longer needed to introduce American children to building construction, airports, or zoos. Except for those in the most underprivileged areas of our cities, American children have ample exposure to such things with their car- and plane-riding families. There are, after all, only a limited number of such excursions possible in the course of a school year. I think visits to a publishing house, research laboratory, computer firm, or art studio would be more enriching than airports and zoos.

Going out into the community in this way, youngsters would observe men and women in their present occupational distribution. By a program of bringing representatives of occupations into the classroom and auditorium, however, the school could broaden the spectrum of occupations young children may link to their own abilities and interests regardless of the present sex typing of occupations, by making a point of having children see and hear a woman scientist or doctor; a man dancer or artist; both women and men who are business executives, writers and architects.[1]

Another way in which the elementary schools could help is making a concerted effort to attract male teachers to work in the lower grades. This would add a rare and important man to the primary group environment of both boys and girls. This might seem a forlorn hope to some, since elementary school teaching has been such a predominantly feminine field, and it may be harder to attract men to it than to attract women to fields presently considered masculine. It may well be that in

---

1. In a large metropolis, resource persons could be invited through the city business and professional organizations, the Chamber of Commerce, art, music and dancing schools, etc. This could constitute a challenging program for PTA groups to handle; or a Community Resources Pool could be formed similar to that the New World Foundation has supported in New York City whereby people from business, the arts and sciences and the professions work with the public schools. Many educators and teachers might hesitate to try such a project in anticipation of parent-resistance. But parent-resistance could be a good opportunity for parent-education, if teachers and school officials were firm and informed about what they are trying to do.

the next decade or so the schools could not attract and keep such men as teachers. But it should be possible for graduate schools of education and also school systems to devise ways of incorporating more men teachers in the lower grades, either as part of their teacher training requirements or in the capacity of specialized teachers: the science, art, or music teacher who works with children at many grade levels rather than just one or two contiguous grade levels.[2] His presence in the lives of very young children could help dispel their expectation that only women are in charge of children, that nurturance is a female attribute or that strength and an aggressive assault on the physical environment is the predominant attribute of man's work.

The suggestions made thus far relate to a change in the sex linking of occupations. There is one crucial way in which the schools could effect a change in the traditional division of labor by sex within the family sphere. The claim that boys and girls are reared in their early years without any differentiation by sex is only partially true. There are classes in all elementary schools which boys and girls take separately or which are offered only to one sex. These are precisely the courses most directly relevant to adult family roles: courses in sex and family living (where communities are brave enough to hold them) are typically offered in separate classes for boys and for girls, or for girls only. Courses in shop and craft work are scheduled for boys only; courses in child care, nursing, and cooking are for girls only. In departing from completely coeducational programs, the schools are reinforcing the traditional division of labor by sex which most children observe in their homes. Fifteen years later, these girls find that they cannot fix a broken plug, set a furnace pilot light, or repair a broken high chair or favorite toy. These things await the return of the child's father and family handyman in the evening. When a child is sick in the middle of the night, his mother takes over; father is only her assistant or helper.

These may seem like minor matters, but I do not think they are. They unwittingly communicate to and reinforce in the child a rigid differentiation of role between men and women in family life. If first

2. Though predominantly a feminine field, there is one man to approximately every two women planning careers in teaching. In the "Great Aspirations" study, there were 11,388 women students planning to teach in elementary and secondary schools, but also 5,038 men. The problem may therefore not be as great as it seems at first: schools of education could surely do more to encourage some of these men to work in the lower grades, in part or for part of their teaching careers.

aid, the rudiments of child care and of cooking have no place in their early years as sons, brothers and schoolboys, then it is little wonder that as husbands and fathers American men learn these things under their wives' tutelage. Even assuming these wives were actively involved in occupations of their own and hence free of the psychological pressure to assert their ascendancy in the family, it would be far better for all concerned—the married pair and the children as well—if men brought such skills with them to marriage.

This is the point where the schools could effect a change: if boys and girls took child care, nursing, cooking, shop, and craft classes together, they would have an opportunity to acquire comparable skills and pave the way for true parental substitutability as adults. They would also be learning something about how to complement each other, not just how to compete with each other.[3] Teamwork should be taught in school in the subjects relevant to adult family roles, not just within each sex on the playground or in the gymnasium. In addition to encouraging more equality in the parental role, such preparation as school children could ease their adjustment to the crises of adult life; illness, separation due to the demands of a job or military service, divorce or death would have far less trauma and panic for the one-parent family—whether mother or father—if such equivalence and substitutability were a part of the general definition of the parental role.

A school curriculum which brought boys and girls into the same classes and trained them in social poise, the healing skills, care of children, handling of interpersonal difficulties and related subjects would also encourage the development of skills which are increasingly needed in our complex economy. Whether the adult job is to be that of a worker in an automated industry, a professional man in law, medicine or scholarship, or an executive in a large bureaucratic organization, the skills which are needed are not physical strength and ruggedness in interpersonal combat but understanding in human dealings, social poise and persuasive skill in interpersonal relations.[4] All too often,

3. Bruno Bettelheim makes the point that American boys and girls learn to compete with each other, but not how to complement each other. He sees this lack of experience in complementarity as part of the difficulty in achieving a satisfactory sexual adjustment in marriage: the girl is used to "performing with males on equal grounds, but she has little sense of how to complement them. She cannot suddenly learn this in bed." See Bruno Bettelheim, "Growing Up Female," *Harper's* (November 1962): 125.

4. These are the same skills which, when found in women, go by the names of charm, tact, intuition. See Helen Mayer Hacker, "The New Burdens of Masculinity," *Marriage and Family Living* 19, no. 3 (August 1957): 227–33.

neither the family nor the school encourages the development of these skills in boys. Hundreds of large business firms look for these qualities in young male applicants but often end up trying to develop them in their young executives through on-the-job training programs.

I have suggested a number of ways in which the educational system could serve as an important catalyst for change toward sex equality. The schools could reduce sex-role stereotypes of appropriate male and female attributes and activities by broadening the spectrum of occupations youngsters may consider for themselves irrespective of present sex-linked notions of man's work and woman's work, and by providing boys as well as girls with training in the tasks they will have as parents and spouses. The specific suggestions for achieving these ends which I have made should be viewed more as illustrative than as definitive, for educators themselves may have far better suggestions for how to implement the goal in the nation's classrooms than I have offered in these pages. Equality between the sexes cannot be achieved by proclamation or decree but only through a multitude of concrete steps, each of which may seem insignificant by itself, but all of which add up to the social blueprint for attaining the general goal.

12

THE STUDY OF SEX ROLES

SHIRLEY S. ANGRIST

Contingency Orientation

The learning of adult sex roles, as indicated earlier, is seen primarily as occupation-directed for males and family-directed for females. While man's straitjacket during socialization is occupational choice and achievement, woman's straitjacket is marriage. This bifurcated picture is accurate in the sense of separate key goals for each sex, but it is inadequate to describe the flexibility phenomenon in sex-role behavior. At this point, I am unprepared to substantiate such a hypothesis for males (although I submit that male role flexibility exists also) but the picture for females should emerge firmly.

My hypothesis is that flexibility in future fulfillment of women's roles is built into socialization both early and late as contingency training. In other words, woman lives by adjusting to and preparing for contingencies. The degree varies by social class, so that the lower the class the higher the contingency orientation. Indeed, women in lower socioeconomic groups have characteristically faced greater unpredictability in life style and greater acceptance of life's hazards as inevitable than higher-class women.[1] Lower-class women may not only be more practical in this respect, but also more realistic.[2] The present discussion centers on middle- and upper-class college-educated women. This contingency orientation is reflected in personality development, in belief systems and in choices.

The Girl Learns to Be "Feminine"

The girl learns to be "feminine"—with all the adjectival subscales that term connotes—relative passivity, deference, low intellectuality, cooperativeness. That is to say, she learns to fit in, "to know her place," to take cues from authoritative males.[3] Catering to people's palates, to their moods, to their needs—these are feminine skills considered necessary to being wife and mother.

Beliefs and expectations about suitable behavior for a girl dwell primarily on the domestic realm of adult women's roles. Given that central theme for girls, an elaborate set of "ifs" surrounds it. For example:

— Douvan refers to the fact that a girl cannot commit herself to

1. Lee Rainwater, *And The Poor Get Children* (Chicago: Quadrangle Books, 1960).

2. Mark Lefton, Shirley Angrist, Simon Dinitz and Benjamin Pasamanick, "Social Class, Expectations, and Performance of Mental Patients," *American Journal of Sociology* 68, no. 1 (July 1962): 79–87.

3. Daryl J. Bem and Sandra L. Bem, "Case Study of a Non-conscious Ideology: Training the Woman to Know Her Place," in *The Psychological Foundations of Beliefs and Attitudes*, ed. Daryl J. Bem (Belmont, Calif.: Brooks/Cole, 1970), pp. 89–99.

anything but marriage; she must remain malleable enough to fit the value system of her potential future spouse.[4] One contingency element, then, is preparation to fit an unknown spousal relationship.

— A second contingency is lack of guarantee that she will marry. Although all but a few women hope and plan to marry, remaining single is both a fear and a possibility—ability to be financially self-supporting is a motivation for vocational training in case one does not marry.

— The economic necessity to work is considered a likely eventuality at some time in the woman's life. She may need to support herself and husband while he completes his education, she may have to supplement or temporarily supply the family income, or earn money for special purposes—a car, vacation, or college costs for children.

— After marriage, temporary or permanent childlessness becomes a possibility, whether by accident or design. Leisure activities or gainful employment, either to fill free time or to provide content to life, may be viewed as resources for filling such a gap.

— When children grow up and leave home, the woman faces a drastic decline, even elimination, of her mothering functions. The need or freedom to fill this void may re-open work or leisure pursuits as realistic options.

— Exmarriage like nonmarriage is a contingency to be prepared for with "security" or "insurance." Divorce or widowhood can require the woman to become a breadwinner. Hence, a common rationale among girls is to be able to work, "just in case."

The Contingencies Are Real

Obviously, the contingencies are real. This does not mean that all growing girls perceive and deliberately plan for them. The research task would be to determine how much rational accounting and preparation for the adult woman's contingencies occurs, how categories of women differ in degree of preparation, and whether some contingencies are more directly prepared for than others.

Not all the possible contingencies are given equal weight. In fact, one

4. Elizabeth Douvan, "Sex Differences in Adolescent Character Process," *Merrill-Palmer Quarterly* 6, no. 4 (July 1960): 203–11.

contingency takes priority during late adolescence and early adulthood rendering others subordinate. It is preparation for, even overstress on, marriage and the marital role. Epitomizing as it does the essence of American conceptions of femininity, this marital role emphasis masks the multiplicity of functions which family life entails for the woman. As the key contingency, preparation to fit the unknown spouse leads girls to tailor their behavior for maximum eligibility. This means acting feminine (passive, cooperative, nonintellectual) in dating situations[5] and high school girls' acceptance of traditional but disliked domestic responsibilities for their married lives.[6] It means perception of limited options in the occupational world. The inability of occupational choice theories to handle women's patterns reflects women's contingency orientations.[7] Women's expectations for adult roles have been dubbed unrealistic; [8] on the contrary, one could argue that they are concretely realistic. While a boy enters college considering types and conditions of work, the girl's primary focus is on marriage. Work is peripheral. College then becomes important—as broadening social experience, for self-development, for mate finding. Whereas during the preteen years boys and girls tentatively consider occupations, only boys consistently pass into the reality stages of exploring, crystallizing, and specifying an occupation. Ginzberg notes that ". . . major adjustments must be made in the general (occupational) theory before it can be applied to girls. . . ." [9]

Longitudinal Research on Role Aspirations

In my current longitudinal research on college women's role aspirations, there is evidence for the extent to which a contingency

5. Mirra Komarovsky, "Cultural Contradictions and Sex Roles," *American Journal of Sociology* 52, no. 3 (November 1946): 184–89.

6. Ruth E. Hartley and Armin Klein, "Sex Role Concepts Among Elementary-School Girls," *Marriage and Family Living* 21, no. 1 (February 1959): 59–64.

7. George Psathas, "Toward a Theory of Occupational Choice for Women," *Sociology and Social Research* 52, no. 2 (January 1968): 253–68.

8. Arnold Rose, "The Adequacy of Women's Expectations for Adult Roles," *Social Forces* 30, no. 1 (October 1951): 69–77.

9. Eli Ginzberg, Sol W. Ginsburg, Sidney Axelrad, and John L. Herma, *Occupational Choice: An Approach to a General Theory* (New York: Columbia University Press, 1963), pp. 160–76.

orientation operates. Study subjects initially consisted of the 188 freshmen entering the women's college of a larger coeducational university. Students were asked to complete a questionnaire each fall and to be interviewed twice during the four years. Attrition over four years left 108 seniors; complete questionnaire data were obtained for 87 of this cohort.

Occupational preferences during freshman and sophomore years show extensive shifting: 37 percent shifted preferences within the first month of freshman year, fully 70 percent had changed by September of sophomore year.[10] Not only did choices change, but early in sophomore year 42 percent still reported feeling undecided about their occupational choice compared with 58 percent who had said so as freshmen. Indecision about or disinterest in occupation is reflected in the low proportion of the cohort of 87 who as freshmen were career salient—30 percent.[11] This percentage is especially noteworthy since the college in which the research was done is reputed as vocationally-professionally oriented. Indeed, by senior year, 43 percent were career salient, perhaps suggestive of the school's influence. But panel analysis of the choice patterns shows radical vacillation between career and noncareer interests. Of the 37 who were career-salient seniors, only 6 had been so consistently over the four years. The others had arrived there via one or more changes in salience. By contrast, girls who are not career salient predominated in all four years and showed considerably less shifting.

Marriage Is the Key Contingency

The extent to which marriage is a key contingency is suggested from my analysis of single women's responses to questions about home vs. career preferences. In a study of educated women's life styles, five- and fifteen-year alumnae of the women's college referred to above completed questionnaires on their leisure and work activities. Details on the

10. These percentages are based on 125 freshmen of the 143 who became sophomores and for whom complete questionnaire data were obtained. Compare with James A. Davis, *Undergraduate Career Decisions* (Chicago: Aldine, 1965); and Walter L. Wallace, *Student Culture* (Chicago: Aldine, 1966).

11. Career salient is defined in terms of answers to two questions about adult roles. Career salient are girls who 15 years from now would like to be career women (either single, married, or with children) and who would work full-time or part-time even if their husbands earned enough so that they would never have to work.

sample and procedures are in Searls and Angrist.[12] Of the 318 respondents, 85 percent were married and mainly homemakers. Of 90 women employed at least part-time, roughly one-third each were single, married without children, or married with children. For the single working women (average age, 27 years) 48 percent said they would most want to concentrate on home and family if they were to marry; only 24 percent and 12 percent of childless working women and working mothers, respectively, picked that option.[13] However, when preferred occupations are compared with actual ones, there is some indication that they now realistically confront the nonmarriage contingency—compared with married working women, the single ones prefer substantially higher level occupations than those they have: 47 percent had professional jobs but 65 percent desired them. This discrepancy was highest for the single women.

Among the small group of 34 alumnae with a median age of 36 who were mothers and working part-time, only 44 percent reported working in fields they preferred. The actual jobs held were generally related to their college major, but often unrelated to jobs they desired. In answer to the question: "What one occupation or field would you most like to work in if you had the necessary training"?—only one person preferred a sales, secretarial, or clerical job, but 5 held such jobs; 7 preferred semiprofessional jobs but only 3 had chosen such. In general, the older the woman, the less likely her preferred job resembled her actual one. Thus, while marriage was an explicitly anticipated contingency, work appears to have been only vaguely prepared for. Although college major is reflected in later work choices, the major itself was probably chosen with the criteria reported by contemporary women in the same college: "to be practical," "to be able to work in case I ever have to." [14]

---

12. Laura Searls, "College Major and the Tasks of Homemaking," *Journal of Home Economics* 58, no. 9 (November 1966): 708–14; and Shirley S. Angrist, "Role Constellation as a Variable in Women's Leisure Activities," *Social Forces* 45, no. 3 (March 1967): 423–31.

13. The question was: Assume that you are trained for the occupation of your choice, that you are married and have children, and that your husband earns enough so that you will never have to work unless you want to. Under these conditions, which of the following would you prefer? (Check one) (1) to participate in clubs or volunteer work, (2) to spend time on hobbies, sports or other activities, (3) to work part-time in your chosen occupation, (4) to work full-time in your chosen occupation, (5) to concentrate on home and family, (6) other (explain briefly).

14. Bailyn describes women's occupational choice process as revokable, irrational and discontinued. See Lotte Bailyn, "Notes on the Role of Choice in the Psychology of Professional Women," *Daedalus* 93, no. 2 (Spring 1964): 700–710.

And After Marriage . . .

After marriage the contingency orientation shows up in new ways. While marriage was an explicit contingency one prepared for, others remained only implicit. Again, drawing on the alumnae data mentioned, one sees the married women's accommodation to stages and features of family life. For example, among full-time homemakers the type of leisure activities pursued varies according to ages of children—women with preschoolers tended to follow recreational and self-enrichment activities which are largely home-centered; women with school-age children pursued predominantly community activities.[15] Similarly, the older homemakers found less enjoyment and mastery in homemaking than the younger women—perhaps they reflected boredom with domesticity, or else their late-found option to like homemaking less as it is less needed by older children.[16]

Statistics on women in the labor force also show this contingency orientation. A pattern of phasing in and out of the work world represents married women's reactions to the family life cycle. Women's lowest participation in the labor force is between the ages of 25 to 34 when family responsibilities are greatest. The peak comes at 45 to 54 years of age when 42 percent of the married-woman population is in the labor force. Whereas one-quarter of women workers in 1940 came from the 45–54 age group, 50 percent did so in 1962; for the 35–44 age group, the figure rose from 29 percent in 1940 to 45 percent in 1962. These new peaks reflect younger ages at which women complete childbearing and become freer of family responsibilities.[17]

Concern over women's work-force trends and the compressed parental years, manifests itself in the "retread" phenomenon. Continuing education programs have arisen to deal explicitly with the presumed crisis of the later years, to help women take a kind of second look at life.[18] Marriage becomes a past or minor contingency and others like filling time or economic self-sufficiency loom large.

Of course, the ideas and data reported above need to be tempered with the work world conditions impinging on women's occupational choice, for example, the difficulties of finding high-level part-time work.

15. Angrist, "Role Constellation," pp. 423–31.

16. Searls, "College Major," pp. 708–14.

17. U.S. Department of Labor, *Handbook on Women Workers* (Washington, D.C.: Women's Bureau Bulletin No. 285, 1963).

18. Center for Continuing Education, *Opportunities for Women Through Education* (Ann Arbor: University of Michigan, 1965).

13

WOMEN'S STUDIES: ITS ORIGINS, ITS ORGANIZATION, AND ITS PROSPECTS

SHEILA TOBIAS

Female Studies is the intellectual examination of the absence of women from history; the fresh look in a non-Freudian way at the social psychology of women; the study of women in literature and the images of women in the arts; the economic and legal history of the family; and speculation about androgyny defined as societies, utopist, primitive or revolutionary, where sex differences have been minimized.

The Origin of Women's Studies

At the beginning, Women's Studies was not a course so much as a discovery. I remember looking over a lengthy multidisciplinary list of about two hundred books that was being circulated in 1968 as "Books about Women" and noting with some surprise that I had read almost all of them, even those in fields far different from my own, and that my friends in anthropology, in literature, in biology and history had read most of them, too. The connection between ourselves and certain books made us certain that the study of women could be a field. Moreover, we had been sensitized by black students to the absence from our "value-free" university curriculum of the history and literature, the experience and the struggles, of nonwhite Americans and of Africans. We had been educated by black students to understand what they meant when they said Black Studies was to be a "critique of the American experience" and how important it was not just to give blacks (and women) "equal time" in the curriculum but to investigate what it was about the dominant point of view that left them (us) out.

When women in universities began to see that they, too, were a "minority" both in terms of numbers and in terms of alienation, then other connections began to be made. At first they read on their own time about women. Soon they began to ask for the opportunity to do this research more seriously. Then they wanted to teach it.

At the same time, the intellectual content of movement literature had been high from the beginning. Betty Friedan's best-seller *The Feminine Mystique* was sociology and not polemic. Kate Millett's notion of patriarchy (summarized in chapter 2 of *Sexual Politics*) challenges assumptions about sex differences (psychology), the rationale for a male-dominated culture (sociology), and the almost universal preference for male writers and male writing (literary criticism). Other feminists had already begun the kind of research that would provide material for women's studies courses. Alice Rossi had analyzed the low incidence of women scientists and engineers and had formed some hypothesis about sex-role socialization. She published in 1969 her model of male-female integration which she described as "hybrid" allowing for an adjustment of male life style to women's needs as well as women's to men's. Sandra and Daryl Bem, at the University of Pittsburgh, had analyzed the educational system in a pithy article entitled "Training a Woman to Know Her Place" and Naomi Weisstein was unforgiving in her exposé of antifeminist biases among professional psychologists in their "value-free" research.

Thus, the women were moving forward with new questions and new research while social science, at least at the beginning, stood still. I remember participating in a conference on women at Cornell in 1969 where the psychologist, anthropologist, political scientist, and sociologist all in their own way denied that the "woman issue" was related to their fields. The "woman problem" was still being examined, like the "Negro problem" of yesteryear as outside and unrelated to the mainstream of American life and thought. It was the reversal of this perspective, together with an aggressive insistence that sex differences be taken as learned (until proven otherwise) that characterized the first new Women's Studies courses.

"From the point of view of the wolf," Linda Nochlin Pommer wrote in her January 1971 article "Why Are There No Great Women Artists?" the lambs have a "lamb problem." From the point of view of the "lambs," the issue is racism, sexism, or systematic exclusion by the majority in power. At the beginning, however, most teachers and students in Women's Studies courses were content to study women. So much had been excluded and so much misrepresented that the study of woman was an appropriate theme. At Cornell, the course was entitled

"The Evolution of Female Personality" (Spring 1970) and it represented quite simply a desire to know more about women. Particular persons in history; perspectives on contemporary women as sociology, economics, and psychology might reveal them to be; types of women: artists, mothers, blacks, Chicanos, and old women; types of child-rearing that puts the nuclear family in a cross-cultural perspective; images of women as portrayed in literature and the arts and popular culture; alternatives for women (and men) in, as the last section of the course was called, an "androgynous" society, which would minimize, instead of emphasize, sex differences.

Like the black academic minority who began by studying black people and then moved on to racism, Women's Studies evolved from this initial interest in female personality and female people to an analysis of Man's World. The progression was not orderly, but followed a series of discoveries of connections between female behavior and the environments in which it is and has been shaped. That progression might be summarized as follows:

1. The Study of Woman—Female Personality.
2. Masculinity and Femininity: What are the implications of these terms? How are they defined? How are the behaviors learned? Are they universally the same?
3. Female Culture: What is it that is common to the female experience? How would it be evaluated in a nonmale society? Is achievement, motivated by need for affiliation for example any worse than achievement motivated by a need for dominance?
4. The Academic Disciplines: Having discovered the absence of women from history and the minimizing of the subject of sex-role socialization, students and teachers proceeded to examine the disciplines themselves for bias. In this period, "feminist criticism" began to appear in literary journals; fundamental critiques of social science methodology as well.
5. Male Society: What are the strengths and weaknesses of the majority when seen as "male" instead of "human?"
6. Male Personality: How has it evolved?

Men's Studies has not yet replaced Women's Studies, but an interest in maleness certainly characterizes my own development and I intend in the next general course on women's social roles in America to devote a block of time to men's roles and personality.

Another reason for the rapid growth of Women's Studies courses, aside from the intellectual concerns of its members, has to do with the fact that from the beginning a large proportion of movement women were university students and teachers. Campus consciousness-raising had, in the initial period, united undergraduates disenchanted with sex stereotyping and with radical (mostly) male students' pretensions, graduate students suffering motivation crises as they approached the professional degree, and bewildered women Ph.D.s who, having mastered the hurdles, some with highest honors, were still unable to get and keep good jobs. In every case, at the large, coeducational institution where my experience began, women staff and women students showed an alienation from the college, and from their male and female peers.

Without the Women's Liberation Movement, there would have been no Women's Studies courses or research. The movement gave women teachers the courage to press reluctant departments and administrators for the relief time and the financial support to start teaching new courses. The movement made women students suddenly interested and supportive of women teachers. Still, the timing was fortuitous as well. Coming on the heels of Black Studies and of the crisis of relevance in the university, Women's Studies was able to employ language and rationale already familiar in other contexts.

In the fall of 1972 there were more than 750 courses on women in 500 universities. Almost every major professional journal had devoted a section if not an issue to the subject of women in the past four years. Every professional association has entertained panels on one or another new subject related to Women's Studies. The press in Pittsburgh that, from the beginning, published syllabi of new courses,[1] now publishes a yearly "Guide to Female Studies" that simply lists names of courses, names of instructors, and universities. There are two Women's Studies journals[2] and a regularly appearing newsletter on Women's Studies funded by a National Endowment grant.

There has not yet been any systematic evaluation of Women's Studies courses, either for content or for impact on student attitudes. But that is probably because the field has moved too fast to be studied.

1. Know, Inc., P.O. Box 10197, Pittsburgh, Pennsylvania 15232.

2. Feminist Studies, c/o Ann Calderwood, 417 Riverside Drive, New York, N.Y. 10025 and Women's Studies, c/o Wendy Martin, Queens College, English Department, Flushing, New York 11367.

The Organization of Women's Studies

In general, the first Women's Studies courses were seminars or small colloquia, held in dorms, as part of a "free-university" curriculum, or for no credit. They were taught by students, "nonladder" faculty, and nonacademic staff. Only where a regular member of the faculty was interested in sponsoring such a course, could Women's Studies appear officially in a college catalogue. Thus, the organization of the courses and programs was from the beginning a series of pragmatic responses to the possibilities that varied from campus to campus.

Unlike the black students, who had to recruit black persons to teach Black Studies, women students could usually find an underpaid but willing woman faculty member to help them out. Often such women faculty were engaged in freshman courses having no particular curriculum (humanities, introduction to social science, etc.) where experimentation could take place without much red tape. In the Cornell case, a woman assistant professor, supported by a male full professor, took formal responsibility for "The Evolution of Female Personality" on behalf of a team of teachers most of whom were not members of the regular faculty.

Where a professor was well established, of course, the new subject matter could be integrated without fuss. Alice Rossi, of Goucher, made "sex" a unit in her course on the sociology of equality. Annette Baxter of Barnard, expanded a course she had been giving since 1965 on women's history. A home economics department chairman at Kansas and another at Stout State in Wisconsin offered new courses on women as part of the curriculum very soon after the material and reading lists began to circulate. Some home economists were old enough to remember when courses on women had been a regular part of their offerings.

Where there was no faculty member willing to teach or underwrite a course on women (and this was by far the most frequent situation), students had to initiate the programs. At Bryn Mawr, students sat-in and forced the administration to hire Kate Millett to teach a one-semester course. At Columbia, students and graduate students met for a year designing a full program on Women's Studies before presenting it as a demand to the administration. At San Diego State, a nationwide write-in campaign was organized on behalf of the pro-Women's Studies caucus, and at SUNY–Buffalo, when Women's

Studies was launched at the same time in the colleges of arts and sciences and in social work, massive student support made the difference.

Once the courses were underway, developments varied. I call "Year Zero" the year in which consciousness is raised, an interuniversity conference on women or a trip to another conference is made by students and faculty; and by the end of which there is a desire for "something" more than noncredit bull sessions about women. "Year One" begins with a course, given either by a cooperative faculty member or by a group of interested students. Few participate, but all are intensely interested in having the course continued and others added.

During "Year Two" a number of alternative organizational possibilities were considered: At San Diego State in 1970 a proposal was written for a large-scale program based both on campus and in the community. The director was to be independent of the university tenure system and would be hired in consultation with a staff made up of students and teachers. At Cornell, in 1971, a more modest budget was requested for a coordinating office that would employ only visiting lecturers and borrow faculty from cooperative departments. At Pittsburgh (1971), five faculty positions were designated joint appointments in English, psychology, etc.—Women's Studies. The director was to be an academic woman who would help recruit, hire, and expand the program. At Wesleyan, on the other hand, "Year Two" brought with it more courses offered by departments but no plan for a program or a major.

By "Year Four," some twenty colleges had developed full-fledged programs in Women's Studies but most were operating on an ad hoc basis with continuing success in attracting students of both sexes. At Sarah Lawrence College, in Bronxville, New York, there is a major at the M.A. level in Women's History. At George Washington University, in Washington, D.C., there is an interdisciplinary M.A. At Goddard College, an experimental college in Vermont, which also attracts nonresident students, there is a major and an M.A. in Women's Studies. At Cornell, there is a program housed in the College of Arts and Sciences.

Just as arrangements have varied from place to place depending on precedent, budget and personal preference of the students and staff, so, too, the problems besetting the courses and programs have varied. At

Cornell, San Diego, Pittsburgh (and probably elsewhere) disagreements developed between the professional staff, sensitive to professional criteria for advancement, and the nonacademic staff, anxious to keep Women's Studies from removing itself to the ivory tower. The distinction was termed: "Street Women's Studies versus Classroom Women's Studies." One aspect had to do with selection of material that is appropriate to courses on women. From one point of view, the subject matter might be radical, but the materials were to be traditional, and the style of learning comparable to Psychology 101. From another point of view, a radical new subject ought not be taught in a traditional way using traditional materials. Moreover, as younger, radical women expressed it, "Every woman knows more about what it's like to be a woman than any author. So why read?"

In some places, Women's Studies had attached itself at the beginning not to a seminar program but to a community-affairs project. For these students, community action in off-campus projects was appropriate for the student of women; and personal experience, personally evaluated, was the goal. My own conclusion after "Year Four" was that it was easier to teach male and female students in a single Women's Studies course than to teach radical and nonradical women at the same time. The issue was particularly damaging because for most women, Women's Studies had to be as rigorous and as impressive as other courses in order to gain respect from faculty, administration, and professional peers.

These views, incompatible in a single course and in a single program, stopped the Women's Studies momentum on a number of campuses. No doubt Black Studies had had similar strains during its development, but these had not surfaced before the white community. The issues are ideological and political; but linked to this is that awful hunger women have for the status and respect that is "inside" the establishment. Junior faculty were especially vulnerable to their colleagues' sneers about their work. Some women, today in "Years Five" and "Six," are being denied tenure because their research is "insignificant." Yet undergraduates, unable to identify with these professional interests, often joined with nonprofessionals to defeat women faculty.

In some cases, but not in many, the issue of male participation became divisive. Can a man teach Women's Studies, its history or psychology, if he is academically qualified but not personally experienced in what it is to be a woman? Ought male students be present in all classes at all times? These questions still concern us as we pause to speculate about the future.

The Future of Women's Studies

What has matured Women's Studies much in the past four years are the books and reprints, anthologies and monographs, none of which were available at the beginning, and all of which reinforce that early certainty that there is a field of study having to do with women that deserves serious attention. The interdisciplinary nature of the field has remained central to its definition, although because of the coincidence that there are more women faculty in literature than in any other field, the lead in some cases has been taken not by the social and behavioral scientists, but by the literature faculties. With the help of this body of material, I now find it possible to offer a coherent analysis of the social roles of women in America that begins with: Sex differences that are biologic, mythic and psychoanalytic in origin; and then to move on to the experience of "Outsider" [3] that most women have; then to tie the role behaviors of family life to those found appropriate to the jobs women do (nurturance makes for good nursing; dependence makes for good secretarial attitudes); then to study a system of division of labor by sex which has survived as a cultural lag other revolutionary changes in female labor force participation; always looking at other cultures for clues as to what is biologic and fundamental about behavior and what is socially learned. We study marriage in Shakespeare (*Taming of the Shrew*), Ibsen (*A Doll's House*), and Chopin (*The Awakening*), and we look at TV shows and films for evidence of the process by which we are made to believe in the cultural stereotypes about ourselves.

Every year my students know more about the subject before the class begins than they knew the year before. Every year I take on more individual tutees who want to do research in women's history or women's roles. Yet every year I resist expanding the number of courses beyond the few that are by now successful and well loved. I discourage students from "majoring" in Women's Studies because I care for their

---

3. Vivian Gornick and Barbara K. Moran, eds., *Woman in Sexist Society: Studies in Power and Powerlessness* (New York: Signet Books, 1972).

professional futures and fear that, like home economics, Women's Studies could become a dead end for women students.

Yet every year, I attend another important conference in which research is reported that tempts me to engage more and more women students in pursuing the truth about women, even at the cost of a traditional preparation for a traditional career.

I am torn, and so I state the future of Women's Studies in the form of the following questions:

1. Should Women's Studies be multidisciplinary, a separate field, or become integrated into traditional disciplines?
2. Should men be permitted and encouraged to study Women's Studies, or should Men's Studies be set up for men interested in gender roles?
3. What are the special opportunities and obligations for Women's Studies at women's colleges?
4. What should be the place of Women's Studies programs in an academic and nonacademic community? What should be the relation of Women's Studies to the political organizations of women on and off the campus?
5. Should there be graduate work in Women's Studies? A Ph.D. minor? An undergraduate major? Should Women's Studies be required of men and women entering professions that involve dealing with people (law, medicine, social work, teaching)?
6. How can research be funded if it is multidisciplinary and if the subject is considered trivial?
7. What should be the level of experimentation in teaching Women's Studies?
8. What should be the relationship of Women's Studies to home economics programs (where they still exist)?

The issues are important but in "Year Five" no longer so urgent to solve. For as we debate the theoretical positions, and ponder how we can make our women students and faculty stronger than they have been able to be in the past, the classes meet; the books are written and published; the papers are delivered and the new material shared.

Nothing is as powerful as an idea whose time has come.

REQUIRED BOOKS

Bardwick, Judith	*Readings on the Psychology of Women*
Freud, Sigmund	*Dora: An Analysis of a Case of Hysteria*
Mead, Margaret	*Sex and Temperament*
Ladner, Joyce	*Tomorrow's Tomorrow*
Angelou, Maya	*I Know Why the Caged Bird Sings*
Gornick, Vivian, and Moran, Barbara	*Woman in Sexist Society*
Sinclair, Andrew	*The Emancipation of the American Woman*
Shakespeare, William	*Taming of the Shrew*
Ibsen, Henrik	*A Doll's House*
Chopin, Kate	*The Awakening*
Kreps, Juanita	*Sex in the Market Place*
Janeway, Elizabeth	*Man's World Woman's Place*

LECTURE	READING

Part One: Sex Differences

LECTURE	READING
Introduction	None
Film: *Growing Up Female*	Bardwick, chaps. 8, 9, 10
	Bardwick/Douvan, Komarovsky, Horner
Sex-role Socialization	Same as above
Biological Basis of Sex Differences	Bardwick, chaps. 1, 3, 5
	Money, Mitchell/Goldberg/Lewis
Mythic and Scientific Conceptions of Sex Differences	Mead, *Sex and Temperament*, chaps. 7, 12, 15
	Bible, Genesis 1:1 to 3:24.

LECTURE	READING
Part II of Myth Lecture	Janeway, *Man's World Woman's Place*, chaps. 1–3, 5, 8, 10, 20 Gadpaille, "The Biological Fallacies of Women's Lib" (Handout)
Matriarchy, Myth, Symbol or Reality	
Discussion of Material Covered So Far	Review, Additional recommended reading: Mead, chaps. 3, 5, 6, 16. Ginsberg, Louis, *Legends of the Jews*, vol. I, pp. 64–89.
Psychoanalytic Basis of Sex Differences	Freud, *Dora: An Analysis of a Case of Hysteria* (entire)
"Freud and Freudianism"	Choice: chap. 4 "Sexual Solipsism of Sigmund Freud" in Friedan, *The Feminine Mystique*; Kate Millett, *Sexual Politics*, pp. 127–56 in chap. 1, part 3, and chap. 2; or Mary McCarthy, "Tyranny of the Orgasm" (Handout)
Modern Theories of Sex Differences, Social Learning, and Identification	Suggested: Bardwick, chaps. 6, 7, 15

Part Two: Sex Roles

Sex Role: Woman as Outsider	Gornick, chap. 4; Bardwick, chaps. 8, 9, 47
Career Role	Bardwick, chaps. 10, 11, 12, 14, 15, 16
Its Limitations: I—Institutional	Kreps, *Sex in the Market Place* (entire)
Its Limitations: II—Cultural	Gornick, part 3

LECTURE	READING
Traditional Role	Bardwick, part 3
Its Limitations	Gornick, chaps. 5, 6, 7; Bardwick, chap. 45
Blue-collar Women	"Inside the Telephone Company," Elinor Langer, *New York Review of Books*, March 12, 1970, and March 27, 1970
Black Women	Ladner, *Tomorrow's Tomorrow* and/or Maya Angelou, *I Know Why the Caged Bird Sings*

Part Three: Marriage in Life and Literature

Marriage in Shakespeare and Ibsen	Shakespeare, *Taming of the Shrew* (entire) Ibsen, *A Doll's House* (entire)
Marriage in Kate Chopin	Chopin, *The Awakening* (entire)
Marriage in America	
Marriage in the Twentieth Century	Film: *The Pumpkin Eater*

Part Four: Past and Present Protest

Women's Suffrage	*The Emancipation of the American Woman*
Part 2	Same
Women's Liberation	Introduction, part 4 in Gornick, *Woman in Sexist Society;* Part 4 in Bardwick
Part 2	Same

B

Attitudes Toward Sex Expression Existing

evidence, limited though it is in terms of quantity of reliable and
systematic studies, indicates that we in America are undergoing a
change popularly termed a "sexual revolution." The change since
1900 is primarily in attitudes and values, rather than behavior, at
least with respect to premarital sex. The change in standards since
the 1930s, moreover, is a moderate one possibly undeserving of its
popular characterization as revolutionary. Specifically, a standard
of "permissiveness with affection" whereby premarital intercourse
is acceptable under the condition of strong affection or love is
making inroads into the still-dominant standard of chastity for
women and the double standard for men.[1]

Reasons for the evolutionary, rather than rapid, change in
norms regulating premarital sexual intercourse among the
relatively advantaged social classes are discussed in the initial
selection by Pope and Knudsen.[2] These sociologists maintain that
it is the middle and upper classes who are most able to proscribe
premarital intercourse as well as most interested in doing so. They
are interested basically because children born to unwed parents
have illegitimate status which makes problematic the family's
maintenance of its privileged position in society. It is likely, then,
that the advantaged classes will continue to try to uphold the
more restrictive sexual standards and make them the legitimate
standards for all in order to differentiate themselves from the more
disadvantaged and to capitalize on their "moral worthiness." On
the other hand, the advantaged will lessen their commitment to
restrictive sexual standards, especially the norm of chastity, to the

1. Ira L. Reiss, *Premarital Sexual Standards in America* (Glencoe, Ill.: Free Press, 1960).

2. The reader should note that this article was written prior to the U.S. Supreme
Court's ruling regarding restrictive abortion laws in Texas and Georgia.

extent that premarital intercourse can be separated from illegitimate birth. Four social arrangements that permit such disassociation in varying degrees involve contraceptive techniques, abortion, adoption, and marriage of couples who conceive out of wedlock.

First, premarital intercourse could be separated from conception (hence, illegitimate birth) by effective contraceptive techniques, which could then foster change toward more permissive norms. At present, however, the general attitude toward sex permits too little formal and informal instruction about it; there is a social-class differential in use as well as knowledge of and access to the most effective techniques; and even the most effective techniques are not perfect. The side effects of oral contraceptives, for example, discussed in the following chapter, give pause to the relatively advantaged women who might otherwise benefit from their use.[3]

Second, premarital intercourse and conception could be separated from illegitimate birth by tolerance or encouragement of abortion. During the past few years, several states have liberalized significantly their abortion laws and, at this writing, the U.S. Supreme Court has declared unconstitutional restrictive abortion laws in Texas and Georgia. This ruling, discussed in the following chapter, can be expected to have ramifications in many states, but the exact nature of the effect and the speed and duration of its occurrence remain to be seen.

A third social arrangement by which premarital intercourse could be disassociated from (acknowledged) illegitimacy could be the availability of adoption. The adoption "demand" for illegitimate babies of white middle-class couples now exceeds the "supply," the latter being low in part because of contraception and abortion. It is more likely that the current adoption market will continue to foster less stringent selection procedures for adopting parents (e.g., permit and encourage interracial adoptions) than support more permissive sexual standards among whites, at least.

The fourth and final social arrangement is marriage for the

---

3. See, in addition, Louis Lasagna, "Caution on the Pill," *Saturday Review* 51, no. 44 (November 1968): 64–69.

couples who conceive. Pope and Knudsen conclude, in fact, that institutionalization of a norm of "permissiveness-with-affection —plus commitment to marry" is the solution most likely to be adopted by the advantaged adults if they cannot maintain chastity standards.

It is recognized, however, that youth groups themselves have considerable influence in the generation of sex norms and that if women were to become more equal in status to men, the outcome might reflect little interest in parents' basic concern to maintain status for themselves and their children. In women's consciousness-raising groups, for example, one commodity marketed in the courtship system is being questioned; that is, the sexual attractiveness of females (for males). It will be remembered from part 1 that Collins views sexual property as the basis for a system of sexual stratification which is separate from but intersects with other stratification systems. In a similar vein, Atkinson discusses sexual intercourse as an institution buttressed normally by the construct of marriage and, when marriage is threatened, by the substitute theoretical construct of vaginal orgasm. She makes clear the political nature of sexual intercourse and poses the question of what its nature could be if, through research on "test-tube babies," [4] sex relations no longer functioned to replace the species. It is possible, she suggests, that under such conditions we might be better able to understand psychological, as opposed to physiological, aspects of the sense of feeling and to determine the nature of sensual characteristics from the point of view of the good of each individual. From this point of view, moreover, there might very well be no grounds for the "cooperative" effort between two people of the opposite sex known as sexual intercourse.

One feminist alternative to the institution of sexual intercourse is lesbianism, defined by Martin and Lyon to include overt sexual activity between two women, psychological homosexual reaction (i.e., an awareness of sexual arousal by seeing, hearing, or thinking about persons of the same sex, often accompanied by physiologic reactions) or both. Contrary to public opinion, lesbianism is currently an alternative to heterosexuality in

---

4. See in this volume the article by Edward Grossman.

a limited sense only, for most homosexuals are also at times heterosexual.[5] Although the etiology of homosexuality in general is still poorly understood, it is believed that human beings have an inherited capacity for erotic responsiveness to both the same and the opposite sex and that social conditioning determines largely the predominance or mix of sexual response which characterizes individuals.[6]

There are great cross-cultural variations in attitudes about and behavior toward homosexuals and in this context our own society appears relatively restrictive. Social conditioning tends to foster in lesbians themselves feelings of fear, guilt, and hostility as well as make extremely difficult their search for self-identity and self-fulfillment. The prescribed role of housewife-mother and the structured inequality of opportunity in social arenas outside the home for women in general are felt to be particularly oppressive to lesbians who will not likely get married or pregnant but, rather, will likely be stable employees who have to support themselves. Given current attitudes in society, then, the lesbian who divulges her identity risks loss of job, family, and friends. Martin and Lyon conclude that until she dares to risk such losses, however, no personal confrontation can occur which, together with formal education of the public, would help dispel stereotypes of her as lesbian.

The necessity for an increased willingness of women to risk loss is a theme which is repeated in the final selection of this section. Here, however, it is celibacy that Densmore proposes be accepted as an honorable alternative to heterosexual relations. We return now to the question raised by Atkinson concerning the basic nature of human sexuality. Consistent with Densmore is evidence that some women (and men) can indeed live with little or no sexual experience without evidencing strain or compensation.[7] In addition, self-stimulation, which Densmore

5. Wardell B. Pomeroy, "Homosexuality, Transvestism, and Transsexualism," in *Human Sexuality in Medical Education and Practice*, ed. Clark E. Vincent (Springfield, Ill.: Charles C Thomas, 1968), pp. 367–87.

6. Clellan S. Ford and Frank A. Beach, "Human Sexual Behavior in Perspective," in *Patterns of Sexual Behavior* (New York: Harper, 1951), pp. 250–67.

7. John H. Simon and William Gagnon, *The Sexual Scene* (Chicago: Trans-action Books, Aldine, 1970).

poses as an alternative to celibacy for some,[8] is harmless physiologically. The risk, then, with either celibacy or masturbation is to open oneself to probable loss of sexual attention—love, desire, and mercy—from those men whose sexual identity is threatened by nontraditional sex roles. These alternatives, however, may facilitate same sex solidarity and may be important in providing normative alternatives to monogamous heterosexual marriage for intimate human relationships.

8. A contrasting view is expressed by Sherfey, whose explorations of implications of women's greater orgasmic capacity leads her to maintain that the "natural" sexual encounter for women is closer to promiscuity than monogamy or celibacy. See Mary Jane Sherfey, *The Nature and Evolution of Female Sexuality* (New York: Random House, 1972).

14

PREMARITAL SEXUAL NORMS, THE FAMILY, AND SOCIAL CHANGE

HALLOWELL POPE and DEAN D. KNUDSEN

Family sociologists have often considered current American family institutions in the context of social change. But, curiously, the causes for the changing American family have not been systematically formulated, largely because the search for causes has not been guided by explicit theory. The family specialist's approach to change has too often been descriptive, with a grab bag of variables being introduced to "account" for change. This vague, eclectic approach has resulted in the inability to identify core arguments, to formulate them precisely, and then to subject them to empirical test. Not only is our understanding of the process of change limited, but we are also faced with the inability to predict future changes. Systematic understanding of the process of social change would provide the tools whereby predictions rather than forecasts could be made; these predictions could be stated so that the passage of time would provide an empirical test of them and more importantly, of the theory on which they were based.[1]

This paper is an attempt to further the systematic investigation of changes in American family institutions by consideration of the so-called sexual revolution against traditional standards—premarital chastity for the woman, the double standard for the man. This revolution has been written about, analyzed, researched, and, above all, worried about by several generations. Except in rare instances, the "revolution" in sexual standards is now accepted as an accomplished fact.[2] Such analysis as there is focuses on the forces that are producing

---

1. Science, of course, phrases future possibilities as predictions rather than as forecasts. Predictions may be incorrect forecasts for three reasons: (1) the necessary and sufficient conditions specified by the prediction do not occur; (2) the prediction is wrong—that is, even though the necessary and sufficient conditions do occur, the predicted events do not take place; and (3) the conditions specified in the prediction are irrelevant for the prediction being attempted. In each case, the implications for the relationship between theory and fact are very different. In the first case, the prediction is wrong, not because adequate understanding is lacking, but because the required antecedent conditions do not occur. In the second and third cases, the prediction is wrong because understanding is faulty. Only in the latter two cases is theoretical revision definitely needed. In this paper, the reader may disagree with the authors' predictions either because of theoretical differences or because he judges the empirical conditions to be different than do the authors. The first type of disagreement calls the theoretical analysis into question; the second, only the assessment of the facts.

The analysis of social change and the American family has a number of classics. Cf. Carle C. Zimmerman, *Family and Civilization* (New York: Harper & Row, 1947); William F. Ogburn, "The Family and Its Functions," in *Recent Social Trends* (New York: McGraw-Hill, 1933), chap. 13; Ernest W. Burgess and Harvey J. Locke, *The Family: From Institution to Companionship* (New York: American Book, 1945); and W. F. Ogburn and Meyer F. Nimkoff, *Technology and the Changing Family* (Boston: Houghton Mifflin, 1955).

In addition, there have been more recent signs of interest in the analysis of change in the family field: Reuben Hill, "The American Family of the Future," *Marriage and Family Living* 26 (February 1964): 20–28; and Bernard Farber, *Family: Organization and Interaction* (San Francisco: Chandler, 1964). Finally, for a world perspective, see William J. Goode, *World Revolution and Family Patterns* (Glencoe, Ill.: Free Press, 1963).

As the above indicates, there are a variety of strategies one might employ to understand social change in the family. The authors have chosen to consider the middle-class family as governed by a normative system and to interpret the impact of extrafamilial social factors (e.g. occupational institutions) or nonsocial factors (e.g., technological) on the norms defining the family structure. The authors further argue that certain features of our family institutions, namely, those governing family formation, serve as structural anchors; that is, variations in norms within the family institution are limited in their variation by those norms defining these systemic anchor points. A basic change in a familial norm must in most cases be associated with a change in these anchor points. For example, if married women are to be allowed employment, traditional patriarchal ideas governing interaction between the spouses will have to be modified.

2. In a paper written in 1937, Theodore Newcomb pointed out that the 1930s were less different from the 1920s in sexual standards than many "scarehead writers" had

---

"sweeping" changes and overlooks the forces promoting maintenance of traditional standards. This paper presents an alternative interpretation of the facts regarding changing sexual standards in the United States during this century; it also points out that there are strong social pressures that are inhibiting changes in our traditional sexual standards. It discusses reasons why norms governing premarital intercourse have *not* become rapidly more permissive, and why they are not likely to do so in the near future, in spite of pressures in that direction. It then characterizes those social conditions under which conservative standards are maintained and those under which permissive standards are allowed. The analysis is intended to apply only to the advantaged—the white-collar worker, the college educated, those with middle- and upper-level incomes. This limitation is necessary because present sexual standards, those that are likely to emerge, as well as the reasons for their emergence are different for the various social strata.[3]

By this paper, the authors hope to accomplish an appreciation of the fact that any valid theory used to explain changes in American sexual standards must account for the social supports of traditional standards as well as the pressures that undermine them. Any simplistic notion that traditional standards maintain themselves only by inertia in the face of pressures toward change will be found wanting.

Changes in Sexual Standards and the Evidence

After the Second World War, the Kinsey Reports stimulated widespread discussion of American sexual standards, particularly those governing premarital intercourse. Many explanations were offered for what often was interpreted as a trend toward permissiveness as the dominant American premarital sexual standard. Among the many contributing factors mentioned were: technological changes, rational-

feared. See "Recent Changes in Attitudes toward Sex and Marriage," *American Sociological Review* 2 (December 1937): 659–67.

3. In a projected paper, the authors intend to examine the social conditions associated with permissive premarital sexual standards. In the United States, permissive standards appear in those same strata in which the matrifocal family is most frequent—among deprived Negroes and whites. In these groups, the woman forms a series of liaisons rather than formally contracting marriage. She does this when marriage offers limited, if any, advantages, and when no wealth or tradition is present to be conserved by and transmitted through a family line.

ity, anonymity, altered familial functions, equal status for women, freedom of the young, the dating system, the romantic love complex, automobiles, an acceptance of play morality, coeducational colleges, and so forth. But several studies show that shifts in American sexual standards, though real, are not nearly as dramatic as trumpeted in the popular press or by pessimistic moralists.

Evidence about shifts in sexual standards is scarce; some "evidence" is no more than inference from studies describing behavior.[4] Kinsey's data, for example, show that no change took place among the middle strata in incidence of premarital intercourse among those women born after 1900. Further, much of the shift occurring for women in the 1920s was due to increased incidence of intercourse with their future husbands.[5] In the late 1940s, Ehrmann interviewed white college students who were unmarried and predominantly middle class. His results indicate how slowly change has occurred in comparison to what some feared would happen following the "gay 'twenties." [6] Many of his college males still adhered to the double standard. Only 24 percent of

---

4. For a discussion of the past trends in behavior and changes in standards, see Ira L. Reiss, *Premarital Sexual Standards in America* (Glencoe, Ill.: Free Press, 1960). Also see: William M. Kephart, *The Family, Society, and the Individual* (Boston: Houghton Mifflin, 1961), pp. 350–52; and Winston Ehrmann, *Premarital Dating Behavior* (New York: Henry Holt, Bantam ed., 1960), who reports on the incidence of premarital sexual intercourse by sex as reported by various investigators, pp. 39–44. See Nelson N. Foote, "Sex as Play," in *Sexual Behavior in American Society*, ed. J. Himelhoch and S. F. Fava (New York: W. W. Norton, 1955), pp. 237–43, for a summary of the evidence from Kinsey's data indicating a decline in the double standard. Finally, see Winston Ehrmann, "Social Determinants of Human Sexual Behavior," in *Determinants of Human Sexual Behavior*, ed. George Winokur (Springfield, Ill.: Charles C Thomas, 1963), pp. 142–43, for a general review of knowledge about sexual behavior from a sociological perspective.

5. The data: among ever-married women born before 1900, 27 percent were sexually experienced; this increased to 51 percent for those born in the 1900–1910 decade and did not increase from this figure even for those women born in the 1920–29 decade. The proportion of ever-married women who experienced coitus with other than their husbands-to-be only increased 1 percent (5.5 percent to 6.5 percent) from those born before 1900 to those born between 1920–29. Reiss, *Premarital Sexual Standards*, p. 230, table 4.

6. One example of a statement forecasting fast change: "In contrast with the slow tempo of many cultural changes, the trend toward premarital sex experience is proceeding with extraordinary rapidity. . . . If the drop should continue at the average rate shown for those born since 1890 virginity at marriage will be close to the vanishing point for males born after 1930 and for females born after 1940. . . . It will be of no small interest to see how long the cultural ideal of virgin marriage will survive as a moral code after its observance has passed into history." Lewis M. Terman, *Psychological Factors in Marital Happiness* (New York: McGraw-Hill, 1938), pp. 321–23.

---

these men experienced intercourse with their love mates, but 60 percent experienced sex relations with girl friends. Their personal codes for behavior allowed less than half (47 percent) of these college men to have sex relations with their love mates, but allowed about three-quarters (72 percent) of them to have sex relations with their girl friends. For the females, behavioral adherence to the abstinence standard was common: 17 percent had experienced intercourse with love mates, less than 10 percent with friends or acquaintances. The personal codes of only 14 percent of the female students allowed them intercourse with their love mates, and less than 10 percent felt that intercourse with boy friends or acquaintances was permissible.[7] In 1959, Ira Reiss found that among white college students in Virginia, 46 percent of the men and only 4 percent of the women held standards that allowed premarital intercourse.[8] In 1963, from a national probability sample of adults, Reiss found that among whites, less than one-third of the men and less than one-tenth of the women held standards accepting premarital coitus.[9]

The available data indicate that since World War II, there has not been a mass retreat from chastity standards among the advantaged groups. The change since World War I in premarital sexual standards among the middle and upper strata seems to have been one of increased permissiveness for women only under certain conditions. Standards intolerant of promiscuous premarital intercourse remain, so that "concurrent" promiscuity is still condemned. However, "serial" promiscuity with different love mates has become more permissible. There appears to have been a decline in adherence to the double standard among men as well as a decreased acceptance of it by women. Convergence toward a single standard for men and women has occurred—a standard of "permissiveness with affection."[10] That is, strong affection or love is becoming an accepted condition for premarital intercourse. This standard has not replaced the formal

7. Ehrmann, "Social Determinants of Human Sexual Behavior," p. 224, table 5.2.

8. Ira L. Reiss, "Sociological Studies of Sexual Standards," *Determinants of Human Sexual Behavior*, p. 134, table 14.

9. Ira L. Reiss, "Premarital Sexual Permissiveness among Negroes and Whites," *American Sociological Review* 29 (October 1964): 691, table 2. See also Ira L. Reiss, "The Scaling of Premarital Sexual Permissiveness," *Journal of Marriage and the Family* 26 (May 1964): 188–98.

10. Here, the authors follow Reiss's terminology. See Reiss, *Premarital Sexual Standards in America.*

standard of chastity for women or the double standard for men, but it is making inroads into both of them.[11]

What accounts for this moderate change in sexual standards, the convergence on a norm of permissiveness with affection, and the associated decline of the double standard? This gradual trend has occurred even though the family is faced with declining functions, the dating system, romantic love, and other forces for change. Following is an analysis of the forces for stability and also a brief conjecture about the future—the next generation or two.

The Advantages of Legitimacy for the Advantaged

Any analysis of premarital sexual norms, as Kingsley Davis has pointed out, must start from an analysis of marriage and parenthood. The first question should be, "Will unmarried motherhood be allowed?" rather than, "Will premarital coitus be permitted?" If the conclusion is that unmarried motherhood will be proscribed normatively, the next question is, "Will parenthood be disassociated normatively from coitus?" [12] The control of premarital intercourse is closely connected with the maintenance of the family; any analysis that deals with change in premarital sexual standards and does so independently of change in norms governing family formation is mistaken—in reasoning, if not in fact.

Those social strata with advantages to protect will strive to maintain their advantaged position. For groups with prestige or power, legitimate birth maintains secure and unambiguous status placement and supports the transmission of social power and honor from generation to generation. Members of these strata have good reason to support norms

---

11. The above is not meant to imply that no significant changes have taken place since 1900. It only argues that *standards* governing premarital intercourse have changed less than is often believed. It is true that some forms of heterosexual behavior defined previously as immoral are now acceptable—for example, petting. Some argue most girls remain "technical" virgins only and that the increase in heavy petting is indicative of the change that has occurred. But this "technical" virginity is crucial sociologically, as the remainder of this paper tries to demonstrate. For a discussion of changes in Western countries in sexual norms and behavior before marriage, see Goode, *World Revolution*, pp. 35–39.

12. See Kingsley Davis, *Human Society* (New York: Macmillan, 1949), pp. 399–401. An analysis consistent with the present one in most respects is found in Robert F. Winch, *The Modern Family* (rev. ed.; New York: Holt, Rinehart, Winston, 1963), pp. 608–35.

ensuring legitimacy and have the means to do so. In addition, because small numbers of persons violate these norms, negative sanctions can be concentrated upon transgressors. Among advantaged strata, premarital intercourse is proscribed because children born to unwed parents have illegitimate status. In a recent article, Goode has supported this argument with cross-cultural data. He found that a stratum's lack of prestige and power is associated with its lack of commitment to the norm of legitimacy.[13]

However, there are social arrangements, some based on technological innovations, that circumvent unwed parenthood in spite of premarital intercourse. These social arrangements include the following:

1. Premarital intercourse may be permitted, but only between those partners who will later marry.
2. Institutionalized means may be available for the legitimation of children born out of wedlock, for example, through adoption.
3. Abortion (or infanticide) may be tolerated or encouraged, allowing the separation of conception from parenthood.
4. Contraception may be permitted, allowing separation of premarital coitus from parenthood.[14]

---

13. William J. Goode, "Illegitimacy in the Caribbean Social Structure," *American Sociological Review* 25 (February 1960): 21–30. For a brief but excellent summary of Goode's views on legitimacy and illegitimacy, see: W. J. Goode, *The Family* (Englewood Cliffs, N.J.: Prentice-Hall, 1964), pp. 19–30.

Contrary to Kingsley Davis' treatment and, in some respects, contrary to Goode's treatment in the above article, there is no need to make assumptions about societies or strata having system properties or maintaining steady states. The only necessity is the assumption that upper-status parents, or those responsive to their influence, will strive to prevent illegitimate births by creating, promulgating, and implementing norms proscribing premarital intercourse. They can effectively do this through political pressure, pressure on educational agencies, influence in religious organizations and over mass media productions, as well as by direct influence over and control of their own children. Before expecting the advantaged strata to tolerate the disruptive consequences of illegitimacy, it would be necessary to expect them to ignore the importance of family in the maintenance of their privileged position.

14. If the authors were to extend their analysis to include cross-cultural variations as well as those through time, they would have to consider the impact of factors other than those applicable to the American situation. For example, infanticide is a possible method of eliminating an illegitimate child; it need not be considered further here because in the United States, adoption and abortion are available as more acceptable cultural alternatives. Sterilization, if it could be made temporary, might be another way of avoiding conception after coitus, but contraception achieves the same effect and is the most likely cultural alternative to be chosen in a country with a high educational level. In the United States, people could learn to use contraceptive techniques effectively.

There are relatively high illegitimacy rates and, at the same time, liberal sexual attitudes, including the widespread acceptance of intercourse between engaged couples, in some modern Western societies—for example, Denmark. There, even the unwed mother and her child are not the objects of opprobrium—the general population in Denmark holds an understanding and sympathetic attitude toward them. This points to the possibility that illegitimacy and permissive sexual norms may be accepted by advantaged strata under conditions other than when cultural alternatives allow the circumvention of illegitimacy after premarital intercourse.

However, an analysis of sexual standards and illegitimacy in Denmark supports the above analysis in large part. The following conditions in Denmark allow the more complete disassociation of premarital intercourse and illegitimate birth than is true in the United States: (1) A long tradition in Scandinavia permits premarital intercourse between potential spouses, but if a child should result, the couple is expected to marry eventually and is held responsible for the "illegitimate" child. Thus, officially recorded illegitimacies may not be illegitimacies socially. (2) Adoptions of illegitimate children are possible, and the unwed mother is aided in the placement of her child. (3) Criminal abortions are widely utilized to avoid the birth of an illegitimate child and are relatively easily obtained. Apparently, the population is more tolerant of abortion than in the United States. (4) Contraception is, of course, practiced. (As in the United States, there is widespread ignorance about it.) These cultural traits and social practices mean that illegitimate status for a child is a less likely outcome after premarital intercourse in Denmark than in the United States; as a result, advantaged groups in Denmark can tolerate more permissive norms.

But in spite of the above, it is likely that advantaged groups in Denmark both experience and tolerate more actual social illegitimacy and, at the same time, hold more permissive norms regarding premarital sexual intercourse than do comparable groups in the United States. Another reason for the greater tolerance of illegitimacy in Denmark is that the unwed mother is given more governmental protection. She is provided less grudging assistance by public agencies than in the United States. Also, the father is legally required to contribute to the support of the child. Because she is helped by the state and little stigma is attached to this help, the unwed mother is better able to get along until she can marry or have her child adopted; she need cause only a minimum of trouble to her family. If legal protection and public assistance were more readily available to the premaritally pregnant daughters of advantaged parents in the United States (and if assistance by social welfare agencies carried no stigma), advantaged parents might be less resistant to the development of permissive sexual attitudes here.

One additional point needs to be made: there has not been an upward trend in the illegitimacy rate in Denmark during this century. It may be that structurally Denmark generates and can tolerate somewhat more illegitimacy than is true for the United States but that the structural factors resulting in illegitimacies have not varied appreciably in recent times in Denmark. Thus, in Denmark, since more permissive sexual attitudes are not related to more and more actual illegitimacy, these liberal standards can be accepted. In the United States, since actual social illegitimacy has increased, liberal sexual standards are likely to be resisted by the advantaged.

See Sydney H. Croog, "Aspects of the Cultural Background of Premarital Pregnancies in Denmark," *Social Forces* 20 (December 1951): 215–19; Goode, *World Revolution and Family Patterns*, pp. 35–39; Harold T. Christensen, "Cultural Relativism and Premarital *illegitimate birth.* So long as premarital intercourse *might* produce an illegitimate child, norms prohibiting it will be supported among the advantaged.[15]

Premarital Coitus, Legitimacy, and Normative Change

These four social arrangements and the degree to which they have been and are likely to become cultural alternatives can now be considered. This allows interpretation of past changes in premarital sexual norms in the United States as well as prediction of future changes.

1. One of the various contraceptive techniques would seem to offer the best possibility of breaking the link between intercourse and conception. In the past, contraception could have allowed norms to develop that condone premarital coitus provided some contraceptive

---

Sex Norms," *American Sociological Review* 25 (February 1960): 31–39; and the articles on Scandinavian countries in *The Encyclopedia of Sexual Behavior*, ed. Albert Ellis and Albert Abarbanel (New York: Hawthorn Books, 1961).

15. An additional reason can be found for why the advantaged will attempt to uphold restrictive sexual standards. The moral stance taken by advantaged strata is not independent of the behavior and standards held by those in more disadvantaged strata. Persons in positions of advantage will attempt to uphold their standards as the legitimate yardstick for all. Thus they differentiate themselves from those who do not hold these standards or who do not conform to them. In addition to avoiding the internal disruption illegitimacy produces in their family system, the advantaged will attempt to maintain restrictive sexual standards as a part of "middle-class morality" in the attempt to capitalize on their moral worthiness as a part of their constant struggle to maintain their high position in the prestige hierarchy.

In the United States, discrimination against ethnic and minority groups has been justified by pointing out the moral unworthiness of such groups. For example, the loose sexual behavior and standards of Negroes is one of the favorite "proofs" by whites that Negroes are inferior. Constant attempts have also been made to question the morality of those being supported by welfare, attempts to define them as the undeserving poor—attempts that will justify decreased welfare allotments. Though this degradation of the disadvantaged is done in a haphazard manner and not by the organized action of class-conscious strata, our educational system, our mass media, and our political system act so that the disadvantaged are defined as unworthy because they do not meet middle-class moral standards. Thus bills are introduced in state legislatures proposing to declare women who have had illegitimate children morally unfit and incompetent mothers so that their children may be placed in foster homes or so that they may be sterilized; in the public mind, these bills give official backing to the definition of lower-class (or ethnic group) behavior as immoral.

technique was used. Contraceptives permitted the violation of chastity standards in the past, but the availability of contraception did not do much to help create more permissive *standards*. Contraceptive techniques *in practice* have been, and still are, too risky—especially for the advantaged girl with everything to lose and only an unwanted child to gain. Even among middle-class married couples practicing birth control, there are large numbers of "accidental" children.[16] Attempted use of contraception among guilt-ridden, poorly informed, and inexperienced couples would often misfire; the number of accidental pregnancies among the unmarried is enough to keep parents fearful and daughters apprehensive. Unless our middle classes develop a much more open attitude toward sex and allow more practically oriented school instruction about it, contraception will not become sufficiently effective to foster a general normative change within the next generation or two.

However, within advantaged groups, some parents will train their children in more liberal sexual attitudes, and these children will be able to take advantage of traditional contraceptive methods or the newer oral contraceptives which have the advantage of keeping one's preparation for "safe" coitus continuous. Students in some colleges will continue to be exposed to liberalizing influences, and this in conjunction with access to information about up-to-date contraceptive techniques will encourage some students to develop permissive sexual attitudes. But the extent of permissiveness on college campuses is often overdrawn or based on information from colleges with liberal atmospheres.[17] To understand the changes that are taking place, it must be

---

16. Married white Protestant women, using appliance methods of contraception only, reported that 21 percent of their pregnancies were accidental (conception occurred when some method was being used to avoid it). See Ronald Freedman, Pascal K. Whelpton, and Arthur A. Campbell, *Family Planning, Sterility, and Population Growth* (New York: McGraw-Hill, 1959), p. 208, table 6–17. This study was based on a national sample chosen to represent white married women between the ages of 18 and 39 who were living with their husbands.

On the basis of numerous talks with girls from colleges throughout the country, journalist Gael Greene reports: "By her own description, the average college girl is 'pitifully naive' about conception and 'even less informed about contraception,' " *Sex and the College Girl* (New York: Dell, 1964), p. 160.

17. The difference between colleges and, presumably, between groups on the same campus can be striking. Reiss, "The Scaling . . . ," p. 195, table 8, reports 62 percent of students in a white Virginia college accepting abstinence whereas the same was true of only 18 percent of students in a white New York college. Such variations need to be explained; in addition, the relation of standards to behavior must be more thoroughly investigated.

determined whether these liberal attitudes are spreading from campus to campus, especially whether they are spreading to and within the bigger universities. And should the conservative pressures exerted in many colleges, especially those with religious affiliations, be ignored?

Even granting that a significant and increasing proportion of college students will develop more liberal standards as a result of their college experiences, will they keep their permissive attitudes and pass them on to their children? Although children are known to perceive their parents as more restrictive than themselves, the reasons for this perception are not known.[18] Is it because of historical change, with each generation becoming progressively more permissive, or is it because each generation becomes more restrictive as it grows older and has children? The authors suspect that both effects are present. Knowing what standards the present generation holds while in college does not indicate what standards they will attempt to pass on to their children. Again, it is wise to remember that accidental and unwanted pregnancies both before and after marriage are not an uncommon experience for recent generations. Will such parents be open and frank regarding sex with their children and have the confidence to instruct and encourage their children in the use of contraceptive techniques when the official morality says safety through restraint is the proper way?

Certain conditions will generate strong pressures against traditional chastity standards; among these pressures is the growing number of women in the labor force. This leads to the association of unmarried men and women on the job. Such couples are often free of family or community controls and in a position to engage discreetly in illicit sex relations. In the case of a premarital pregnancy, the girl has the financial resources, mobility, and independence necessary to dispose of the baby with a minimum of fuss—through adoption or abortion. Opportunity for heterosexual contact within the context of the search for intimacy and the American emphasis on fun morality, freedom, and the commercialization of sex generates strong pressures against restric-

---

18. For evidence that the younger generation sees their parents as more restrictive than themselves plus evidence that the older generations are, in fact, more restrictive, see Harry A. Grater, "Behavior Standards Held by University Females and Their Mothers," *Personnel and Guidance Journal* 38 (January 1960): 369–72, and Reiss, "Premarital Sexual Permissiveness . . . ," p. 692. See also Robert R. Bell and Jack V. Buerkle, "Mother and Daughter Attitudes toward Premarital Sexual Behavior," *Marriage and Family Living* 23 (November 1961): 390–92.

tive standards among working couples.[19] Under such conditions, norms emphasizing mutual satisfaction and responsibility toward one another rather than toward family and community may develop. But will such standards be carried away from the situations that generate them? After marriage and parenthood, the authors would expect many to retreat from the liberal standards of their "irresponsible youth."

2. Abortion is technically available for prevention of a birth after an unwanted pregnancy. A number of women have used this currently illegal avenue to avoid the stigma of an illicit birth.[20] Abortion avoids the social problems that are caused by the birth of a fatherless child. Seemingly, this would provide a practical means of avoiding illegitimacy, and if it were to be encouraged or even just tolerated, a more permissive attitude could be expected to develop toward premarital intercourse. What is the likelihood that within the next few generations, abortion will become a legal and subsequently a generally accepted means of avoiding illegitimate births?

Abortion has never been normatively prescribed in the United States and is generally considered by religious and social agencies alike to be a negative and antisocial control of birth.[21] The abhorrence with which abortion is publicly greeted precludes its consideration as a way to avoid illicit birth, either by the person contemplating illicit sex relations or by parents suspicious about what happens to their daughter while out on a date. Our cultural tradition even blocks use of abortion as a means of resolving pregnancies within wedlock except when the health of the mother and/or the fetus is endangered. In the future, as in the

---

19. The above is based on Vincent's discussion in his study of unwed mothers in California. It is notable that the greatest increase in the illegitimacy rate has been among women aged between 25 and 34 between 1938 and 1957—over three times that of the 15–19 age group. These are the women most likely to be working and independent of their families. In spite of the large increase in the illegitimacy rate among older women, the greatest concern is with the adolescent unwed mother. The older women and their children are not a social problem because they do not burden the taxpayer and because they provide childless couples with adoptable infants. See Clark E. Vincent, *Unmarried Mothers* (Glencoe, Ill.: Free Press, 1961), p. 54 and pp. 86–96.

20. For a summary of the Kinsey figures on abortion, see Clifford Kirkpatrick, *The Family* (2nd ed.; New York: Ronald Press, 1963), pp. 359–60.

21. "The woman who has an abortion has, from the Planned-Parenthood point of view, wasted life. . . . Abortion destroys life; . . . [and] is negative and anti-social." Edward F. Griffith, *A Sex Guide to Happy Marriage* (New York: Emerson, 1952). See also the discussion of penalties for abortion as they are associated with the Judeo-Christian tradition in Richard M. Fagley, *The Population Explosion and Christian Responsibility* (New York: Oxford University Press, 1960), p. 108.

past, religious and most legal and medical professional groups will resist attempts to legalize abortion except under restricted conditions. More likely than any sudden change is a process of relaxation of the restrictions placed on legal abortion—such as making abortion permissible for not only physical but also for mental health reasons. It is highly unlikely that abortion will in the near future become tolerated as the means whereby illegitimacy will be circumvented after a premarital pregnancy.[22]

3. In the past, the ease with which the advantaged girl left home temporarily, had her child adopted, and then returned home to reenter the marriage market unencumbered may have contributed to a change in sexual standards. Adoption could, if properly handled, avoid the stigma of an acknowledged illegitimacy, dispose of the baby in an acceptable manner, and avoid unpleasantness with the father's family. If there is a continued high demand for illegitimate babies of middle-class couples, this will contribute to a slackening public and private concern over illegitimacy. Norms could develop which would make it permissible for a middle-class girl to have a baby if she put it up for adoption. However, the adoption market may become overloaded, due either to an oversupply of babies or to increased stringency of selection procedures for adopting parents.[23] Heightened concern over

---

22. It is possible that conditions such as extreme population pressure would lead to the acceptance of abortion as a corrective measure (cf. Japan), but in a Western-educated society, with its Judeo-Christian background, contraception would probably be tried first. In contrast to abortion, contraception may be practiced in private by illicit lovers. Thus, there may be a split between public morality and private behavior and morality—witness the data on sexual practices reported by Kinsey and the public reaction to them. Use of contraception and private acceptance of it may increase without public acknowledgment or acceptance. Such a condition may pave the way for a sudden shift toward public acceptance of contraception used by unmarried couples when it is suddenly realized that many such couples have been using contraception for some time.

Unlike contraception, abortion cannot usually be kept a private matter between the illicit lovers. Also, the abortionist involved is subject to legal and professional controls. Changes in the number of abortions or individual shifts in attitudes toward abortion will generate discussion within professional groups and by the public. (The inaccessibility of information about this illegal practice may lead to an exaggerated fear of its extent and the threat it poses to society.) Shifts toward a more liberal view of abortion are less likely to have their way paved by prior widespread private use of abortion and by an acceptance of it by the private morality. This would be changed if an easy, reliable, and safe technique for induced abortion were developed which would be carried out by the pregnant girl herself—if such a technique were allowed to become widely known.

23. "One of the most important factors influencing adoption for a number of years has been the discrepancy between the number of families wanting to adopt a child and the

---

illegitimate children could then be expected among middle-class parents. The end result would be attempts to promulgate and enforce chastity standards. Because it is unlikely that adoption will ever conveniently absorb enough illegitimate children, this social arrangement will not support more permissive sexual standards.

4. A final social arrangement, namely, marriage between sex partners who conceive a child out of wedlock, avoids illegitimate birth. By establishing and strengthening norms that ensure marriage between couples who premaritally conceive, the middle-class parent would protect the position of his family. Within the context of American culture, the following norms, which are mutually reinforcing, are likely to be supported: (1) couples should be committed to marriage before engaging in premarital sex relations; (2) couples considering marriage or sex relations should be in love with one another; and (3) marriage between the natural parents should take place following a premarital pregnancy. The linking of commitment to marry with the emotional attachment of love would make the desired outcome—marriage— highly likely in case of a premarital pregnancy. It is the normative solution most likely to be adopted by advantaged strata if they are forced to retreat from chastity standards. The trend in changing sexual norms, if any is yet clearly discernible, is in this direction.

This "solution" to the problem of premarital sexual relations is compatible with other changes that are taking place in American family institutions: (1) As women gain social equality, the double standard becomes increasingly more difficult to maintain. The middle-class woman seeking premarital sexual privileges will seek them with the man she loves. (2) The "irrationality" of romantic love has been under attack from family life professionals, such as family sociologists, who have some influence over the education of youth. With parental support, these professionals would be able to encourage young people even more than now to pick their courtship partners on the basis of marriageability. This would allow an easy resolution of the dilemma created by a premarital pregnancy. Such changes will cause more

---

number of children legally available for adoption. With ten or more families applying to adopt for every child legally available for adoption, it was impossible for adoption agencies to meet the demand for children. . . . Recently there seems to be a tendency in the opposite direction. A number of agencies are concerned about the decrease in applications for adoption of normal white infants." *Readings in Adoption*, ed. Evelyn I. Smith (New York: Philosophical Library, 1963), pp. 530–31.

---

advantaged persons in the future to condone intercourse, but only between potential marital partners.[24]

This paper has drawn its conclusions primarily from the premise that the threat illegitimacy poses to the social position of the advantaged will cause them to institute the norm of permissiveness-with-affection-plus-commitment-to-marry. However, there are obviously other forces that will generate norms different from and more permissive than this one. Such a factor is the relative freedom with which our youth interact during the courtship period and the relative absence of adult surveil-

---

24. The pattern of marriage following premarital conception is common now. Christensen's work using record linkage shows that nearly one-fifth of first marital births in an Ohio sample were premaritally conceived. However, it is likely that these couples marry more from fear of detection than from following a norm of marriage to the person with whom one premaritally conceives. This is indicated by the large number of couples who marry almost immediately after the pregnancy is determined or even suspected. As the pattern of marriage after premarital conception became accepted and institutionalized, there would be much less anxiety generated and fewer quick marriages. This is the pattern shown by a more sexually permissive culture investigated by Christensen. It should be clear from the present argument, however, that postconception marriages will become required normatively among the advantaged and will not remain a matter of personal choice. Otherwise, the threat to social position and honor would remain.

For a recent summary of Christensen's work, see Harold T. Christensen, "Child Spacing Via Record Linkage: New Data Plus a Summing Up from Earlier Reports," *Marriage and Family Living* 25 (August 1963): 272–80.

Clark E. Vincent reports from his study of unwed mothers in California (*Unmarried Mothers*, pp. 82–91) that those from advantaged groups had predominantly felt themselves to have been in a "love relationship of some duration" with their sex partners. Can this data be interpreted as indicating that the norm of permissiveness with affection but *without* commitment to marry is already spreading among the advantaged? The present authors think not. Many of these women probably expected or assumed that they would marry the father of their child—especially if they became pregnant. They were most likely following the norm of permissiveness-with-affection-plus-commitment-to-marry, but the commitment may not have been mutual.

Below is described a likely result for those women engaging in premarital intercourse in a culture with restrictive sexual attitudes. Once the woman finds that she is pregnant premaritally, she develops guilt feelings and blames her erstwhile lover for her plight. Her family and friends are likely to interpret the male as the "sexual exploiter" (see Vincent, ibid., pp. 73–82) and to consider him unworthy as a marriage partner. The premaritally pregnant girl is charged with finding someone more suitable. A girl who is genuinely in love with an illicit sex partner can decide that she does not want to marry him, especially if he is hesitant about "making an honest woman of her." Evidence from the study of unwed motherhood in North Carolina comparing whites (more restrictive standards) and Negroes (more permissive standards) supports this interpretation: whites who are premaritally pregnant more often marry (usually the child's father) before giving birth; but among those who have given birth and who marry, whites less frequently marry the natural father than do Negroes.

---

lance of them. Our courtship system is to a great degree participant-run; youths themselves are in control of the role bargains made in the courtship market.[25] Parents attempt to teach restraint to their children, especially their daughters, but when a child enters high school, and even more so when he or she departs for college, peer-group influences compete with direct parental control and with attitudes internalized within the family of orientation. The pressures on youths in their peer groups are different from those acting on their parents and tend to generate different sets of norms than those supported by their parents.

Under conditions of relative status equality between the sexes, one would expect that the bargaining power of each partner in a dating relationship would be relatively equal and that norms stressing equal commitment and mutual responsibility would develop. Male exploitation of affection to obtain sexual favors or female exploitation of sex to obtain affection will be rejected, and norms of mutual responsibility will be stressed. Affection and sex will have to come from both sides of the partnership in equal measure. However, illegitimacy is less salient a threat to youth than to parents of established families, and youth will not stress the commitment to marry as much as their parents. And to the extent that contraceptive techniques are available and believed effective, there will be further pressure to disassociate sex and affection from a commitment to marry. The pressures toward acquiring the safety of a "steady" in a competitive dating market, the relatively equal bargaining power of the sexes, and the fear of exploitation of one's feelings will lead youth to prescribe sex relations only within the protective cocoon of mutual affection. The youth norm of permissiveness with affection can be expected to compete with the adult norm of permissiveness-with-affection-plus-commitment-to-marry.[26]

---

25. See Goode, "Illegitimacy in the Caribbean Social Structure," for a discussion of courtship systems as market systems in which role bargains are struck. That is, ". . . in any role relationship both ego and alter are restricted in what services they may agree to perform for one another, by the expectations of others and thus by the sanctions which others will apply. . . . All courtship systems are market systems in which role bargains are struck. They differ from one another with respect to the commodities which are more or less valuable on that market (beauty, personality, kinship position, family prestige, wealth) and who has the authority to do the marketing. Modern Western societies seem to constitute the only major historical civilization in which youngsters have been given a substantial voice in this bargaining (Imperial Rome might be added by some historians)," p. 28.

26. In a recent book written for teen-agers, one widely read family life specialist stresses mutual responsibility in her discussion of sex controls. She also tells the teen-ager

Other forces will also lead to support of the norm of permissiveness-with-affection-plus-commitment-to-marry, or even of the more conservative norm of premarital chastity. These forces will act more on youth than on the parental generation. If there is an increased emphasis on rational-scientific criteria for mate selection (e.g., through the influence of marriage and the family courses[27]), there will be increased fear of the "affection trap." Dating couples will avoid overcommitting themselves, either through sex or affection, so as to avoid a premature marriage. Either partner will be wary of committing himself or herself to premarital intercourse, fearing it might lead to marriage (due to pregnancy or to premature emotional involvement). Partners will delay committing themselves to one another as long as possible—until they are sure. This kind of courtship will be a progressive commitment, weighed at every step. Intercourse would result only when each partner was definitely willing to marry. Such courting procedures foster the same norms that advantaged parents would support, but for different reasons—not for fear of illegitimacy but for fear of acquiring an undesirable marital partner.

---

to recognize the investment parents have in their children and that parents want children to be a credit to the family ("one impulsive moment may break the social standing of years"). Teen-agers are urged to view their sexual behavior within the context of the larger goals they have in life and are told that the ability to achieve depends on deferring immediate gratifications. For the most part, this book represents the normative position which advantaged parents are expected to take, but, in addition, it recognizes the position that advantaged youths are formulating. The author attempts to interpret the parental position to teen-agers, stressing the ruined reputations and damaged life chances which premarital intercourse can cause. See Evelyn Millis Duvall, *Love and the Facts of Life* (New York: Association Press, 1963), especially pp. 228–30, 260–63, and 334–42.

27. Reuben Hill compared the emphasis given to different concerns by the first marriage textbook in 1934 and by three 1963 marriage texts. This comparison can be an index to how the family professionals, through their writing, teaching, and counseling, will attempt to shape the future of our family system. Hill's content analysis shows that in 1963, the most frequently mentioned area of concern is the general topic of "better mate selection." This topic is getting about twice as much attention in 1963 as it did in the 1934 text. And, interestingly enough, Hill lists the following as subtopics under this general heading: "More mutuality in sex relations, less exploitation," and "Single high or single permissive standard for premarital sex." Neither topic is mentioned as a concern of the 1934 text. See Hill, "American Family of the Future," pp. 24–28.

Advantage, Legitimacy, and Social Change: A Summary

Premarital sexual norms are intimately connected with maintenance of family lines and position. Through group pressures and control over sanctions, advantaged strata will resist the development of norms that threaten their high position and support those that maintain family prestige and continuity. Among the advantaged, changes in sexual standards have successfully been resisted for the past thirty years. In the future, some concession to changed social conditions will cause more of the advantaged to adopt the premarital sexual standard of permissiveness with affection. But this step will be resisted strongly unless those social arrangements that allow separation of premarital coitus from unwed parenthood are also adopted.

The desire of those in advantaged social positions to maintain a high position for themselves and their children comprises an important element in the dynamic situation that determines change or stability in standards governing sexual intercourse before marriage. The traditional chastity standard cannot be treated merely as a brake that slows down but cannot stop changes toward permissiveness. The struggle between those forces fostering permissiveness, such as equal rights for women and the dating system, and those forces fostering restrictiveness outlined above will be continued in the families of the future. Because these two opposing forces are nearly equal in strength, change in the foreseeable future will be gradual, and the American sexual revolution will remain but a continuing evolution.[28]

---

28. As contraceptives become more efficient and gain wider acceptance, confidence in them will increase. Among groups that gain complete confidence in available contraceptive techniques, a norm of permissiveness with contraception will likely develop. Though this norm is probably developing now, its wide acceptance is several generations in the future.

15

THE INSTITUTION[1] OF SEXUAL INTERCOURSE

TI-GRACE ATKINSON

> . . . our "society," . . . if it's not deflected from its present course and if the Bomb doesn't drop on it, will hump itself to death.
>
> Valerie Solanas

The debate on vaginal orgasm is not central to feminism as a whole. The theory of vaginal orgasm was created quite recently to shore up that part of the foundation of a social institution that was being threatened by the increasing demand by women for freedom for women. The political institution I am referring to is the institution of sexual intercourse. The purpose, i.e., the social function, of the institution is to maintain the human species.

It used to be that the construct of marriage guaranteed the institution of sexual intercourse. It is still true that, when and where that construct in any of its original variants is properly entered into and protected, the activities sufficient to the definition of this construct and, thus, the purposes of the institution of sexual intercourse, are protected. The substitute theoretical construct of vaginal orgasm is necessary only when marriage is threatened.

The theory of vaginal orgasm was the concoction of a man, Freud, whose theories generally place women in an inhumane and exploited role. His theory of vaginal orgasm reaches the apex of these. The theory was inspired by his confrontations with women who were sick to death of the female role, and it adjusted women back into this female role by conning them that it was in a woman's interest, *by her very nature* (i.e., it

---

1. The definition of "institution" used in this article = (John Rawls' df. of "practice" = any form of activity specified by a system of rules which defines offices, roles, moves, penalties, defenses, and so on, and which gives the activity its structure) + (Webster's df. of "institutional" = organized so as to function in social, charitable, and educational activities).

is in the interest of her vagina), to be dehumanized and exploited. While Freud's theory is inconsistent with female anatomy, it is excellent evidence in support of the theory that the concept of sexual intercourse is a political construct, reified into an institution.

The construct of vaginal orgasm is most in vogue whenever and wherever the institution of sexual intercourse is threatened. As women become freer, more independent, more self-sufficient, their interest (i.e., their need) in men decreases, and their desire for the construct of marriage which properly entails children (i.e., a family) decreases proportionate to the increase in their self-sufficiency. It is for this reason that the construct of *vaginal* orgasm is coming under attack among women radicals in the feminist movement (as opposed to radical feminists) while at the same time the construct of marriage is coming under attack among women in the feminist movement who are either politically conservative, or liberal-to-the-right (e.g., a McCarthyite), or, as is the case with most women, apolitical in the main. The latter group is both presently and potentially far larger than the former, which is the only reason the debate on the marriage-family[2] construct is central to feminism as a whole, whereas its more recent substitute, vaginal orgasm, is not.

Vaginal orgasm is, then, a substitute construct for marriage. Unfortunately for those women who are accepting the substitute, vaginal orgasm as a political construct is less in their interests than marriage. It takes time for women, simply because they are so much weaker politically, to build in compensations for themselves in any political construct in which they are a necessary member.

It is interesting to compare the correlative structures of these two political constructs. (I will not consider those protections built in at a later date into marriage so that the two constructs can be compared in their original and definitive forms.) The salient feature of both is that both constructs are in the interests of the male and against the interests

---

2. This article is not on the interdependence of the two political constructs of marriage and the family, but the comments on the biological theory contained in the construct of marriage assumes this interdependence. The goal of the institution of sexual intercourse, i.e., childbearing by women, is the bridge between the two constructs of marriage and family. If this article were not concentrating on political constructs by definition limited to two persons and as pertains to the institution of sexual intercourse, it might be more accurate to refer to the marriage-family construct. At the present time and in the foreseeable future, without the construct of the family, the marriage construct would serve no political purpose, i.e., there would be nothing to protect, and it would evolve out.

of the female, and both constructs were, not surprisingly, conceived of by men. Both constructs limit a woman's human possibilities (the double standard is built into any double-role theory). Both constructs incorporate attempted justifications (excuses?) for the role assigned to women in sexual intercourse, which however in no way mitigates the initial exploitation.

1. Both constructs contain conveniently supportive unknown or unrecognized biological theories:

A. In marriage the supportive biological theory is the theory of maternal instinct. The biological argument for the maternal instinct goes something like this: Women *need* to have children, it's part of their *nature*. Can't you see that that's what their bodies were built for? And if women didn't *like* to have children, they wouldn't; this proves women *choose* to have children. And since they choose to have children in such large numbers, having children must come naturally to women. It's an *instinct*, the *maternal* instinct.

(i.) There's a confusion of priorities here: a capacity for some activity is not the same as a need for that activity, so that even if women's bodies *were* suitably formed for the activity of childbearing, this in no way necessarily entails that they *want* to bear children, much less need to. Unfortunately for women, childbearing wreaks havoc on their bodies and can hardly be defended as healthy. (a) Pregnancy and birth distend and tear women's bodies out of their natural forms as women (as opposed to mothers), so that it hardly can be held that women's bodies are constructed appropriately for the activity of childbearing. (b) Reliable estimates indicate that in the United States, the *maternal* death rate was 29.1 out of every 1,000, the *female* death rate in 1966 was 8.1 out of every 1,000 (*U.S. Vital Statistics*). Maternity triples the risk of death for the average woman in the years of her pregnancy. The maternal death rate for the entire world in 1966 was at least twice that of the United States, so that the average woman, appropriately enough, sextupled her chance of death by becoming pregnant (UN figures). There is no other activity in the world, short of war, with that high a mortality rate that would be legalized. (It's interesting, albeit chilling, that the maternal death rate is almost never publicized, whereas the infant mortality rate is often seen: This is another indication of the low value placed on women.)

(ii.) At this point, it might be countered that while it might not make *sense* to engage in such an activity as pregnancy, that this is proof that maternity is indeed an instinct: It is an activity engaged in in spite of its being contrary to the interest of the agent.

(It is easy to see how nicely this argument feeds the theory of innate masochism into female psychology. The institutional strangleholds that coerce women into childbearing are always overlooked here, but it is in fact these institutions that transform the alleged maternal instinct from what would appear to be a kind of death wish into an instinct for her own political survival.)

It is claimed then that women enjoy having or, at least, wish to have children. The evidence is against this, too. (a) Does anyone wish to try to hold that the blood-curdling screams that can be heard from delivery rooms are really cries of joy? (b) How are you going to account for the fact that as much as two-thirds of the women bearing children suffer postpartum blues, and that these depressions are expressed in large numbers by these women killing their infants, or deserting them, or internalizing their hostility to such an extent that the woman must be confined in mental hospitals for "severe depression" (often a euphemism for attempted murder). Either it's necessary to fall back on some physiological explanation which will irrevocably damage the claim that childbearing is good for a woman's health, or it's necessary to admit that an overwhelming number of women do not *like* to bear children regardless of whether or not there is some theory that it is a woman's natural function to bear children. (c) As for women wishing to possess children, it will be necessary to account for the fact that parents (and we all know who that is) are the second highest cause of children's deaths ("accidents" rank first). If the theory is still maintained that women by their nature like to have, or take care of, children, and that this constitutes at least a necessary part of what is called "maternal instinct," it would seem that it is the duty of men, i.e., society, to protect children from women's care just because of this instinct.

(iii.) It seems clear that there is far too large a body of counter evidence to try to maintain any biological theory of maternal instinct.

B. In vaginal orgasm, the supportive biological theory is that the institution of sexual intercourse is in the interests of woman's sexual instinct. The argument goes something like this: Man has a sexual instinct, and we know this because men like to have sexual intercourse so much. Since his desire for sexual intercourse is not determined by the recipient, it must be the activity itself which is desired. The activity is defined essentially as the penetration by the penis into the vagina. But the man may have an intense experience, called "orgasm," caused by some activity of his own within the particular environment of the vagina. The completion of his experience, or orgasm, is indicated by certain signs, e.g., ejaculation. This experience has been judged by society to be pleasurable. The environment of the vagina is necessary for sexual intercourse. Either a woman must be forced to provide this environment or it must be in her interests to do so. It's illegal to force her: that's called rape. Therefore, it must be in her interest to provide this environment. Therefore, it must be that she experiences the same experience that the man does because of the same activity. This will be called vaginal orgasm to distinguish it from the original sense of "orgasm," i.e., male orgasm. And it is pleasurable for the woman. If it is the same experience as the male orgasm, there should be no discrepancy between either the amount or conditions of the experience. Therefore, women also have a sexual instinct.

(i.) The maternal instinct is obviously too indirect an interest to justify sexual intercourse to a free woman. There has to be some direct connection between the act and the woman's interests. As exterior coercion lessens, it must be projected inside the victim.

(ii.) The construct of vaginal orgasm as even a second order biological need for women has been absurd from the beginning. First of all, animals don't have this need, that is, they don't have vaginal orgasm. The whole point of vaginal orgasm is that it supports the view that vaginal penetration is a good in and for itself. It justifies vaginal penetration, i.e., a necessary condition of the institution of sexual intercourse, as in the direct interests of women. Since a necessary condition for a biological need is that it cover the species of mammals, the fact that animals do not experience vaginal orgasm is an extremely strong argument against its biological nature. Secondly, women don't possess the receptors in the vagina for any sensations that could *cause* anything like a male orgasm, that is, what has been proposed as vaginal orgasm.

2. Both the construct of marriage and the construct of vaginal orgasm contain conveniently supportive psychological theories to justify the institution of sexual intercourse to the female. These psychological theories are dependent on their respective physiological theories; without the biological basis, the psychological theory, instead of justifying, exposes the exploitative nature of the institution of sexual intercourse.

A. In marriage, the psychological theory is an analysis of the psychological characteristics inherent in the alleged maternal instinct. This varies somewhat from time to time depending on what sacrifices society deems necessary from the parent to keep the child in line, and how the political system needs, or regards as a liability, women in the outside world. The main constants are that woman, i.e., a mother, whether actual or potential, is adaptable and giving. It is the woman's role in marriage to meet the needs of others, and her joy to do so. But in the circular argument of the marriage construct, the woman's role is called her will and from there is transformed into her essential nature.

B. In vaginal orgasm, the psychological theory is based on the assumption of the physiological fact of vaginal orgasm, and the further assumption that that orgasm is caused not psychologically but physiologically by the penetration of the penis into the vagina. There is an equivocation at this point in the argument for the theory that even further assumes that what was defined by a male as vaginal orgasm is analogous to the orgasm the male experiences by penetration. It is only by claiming some such responsive equivalence that the institution of sexual intercourse can be justified between free parties.

So far here, sexual intercourse has been referred to as an institution. Since our society has never known a time when sex in all its aspects was not exploitative and relations based on sex, e.g., the male-female relationship, were not extremely hostile, it is difficult to understand how sexual intercourse can even be salvaged as a practice, that is, assuming that our society would desire positive relationships between individuals.

The first step that would have to be taken before we could see exactly what the status of sexual intercourse is as a practice is surely to remove all its institutional aspects: We would have to eliminate the functional aspect. Sexual intercourse would have to cease to be society's means to population renewal. This change is beginning to be within our grasp with the work now being done on extrauterine conception and incubation. But the possibilities of this research for the woman's movement have been barely suggested and there would have to be very concentrated research to perfect as quickly as possible this extrauterine method of pre-natal development so that this could be a truly optional method, at the very least.

This step alone would reduce sexual intercourse, in terms of its political status, to a practice. But the biological theories as well as the psychological ones would fall with the institutional purposes: Sexual "drives" and "needs" would disappear with their functions. But since a practice must have some sort of structure, and without a social function sexual relations would be individually determined and socially unpatterned, sexual intercourse could not be a practice either.

It is necessary to at least speculate on just what the status or place of sexual relations would be once the institutional aspects disappeared. If for no other reason, it is necessary to figure out some sort of projection because an idea like this frightens people so badly. Because of the implications of such a change, people must have some idea of a possible future. It should still be understood, however, that such projections must be very tentative guesswork because so many possible variables could appear later that can't be foreseen now.

Having lost their political function, one possibility is that perhaps we could discover what the nature of the human sensual characteristics are from the point of view of the good of each individual instead of what we have now which is a sort of psychological draft system of our sexualities. Perhaps the human sensual characteristics would have the status of a sense organ; they might even properly be called a sort of "sixth sense." This sense organ, like the other five, would receive stimuli via the brain and the more direct contact appropriate to that sense. In the case of the sexual organs (although they would probably not be called that anymore since the term "sexual organs" assumes two sexes: the purpose of transforming that distinction into a definitive property has been the procreative function of the sexual organs), the direct stimuli would be tactile and the indirect stimuli would be the thought of someone or something that you would like to touch or be touched by.

Now since, for the sake of the argument, we will assume that the direct stimulus is a living being, even a human being, and that this human being is other than the human being stimulated, and that the procreative function of the activity is absent even in the concept of the activity (that is, it is not regarded as a practice since it is not a structured activity), why should there be this tactile contact with another person? We assume at this point that sexual contact is not a biological need and was formerly only the means to satisfy the social need of survival of the species.

It will be argued no doubt that this tactile contact is pleasurable. But what exactly is meant by this? Why is it more pleasurable than auto-contact? In whose interest is this physical contact between two persons, and what are the grounds of this interest? If masturbation has such strong arguments in its favor (assuming the sexual organs are a kind of sense organ) such as technical proficiency, convenience, egocentricity, on what grounds is an outside party involved? On what grounds is this party a positive addition to the experience?

Must this alleged pleasure be mutual? And if so, why? What motivates the desire to touch other people, and without the procreative function of sex, what would distinguish (for the average person) touching a child and touching an adult in whom one had an alleged "sexual" interest. Would you want to make an important distinction between an erotic and a sexual contact? Isn't it crucial to the argument for tactile contact as innately pleasurable whether or not you can hold the claim that touching the other person is directly pleasurable to the toucher, not only indirectly pleasurable to the toucher by witnessing the pleasure of the touched? How could it be claimed that the fingertips are as sensitive as the alleged erogenous areas of the body? Or would you have to establish some separate but equal, synchronized system of mutual indirect/direct stimuli? But wouldn't that force you back into a practice, and under what justification? Wouldn't you be institutionalizing sex again? Given the nature of sex, once you deinstitutionalize it and it has no social function, and there is no longer any need for a cooperative effort, and when the physical possibilities of this sense can be fully realized alone, on what possible grounds could you have anything remotely like what we know today as sexual relations?

If the sense of touch alone were under discussion, it would be surely less complicated simply because there would be only one, in any way relevant to our discussion, fluctuating (i.e., changeable) party. And even more important to any ethical consideration, it wouldn't matter whether the touched wished to be touched. (The constructs of marriage and of vaginal orgasm as supportive practices to the institution of sexual intercourse are both based on the assumption that "it wouldn't matter whether or not the touched wished to be touched." The construct of vaginal orgasm differs from marriage only in that the coercive aspect is internalized in the female.)

The important distinction between "the sense of touch" and what is being called here the "sixth sense," the "sense of *being* touched," or the "sense of feeling," is the addition of a strong passive element. Since what is being received cannot be a technical or physical improvement

---

on that same auto-experience, any positive external component must be a psychological component. It must be some attitude or judgment held by the person doing the touching, or the agent, about the person being touched, that is satisfactory to the person being touched most of the time and at other times is supportive to the person being touched. In short, the agent is trusted to either add to or to reinforce and diffuse the pleasure of the sensual experience. The contribution of the agent is firstly to extend the area of the sensual experience in the quite literal way of touching the recipient's body and being touched by it; this reinforces the auto-erotic sense by extending the feelings of pleasure and of well-being. The second, more important, contribution is that the recipient must make a psychological extension from the agent touching and giving pleasure and the attitude of good will the recipient deduces from that action to the outside world and its attitude toward the recipient. The extension of the recipient's intention for its own pleasure to the world's intentions toward the recipient must be at least one good motive for the socialization of the sensual experience.

The most difficult component to define in this projected, seemingly gratuitously, cooperative act is the psychological attitude of the participants each to the other. What is it about this psychological attitude, the two attitudes together transmitted through various physical contact being the relationship, that could render the two-party experience (1) relevant to what is essentially an independent experience, and (2) an improvement upon such an independent experience?

The first step might be to determine what the components of such a cooperative experience would be: two individuals and their respective erotic sensibilities. Since neither individual can *add* to the physical experience of the other, it must be that the contribution is a mental one, that it consists of the agent forming certain concepts and expressing these concepts in statements to the recipient. These statements, or thoughts, are not translated into a verbal medium but into a medium of gestures (or physical actions). These gestures are most fully understood when they are received directly, that is, in physical contact, by the person to whom they are addressed. This is because of the nature of the language, that it is not primarily heard but *felt* through being touched.

The most plausible explanation for a theory of cooperative sensual experience is probably some theory of psychic language, that is, a mime expressive of the agent's attitude toward the recipient and transcribed into gestures appropriate to a particular experience. (It must be remembered that this is the roughest sketch of some alternatives to institutionalized sex.) Some account must be given of this language which would be common to many different cultural languages, such as that it is emotive, that it is expressed by touch; some account must be given of its structure, whether some attitudes are required or some emotions must be expressed before someone could claim the use of the language; some account must be given of how the concept of style is relevant to the language, at what point do you have a dialect? what would count as a metaphor?

The agent is present to convey certain feelings. Assuming a healthy relationship, it's probably safe to say that these feelings would be positive toward the recipient. But what would "positive" mean? It would have to satisfy the recipient, since the gesture would be received by that person and simultaneously interpreted. But why would such feelings have to be expressed by touching instead of verbally? What is significant about the connection between certain emotions and the sense of touch? But most important, what is the significance of this combination to the recipient?

How is the expression of approval related to the sensual experience? It must mean something that it is a joining of extreme examples of the public (approval being a conventional judgment) and of the private (the auto-erotic). It must be that this mime has a symbolic aspect, and that in this essentially private act the outside participant expresses by its presence an identification with the recipient's feelings for itself. This could serve as a reinforcement to the ego and to a generalization from the attitude of the agent toward the recipient to the attitude of the public as a whole toward the recipient.

These are only a few suggestions. Our understanding of the sense of feeling, or intuition, is almost nonexistent, and few people probably even realize that there is such a sense. It is as if our understanding of the sense of sight were modeled on the experience of being punched in the eye instead of on experiences such as seeing a Tunisian watercolor from Paul Klee. One might infer the possibility of assault from the art but not the possibility of art from the assault. We are unfortunately in the latter position, and there's not much hope of inferring an understanding of the sense of feeling from the institution of sexual intercourse. It has to be approached from some other direction. I have tried to suggest a possibility.

16

THE REALITIES OF LESBIANISM

DEL MARTIN and PHYLLIS LYON

The lesbian minority in America, which may run as high as 10 million women, is probably the least understood of all minorities and the most downtrodden. She has two strikes on her from the start; she is a woman and she is a homosexual, a minority scorned by the vast majority of people in our country. If, in addition, she is a member of a racial minority, it is hard sometimes to understand how she survives.

A lesbian is a woman who prefers another woman as a sexual partner; a woman who is drawn erotically to women rather than to men. This definition includes women who have never experienced overt sexual relations with a woman—the key word is "prefers." There is really no other valid way to define the lesbian, for outside of the sexual area she is as different in her actions, dress, status and behavior as anyone else. Just as there is no typical heterosexual woman, neither is there any typical lesbian.

However, there is a popular misconception, or stereotype, of the lesbian. She is believed to embody all the worst masculine attributes of toughness, aggressiveness, lack of emotion, lack of sentiment, overemphasis on sex, lack of stability—the need and desire to dress as a man or, at least, as much like a man as possible.

At some time in her life the lesbian may fit this stereotype—usually when she is very young and just finding out about herself. After all, the lesbian is a product of her heterosexual environment and all she has to go on, at her first awareness of lesbian feeling in herself, is society's image. Part of the reason for her overmasculinization is the sexual identity of being attracted to women. At this point the lesbian feels that in order to be attractive to another woman she must appear masculine. Another reason is for identification purposes. How will she meet other lesbians? How will they know her to be one of them unless she indicates herself in her outward appearance? A third reason is one of releasing her hostility against society, of defying the mores which she finds stifling to what she considers her very being. A fourth reason is comfort. Any woman who says that girdles and high heels are comfortable is simply lying.

While it is true that occasionally a lesbian gets trapped in this way of life (emulation of the male) and never finds her way to being a person rather than a symbol, the vast majority pass through this phase and learn to accept their femininity. As a lesbian she comes to realize she is a human being first, a woman second, and a lesbian only third. Unfortunately, however, society places the emphasis on the third—sexual identification—and does not acknowledge the lesbian as a woman or a person.

But the average lesbian (if there can be anything approaching "average" in our very complex world) is indistinguishable from other women in dress, in manner, in goals and desires, in actions and in interests. The difference lies only in that she looks to women for her emotional and sexual fulfillment. She is a member of the family—a distant cousin, or perhaps, a maiden aunt. But more than likely she's closer to home—maybe a daughter, a wife and mother, a grandmother or a sister. She may work in an office, in a factory production line, in the public school system, at the corner grocery. She is not bound by lines of class distinction or educational level, race or religion.

What causes a woman to become a lesbian? How can it be that two sisters, raised by the same parents in the same home, can turn in two different directions—one toward heterosexuality, the other toward homosexuality? Very simply, the answer is that no one knows. A great deal of research and study has been done in this country on the male homosexual, but very little has been done on the lesbian. The reason for this, we suspect, lies in the status of women in our country. Because the male—masculinity—is so highly valued, it has been deemed to be imperative to search out the reasons for any deviation from this American norm. Also, the majority of persons working in research are men. Research on the lesbian has, for the most part, been confined to women who were either psychiatric patients or in prison—which hasn't made for a very full or accurate picture.

Nevertheless, if you begin reading about the "causes" of homosexuality you will find that, as in the Bible, the answer you want to find will be somewhere. Each "expert" on the subject presents a different "cause." Our feeling, which is supported by a growing number of professional persons, is that homosexuality (in both men and women) is merely one dimension of the vastly complicated and varied spectrum of human sexuality. There has always been homosexuality; it has appeared in almost every culture in recorded history; it occurs in every species of animal.

Perhaps the most logical and least hysterical of all statements about homosexuality is the following made by Dr. Joel Fort, psychiatrist and public health specialist; Dr. Evelyn G. Hooker, research psychologist at the University of California at Los Angeles; Dr. Joe K. Adams, psychologist and former mental health officer in California. The statement, made in August 1966, is as follows:

> Homosexuals, like heterosexuals, should be treated as individual human beings, not as a special group, either by law or social agencies or employers.
>
> Laws governing sexual behavior should be reformed to deal only with clearly antisocial behavior, such as behavior involving violence or youth. The sexual behavior of individual adults by mutual consent in private should not be a matter of public concern.
>
> Some homosexuals, like some heterosexuals, are ill; some homosexuals, like some heterosexuals, are preoccupied with sex as a way of life. But probably for a majority of adults their sexual orientation constitutes only one component of a much more complicated life style.

Why then, if the lesbian is by and large indistinguishable from other women and if her sexuality is not abnormal, does she face such genuine problems in her search for self-fulfillment? For struggle she does against myriad obstacles presented to her by a hostile society. Through our work with the Daughters of Bilitis, Inc., a lesbian organization started in San Francisco in 1955, we have talked to literally thousands of lesbians (and almost as many male homosexuals). And, although each case is different, each person individual, through all is a searching for self-identity and self-fulfillment to the utmost of the person's ability.

Consider the stereotyped "box" most women in this country are placed in from birth: that of becoming wife and mother, nothing else. Consider then, the girl brought up in this box who finds her sexual identification to be lesbian. How then express the "wife-and-mother" role? This conflict often starts the process of self-searching which goes on for years and which, for some, is never resolved.

Toward a Quaker View of Sex, which came out of England and is more enlightened than most religious treatises on male homosexuality, fails utterly in its chapter on the female homosexual. The only statement with which we can agree is the first sentence: "Homosexuality is probably as common in women as it is in men." The Quaker view of the lesbian is apparently that of the wishy-washy, namby-pamby old maid who holds hands with another old maid (or preferably an adoring younger girl, if available) because she never was able to catch a man and fulfill her deep yearning for the rewards of the pangs of childbirth. At least the American stereotype of the predatory, aggressive masculine woman has a little more color!

The Quaker view indicates that woman's prime requisite is her "maternal tenderness," that her only reason for being is to have babies, and that the lesbian is warped and frustrated because she isn't doing her fair share toward the population explosion. To this question of maternity we must point out that the mere possession of biological machinery to produce babies has no correlation whatever with the attributes of motherhood. Let's face it—many women can have babies but make lousy mothers.

The art of motherhood in the human species is not instinctual. It is learned. We have courses in the care of the baby, and there are countless books on the market to help the young mother with the problems she may encounter during the course of her child's growth and development. In some cultures, babies are taken from the mothers and raised by the community without any apparent psychically traumatic results for the biological mothers or their offspring. In other cultures it is the male who tends the young.

It simply does not follow, then, that every lesbian is suffering untold qualms because she is frustrating her "natural" birthright for giving birth. There are many other ways for women to contribute creatively to society, and at this particular point in the history of the population of our globe, they may also be highly desirable. The lesbian who does feel frustrated because she doesn't have any children of her own may work in the teaching profession, she may be a playground director or a social worker who comes in contact with families and children. But the majority of lesbians we have known have not expressed in any way the "void" they feel because they have no children. To the contrary, the expression, "I would prefer to lead a heterosexual life if I could," is much more apt to come from the male homosexual than from the female.

It must be said, however, that there are many lesbians who are raising children—some successfully, some not so successfully. The rate of success is, of course, determined by the degree of self-acceptance and self-assurance of the mother, and the permanence and stability of her relationship to her lesbian partner. It takes guts, grit, and determination. For if a mother is determined to be a lesbian the courts will assume she is an "unfit mother" on the face of it and take her children away from her. It seems children must have the protection of heterosexuals, regardless. The fact that *all homosexuals are products of heterosexuality* seems to escape those who would judge the homosexual relationship.

The teen-age lesbian has a particular problem which has not been met. Homophile organizations, like the Daughters of Bilitis, have had to refuse membership to those under twenty-one for fear that they will be charged with "contributing to the delinquency of a minor." The teen-ager has no one to turn to. Society thinks only in terms of counseling of the variety that would tend toward reestablishing the sexual identity in a heterosexual vein, and the teen-age lesbian is whisked off by her parents to the family doctor or clergyman to put a stop to this nonsense. However, in the cases that have come to our attention, the teen-ager has no doubt about her sexual orientation. What she wants to know is what to do about it. She wants to meet others like herself; she wants to socialize and to discuss the problems she faces. She is looking for lesbian models, those who have worked out their problems and have established long-term relationships.

When she is denied this social outlet, she very often winds up in unsavory areas of a city like the Tenderloin in San Francisco. There she may find other youth, but she also finds herself in the company of prostitutes, pimps, drug addicts and dope peddlers. There have been several attempts in various cities to set up coffee houses where there is dancing for the teen-age homosexual. But they have lacked the influential backing of, say, the church, to provide protection against police harassment while creating a wholesome social fabric for the teen-age homosexual.

Because of the absence of role models in working out her way of life, and because the only marriage she has known is that of Mom and Dad, the young lesbian usually gets hung up in the "butch-femme" syndrome in her early relationships. It is only with painful experience that she learns the lesbian is attracted to a woman—not a cheap imitation of a man. The lasting lesbian liaison (and there are many) is one based on mutuality of concern, love, companionship, responsibility, household chores, outside interests, and sex.

The successful lesbian relationship cannot be based on society's exaggerated male-female, dominant-passive roles, as depicted in the flood of lesbian novels on the newsstands which are, for the most part, written by men for heterosexual male consumption. It is the realization that, contrary to cultural myths, all human beings have both feminine and masculine traits and that a person has to find her own identity as a woman and as a partner in this love relationship that makes for success. The fact that lesbian relationships are generally long-lasting without benefit of religious ceremony or legal sanction is indicative of a strong bond of love and respect which sees the couple through all the obstacles society places in their way.

Fortunately for all women, there is a growing awareness in this country that a woman needs, and is more openly demanding, an identity for herself as a human being, an identity over and beyond the societal role of housewife and mother. This awareness, coupled with more openness about sexuality and homosexuality, is making it easier now for the young girl, newly aware of her lesbianism, to cope with the negative sanctions of society. But it is still true that in most areas of our country she has no place to turn for counsel, no one with whom she can talk about her feelings without running the very real risk that the counselor will turn away from her with horror and revulsion.

The Quakers state: "Female homosexuality is free from the legal and, to a large extent, the social sanctions which are so important in the problems of male homosexuals." This is a myth that even the male homosexual has come to believe. It is true that in England there were never any laws pertaining to female homosexuality. But this is not true in the United States. The lesbian is just as subject to the sanctions of certain laws as the male homosexual; she is just as subject to arrest when she sets foot in a "gay bar"; she is just as subject to blackmail and police harassment. The stigma attached to homosexuality has just as much effect on the lesbian as she tries to deal with fear and society-imposed guilt in the problem areas of employment, family relationships, and religion. Just because the record of arrests is so much smaller is no indication that the lesbian is relatively free from legal or social sanction. It only means that she is less obvious and less promiscuous. She has done a better job of covering up.

Lesbian problems we have dealt with over the years include the

---

twenty-year-old driven to thoughts of suicide because she could not resolve the conflict between her identity as a lesbian and as a Christian. Or the forty-year-old mother who telephoned Daughters of Bilitis 3,000 miles across the country to break "18 years of silence" after reading a book called *The Grapevine* by Jess Stearn. Then there was the nurse with a "perfect work record" in a federal hospital who was interrogated by a government investigator, flown from Washington, D.C., at the tax-payers' expense, because someone wrote to a Congressman accusing her of being a lesbian.

There was the nineteen-year-old who was trying to find out what homosexuality was all about because she was drummed out of the armed services on a charge she didn't understand. The daughter who receives a monthly allowance from her wealthy family in the Midwest to stay on the coast lest her district attorney father be threatened with a "family skeleton" by his political foes. And the twenty-five-year-old who, after five years of psychiatric therapy, decides she must make the best of herself as herself—a lesbian.

The most serious problem a lesbian faces in life is that of self-accept-ance. Like everyone else, she has been taught the cultural folklore that a lesbian is something less than human—a sick, perverted, illegal, immoral animal to be shunned and despised. Needless to say, with the first glimmering of self-knowledge, of awareness that she has lesbian tendencies, she becomes bogged down in doubt, fear, guilt, and hostility.

Some lesbians claim they have been aware of their lesbianism since early childhood. Others first become aware during adolescence. Yet there are some women who make this discovery about themselves much later in life—after they have been married and have had children. Still others, either by choice or lack of opportunity, never admit or act out their lesbianism.

It isn't easy for a woman to say to herself, let alone anyone else, "I am a lesbian." But once the words are said, has she really changed? Isn't she still the same person she was—the dear friend, the competent employee, the loving sister? And yet the words become a barrier in her personal and working relationships. To protect her family and her job, she is forced to live a lie, to take on a dual life. No wonder many lesbians seek out some type of psychiatric or therapeutic help. The miracle is that so many are able to function so well and to contribute so much to society.

The lesbian is thus a secretive, chameleon creature. She is not easily recognized. The old adage, "It takes one to know one," is not true. Not being distinguishable from other women, she has difficulty meeting others like herself. The "gay bar" is still a meeting place, but there are few such bars which cater to women exclusively because they do not constitute a steady clientele. Besides, a lesbian, as a woman, has no doubt heard many times the old saw "nice girls don't go into bars," or "no lady would ever go into a bar alone." The lesbian goes out on the town only occasionally and is more apt to settle down with a partner, to build a home and a lasting relationship, and to develop a small circle of friends—usually both homosexual and heterosexual. Another social outlet for the lesbian can be homophile organizations throughout the country (if she knows about them), such as Daughters of Bilitis, which has chapters in New York and San Francisco.

The lesbian, being a woman, comes out of the same cultural pool as do heterosexual women. Therefore, on top of everything else, she may have the same hangups and inhibitions about sex, dress, work, actions, etc., as do her heterosexual sisters. Since women have been taught to be passive, to shun the role of the aggressor, the lesbian finds herself without the slightest idea of how to approach another woman for a date, for a conversation, for sex. It is a rarity for a heterosexual woman to be approached by a lesbian unless she has given much indication that such advances are welcome.

Even when the lesbian accepts her sexual identity and herself as a person, she still faces very real discrimination from society. If she has educated herself to a profession (a role doubly difficult for any woman), she can lose her professional status merely because someone points a finger. This is especially true of teachers, attorneys, doctors, social workers, and other professions licensed by the state. But it can also be true for file clerks and secretaries. Very few employers are aware enough to realize that in the lesbian he has an employee who must work, who will not get married or pregnant, who will devote her energies and capabilities to her job because she will always have to support herself.

As Rabbi Elliot Grafman has stated, "People fear that which they do not understand, and what they fear they despise." It is only through more knowledge and more personal confrontation that the stereotype of the lesbian can be dispelled. However, to accomplish this feat is to overcome the vicious circle that now envelops the lesbian who tries to be honest.

If she divulges her identity, she automatically becomes vulnerable. She faces loss of job, family, and friends. Yet, until she opens herself to such possibilities, no one will have the opportunity to come to know and to understand her as the whole person she is.

Through the Council on Religion and the Homosexual, which was formed in San Francisco in 1964 after a three-day retreat attended by clergymen and male and female representatives of the homophile community, such a dialogue began in earnest. Avenues of communication have been opened up not only with the religious community (seminaries and other church groups), but with governmental agencies, the police, business and professional groups, college and high school students. But the task of demythologizing, of education and redefinition of the homosexual is a long and arduous one.

17

ON CELIBACY

DANA DENSMORE

One hangup to liberation is a supposed "need" for sex. It is something that must be refuted, coped with, demythified, or the cause of female liberation is doomed.

Already we see girls, thoroughly liberated in their own heads, understanding their oppression with terrible clarity trying, deliberately and a trace hysterically, to make themselves attractive to men, men for whom they have no respect, men they may even hate, because of "a basic sexual-emotional need."

Sex is not essential to life, as eating is. Some people go through their whole lives without engaging in it at all, including fine, warm, happy people. It is a myth that this makes one bitter, shriveled up, twisted.

The big stigma of lifelong virginity is on women anyway, created by men because woman's purpose in life is biological and if she doesn't fulfill that she's warped and unnatural and "must be all cobwebs inside."

Men are suspected at worst of being self-centered or afraid of sex, but do not carry any stigma of being unnatural. A man's life is taken as a whole on its merits. He was busy, it may be thought, dedicated, a great man who couldn't spare the time and energy for demanding relationships with women.

The guerrillas don't screw. They eat, when they can, but they don't screw. They have important things to do, things that require all their energy.

Everyone of us must have noticed occasions when he was very involved in something, fighting, working, thinking, writing, involved to the extent that eating was haphazard, sleeping deliberately cheated. But the first thing that goes is sex. It's inconvenient, time consuming, energy draining, and irrelevant.

We are programmed to crave sex. It sells consumer goods. It gives a lift and promises a spark of individual self-assertion in a dull and routinized world. It is a means to power (the only means they have) for women.

It is also, conversely, a means of power for men, exercized over women, because her sexual desire is directed to men.

Few women ever are actually satisfied, of course, but they blame the particular man and nurse the myth that they can be satisfied and that this nirvana is one which a man and only a man can bring her.

Moreover, sexual freedom is the first freedom a woman is awarded and she thinks it is very important because it's all she has; compared to the dullness and restrictiveness of the rest of her life it glows very brightly.

But we must come to realize that sex is actually a minor need, blown out of proportion, misunderstood (usually what passes for sexual need is actually desire to be stroked, desire for recognition or love, desire to conquer, humiliate, or wield power, or desire to communicate).

We must come to realize that we don't need sex, that celibacy is not a dragon but even a state that could be desirable, in many cases preferable to sex. How repugnant it really is, after all, to make love to a man who despises you, who fears you and wants to hold you down!

Doesn't screwing in an atmosphere devoid of respect get pretty grim? Why bother? You don't need it.

Erotic energy is just life energy and is quickly worked off if you are doing interesting, absorbing things. Love and affection and recognition can easily be found in comrades, a more honest and open love that loves you for yourself and not for how docile and cute and sexy and ego building you are, a love in which you are always subject, never merely object, always active, never merely relative. And if despite all this genital tensions persist you can still masturbate. Isn't that a lot easier anyway?

This is a call not for celibacy but for an acceptance of celibacy as an honorable alternative, one preferable to the degradation of most male-female sexual relationships. But it is only when we accept the idea of celibacy completely that we will ever be able to liberate ourselves.

Until we accept it completely, until we say, "I control my own body and I don't need any insolent male with an overbearing presumptuous prick to come and clean out my pipes," they will always have over us the devastating threat of withdrawing their sexual attentions and worse, the threat of our ceasing even to be sexually attractive.

And that devastating rejection is absolutely inevitable. If you are serious and men realize it they will cease being attracted to you.

If you don't play the game, the role, you are not a woman and they will *not* be attracted. You will be sexless and worse, unnatural and threatening.

You will be feared and despised and viciously maligned, all by men you know perfectly well you could charm utterly and wrap around your finger just by falling into the female role, even by men who have worshiped you in the past.

How is that possible? Obviously, because they never were worshiping you. That's the bitter truth, and you'd better catch on now.

Whenever they're nice to us, it isn't us they're being nice to but their own solipsistic creations, the versions of us they manufacture for their own amusement and pleasure and purposes. How presumptuous it is of us to accept the love and admiration, to crave it even, as if it were meant for us!

It's their female ideal they adore and they will be resentful and angry if you mar that image and will turn against you to a man if you try to destroy it.

Unless you accept the idea that you don't need them, don't need sex from them, it will be utterly impossible for you to carry through, it will be absolutely necessary to lead a double life, pretending with men to be something other than what you know you are. The strain of this would be unimaginable and could end in any number of disastrous ways.

You, who have had such heady power to charm and arouse and win men's total admiration and respect, must be willing to give it up. You must be willing that they cease to be attracted to you, even find you repulsive, that they cease to respect you, even despise you, that they cease to admire you, even find you unnatural and warped and perverted sexually.

These men who were so tenderly protective will try to destroy you, to stab you in the back, to use any underhanded means to get back at you for posing this threat to them. You have done them the incalculable offense of not deferring to their sex, of daring to be yourself (putting your needs ahead of his), of stepping out of your role, of rejecting the phony sexual differentiations that make each of them feel like a man.

If you don't act like a woman he doesn't see himself as a man, since his sexual identity depends on the differences, and so he feels actually castrated. Expect no love, no desire, no mercy from this man.

You have to be prepared, then, to be not just unattractive but actually sexually repulsive to most men, perhaps including all the men you currently admire.

We've spent many years learning to be appealing to men, to all men, whether we are specifically interested in them or not. We dress, we walk, we laugh, we talk, we move our hands and our heads, we sit, we speak, all in a way carefully cultivated to be feminine and charming.

We need to be thought charming and appealing even by men who bore us or repulse us, by strangers who may be trying to pick us up; we have a horror of appearing vulgar and repulsive even to the most nauseating creep. The creeps must all be brushed off gracefully, in a way that leaves their egos intact and consequently leaves them with a friendly impression of us.

It's so important that our image be favorable, we are willing to put up with the fact that it is false, distorted, that we are being loved for our weaknesses, or for qualities we don't have at all, and our strengths are denied or ridiculed.

If we are going to be liberated we must reject the false image that makes men love us, and this will make men cease to love us.

Unless we can accept this we will crumble under the first look of fear and disgust; or certainly under the first such look from a man we love and admire.

Ultimately, of course, we will cease to love and admire such men. We will have contempt for men who show that they cannot love us for ourselves, men whose egos demand and require falsehoods.

It will be a less friendly world, but there will be no unrequited longing. What we're really after is to be loved for ourselves and if that's impossible, why should we care about love at all? Friends and enemies will be clearly lined up, and the friends will be real friends and the enemies unable to hide behind phony benevolence—nor will we have to toady to them.

An end to this constant remaking of ourselves according to what the male ego demands! Let us be ourselves and good riddance to those who are then repulsed by us!

August 1968

C

Birth Control
Concern about environmental pollution and depletion of resources has rekindled the long-standing discussion and debate regarding the concept of "optimum population." One question of great interest nationally centers on the determination of the best means to further reduce fertility levels. The adequacy of voluntary public family-planning programs as a population control measure is being questioned because most Americans are already effective users of birth-control methods and want three or four children which is more than is necessary for replacement.[1] The philosophy behind Planned Parenthood stresses that parents—and not the state or some organization—shall have freedom to bear whatever number of children they want, when they are wanted. This philosophy simply does not solve the problem of too many wanted children even though the small family is advocated among many family planners.

In contrast to the "average" American, the poor in our society are not effective practitioners of birth-control methods. There is some public interest in a policy whereby the federal government would make contraceptives available to the poor in particular in an attempt to control population growth. The fact is, however, that Planned Parenthood clinics have been generally unsuccessful in reaching the poor. There are, furthermore, certain undesirable aspects about having a population policy aimed specifically at the less advantaged.

A critical perspective of one racial minority group on national population policy is presented in the initial selection by Willie. He

1. Kingsley Davis, "Population Policy: Will Current Programs Succeed?" *Science* 158, no. 3802 (November 1967): 730–39.

indicates that there is suspicion among blacks of any national program which focuses on family planning. Militant black males in particular are concerned that such a focus represents an attempt by whites to maintain control over, and possibly exterminate, black people. Greater concern about sexism than racism, however, characterizes many black women who see in contraception a means to limit their own sexual exploitation—the genocide of black women and children.[2]

Consideration of family-planning programs as a means of increasing the freedom of women, rather than as a way to deal with poverty, pollution, and other problems, was basic to the thinking of Margaret Sanger whose ardent support for birth control early in this century was largely responsible for making Americans generally aware of contraceptive practices.[3] Her terms for birth control of "voluntary birth prevention" and "voluntary motherhood," however, have been replaced with "family planning," which implies that women using contraceptives (and women are the only people defined as family-planning "patients") are expected to become mothers. This, of course, is consistent with the pronatalism of the family as indicated importantly by the definition of sexual roles—for both men and women—as basically reproductive roles and by the definition of women's career in particular as basically childbearing and child rearing.[4] It is just such pronatalism in our society and the lack of acceptable and rewarding alternatives to motherhood which lead most women to want several children.

Despite elements of sexism in family planning, including male dominance generally in the development and distribution of contraceptives,[5] to what extent can women control their own bodies (i.e., prevent unwanted pregnancies) via contraception? There is no doubt that highly effective birth control is now possible especially through use of oral contraceptives. The pill is,

2. See, for example, Toni Cade, ed., *The Black Women* (New York: Signet Books, 1970): 162–69.

3. Margaret Sanger, *Women and the New Race* (New York: Truth Publishing, 1921).

4. Judith Blake, "Population Policy for Americans: Is the Government Being Misled?" *Science* 164, no. 3879 (May 1969): 522–29.

5. Barbara R. Bradshaw, "Sexism and Family Planning," *Women: A Journal of Liberation* 3, no. 1 (Fall 1972): 47–48.

moreover, easy to use; it does not have to be timed to intercourse and it does not delay, interrupt, or mechanically impede the sexual act. As the *Time* article indicates there are drawbacks, nevertheless, including cost, and evidence regarding side effects makes the pill an unsuitable contraceptive technique for a number of women in addition to the poor, including those with a history of breast or cervical cancer, a likelihood of clotting or circulatory problems, diabetes, or a history of migraine headaches or of jaundice during pregnancy.

Aside from oral contraceptives, of course, there are a variety of mechanical devices on the market. The failure rate with these devices is very low, especially among highly motivated women. Unfortunately, they too are unsuitable contraceptive methods for many women; namely, those who will not or cannot use them because of anatomic, psychological, or religious reasons.

A final technique, which enables women to control unwanted births, if not conception, is abortion. Since 1967 four states (New York, Washington, Alaska, and Hawaii) have liberalized their laws making a safe, legal abortion accessible at moderate cost.[6] In thirty-one other states laws permit abortion only to save the life of the mother; and in fifteen others abortion is subject to qualifications including cases in which there is danger to the woman's physical or mental health; there is risk of fetal deformity; or because the pregnancy resulted from rape or incest.[7] Restrictive laws in forty-six states, then, were recently (January 1973) voided by the U.S. Supreme Court's rulings regarding provisions of abortion laws in Texas and Georgia. According to the Court, a woman has the right of personal privacy which is qualified by state interests of setting health standards and of protecting prenatal life. This means that during the first trimester the termination of an unwanted pregnancy is the decision of a woman and her doctor. In the second trimester the states may intrude on a pregnant woman's right of privacy in order to preserve and protect her health via health regulations (e.g., legislate a stipulation that abortions be performed in hospitals and not elsewhere). In the third trimester states may proscribe abortion in the interests of

6. "Legal Abortion: How Safe? How Available? How Costly?" *Consumer Reports* 37, no. 7 (July 1972): 466–70.

7. "Abortion: What Happens Now," *Newsweek* 81, no. 6 (February 1973): 66, 69.

"potential life," except when abortion is necessary to preserve the life or health of the mother.[8]

Sweeping though it is, from a feminist perspective, this Supreme Court decision leaves many things to be desired. As Cisler warns, it, like some earlier attempts at reform, stops short of asserting that any woman can have an abortion on request. The requirements that abortions be performed by doctors and in hospitals after the initial trimester may continue to put costs beyond the reach of poor women, although some relief may be possible if paramedics are permitted to do the work under the direction of a physician. Lastly, despite a woman's own wishes, even if she has the money and the willingness of a physician, beyond a certain time in pregnancy, she can be forced by state law to bear an unwanted child.

We can expect, nevertheless, a continuation of the positive impact of legalized abortion already reported from New York and California.[9] This includes such consequences as reduced septic abortion; reduced maternal mortality and a decrease in the number of illegitimate births. The need to travel to states with liberal laws will disappear. A greater proportion of women will apply for abortion early in pregnancy and benefit from lower-risk and lower-cost procedures. Finally, it is important to note that several recent studies which attempt to define the effects of abortion on a woman's mental state conclude generally what feminists have known all along—that the mental health of most women, especially the "normal" ones, is improved by their abortion.

---

8. "The Abortion Revolution," *Newsweek* 81, no. 6 (February 1973): 27–28.

9. "Health, Social Impact of Legalized Abortion," *Family Planning Digest* 1, no. 4 (July 1972): 13–15.

18

POPULATION POLICY AND GROWTH: PERSPECTIVES FROM THE BLACK COMMUNITY—A POSITION PAPER

CHARLES V. WILLIE

My intention is to present a perspective on national population policy from the point of view of a social scientist who is black, has lived in both northern and southern regions of the United States, and has experienced poverty and a measure of affluence.

My name is Charles Willie. I was born in Dallas, Texas, and now live in Syracuse, New York. Currently, I am professor and chairman of the department of sociology at Syracuse University.

First, I must state categorically that many people in the black community are deeply suspicious of any family-planning program initiated by whites. You probably have heard about but not taken seriously the call by some male-dominated black militant groups for females to eschew the use of contraceptives because they are pushed in the black community as "a method of exterminating black people." While black females often take a different view about contraceptives than their male militant companions, they too are concerned about the possibility of black genocide in America.

The genocidal charge is neither "absurd" nor "hollow" as some whites have contended. Neither is it limited to residents of the ghetto, whether they be low-income black militants or middle-aged black moderates. Indeed my studies of black students at white colleges indicate that young educated blacks also fear black genocide.

This statement from a black female student in the spring of 1970 is representative of the thinking of so many other blacks. She said: "The institutions in society are so strong. The CIA is everywhere. I believe that America desires to perpetuate concentration camps for political opponents of the system of this country. People who speak out against the system are being systematically cut down—Eldridge Cleaver, the Chicago Seven, the Black Panthers." She concluded her recitation of despair with this depressing thought: "I wouldn't say that this society is against all-out genocide for black people." While there is uncertainty in her accusation, there is no mood of hope.

I designate the death of Martin Luther King, Jr. as the beginning of this serious concern among blacks about the possibility of genocide in America. There were lynchings, murders, and manslaughters in the past. But the assassination of Dr. King was too much. In Dr. King, many blacks believed they had presented their best. He was scorned, spat upon, and slain. If America could not accept Dr. King, then many felt that no black person in America was safe. For none other could match the magnificent qualities of this great man. Yet they were not enough; and so he was cut down by the bullet of a white assassin in a crime that remains mysterious, considering the help that the assassin received in escaping to a foreign land.

I dwell upon this event of our modern history because the Commission on Population Growth and the American Future must consider the present as well as the recent past, which is the context within which it must plan. This context cannot be ignored. Unless the American society can assure black people that it is committed to their survival with dignity and equality, they will refuse to cooperate with any national population plan. The Commission must demonstrate that participation in any national plan will serve the self-interests of blacks.

This Commission on Population Growth is carrying excess baggage which it did not pack and which it does not need. To some blacks, any call today by a federal commission for a national population policy, especially if it focuses on family planning, sounds similar to a call yesterday by a federal official for a national program to stabilize the black family. That call was set forth in *The Negro Family, A Case for National Action*, which was prepared by the U.S. Labor Department and published in 1965. Its chief author was Daniel Patrick Moynihan. I need not remind you of the negative reaction of blacks to the Moynihan report. Many blacks got the idea that the national policy Dr. Moynihan was pushing was designed to make over blacks in the image of whites. They got this idea from his allegation that a matriarchal family structure exists among blacks, and has seriously retarded their progress, *"because it is so out of line with the rest of the American society."* [1] In an article published later in *Daedalus*, Dr. Moynihan described the

---

1. U.S. Department of Labor, *The Negro Family* (Washington, D.C.: Government Printing Office, 1965), p. 29.

Negro family as being in a state of "unmistakable crisis." He concluded that the crisis was acute because of "the extraordinary rise in Negro population." [2]

While Dr. Moynihan may not have intended to give this impression, his two statements seem to me to call for a national policy to obliterate any family forms among blacks which might be different from the family forms found among whites. Moreover, he suggested that the nation should act fast to make over blacks in the image of whites because blacks were gaining on whites in numbers. These statements came from one who has been an intimate consultant to two presidents, including President Richard Nixon. Blacks were suspicious of Dr. Moynihan's call for a national policy which focused upon the black family. The Moynihan report on the black family therefore is excess baggage which this Commission does not need and from which it should separate itself. *The Commission should make it clear to the public that the national population policy which it is attempting to formulate is not merely an extension and a refinement of the Moynihan call for a national program to stabilize the black family.*

If the Commission on Population Growth and the American Future is to promulgate a national population policy which will gain the cooperation of black people, such a policy must gather up the goals and aspirations which blacks themselves have identified as important. A national population policy must demonstrate that it is more concerned about the *health* and *wealth* of black people than it is about the number of children they have. I am talking about a *positive population policy* which is the preferred way to deal with a negative effect.

Social scientists know that people tend to act in accordance with their beliefs. If blacks *believe* that family-planning programs are insidiously designed by whites to exterminate blacks, then blacks will not cooperate with any national population policy which focuses upon family planning only.

Let me explain why blacks believe any national program for family stability which focuses largely upon family planning is a desperation move on the part of whites to remain in control. Whites were not concerned about the family structure of blacks a century and a half ago. Then blacks were nearly one-fifth (18.4 percent) of the total population.

---

2. Daniel P. Moynihan, "The Ordeal of the Negro Family," in *The Family Life of Black People*, ed. Charles V. Willie (Columbus: Charles E. Merrill, 1970), p. 175.

This, of course, was during the age of slavery, during the 1820s. Then, blacks were not free. They were no challenge to whites. Although they represented one out of every five persons in the United States, and although the family assumed even more functions for the growth, development, and well-being of individuals then than it probably does today, American whites were not concerned about the fertility or stability of the black family. Indeed, there were attempts to breed healthy male black slaves with healthy female black slaves disregarding any family connections and even prohibiting marriage. In his famous book, *An American Dilemma*, Gunnar Myrdal wrote, "most slave owners . . . did not care about the marital state of their slaves. . . ." In fact, "the internal slave trade broke up many slave families." [3] Neither the size of the black population nor their circumstances of family life worried white Americans before black people were free.

But come the mid-1960s, when the throttle to the Freedom Movement was open and demonstrations for self-determination were going full blast, white Americans became concerned about the size and the stability of the black family. Daniel Patrick Moynihan tipped off blacks about what was in the minds of whites when he described the situation as "acute" because of the "*extraordinary* rise in Negro population." The size and stability of the black family was of no concern to white Americans when black people were enslaved. The size and stability of the black family is a cause for alarm among white Americans, requiring a national program of family control, now that black people are beginning to achieve freedom and equality.

Blacks, of course, would not claim that there has been an extraordinary rise in the black population. The black population in America has increased from 9.9 percent in 1920 to approximately 11.4 percent today—no cause for alarm. But then maybe an increase of between one and two percentage points of the total population is an extraordinary rise if one believes it is. Social scientists know that if people believe a situation is real, it tends to be real in its consequences. Sociologist Robert Merton of Columbia University has written that "self-hypnosis through one's own propaganda is a not infrequent phase of the self-fulfilling prophecy." [4]

Moreover, a population increase of one to two percentage points of

3. Gunnar Myrdal, *An American Dilemma* (New York: Harper & Row, 1944), p. 931.
4. Robert K. Merton, *Social Theory and Social Structure* (Glencoe: Free Press, 1949), p. 185.

the total creates an acute situation and is cause for alarm if the ultimate national goal is to eliminate black people; for such an increase, although small, indicates that they will not go away.

The genocidal charge of black people is anchored in good data. Blacks point out that a leading government spokesman has declared that an increase in black people of one to two percentage points of the total population is "extraordinary." Blacks also point out that whites were not concerned about their family form and size during the age of slavery. Even after the days of slavery, blacks point out that over the years the greatest contributor to family instability among the members of their race has been the death of the male spouse rather than divorce or desertion. Moreover, blacks point out that the major control upon their fertility rate in the past has been the deaths of their very young children.

Back in 1910, 27 percent of black females were members of broken families because their husbands were dead. During that same year, only 6 percent of the black families were broken because of divorce or desertion of the male spouse. Thus, death was four times more frequently a contributor to family disruption than other social causes. I should add that death of the husband was the chief cause for marital breakup for black families compared with desertion or divorce up through 1963. And death of the male spouse broke up black families more frequently than divorce and desertion combined up through 1958. Thus, divorce and desertion which were highlighted by Dr. Moynihan as reasons why a national program to stabilize the black family was needed are newcomers as chief causes of family breakup for black people. The information on trends in marital status comparing the relative contributions of death, desertion and divorce to family breakup among blacks was obtained from an article written by Dr. Reynolds Farley of the University of Michigan and may be found in a recent book which I edited on the *Family Life of Black People* (see footnote 2, p. 4).

It would seem that whites were not concerned about the stability of the black family when it was broken largely because black men were dying prematurely. It would seem that whites are concerned about the size and stability of the black family now only because the number of *black men who are dying prematurely is decreasing and the number of black children born who survive is increasing.* If you can understand the basis of the alarm among white liberals about this situation, then you can understand the basis for the charge of genocide which is made by black militants.

Essentially, I am saying what several distinguished demographers already have said. Irene Taeuber of the Office of Population Research at Princeton University, for example, has said that "the test of future population policies, planned and unplanned, will be in the speed and the completeness of the obliteration of those demographies that can be categorized by the color of the skin or the subcultures of origin." [5] In other words, Dr. Taeuber was saying that "the demography of black Americans is a product of, and component in, the demography of all Americans." [6] This must be a guiding principle for the Commission on Population Growth. Professor Kingsley Davis of the University of California at Berkeley has pointed out often in his writings and lectures that a population policy for any geographic area is a policy for the entire citizenry. My advice is that the Population Commission should avoid the pitfall of the Moynihan report. It should promulgate a national population policy for all people in the United States and not attempt to limit a policy to only a black, brown, or white segment of the people. A national policy, however, must consider the differential experiences of different population groups.

All that has been said thus far should clearly indicate that a national population policy cannot succeed if it focuses only on reproduction, family size or family planning. Analysis of past experiences has revealed that family planning, particularly with reference to size, is often a function of other socioeconomic opportunities. Clyde Kiser, an outstanding demographer with the Milbank Memorial Fund, and Myrna Frank have discovered *that black women over twenty-five years of age who have a college education or who are married to professional men tend to have a fertility rate that is much lower than that for whites of similar circumstances.*[7]

Dr. Taeuber also refers to the socioeconomic facts of life. She states that "trends in the fertility of the blacks in future years will be influenced both by rapidity of the upward economic and social movements and by that complex of factors that influences national fertility, white or black. . . ." [8]

It can be stated in general that an inverse relationship exists between

5. Irene B. Taeuber, Discussion at Milbank Round Table on Demographic Aspects of the Black Community, *The Milbank Memorial Fund Quarterly* 48, part 2 (April 1970): 37.
6. Ibid.
7. Clyde V. Kiser and Myrna E. Frank, "Factors Associated with Low Fertility of Nonwhite Women of College Attainment," in *The Family Life of Black People*, pp. 42–43.
8. Taeuber, Milbank Discussion, p. 39.

fertility and socioeconomic status factors. People of higher income, occupation, and education tend to have fewer children.

However, the association between fertility and socioeconomic factors is a bit more complex when one is dealing with blacks. Reynolds Farley of the University of Michigan tells us that among urban blacks, "after 1940, fertility rate . . . increased rapidly . . ." and that in 1960 "urban fertility rates [for blacks] were higher than those in rural areas."[9] He further points out that a general increase in fertility has occurred among blacks which has involved all social classes and concludes that this is probably due to improved health conditions resulting in decreased death rates, particularly infant and maternal mortality.[10]

The Commission should understand that blacks have begun to make only modest gains in fertility only because of increased health care. The historical adversities and recent opportunities of blacks must be taken into consideration when formulating a national population policy.

Because so little trust exists between the races in the United States, when whites speak of limiting fertility or controlling the family in any way, many blacks believe that whites are planning to return to a modified Malthusian plan which has controlled black family life in the past. Blacks know that their families have been disrupted and limited in the past because of deaths. They therefore are suspicious of any plan that does not assure them that death again, individually or collectively, will not be the chief controlling variable.

In a jocular vein, Dr. Moynihan, writing for *America* magazine, the national Catholic weekly review, said "while the rich of America do whatever it is they do, the poor are begetting children."[11]

I should point out in a not so jocular vein that many of the children begotten by the black poor in the past died before reaching manhood or womanhood and that these children are beginning to live today, so that the proportion of black people in the total population is increased by one to two percentage points of the total. The increase in fertility due to these achievements in health care therefore is no cause for alarm.

---

9. Reynolds Farley, "Fertility Among Urban Blacks," *Milbank Memorial Fund Quarterly* 48, part 2 (April 1970): 189.

10. Ibid. pp. 194–95.

11. Daniel P. Moynihan, "A Family Policy for the Nation," in *The Moynihan Report and the Politics of Controversy*, ed. Lee Rainwater and William L. Yancey (Cambridge, Mass.: MIT Press, 1967), p. 392.

Indeed, the Commission on Population Growth should urge and encourage a fertility that is not impeded by disease and death.

If the poor beget children and if the number they beget is counterproductive for the future welfare of the total nation, and if there is an inverse association between fertility and socioeconomic status, then it would seem that a national population policy should have as a major plank a program to guarantee equality in economic and educational opportunities for all people in this nation. This means that a national population policy must come out strong against racial and ethnic discrimination. Herman Miller of the U.S. Census Bureau tells us that "the average Negro earns less than the average white, even when he has the same years of schooling and does the same kind of work." This conclusion comes from the analysis of income figures which, according to Dr. Miller, "provide the unarguable evidence on which public policy should rest." [12]

It is for this reason that I conclude that a national population policy which would serve the best interests of blacks as well as the other citizens of this nation should focus not only on family planning, family size, or family stability, but also on enhancing the *health* and *wealth* of every household in America.

---

12. Herman P. Miller, *Rich Man, Poor Man* (New York: Thomas Y. Crowell, 1964), p. xxi.

19

THE PROS AND CONS OF THE PILL

FROM *TIME*, THE WEEKLY NEWSMAGAZINE

Since oral contraceptives were introduced for general prescription in 1961, at least 10 million U.S. women have taken them; about 7 million are using them now. Despite the natural assumption that such popularity must be deserved, the Pill has provoked an almost equally

---

strong countercurrent of opposition and denunciation. Anti-Pill crusaders demand that it be taken off the market, claiming that it is killing scores if not hundreds of American women every year, maiming ten times as many, and making others infertile. More than a hundred lawsuits are pending against manufacturers.

The *Ladies' Home Journal* is editorially allergic to the Pill, and has published articles under such titles as "The Terrible Trouble with the Birth-Control Pills." *McCall's* has printed a review of dropouts, called "Why They Quit the Pill." Columnist Drew Pearson reported in his more than 600 subscribing newspapers that "at least 10% of all adverse-reaction reports are fatalities and that one-third of the recent reports on one specific pill involve death."

Such impassioned distortions only becloud the truth about the Pill, which is difficult enough to establish. From the most recent technical reports, however, these conclusions emerge: (1) the Pill is the most effective contraceptive yet devised; (2) like any other potent drug, it sometimes produces side effects that may be crippling or fatal to a minute proportion of users; (3) while the risks of such side effects appear to have been wildly exaggerated, there are some women for whom the Pill should never be prescribed.

The Pill on the U.S. market today contains two synthetic chemical components, one resembling the natural female hormone estrogen, the other a progestin that resembles progesterone, which women secrete chiefly during pregnancy. Some are combinations in which both the estrogen and the progestin are taken for 21 days a month; others are "sequentials," in which the estrogen alone is taken for 14 to 16 days, and estrogen with progestin for 5 or 6.

The most recent assessments of the Pill were given last month to the American Association of Planned Parenthood Physicians and the American College of Physicians. No two of the assembled experts agreed completely on the relative advantages and risks of the Pill, or in defining the patients for whom they would prescribe or proscribe it. Nevertheless, they reached a reasonable consensus on the most important and potentially dangerous side effects.

Blood and Clots. Hormone components of the Pill appear to "rev up" the chain reaction of yet other hormones that regulate blood pressure. Columbia University's Dr. John H. Laragh has seen twenty women whose blood pressure skyrocketed while they were on the Pill; presumably they were unusually sensitive to the hormonal effect.

Women with kidney disease are especially susceptible. A related mechanism, said Laragh, explains some complaints of "feeling bloated" and gaining weight, usually during the first three or four months that a woman is taking the Pill; some of the hormones involved cause retention of salt and water.

The estrogen component of the Pill is known to increase the coagulability of blood and therefore the risk of clot formation. British researchers have shown that women under forty risk a clotting problem that is seven to nine times greater than the minuscule risk among nonpregnant women of the same age not on the Pill. Clots may form in either superficial or deep veins of the legs (thrombophlebitis), and may travel to the lungs, causing pulmonary embolism, which carries a high death rate. Or they may form in the brain, causing strokes. There are also a few cases in which a myriad of minute clots have blocked circulation in the heart and in intestinal arteries.

These dangers must be set against the greater hazards of pregnancy. For three weeks after a normal pregnancy and delivery, the risks of thromboembolism (including pulmonary embolism) are greatly increased, and even during pregnancy may be slightly increased. Northwestern University's Dr. David Danforth calculated for the College of Physicians that there are .55 cases of thromboembolism per 1,000 women a year among Pill takers compared with .74 per 1,000 during pregnancy and 3 to 10 cases per 1,000 after delivery. Clotting problems aside, pregnancy carries other risks, including fatal complications associated with high blood pressure and kidney disorders. And unwanted pregnancy involves the risk of illegal, septic abortion, which is notoriously hazardous to life. Nonetheless, a one-to-one comparison of the risks of the Pill and those of pregnancy would be invalid. That is largely because a woman who chooses not to use the Pill has other alternatives for avoiding pregnancy—such as the diaphragm, foam, the intrauterine device, or her husband's condom.

Brain and Eyes. High blood pressure increases the risk of strokes of both major kinds—the thromboembolic, caused by traveling clots, and the hemorrhagic, in which a blood vessel bursts. Strokes are uncommon among women under forty, but several neurologists say they have seen as many as ten cases in a year among women on the Pill, where they used to see only one or two before the Pill. Both the increased blood pressure and the estrogen's effect on the clotting mechanism may be responsible. There are a few authenticated cases of severely impaired vision, even to the extent of blindness, as the result of clotting in the minute retinal arteries.

Because migraine headaches result from dilation of small arteries near the surface of the skull, they might be related to the Pill's effects on blood vessels. Thus some physicians never prescribe the Pill for a woman who has any history of migraine, and stop it promptly if a woman with no such history complains of migraine while on it. Others counter that this could rule out five percent or more of the female population.

Metabolism. Estrogens, but not progesterone, have long been known to influence the metabolism of fats—to the point where they have been given to men in the hope of lowering their blood-cholesterol levels and protecting them against heart attacks. In fact, says the University of Miami's Dr. William N. Spellacy, their effect on cholesterol is still debatable; they seem to increase the proportion of big, "flabby" fat molecules circulating in the blood. The most consistent finding, said Spellacy, is that increased estrogen levels cause increased blood levels of triglycerides, the complex, fat-containing molecules involved in athero-sclerosis and heart disease. But, Spellacy emphasized, there is as yet no evidence linking the Pill with these diseases in women.

The Pill's effect on insulin and carbohydrate (sugar and starch) metabolism is somewhat clearer. In many women, the blood-sugar level goes up, and with it the level of circulating insulin. There is no reason to believe that the Pill causes diabetes, but it may, in some cases, accelerate the onset of the disease. Then again, so does pregnancy.

Liver. If a woman has had pregnancies marked by either jaundice or pruritus (diffuse itching), she should not go on the Pill, suggests Dr. Robert A. Hartley of Baltimore. Both these conditions result from impaired liver function, and the Pill is likely to reproduce the effects of pregnancy. Some gynecologists, however, believe the Pill is safe if the woman has had infectious hepatitis and has fully recovered from her jaundice.

Fertility. In the early days of enthusiasm for the Pill, the word was that, far from interfering with fertility, it seemed to enhance it. Women who had just stopped taking the Pill seemed more likely to become pregnant within a couple of months. This is not true, certainly not for all women, says Dr. Alan F. Guttmacher, president of the Planned Parenthood Federation of America. Some who have taken it for two years or more, then stopped because they wanted a baby, have failed to menstruate and ovulate, and therefore to conceive, for as long as eighteen months. Guttmacher prefers not to prescribe the Pill for a young woman with irregular menstruation, or no periods at all, who has not completed her family.

Cancer. The claim was once made that while estrogens may cause cancer, as they do in many laboratory animals, the Pill seemed actually to afford some protection against breast cancer. More cautious now, the experts claim no protective effect, but assert unequivocally that they have seen no case of breast cancer that might have been caused by the Pill. Still, to stay on the safe side, they will not prescribe it for any woman who has cancer or any suspicious change in a breast.

The greatest controversy today concerns cancer of the cervix. Again the trouble is insufficient data. What is indisputable is that many, if not most, women on the Pill undergo cellular changes in the cervical region. The question is whether these are precancerous. Two researchers, Drs. Hilliard Dubrow and Myron R. Melamed, conducted a three-year study of almost 35,000 women at Manhattan Planned Parenthood clinics. Their report has not been published, and may never be, because technical reviews of the study suggest that it was badly designed. But bits and pieces of the findings have been carefully leaked to the press by anti-Pill crusaders. The essence: among women on the Pill, Dubrow and Melamed found twice as many cases of cell changes as among women using diaphragms. They call these changes "carcinoma *in situ*" (literally "cancer in place," as distinct from cancer that has spread). This condition is also known as "carcinoma, stage zero," and as a "precancerous condition," although it does not always lead to cancer. What is not clear is whether these women had any greater incidence of cell abnormalities than did other women who did not use diaphragms (some physicians consider the diaphragm to be a protective factor).

Not even the most enthusiastic supporters of the Pill in its present form believe that it is the ideal contraceptive. In addition to its side effects, it has the disadvantage of requiring close calendar watching. Researchers are working strenuously to produce a morning-after pill, a one-a-month pill or a once-a-year injection to achieve the same result with greater certainty and less fuss. What may well be the second generation of oral contraceptives is already undergoing extensive tests.

In Manhattan, at city-owned Metropolitan Hospital, Dr. Elizabeth B. Connell has had more than one thousand women, some for as long as four years, taking a pill consisting only of chloramadinone, a progestin, every day of the year. Side effects seem to be fewer and less severe than those from pills containing estrogens, and the number of unwanted pregnancies has been negligible. The remarkable thing about these pills is that most women taking them still ovulate regularly, and so are theoretically exposed to conception. For reasons unknown, conception does not occur.

A similar progestin is being tested by the Upjohn Company in a novel form. Upjohn technicians have made vaginal rings of Silastic (silicone rubber) impregnated with medroxyprogesterone (Provera). The rings are of the same spring-reinforced design as the ring of a diaphragm, but there is no cap. The woman inserts the ring five days after the beginning of a menstrual period, removes it after twenty-one days, and throws it away. She should menstruate within two days, and start the twenty-eight day cycle again with a new ring five days later.

As for the Pill in its present forms, as sensible an opinion as any was expressed at last week's meeting of the College of Physicians by Dr. Ann Lawrence, a hormone specialist at the University of Chicago. She would not, she said, prescribe it for women with a family history of breast or cervical cancer, or the likelihood of clotting or circulatory problems, or diabetes. "I am one of what I would call the concerned physicians, simply pleading that the drug be used with a certain circumspection," said Dr. Lawrence. "But I wouldn't even try to deny that the Pill has been a boon to millions of women." For all but the most fanatical opponents or proponents of the Pill, Dr. Lawrence's attitude seems the soundest of all.

20

ABORTION LAW REPEAL (SORT OF): A WARNING TO WOMEN

LUCINDA CISLER

One of the few things everyone in the women's movement seems to agree on is that we have to get rid of the abortion laws and make sure that any woman who wants an abortion can get one. We all recognize how basic this demand is; it sounds like a pretty clear and simple demand, too—hard to achieve, of course, but obviously a fundamental right just like any other method of birth control.

But just because it *sounds* so simple and so obvious and is such a great point of unity, a lot of us haven't really looked below the surface of the abortion fight and seen how complicated it may be to get what we want. The most important thing feminists have done and have to keep doing is to insist that the basic reason for repealing the laws and making abortions available is *justice*: women's right to abortion.

Everyone recognizes the cruder forms of opposition to abortion traditionally used by the forces of sexism and religious reaction. But a feminist philosophy must be able to deal with *all* the stumbling blocks that keep us from reaching our goal, and must develop a consciousness about the far more subtle dangers we face from many who honestly believe they are our friends.

In our disgust with the extreme oppression women experience under the present abortion laws, many of us are understandably tempted to accept insulting token changes that we would angrily shout down if they were offered to us in any other field of the struggle for women's liberation. We've waited so long for anything to happen that when we see our demands having any effect at all we're sorely tempted to convince ourselves that everything that sounds good in the short run will turn out to be good for women in the long run. And a lot of us are so fed up with "the system" that we don't even bother to find out what it's doing so we can fight it and demand what *we* want. This is the measure of our present oppression: a chain of aluminum *does* feel lighter around our necks than one made of iron, but it's still a chain, and our task is still to burst entirely free.

The abortion issue is one of the very few issues vital to the women's movement that well-meaning people outside the movement were dealing with on an organized basis even before the new feminism began to explode a couple of years ago. Whatever we may like to think, there *is* quite definitely an abortion movement that is distinct from the feminist movement, and the good intentions of most of the people in it can turn out to be either a tremendous source of support for our goals or the most tragic barrier to our ever achieving them. The choice is up to us: we must subject every proposal for change and every tactic to the clearest feminist scrutiny, demand only what is good for *all* women, and not let some of us be bought off at the expense of the rest.

Until just a couple of years ago the abortion movement was a tiny handful of good people who were still having to concentrate just on getting the taboo lifted from public discussions of the topic. They dared not even think about any proposals for legal change *beyond* "reform" (in which abortion is grudgingly parceled out by hospital committee fiat to the few women who can "prove" they've been raped, or who are crazy, or are in danger of bearing a defective baby). They spent a lot of time debating with priests about When Life Begins, and Which Abortions Are Justified. They were mostly doctors, lawyers, social workers, clergymen, professors, writers, and a few were just plain women—usually not particularly feminist.

Part of the reason the reform movement was very small was that it appealed mostly to altruism and very little to people's self-interest: the circumstances covered by "reform" *are* tragic but they affect very few women's lives, whereas repeal is compelling because most women know the fear of unwanted pregnancy and in fact get abortions for that reason.

Some people were involved with "reform"—and are in the abortion movement today—for very good reasons: they are concerned with important issues like the public health problem presented by illegal abortions, the doctor's right to provide patients with good medical care, the suffering of unwanted children and unhappy families, and the burgeoning of our population at a rate too high for *any* economic system to handle.

But the basis for all these good reasons to be concerned with abortion is, in the final analysis, simple expediency. Such reasons are peripheral to the central rationale for making abortion available: justice for

---

women. And unless a well-thought-out feminism underlies the dedication of these people, they will accept all kinds of token gains from legislators and judges and the medical establishment in the name of "getting something done *now*"—never mind what that is, or how much it cuts the chances for real changes later by lulling the public into a false sense of accomplishment.

These people do deserve a lot of credit for their lonely and dogged insistence on raising the issue when everybody else wanted to pretend it didn't exist. But because they invested so much energy earlier in working for "reform" (and got it in ten states), they have an important stake in believing that their approach is the "realistic" one—that one must accept the small, so-called steps in the right direction that can be wrested from reluctant politicians, that it isn't quite dignified to demonstrate or shout what you want, that raising the women's rights issue will "alienate" politicians, and so on.

Others, however (especially in centers of stylish liberalism like New York City), are interested in abortion because they are essentially political fashion mongers: some of them aspire to public office and some just like to play around the pool. For them, it's "groovy" to be for something racy like abortion. You can make a name for yourself faster in a small movement, such as this one still is, than in something huge like the peace movement, and it's sexier than supporting the grape strikers in their struggle.

Unfortunately, the "good people" share with these pseudo-militants an overawed attitude toward politicians, doctors, lawyers, and traditional "experts" of all kinds; they tend to view the women's movement as rather eccentric troops they can call upon to help them with colorful things like unavoidable demonstrations, rather than as the grass-roots force whose feminist philosophy should be leading *them* in the right direction. Even those who have begun to say that the woman's right to abortion *is* the central issue show a good deal of half-concealed condescension toward the very movement that has brought this issue to the fore and inspired the fantastic change in public opinion witnessed in the last year or so.

Because of course, it *is* the women's movement whose demand for *repeal*—rather than "reform"—of the abortion laws has spurred the general acceleration in the abortion movement and its influence. Unfortunately, and ironically, the very rapidity of the change for which we are responsible is threatening to bring us to the point where we are offered something so close to what we want that our demands for true radical change may never be achieved.

Most of us recognize that "reforms" of the old rape-incest-fetal deformity variety are not in women's interest and in fact, in their very specificity, are almost more of an insult to our dignity as active, self-determining humans than are the old laws that simply forbid us to have abortions unless we are about to die. But the *new* reform legislation now being proposed all over the country is not in our interest either: it looks pretty good, and the improvements it seems to promise (at least for middle-class women) are almost irresistible to those who haven't informed themselves about the complexities of the abortion situation or developed a feminist critique of abortion that goes beyond "it's our right." And the courts are now handing down decisions that look good at a glance but that contain the same restrictions as the legislation.

All the restrictions are of the kind that would be extremely difficult to get judges and legislators to throw out later (unlike the obvious grotesqueries in the old "reform" laws, which are already being challenged successfully in some courts and legislatures). A lot of people are being seriously misled because the legislation and the court decisions that incorporate these insidious limitations are being called abortion law "repeal" by the media. It is true that the media are not particularly interested in accuracy when they report news of interest to women, but the chief reason for this dangerous misuse of language is that media people are getting their information from the established abortion movement, which wants very badly to think that these laws and decisions *are* somehow repeal. (It seems pretty clear that when you repeal an abortion law you just get rid of it; you do not put things back into the statutes or make special rules that apply to abortion but not to other medical procedures.)

The following are the four major restrictions that have been cropping up lately in "repeal" bills, and some highly condensed reasons why feminists (and indeed anyone) must oppose them. No one can say for sure whether sexist ill-will, political horse-trading, or simple ignorance played the largest part in the lawmakers' decisions to include them, but all of them codify outmoded notions about medical technology, religion, or women's "role":

1. Abortions may only be performed in licensed hospitals. Abortion is almost always a simple procedure that can be carried out in a clinic or a doctor's office. Most women do need a place to lie down and rest for a while after a D&C or even a vacuum aspiration abortion, but they hardly need to occupy scarce hospital beds and go through all the hospital rigmarole that ties up the woman's money and the time of overworked staff people.

Hospital boards are extremely conservative and have always wanted to minimize the number of abortions performed within their walls: the "abortion committees" we now have were not invented by lawmakers but by hospital administrators. New laws that ensure a hospital monopoly will hardly change this attitude. (The same committees regulate which women will be able to get the sterilizations they seek—even though voluntary sterilization is perfectly legal in all but one or two states.) The hospitals and accreditation agencies set up their own controls on who will get medical care, and doctors who want to retain their attending status are quite careful not to do "too many" abortions or sterilizations.

Hawaii's new law has this kind of restriction, and hospitals there are already busy setting up a new catechism of "guidelines," none of which ensures that women will get more abortions and all of which ensure that they will have to ask a lot of strangers for "permission" before they are allowed to spend the considerable amount of money hospitalizations inevitably cost. Maryland's bill and the legislation proposed in several other states contain the same provisions that essentially shift the locus of control over women's decisions from the state to the hospital bureaucracies and their quasi-legal "regulations."

2. Abortions may only be performed by licensed physicians. This restriction sounds almost reasonable to most women who have always been fairly healthy and fairly prosperous, who are caught up in the medical mystique so many doctors have cultivated, and who accept the myth that abortion is incredibly risky and thus should cost a lot. But it is one of the most insidious restrictions of all, and is most oppressive to poor women.

Most doctors are not at all interested in performing abortions: even the ones who don't think it's dirty and who favor increasing the availability of abortion generally consider it a pretty boring procedure that they don't especially want to do. One reason they do find it tedious is that it is basically quite a simple operation, especially when the new vacuum aspiration technique is used, rather than the old dilation and curettage. The physicians who would like to see paramedical specialists trained to perform abortions with the aspirator (or who would like to perfect other promising new methods, such as hormone injections) would be completely thwarted by this restriction in their desire to provide efficient, inexpensive care on a mass basis. The general crisis in the medical delivery system in fact demands that paramedical people be trained to do a great many things that physicians do now.

If physicians themselves were to try to perform all the abortions that are needed, they would be swamped with requests and would have to charge a great deal for their specialized training. Childbirth is statistically eight or ten times more dangerous than abortion, and yet nurses are now being trained as midwives in many medical centers. Why can't they and other medical personnel also be specially trained to use the aspirator so that five or six of them can perform clinic abortions under the general supervision of one physician? Only if paramedicals are allowed to do abortions can we expect to have truly inexpensive (and eventually free) abortions available to all women.

In the fall of 1969 a Washington, D.C., court threw out the District's limitations on a doctor's right to perform abortions—but upheld the conviction of a doctor's paramedical aide who said she had wanted to help poor women. Anyone who knows what the present situation in D.C. is will know that abortion is *not* readily available when its performance is limited to doctors only. The public hospital where poor women go has clamped down on abortions almost completely; private hospitals that serve middle-class women still operate restrictively and charge a lot; a few doctors willing to brave the stigma of being "abortionists" are performing abortions in their offices for $300 or so. Although they work long hours, they are inundated with patients (one has a backlog of five weeks). Another is so swamped, partly because he continues to muddle through with D&C, that he does not even take the time to give the women an anesthetic (although they are assured before they arrive that they will get one).

Several attempts have been made to get D.C. doctors to devote a few volunteer hours each week to a free clinic for the poor; doctors have refused, expressing either indifference or fear of professional censure.

Some women insist that because *they* would prefer to go to a doctor, *all* women must be compelled by law to go to one. It is each woman's right to choose to spend $300 for an abortion from a doctor, but she is obviously oppressing other women when she insists that all must do as she does. An abortion performed by a paramedical person with special training in a given modern procedure could easily, in fact, be safer than

---

a D&C performed by a physician who hasn't done many abortions before.

In any case, it is only when doctors have the right to train the people they need to help them meet the demand, and women have the right to get medical care at a price they can afford, that butchers and quacks will be put out of business. Existing medical practice codes provide for the punishment of quacks, but as long as poor women cannot find good abortions at a price they can pay, so long will butchers elude the law and women continue to die from their ministrations.

Looking not so far into the future, this restriction would also deny women themselves the right to use self-abortifacients when they are developed—and who is to say they will not be developed soon? The laws regulating contraception that still exist in thirty-one states were made before contraceptive foam was invented, at a time when all effective female contraception involved a visit to the doctor. That visit was frozen into a legal requirement in some states, and we still have the sad and ludicrous example of Massachusetts, where nonprescriptive foam cannot legally be bought without a prescription.

The "doctors only" clause is a favorite in legislation that masquerades as repeal. Hawaii, Maryland, Washington State, and New York are among the important states where this restriction was (rather quietly) included.

3. *Abortions may not be performed beyond a certain time in pregnancy, unless the woman's life is at stake.* Significantly enough, the magic time limit varies from bill to bill, from court decision to court decision, but this kind of restriction essentially says two things to women: (a) at a certain stage, your body suddenly belongs to the state and it can force you to have a child, whatever your own reasons for wanting an abortion late in pregnancy; (b) because late abortion entails more risk to you than early abortion, the state must "protect" you even if your considered decision is that you want to run that risk and your doctor is willing to help you. This restriction insults women in the same way the present "preservation-of-life" laws do: it assumes that we must be in a state of tutelage and cannot assume responsibility for our own acts. Even many women's liberation writers are guilty of repeating the paternalistic explanation given to excuse the original passage of U.S. laws against abortion: in the nineteenth century abortion was more dangerous than childbirth, and women had to be protected against it. Was it somehow less dangerous in the eighteenth century? Were other kinds of surgery safe

then? And, most important, weren't women wanting and getting abortions, even though they knew how much they were risking? "Protection" has often turned out to be but another means of control over the protected; labor law offers many examples. When childbirth becomes as safe as it should be, perhaps it will be safer than abortion: will we put back our abortion laws, to "protect women"?

And basically, of course, no one can ever know exactly when *any* stage of pregnancy is reached until birth itself. Conception can take place at any time within about three days of intercourse, so that any legal time limit reckoned from "conception" is meaningless because it cannot be determined precisely. All the talk about "quickening," "viability," and so on, is based on old religious myths (if the woman believes in them, of course, she won't look for an abortion) or tied to ever-shifting technology (who knows how soon a three-day-old fertilized egg may be considered "viable" because heroic mechanical devices allow it to survive and grow outside the woman's uterus?). To listen to judges and legislators play with the ghostly arithmetic of months and weeks is to hear the music by which angels used to dance on the head of a pin.

There are many reasons why a woman might seek a late abortion, and she should be able to find one legally if she wants it. She may suddenly discover that she had German measles in early pregnancy and that her fetus is deformed; she may have had a sudden mental breakdown; or some calamity may have changed the circumstances of her life: whatever her reasons, *she belongs to herself and not to the state.*

This limitation speaks to the hangups many people have, and it would be almost impossible to erase from a law once it were enacted—despite its possible constitutional vulnerability on the grounds of vagueness. It is incorporated in New York State's abortion bill, among many others, and in a recent federal court decision in Wisconsin that has been gravely misrepresented as judicial "repeal." The Washington, D.C., decision discussed the "issue," and concluded that Congress should probably enact new laws for different stages of pregnancy. This is not repeal, it is a last-ditch attempt at retaining a little of the state ownership of pregnant women provided for under the worst laws we have now.

4. Abortions may only be performed when the married woman's husband or the young single woman's parents give their consent. The feminist objection to vesting a veto power in anyone other than the pregnant woman is too obvious to need any elaboration. It is utterly fantastic, then, to hear that some women's liberation groups in Washington State have actually been *supporting* an abortion bill with a consent provision. Although such a debasing restriction is written into law in most of the states that have "reform," some legal writers consider it of such little consequence that they fail to mention it in otherwise accurate summaries of U.S. abortion laws. The women's collective now putting out *Rat* in New York recently printed a very good map of the United States, showing in ironic symbols the various restrictions on abortion in each state. For their source these radical women had used a legal check list that did not include a mention of husband's consent—so their map didn't show this sexist restriction existing anywhere.

This may be the easiest of these restrictions to challenge constitutionally, but why should we have to? Instead we could prevent its enactment and fight to eradicate the hospital regulations that frequently impose it even where the law does not.

All women are oppressed by the present abortion laws, by old-style "reforms," and by seductive new fake-repeal bills and court decisions. But the possibility of fake repeal—if it becomes reality—is the most dangerous: it will divide women from each other. It can buy off most middle-class women and make them believe things have really changed, while it leaves poor women to suffer and keeps us all saddled with abortion laws for many more years to come. There are many nice people who would like to see abortion made more or less legal, but their reasons are fuzzy and their tactics acquiescent. Because no one else except the women's movement is going to cry out against these restrictions, it is up to feminists to make the strongest and most precise demands upon the lawmakers—who ostensibly exist to serve *us*. We will not accept insults and call them "steps in the right direction."

Only if we know what we *don't* want, and why, and say so over and over again, will we be able to recognize and reject all the clever plastic imitations of our goal.

April 1970

PART THREE

THE
SOCIAL
AND
ECONOMIC
ASPECTS
OF
MARRIAGE

Marital Roles
and Selected Alternatives

Marital Roles
and Selected Alternatives
Social roles, for
example, those of student and teacher, are usually described in
terms of rights and obligations. Marital roles are no exception.
Although there is debate over whether or not marriage roles
originated historically from cooperation or conflict, there is
general agreement that marriage roles can currently be
conceptualized in terms of exchange. From the woman's
perspective, therefore, she can expect to contribute to the
marriage and to benefit from it as well. At this time in history,
according to Kirkpatrick,[1] women have available to them three
standard definitions of the role of wife. First, women who assume
the traditional housewife role expect financial support and sexual
fidelity from their husbands as well as the right to limited authority
over their domestic domains. In exchange, women are expected to
reproduce and socialize their offspring, to sustain physically and
emotionally the members of the household and to subordinate
themselves economically and socially to their husbands.

Second is the companion role, an ideal which is most
appropriate to privileged classes. Historically, the companion role
parallels the mistress role. This parallel was recently made explicit
by an advertisement for mink coats which admonished wives to
persuade their husbands to treat them as expensive mistresses!
The companion strikes a bargain with her husband different from
that of the housewife-mother, but she is no less dependent on
him. In exchange for romantic companionship with the husband,
physical admiration, and a luxurious life style, the companion wife
is expected to maintain a high level of sexual and intellectual

1. Clifford Kirkpatrick, *The Family As Process and Institution* (New York: Ronald Press, 1963), pp. 168–69.

attractiveness, to be a social asset to her husband's career, and to be an exciting source of satisfaction generally to her husband.

The third standard view of the woman's role in marriage is the partner role, often exemplified by families in which both spouses pursue a career. As an ideal type, this role includes the rights of economic independence, equal authority in regard to family decision making, and equality in social and moral action. Conversely, this role implies obligations which include an appropriate contribution in both the economic and domestic responsibilities of the family.

Critics of the traditional definition of marital roles have indicted the important economic bases of what they believe should be basically an emotional relationship between individuals. Moreover, the feminist critique, while not ignoring the price the husband has to pay, contends that the woman has to make too large a sacrifice for tenuous financial security. Because of women's expectation of economic dependence on her husband and because of the general stress on social mobility in modern industrialized societies, women are socialized to view prospective husbands in terms of their financial potential. With a novelist's sensitive understanding, Doris Lessing, in the short story "Notes for a Case History," [2] portrays one young woman's self-conscious awareness of herself as an object for sale on the marriage market and the process through which she seeks to package herself so as to find a husband with good economic prospects.

Not only is marriage an insurance pact, according to Emma Goldman,[3] but the premium women have to pay is too high. Women give up their names, their independence, their privacy, and ultimately their sense of self. Entrance into marriage commits a woman to parasitic dependence on her husband, ultimately

---

2. *A Man and Two Women*, Doris Lessing (New York: Simon & Schuster, 1963), pp. 248–67.

3. This topical selection, unlike the others in this reader, was not written by a contemporary author. Emma Goldman lived in the United States from August 15, 1889, to December 12, 1919. During that time, she argued through her speeches and writings for positive changes in a wide range of social and political ills afflicting society. She agitated for such modern causes as freedom in love, availability of birth control, and understanding of homosexuals, and against subjugation of women, the draft, war, oppression of workers, and organized government. For a sample of her essays, see *Anarchism and Other Essays* (New York: Mother Earth Publishing Association, 1911).

relegating her to "complete uselessness, individual as well as social."

While not entirely abandoning the traditional image of the American wife and mother, the media emphasize the companion role for women. Sutheim concentrates her critique on this image of women in magazines. The importance of women's magazines in promoting the positive image of the housewife immediately after World War II when women were no longer needed in industry was brought to popular attention by Betty Friedan. During the 1960s articles in women's magazines began to introduce the image of a new and exciting woman. Sutheim labels these intellectually stimulating and physically attractive women, "Bubbling Bettys." "Bubbling Betty" began appearing at a time when there was, for the first time since World War II, both a demand for women in the labor force and a supply of women disillusioned with the housewife role who wanted to enter the labor force.[4] The popularization of the companion image served to thwart any drastic redefinition of the wife role which might have occurred as a result of women entering work roles. The companion role was simply tacked on to the housewife role. The media still clearly picture women as owing primary allegiance to the family. This is possible because the companion role possesses the curious ability to combine dependence on the husband with the "freedom" to work part-time, resulting, as Sutheim notes, in increased sales of consumer goods. An analogous process occurred when the accepted definition of female marital roles (which includes an emphasis on material consumption) was threatened by experiments in living together. Living together was simply redefined as a prelude rather than an alternative to marriage.[5]

The partnership form of marriage faces difficulties from outside sources such as the media and from the internal tendency of spouses to drift into more traditional sex roles. One example of

---

4. Alice Rossi, "Women—The Terms of Liberation," *Dissent* 17, no. 6 (November–December 1970): 535–36.

5. Viewed cross-culturally, marriage is a social institution that most characteristically functions to license parenthood and legitimize children. Since no society prescribes conception outside of marriage, the definition of living together as a prelude to marriage is quite consistent with other social arrangements (discussed in part 4) to circumvent unwed parenthood in spite of the occurrence of premarital intercourse.

an attempt to maintain a partnership within marriage is the marriage contract drawn up by Alix Shulman and her husband. The idea of such a contract within marriage has been criticized as highlighting instead of destroying the business relationship of marriage. As Rossi notes, for example, we need to inject expressive values into the work world rather than increase instrumental values in the family.[6] We would agree with this criticism. However, the Shulmans seem to see their contract, which details explicitly the domestic obligations of each partner, as an interim arrangement until domestic sharing becomes established as a pattern. They drew up a written agreement because verbal agreement seemed to relapse into a traditional division of labor. As Alix Shulman aptly states, "Good intentions are simply not enough." Their agreement is offered as an example of one couple's partnership and any other couple wishing to adopt partner roles in marriage would have to develop their own.

It is when the normal course of marriage is disrupted, perhaps, that we can see most clearly the societal assumptions about marriage generally and about the position of women specifically. In her discussion of the mechanics of divorce, Tomasson indicates clearly that women are still considered to be the property of their husbands. Further, she refutes the contention that women who assume either the traditional or companion wife role can expect an adequate amount of alimony. Disregarding the usual marriage stipulation that women should concentrate their efforts within the home and not develop employment skills (and certainly not valuable employment skills), the courts often limit alimony while admonishing the divorcee to earn her own income. Furthermore, the definition of alimony itself is an insult to women because it is not considered a payment for work done.

The typical operation of the courts belies a double standard—males are considered important; females are considered unimportant. Men are respected for their work whereas women are expected to be passive and deferential in court. Several recommendations that would repair current legal divorce problems are presented by Tomasson.

---

6. Gordon Bermant, "Sisterhood Is Beautiful, A Conversation with Alice S. Rossi," *Psychology Today* 6, no. 3 (August 1972): 74.

While Scott and Oken concur that the legal system is a barrier to obtaining a divorce and a fair settlement, they focus their attention on the positive aspects of recapturing an individual identity and of extricating oneself from a dissatisfying and destructive marriage relationship.

In discussion of an individual case of divorce, they locate the problems with the institution of marriage itself. For most women, marriage means continual deference to others' needs. Typically women who have been unable to adjust to this marital situation have faced problems. For the longest time these problems were conceptualized as personal troubles and women either suffered silently at home or underwent treatment for psychological ailments. It is only within the past decade as a result of social analyses by Betty Friedan and others in the movement that a substantial number of women began to place blame within the institution of marriage rather than within themselves.

21

MARRIAGE AND LOVE

EMMA GOLDMAN

The popular notion about marriage and love is that they are synonymous, that they spring from the same motives, and cover the same human needs. Like most popular notions, this also rests not on actual facts, but on superstition.

Marriage and love have nothing in common; they are as far apart as the poles; are, in fact, antagonistic to each other. No doubt some marriages have been the result of love. Not, however, because love could assert itself only in marriage; much rather is it because few people can completely outgrow a convention. There are today large numbers of men and women to whom marriage is naught but a farce, but who submit to it for the sake of public opinion. At any rate, while it is true that some marriages are based on love, and while it is equally true that in some cases love continues in married life, I maintain that it does so regardless of marriage, and not because of it.

On the other hand, it is utterly false that love results from marriage. On rare occasions one does hear of a miraculous case of a married couple falling in love after marriage, but on close examination it will be found that it is a mere adjustment to the inevitable. Certainly the growing used to each other is far away from the spontaneity, the intensity, and beauty of love, without which the intimacy of marriage must prove degrading to both the woman and the man.

Marriage is primarily an economic arrangement, an insurance pact. It differs from the ordinary life insurance agreement only in that it is more binding, more exacting. Its returns are insignificantly small compared with the investments. In taking out an insurance policy one pays for it in dollars and cents, always at liberty to discontinue payments. If, however, woman's premium is a husband, she pays for it with her name, her privacy, her self-respect, her very life, "until death doth part." Moreover, the marriage insurance condemns her to lifelong dependency, to parasitism, to complete uselessness, individual as well as social. Man, too, pays his toll, but as his sphere is wider, marriage does not limit him as much as woman. He feels his chains more in an economic sense.

Thus Dante's motto over Inferno applies with equal force to marriage: "Ye who enter here leave all hope behind."

That marriage is a failure none but the very stupid will deny. One has but to glance over the statistics of divorce to realize how bitter a failure marriage really is. Nor will the stereotyped Philistine argument that the laxity of divorce laws and the growing looseness of woman account for the fact that: first, every twelfth marriage ends in divorce; second, that since 1870 divorces have increased from 28 to 73 for every 100,000 population; third, that adultery, since 1867, as ground for divorce, has increased 270.8 percent; fourth, that desertion increased 369.8 percent.

Added to these startling figures is a vast amount of material, dramatic and literary, further elucidating this subject. Robert Herrick, in *Together*; Pinero, in *Mid-Channel*; Eugene Walter, in *Paid in Full*, and scores of other writers are discussing the barrenness, the monotony, the sordidness, the inadequacy of marriage as a factor for harmony and understanding.

The thoughtful social student will not content himself with the popular superficial excuse for this phenomenon. He will have to dig down deeper into the very life of the sexes to know why marriage proves so disastrous.

Edward Carpenter says that behind every marriage stands the lifelong environment of the two sexes; an environment so different from each other that man and woman must remain strangers. Separated by an insurmountable wall of superstition, custom, and habit, marriage has not the potentiality of developing knowledge of, and respect for, each other, without which every union is doomed to failure.

Henrik Ibsen, the hater of all social shams, was probably the first to realize this great truth. Nora leaves her husband, not—as the stupid critic would have it—because she is tired of her responsibilities or feels the need of woman's rights, but because she has come to know that for eight years she had lived with a stranger and borne him children. Can there be anything more humiliating, more degrading than a lifelong proximity between two strangers? No need for the woman to know anything of the man, save his income. As to the knowledge of the woman—what is there to know except that she has a pleasing appearance? We have not yet outgrown the theologic myth that woman has no soul, that she is a mere appendix to man, made out of his rib just for the convenience of the gentleman who was so strong that he was afraid of his own shadow.

Perchance the poor quality of the material whence woman comes is responsible for her inferiority. At any rate, woman has no soul—what is there to know about her? Besides, the less soul a woman has the greater her asset as a wife, the more readily will she absorb herself in her husband. It is this slavish acquiescence to man's superiority that has kept the marriage institution seemingly intact for so long a period. Now that woman is coming into her own, now that she is actually growing aware of herself as a being outside of the master's grace, the sacred institution of marriage is gradually being undermined, and no amount of sentimental lamentation can stay it.

From infancy, almost, the average girl is told that marriage is her ultimate goal; therefore her training and education must be directed towards that end. Like the mute beast fattened for slaughter, she is prepared for that. Yet, strange to say, she is allowed to know much less about her function as wife and mother than the ordinary artisan of his trade. It is indecent and filthy for a respectable girl to know anything of the marital relation. Oh, for the inconsistency of respectability, that needs the marriage vow to turn something which is filthy into the purest and most sacred arrangement that none dare question or criticize. Yet that is exactly the attitude of the average upholder of marriage. The prospective wife and mother is kept in complete ignorance of her only asset in the competitive field—sex. Thus she enters into lifelong relations with a man only to find herself shocked, repelled, outraged beyond measure by the most natural and healthy instinct, sex. It is safe to say that a large percentage of the unhappiness, misery, distress, and physical suffering of matrimony is due to the criminal ignorance in sex matters that is being extolled as a great virtue. Nor is it at all an exaggeration when I say that more than one home has been broken up because of this deplorable fact.

If, however, woman is free and big enough to learn the mystery of sex without the sanction of state or church, she will stand condemned as utterly unfit to become the wife of a "good" man, his goodness consisting of an empty head and plenty of money. Can there be anything more outrageous than the idea that a healthy, grown woman, full of life and passion, must deny nature's demand, must subdue her most intense craving, undermine her health and break her spirit, must stunt her vision, abstain from the depth and glory of sex experience until a "good" man comes along to take her unto himself as a wife? That is precisely what marriage means. How can such an arrangement end except in failure? This is one, though not the least important, factor of marriage, which differentiates it from love.

Ours is a practical age. The time when Romeo and Juliet risked the wrath of their fathers for love, when Gretchen exposed herself to the gossip of her neighbors for love, is no more. If, on rare occasions, young people allow themselves the luxury of romance, they are taken in care by the elders, drilled and pounded until they become "sensible."

The moral lesson instilled in the girl is not whether the man has aroused her love, but rather is it, "How much?" The important and only God of practical American life: Can the man make a living? Can he support a wife? That is the only thing that justifies marriage. Gradually this saturates every thought of the girl; her dreams are not of moonlight and kisses, of laughter and tears; she dreams of shopping tours and bargain counters. This soul-poverty and sordidness are the elements inherent in the marriage institution. The state and the church approve of no other ideal, simply because it is the one that necessitates the state and church control of men and women.

Doubtless there are people who continue to consider love above dollars and cents. Particularly is this true of that class whom economic necessity has forced to become self-supporting. The tremendous change in woman's position, wrought by that mighty factor, is indeed phenomenal when we reflect that it is but a short time since she has entered the industrial arena. Six million women wage earners; six million women, who have the equal right with men to be exploited, to be robbed, to go on strike; aye, to starve even. Anything more, my lord? Yes, six million wage workers in every walk of life, from the highest brain work to the most difficult menial labor in the mines and on the railroad tracks; yes, even detectives and policemen. Surely the emancipation is complete.

Yet with all that, but a very small number of the vast army of women wage workers look upon work as a permanent issue, in the same light as does man. No matter how decrepit the latter, he has been taught to be independent, self-supporting. Oh, I know that no one is really independent in our economic treadmill; still, the poorest specimen of a man hates to be a parasite; to be known as such, at any rate.

The woman considers her position as worker transitory, to be thrown aside for the first bidder. That is why it is infinitely harder to organize women than men. "Why should I join a union? I am going to get married, to have a home." Has she not been taught from infancy to look upon that as her ultimate calling? She learns soon enough that the home, though not so large a prison as the factory, has more solid doors and bars. It has a keeper so faithful that naught can escape him. The most tragic part, however, is that the home no longer frees her from wage slavery; it only increases her task.

According to the latest statistics submitted before a Committee "on labor and wages, and congestion of population," 10 percent of the wage workers in New York City alone are married, yet they must continue to work at the most poorly paid labor in the world. Add to this horrible aspect the drudgery of housework, and what remains of the protection and glory of the home? As a matter of fact, even the middle-class girl in marriage can not speak of her home, since it is the man who creates her sphere. It is not important whether the husband is a brute or a darling. What I wish to prove is that marriage guarantees woman a home only by the grace of her husband. There she moves about in *his* home, year after year, until her aspect of life and human affairs becomes as flat, narrow, and drab as her surroundings. Small wonder if she becomes a nag, petty, quarrelsome, gossipy, unbearable, thus driving the man from the house. She could not go, if she wanted to; there is no place to go. Besides, a short period of married life, of complete surrender of all faculties, absolutely incapacitates the average woman for the outside world. She becomes reckless in appearance, clumsy in her movements, dependent in her decisions, cowardly in her judgment, a weight and a bore, which most men grow to hate and despise. Wonderfully inspiring atmosphere for the bearing of life, is it not?

But the child, how is it to be protected, if not for marriage? After all, is not that the most important consideration? The sham, the hypocrisy of it! Marriage protecting the child, yet thousands of children destitute and homeless. Marriage protecting the child, yet orphan asylums and reformatories overcrowded, the Society for the Prevention of Cruelty to Children keeping busy in rescuing the little victims from "loving" parents, to place them under more loving care, the Gerry Society. Oh, the mockery of it!

Marriage may have the power to "bring the horse to water," but has it ever made him drink? The law will place the father under arrest, and put him in convict's clothes; but has that ever stilled the hunger of the child? If the parent has no work, or if he hides his identity, what does marriage do then? It invokes the law to bring the man to "justice," to put him safely behind closed doors; his labor, however, goes not to the child, but to the state. The child receives but a blighted memory of its father's stripes.

As to the protection of the woman—therein lies the curse of marriage. Not that it really protects her, but the very idea is so revolting, such an outrage and insult on life, so degrading to human dignity, as to forever condemn this parasitic institution.

It is like that other paternal arrangement—capitalism. It robs man of his birthright, stunts his growth, poisons his body, keeps him in ignorance, in poverty and dependence, and then institutes charities that thrive on the last vestige of man's self-respect.

The institution of marriage makes a parasite of woman, an absolute dependent. It incapacitates her for life's struggle, annihilates her social consciousness, paralyzes her imagination, and then imposes its gracious protection, which is in reality a snare, a travesty on human character.

If motherhood is the highest fulfillment of woman's nature, what other protection does it need save love and freedom? Marriage but defiles, outrages, and corrupts her fulfillment. Does it not say to woman, Only when you follow me shall you bring forth life? Does it not condemn her to the block, does it not degrade and shame her if she refuses to buy her right to motherhood by selling herself? Does not marriage only sanction motherhood, even though conceived in hatred, in compulsion? Yet, if motherhood be of free choice, of love, of ecstasy, of defiant passion, does it not place a crown of thorns upon an innocent head and carve in letters of blood the hideous epithet, Bastard? Were marriage to contain all the virtues claimed for it, its crimes against motherhood would exclude it forever from the realm of love.

Love, the strongest and deepest element in all life, the harbinger of hope, of joy, of ecstasy; love, the defier of all laws, of all conventions; love, the freest, the most powerful moulder of human destiny; how can such an all-compelling force be synonymous with that poor little state- and church-begotten weed, marriage?

Free love? As if love is anything but free! Man has bought brains, but all the millions in the world have failed to buy love. Man has subdued bodies, but all the power on earth has been unable to subdue love. Man has conquered whole nations, but all his armies could not conquer love. Man has chained and fettered the spirit, but he has been utterly helpless before love. High on a throne, with all the splendor and pomp his gold can command, man is yet poor and desolate, if love passes him by. And if it stays, the poorest hovel is radiant with warmth, with life and color. Thus love has the magic power to make of a beggar a king. Yes, love is free; it can dwell in no other atmosphere. In freedom it gives itself unreservedly, abundantly, completely. All the laws on the statutes, all the courts in the universe, cannot tear it from the soil, once love has taken root. If, however, the soil is sterile, how can marriage make it bear fruit? It is like the last desperate struggle of fleeting life against death.

Love needs no protection; it is its own protection. So long as love begets life no child is deserted, or hungry, or famished for the want of affection. I know this to be true. I know women who became mothers in freedom by the men they loved. Few children in wedlock enjoy the care, the protection, the devotion free motherhood is capable of bestowing.

The defenders of authority dread the advent of a free motherhood, lest it will rob them of their prey. Who would fight wars? Who would create wealth? Who would make the policeman, the jailer, if woman were to refuse the indiscriminate breeding of children? The race, the race! shouts the king, the president, the capitalist, the priest. The race must be preserved, though woman be degraded to a mere machine,— and the marriage institution is our only safety valve against the pernicious sex-awakening of woman. But in vain these frantic efforts to maintain a state of bondage. In vain, too, the edicts of the church, the mad attacks of rulers, in vain even the arm of the law. Woman no longer wants to be a party to the production of a race of sickly, feeble, decrepit, wretched human beings, who have neither the strength nor moral courage to throw off the yoke of poverty and slavery. Instead she desires fewer and better children, begotten and reared in love and through free choice; not by compulsion, as marriage imposes. Our pseudo moralists have yet to learn the deep sense of responsibility toward the child, that love in freedom has awakened in the breast of woman. Rather would she forgo forever the glory of motherhood than bring forth life in an atmosphere that breathes only destruction and death. And if she does become a mother, it is to give to the child the deepest and best her being can yield. To grow with the child is her motto; she knows that in that manner alone can she help build true manhood and womanhood.

Ibsen must have had a vision of a free mother, when, with a master stroke, he portrayed Mrs. Alving. She was the ideal mother because she had outgrown marriage and all its horrors, because she had broken her chains, and set her spirit free to soar until it returned a personality, regenerated and strong. Alas, it was too late to rescue her life's joy, her Oswald; but not too late to realize that love in freedom is the only condition of a beautiful life. Those who, like Mrs. Alving, have paid with blood and tears for their spiritual awakening, repudiate marriage as an imposition, a shallow, empty mockery. They know, whether love last but one brief span of time or for eternity, it is the only creative, inspiring, elevating basis for a new race, a new world.

In our present pygmy state love is indeed a stranger to most people. Misunderstood and shunned, it rarely takes root; or if it does, it soon withers and dies. Its delicate fiber can not endure the stress and strain of the daily grind. Its soul is too complex to adjust itself to the slimy woof of our social fabric. It weeps and moans and suffers with those who have need of it, yet lack the capacity to rise to love's summit.

Someday, someday men and women will rise, they will reach the mountain peak, they will meet big and strong and free, ready to receive, to partake, and to bask in the golden rays of love. What fancy, what imagination, what poetic genius can foresee even approximately the potentialities of such a force in the life of men and women. If the world is ever to give birth to true companionship and oneness, not marriage, but love will be the parent.

22

THE SUBVERSION OF BETTY CROCKER

SUSAN SUTHEIM

Next time you pass a newsstand or magazine counter, notice what's on sale. Here in New York, typically, you'll find about three dozen magazines, nearly two dozen of which will be women's magazines. Why? Because they sell. Notice also the variety: general-interest magazines aimed mostly (although not exclusively) at housewives—*Ladies' Home Journal, McCall's, Good Housekeeping, Redbook*; general-interest magazines aimed mostly at unmarried women—*Seventeen* and *Ingénue* for younger women, *Cosmopolitan* and *Single Girl* for older ones; special-subject magazines—*Modern Bride* and others aimed at about-to-be-married women, magazines about hairstyles and care, cosmetics, knitting, sewing; fashion/beauty magazines—*Glamour* and *Mademoiselle*, *Vogue*, and *Harper's Bazaar*; plus *True Confessions, Modern Romance, Screenlife, Silver Screen*, and countless other romance magazines and comic books.

Each of these magazines is aimed at a slightly different audience and thus emphasizes different aspects of the image of American women (their readers). *Seventeen* and *Ingénue* for the teen-age-into-early-college-age bracket; *Glamour* and *Mademoiselle* for the college/young working girl/young mother group; *Vogue* and *Harper's Bazaar* for the very rich and for those of us who like to peek at the way the rich live. Then there's a bundle directed at married women (predominantly)—*Ladies' Home Journal, McCall's, Family Circle, Good Housekeeping, Better Homes & Gardens, Woman's Day, House Beautiful, Redbook*—each of which has (or tries to have) a special emphasis. *Better Homes & Gardens* carries gardening features that the others don't (or don't regularly). *Good Housekeeping* and *Family Circle* emphasize food, often budget food. *Woman's Day* goes in for do-it-yourself projects. *McCall's* and the *Ladies' Home Journal* are "more sophisticated" in fashions, food, beauty features: which means they're aimed at a more upwardly mobile, urban-suburban audience than, e.g., *Redbook*.

Any woman could probably produce the same rundown of women's magazines, and supply all sorts of details and point out distinctions I've skipped. This may be partially because most women buy one or more women's magazines from time to time. This familiarity also stems from the fact—and this is important—that we read our mothers' magazines from the time we're seven or eight. I can recall, at age nine, telling my mother about an article I'd just read in the *Ladies' Home Journal* about how Russians are just ordinary nice people. This, in 1951, produced a rather hysterical reaction from my mother, who threatened to cancel her subscription. Subversive literature right in her own living room!

Which was precisely the point; if the mothers are resistant, you can indoctrinate the kids. (Skeptics who think girls don't read their mothers' magazines should take a look at the February 1969 *McCall's*, in which the beginning of a new feature by and for under-fourteen-year-olds is announced.)

I said magazines indoctrinate their readers. That's a strong word, and it demands explanation. Just who is indoctrinating whom, and to what end?

I worked for a year in the food department of the *Ladies' Home Journal*. During that year I learned how editorial decisions are generally made, about who has the power to veto editorial material, about how it gets in in the first place. I gather, from friends who work for other magazines and from reading advertising trade journals, that my experience was typical of the trade.

In magazines, you're dealing with two sets of people in business to make a profit: the publishers and hundreds of advertisers. The publisher earns his money by selling the magazine (subscriptions, newsstand sales), but more importantly, from the sale of advertising space in the pages of his magazine. (No magazine could sustain itself on subscriptions alone without raising subscription prices out of sight—and out of competitive range. So either you have foundation support or some other form of donated money, or you sell lots of ads.) Thus, from the publisher's and advertisers' points of view, a magazine exists to sell (run) ads; and the advertisers' desires (which are anyhow pretty much the same as the publisher's) generally determine editorial content.

Advertising space is access to a consumer market—the people who read the magazine. Hence elaborate, constant, and expensive reader surveys: advertisers want to know where your readers live, what their educational level is, what occupations they (and/or their husbands) are in, how many children are in the average reader's family, what the average reader's income is, etc.

All this because in order to sell whatsoever it is you have to sell, you have to know who you're talking to. The advertising copy—and to some extent, the product—you offer to a noncollege-educated, $8,000-per-year suburban woman is not the same as that you address to a college-educated working mother in a large city, or to a single woman.

Given the fact that, from the viewpoint of publisher and advertiser, the ultimate goal of a women's magazine is to *sell* (the magazine, the products it advertises), what—in their estimation and experience—makes women buy? A quick survey of ads and the editorial copy that supplements them yields some obvious answers.

To wit: How does a wife and mother demonstrate her concern/love/devotion to her family? She bakes them a Betty Crocker/Pillsbury/ Swans Down just-like-homemade cake. How does a woman secure her husband's wandering attention? She acts "like an expensive mistress" (demands a mink coat), as a recent *New York Times* ad put it. How does a woman explore and express her individuality? She tries an "exotic" or "offbeat" or "romantic" new lipstick, perfume, paint for the kitchen; she takes an exciting trip to Paris; she buys a cookbook and tries out an exotic recipe. In short, how does a woman (or any proper American) express who she is and how she relates to other people? She buys, buys, buys.

And if you don't have life insurance (get your husband to buy it), you're neglecting the future interests of your children. If you don't have a set of "good" china as well as dishes for everyday use, you're a bit plain, a bit common, a bit of a drag. If you don't treat yourself to a new dress/hairdo/makeup once in a while, well, that's your business, but you really are needlessly denying yourself.

All of which is not to say that one ought not to enjoy a new dress, a trip to Paris, a new paint job for the kitchen, or whatever. All of which *is* to say that if you think such things—*things*—are sufficient satisfaction of basic human needs, sufficient expression of human relationships, you're in trouble. And given the overriding social pressure we live under, when in some corner of your mind you realize that something's missing, your urge will be to fill the gap with still another thing. Including such *things* as psychiatric therapy, going to a good movie, taking a course at a museum—in all cases one pays the price and gets what's paid for. (Even on the emotional level we deal in terms of prices exacted and paid. Consider the human meaning of familiar turns of phrase like "What is that relationship costing you emotionally? . . . I just can't afford an involvement, or commitment, of that sort.")

One of the main props of this commodity culture is the current—and classic—image of the American woman. She is feminine: nonaggressive, noncompetitive (with men), intuitive, and instinctual (more than rational). She is physically beautiful (or at least committed to trying to be). She is loving, warm, sympathetic, mothering; as distinguished from (often opposed to) men, who are hard-headed, cold-blooded, selfish, and authoritarian. Since the World War II era, when women were needed in large numbers to work in jobs left vacant by men going into the army, it has become generally acceptable, even desirable, for women to work.

Over the last twenty years, the image of American women one commonly finds in women's magazines has changed. It has also remained basically unchanged. If you were to skim through all the back issues of a woman's magazine for the last twenty years (as I often did when I worked at the *Ladies' Home Journal*), you'd find the changes rather striking. Shortly after the end of World War II, when the men came home and women were no longer needed in the labor market in large numbers, there was a flood of articles, the general theme of which was: "I used to work from nine to five and it was good because it was patriotic, but now I have returned to being 'just' a housewife again and it's great." This was supplemented by articles on the joys of mother-hood, and how there's no such thing as "just" a housewife (a wife is a psychiatrist, a chauffeur, a mediator of disputes, a gourmet cook, a hobby expert, a laundress, seamstress, Girl Scout leader, civic helper, etc.).

By the late 1950s, this theme was not so frequent. And as the 1960s advanced, there began to appear another—and apparently quite contradictory—theme. Articles popped up which discussed whether one could manage to work and be a proper mother at the same time. Strictly family-oriented magazines introduced regular features aimed at the young, unmarried working girl. Feature articles about how it's possible (and desirable) to get away from the kids for a day or a week cropped up, along with articles about going back to school (often to get teaching credentials) at age forty ("My Daughter and I Are Class-mates").

Supplementing this came ads whose general message was: explore your creative potential; don't (just) sit by the hearth; be a little wild, be a little extravagant; indulge yourself. Lipsticks were given exotic names—Pago Pago Peach, Mad Mocha. Perfumes hinted at indiscretion and just-this-side-of-illicit romance—Sirocco, Intimate, Indiscrète.

The new image of an adventurous, assertive, nonhomebound woman seemed at odds with the stereotype of the passive, mothering, feminine woman. What happened to all those myths about how a career woman loses her femininity and becomes cold and competitive? If a woman makes a good consumer precisely because she's passive, relying on buying things to establish her identity and to express her purpose and relationships, wasn't this new image rather subversive—at least potentially?

Dead wrong. Point number one: all the adventurousness and it's-OK-to-have-a-career propaganda was, and is, firmly placed in an unchanged context: it's OK (good, even) to pursue a career—before you're married (or have kids), after your kids are grown, and/or while you're raising kids (if you can manage it, and plenty of women do). It's fine to be adventurous, go back to school, take a trip—but of course that doesn't mean *sacrificing* your role as wife and/or mother.

Point number two: an active, curious, well-educated, assertive woman is a much *better* consumer than a plain old passive woman. Not that there's anything wrong with passivity—it's just a bit old-fashioned, not very with-it, a bit hickish. An active woman develops all sorts of new tastes, new interests, new ways of fulfilling basic needs—and that means you can sell her all sorts of new products. Plain Jane might be so content with her domestic routine and so devoted to her family that she'd never buy a set of golf clubs, never indulge herself with a special beauty treatment, never slip away for a week alone in the sun. (Furthermore, Plain Jane is not likely to enjoy a family income great enough to do that sort of thing.) Bubbling Betty, on the other hand, finds time to golf on weekends, took a trip to Paris last year and flipped on French cooking (cookbooks, special cooking utensils, special food products), and has been thinking of spending a day in the city treating herself to a once-over facial and hairstyling. Bubbling Betty's husband probably earns upward of $15,000 a year, and Betty herself may work part-time.

Confirmation that who and what women are supposed to be is comparable to what our grandmothers were supposed to be (with added fillips) comes in the February 1969 issue of several women's magazines. *McCall's*, *Glamour*, and *Single Girl* include articles about "the sexual revolution" and its attendant problems. What they mean by "sexual revolution" is that many young people today are "cohabiting in an unmarried state." All the articles take it for granted that this is not a revolution in practice, but in frankness: our parents may have slept together, even lived together, before they were married; but they didn't do it openly.

OK, it's not that much of a revolution. But something is going on that women's magazines which never had touched this heretofore awkward subject have to deal with. On one level, women with teen-age daughters have to figure out what to tell them about living with a man. Is it OK? Not OK? Sometimes OK? What are the limits of acceptability? From another angle, young women living with a man have to decide on what basis the relationship exists. Do they, should they, intend to get married? How soon? Why?

The parameters of acceptability are these: *Of course* marriage is the eventual goal of a living arrangement. *Single Girl* features an article on "How to Get the Man You're Living with to Marry You." The *McCall's* article thinks living arrangements are acceptable "because . . . they [young women] will be released from the pressures of early marriage, hasty marriage. . . ." The *Glamour* article details the agonies of several young women trying to figure out how to broach the subject, trying to decide whether to stick it out until the man in question is ready.

Parameter of acceptability number two: *of course* (OF COURSE) if you want to have children, you get married. In this case, much more is conveyed by what isn't said than by what is. None of the articles even remotely considers that a man and a woman might have a child and stay together, but not marry. A woman might raise a child by herself if, for whatever reason, she and the father split up; that's tough but not unheard of. What is entirely and literally unheard of is nonmarriage *and* sticking together *and* raising a family.

The point: the much-publicized sexual revolution is—or at least women's magazines say it is—no revolution at all when you consider what, under all the trimmings, the woman's role is. Even less of a revolution when you look at it in terms of social organization and not only in terms of a single person or family unit: the nuclear family remains the institution within which childbearing and child rearing take place; the nuclear family remains the single most important institution for the purchase of consumer goods. Tamper seriously with the nuclear family, and you're threatening the entire economy, the entire society.

Evidence: the article in *Glamour* notes that there are no statistics available on how many people are living together unmarried. Why? Because according to the Census Bureau, "cohabiting couples are not 'an important consumer entity.'" Consumer entity. Marriage, as they say on Madison Avenue (they really do say this) makes business; living arrangements don't. Sure, if you're living with someone you have to have dishes, food, blankets, clothes, plenty of things. But you're not going to buy life insurance, expensive rugs, "good" china or silver, or any of hundreds of major durable consumer goods (washing machine, vacuum cleaner, etc.). Which is to say, living arrangements that don't transform into marriage could be a sticky wicket for the people who sell life insurance, washing machines and so on.

More evidence about potential problems with living arrangements: the *McCall's* article has buried in it a dead-giveaway sentence. From the businessman's point of view the logic is backward; it nevertheless is sound: "I need to find fixed and immutable aspects to the relationship of man and woman, and so I find them. I find them by refusing to accept a viable alternative to a stable family for the rearing of offspring."

Viable alternative for the rearing of offspring? Viable alternative to the nuclear family, the single most important motor of our consumption-crazy economy? If you're selling washing machines, that's not funny. It is very threatening. Moreover, it's not a vague off-in-the-future threat; it is happening.

It has begun to happen in and around the New Left, that multiorganizational, cultural/political monster that has already caused at least minor problems for American capitalism (take a look at *Fortune* magazine for January 1969 for an idea of how serious, potentially, the problems are). It's not yet a fully conscious or fully political phenomenon. People just live together. Why marry? It's a hassle—forms, licenses, bureaucracy, all of it meaningless. And it's much more of a hassle to get unmarried. So far, every New Left couple I know of who has a child is married (I think, and/or they say). Some people are speculating about what would happen if you had a child and didn't marry. No one really knows—yet. Much talk, also, about setting up day-care centers, about how to deal with raising our kids (not this couple's kids or that couple's; *our* kids). Plus, with very little talk (except some unfortunate pompousness that seems now to have ended), a lovely freedom from "things" has happened. Not that people don't enjoy a new record, not that we give up things and turn ascetic; we've broken the *compulsiveness* of consumption.

And with this, another political event has begun to connect hundreds of groups all over the country. There's no single, no central organization, but it is collectively known as the Women's Liberation Movement. This movement has diverse sources; women who have been active in various New Left groups are into Women's Liberation, and so are women who never before in their lives have been politically aware or involved. One common element amid the considerable diversity is an understanding/conviction/feeling that the image of womanhood we've been brought up with (the image that women's magazines convey) is wrong, bad, destructive. The fundamental wrongness is that we're supposed to believe we can satisfy our real needs by buying things and by buying things only. And of course we can't—which is precisely the point. Unsatisfied, we buy more, more, and more. Always a little hungry. Always seeing fulfillment just a little out of reach.

The political potential, the human potential, of this movement is enormous. We are half of humankind; we are 53 percent of America. We've been pinched and repressed and distorted in a thousand ways for a thousand years and more. Tap that sublimated and misdirected energy, and something's going to happen. Is happening. Soon it will become stylish; the *New York Times* printed in February a long—and quite sympathetic—article about the "women of the American revolution, 1969." Stylishness will not kill it, any more than the media really killed what was strong and liberating in the early hippie movement.

And the women's magazines? How will they accommodate this upheaval? Soon we will start seeing articles about furniture fashions for the liberated woman living with the liberated (swinging, chic, young) man. Soon will come articles about honeymoonlike vacations for the unmarried set. Soon will come articles detailing the horrors of being thirty-five and having lived with a man (or men) contentedly for years, and suddenly realizing you're all alone. And not quite so soon, but certainly on the agenda, are articles about the entirely disastrous consequences of trying to raise a child with a man you're not married to.

The consequences—plenty of them—will be disastrous, precisely to the degree to which people are left to deal with them alone. Enter once more the Women's Liberation Movement and the New Left (of which it is a part), which bears promise of not having to deal with the consequences alone. If cohabitation without marriage and child rearing without marriage (without relying on the nuclear family) are dealt with socially and politically—along with a vast number of other things, to be sure—we stand a chance of beginning to transform our society profoundly, and in immensely healthy ways.

Think of it just in terms of the development of a healthy, curious, confident, loving child. A hundred years ago, a child grew up in an extended family (parents, lots of brothers and sisters, grandparents, aunts, uncles, and their families). Grew up, in other words, used to being around a variety of people and not dependent only upon his parents for love, for identity formation, for early learning. Contrast that with a child (I know too many) who grows up, until age three or four maybe, knowing the adult world only through his parents, with his parents as his only stable/frequent/reliable reference points. It's bad. It means (comparatively) limited ability to accept and relate to people who aren't your parents, it means your early (and partially definitive) interests, prejudices and skills are limited by those of your parents; it means, in short, going through critical formative years in a semideprived environment.

The Women's Liberation Movement is real. It's growing so quickly that a standard complaint of every women's group I know of is that they don't know how to absorb new members fast enough. And one of the top items on our agenda is a redefinition of who we are. Step one in that redefinition is that we aren't who the women's magazines say we are, or ought to be. And redefining ourselves and how we live—*we're* doing the defining this time, not the guys that sell shampoo and refrigerators (and make a little napalm on the side). Redefining ourselves is what liberation is about.

23

A MARRIAGE AGREEMENT

ALIX SHULMAN

When my husband and I were first married a decade ago, "keeping house" was less of a burden than a game. We both worked full-time at jobs and we each pretty much took care of ourselves. We had a small apartment which stayed empty most of each day so that taking care of it was very little trouble. Every couple of weeks we'd spend a Saturday morning cleaning and taking our laundry to the laundromat. Though I usually did the cooking, our meals were casual and simple. We shopped for food together after work; sometimes we ate out; we had our breakfast at a diner near work; sometimes my husband cooked; there were few dishes. In the evenings we went for long walks and weekends we spent in Central Park. Our domestic life was beautifully uncomplicated.

Then our first child was born. I quit my job to stay home with him. Our domestic life was suddenly very complicated. When our second child was born, domestic life, the only life I had any longer, became a tremendous burden.

Once we had children, we totally accepted the sex roles society assigns. My husband worked all day in an office and I was at home, so the domestic burden fell almost entirely on me. We had to move to a larger apartment to accommodate the children. Keeping it minimally livable was no longer a matter of an hour or two a week but took hours of every day: children make unbelievable messes. Our one meal a day for two people turned into a half dozen meals a day for anywhere from one to four people at a time, and everyone ate different food. To shop for this brood—or even just to run out for a quart of milk—became a major project. It meant putting on snowsuits, boots, and mittens, getting strollers or carriages up and down stairs, and scheduling the trip so it not interfere with someone's feeding or nap or illness or some other domestic job. Laundry turned from a weekly to a daily chore. And all this tumult started for me at six in the morning and didn't let up until nine at night, and *still* there wasn't time enough to do everything.

But even more burdensome than the physical work of child rearing was the relentless responsibility I had for the children. There was literally nothing I could do or even contemplate without having to consider first how the children would be affected. Answering their questions alone ruled out for me such a minimum of privacy as a private *mental* life. They were always *there*. I couldn't read or think. If there ever was a moment to read, I read to them.

My husband's job began keeping him at work later and later, and sometimes took him out of town. If I suffered from too much domesticity, he suffered from too little. The children were usually asleep when he got home and I was too exhausted to talk. He became a stranger. Though he had sometimes, when we were first married, cooked for the two of us, that was no longer possible. A meal had become a major complicated production, in which timing counted heavily and someone might be crying in the background. No longer could we decide at the last moment what we felt like having for supper. And there were always dishes in the sink.

As the children grew up, our domestic arrangement seemed increasingly odious to me. I took freelance work to do at home in order to keep some contact with the world, but I had to squeeze it into my "free" time. My husband, I felt, could always change his job if the pressure was too great, but I could never change mine. When I finally began to see my situation from a Women's Liberation point of view, I realized that the only way we could possibly survive as a family (which we wanted to do) was to throw out the old sex roles we had been living by and start again. Wishing to be once more equal and independent as we had been when we had met, we decided to make an agreement in which we could define our roles our own way. We wanted to share completely the responsibility for caring for our household and for raising our children, by then five and seven. We recognized that after a decade of following the traditional sex roles we would have to be extremely vigilant and wary of backsliding into our old domestic habits. If it was my husband's night to take care of the children, I would have to be careful not to check up on how he was managing; if the baby sitter didn't show up for him, it would have to be *his* problem.

When our agreement was merely verbal, it didn't work; our old habits were too firmly established. So we made a formal agreement instead, based on a detailed schedule of family duties and assignments. Eventually, as the old roles and habits are replaced, we may be able to abandon the formality of our arrangement, but now the formality is imperative. Good intentions are simply not enough.

Our agreement is designed for our particular situation only in which my husband works all day at a job of his choice, and I work at home on a freelance basis during the hours the children are in school (from 8:30 till 3:00). If my husband or I should change jobs, income, or working hours, we would probably have to adjust our agreement to the altered circumstances. Now, as my husband makes much more money than I do, he pays for most of our expenses.

Marriage Agreement

I. Principles

We reject the notion that the work which brings in more money is the more valuable. The ability to earn more money is already a privilege which must not be compounded by enabling the larger earner to buy out of his/her duties and put the burden on the one who earns less, or on someone hired from outside.

We believe that each member of the family has an equal right to his/her own time, work, value, choices. As long as all duties are performed, each person may use his/her extra time any way he/she chooses. If he/she wants to use it making money, fine. If he/she wants to spend it with spouse, fine. If not, fine.

As parents we believe we must share all responsibility for taking care of our children and home—not only the work, but the responsibility. At least during the first year of this agreement, *sharing responsibility* shall mean:

1. Dividing the *jobs* (see "Job Breakdown" below); and

2. dividing the *time* (see "Schedule" below) for which each parent is responsible.

In principle, jobs should be shared equally, 50-50, but deals may be made by mutual agreement. If jobs and schedule are divided on any other than a 50-50 basis, then either party may call for a reexamination and redistribution of jobs or a revision of the schedule at any time. Any deviation from 50-50 must be for the convenience of both parties. If one party works overtime in any domestic job, she/he must be compensated by equal extra work by the other. For convenience, the schedule may be flexible, but changes must be formally agreed upon. The terms of this agreement are rights and duties, not privileges and favors.

II. Job Breakdown

A. Children

1. Mornings: waking children; getting their clothes out, making their lunches; seeing that they have notes, homework, money, passes, books, etc.; brushing their hair; giving them breakfast; making coffee for us.

2. Transportation: getting children to and from lessons, doctors, dentists, friends' houses, park, parties, movies, library, etc.; making appointments.

3. Help: helping with homework, personal problems, projects like cooking, making gifts, experiments, planting, etc.; answering questions, explaining things.

4. Nighttime: getting children to take baths, brush their teeth, go to bed, put away their toys and clothes; reading with them; tucking them in and having night-talks; handling if they wake and call in the night.

5. Babysitters: getting babysitters, which sometimes takes an hour of phoning.

6. Sick Care: calling doctors, checking out symptoms, getting prescriptions filled, remembering to give medicine, taking days off to stay home with sick child; providing special activities.

7. Weekends: all above, plus special activities (beach, park, zoo, etc.).

B. Housework

8. Cooking: breakfasts; dinners (children, parents, guests).

9. Shopping: food for all meals; housewares; clothing and supplies for children.

10. Cleaning: dishes daily; apartment weekly, biweekly, or monthly,

11. Laundry: home laundry; making beds; dry cleaning (take and pick up).

III. Schedule

(The numbers on the following schedule refer to Job Breakdown list.)

1. Mornings: every other week each parent does all.

2. and 3. Transportation and Help: parts occurring between 3:00 and 6:30 P.M., fall to wife. She must be compensated (see 10 below). Husband does all weekend transportation and pickups after 6:00. The rest is split.

4. Nighttime (and all Help after 6:30): husband does Tuesday, Thursday, and Sunday. Wife does Monday, Wednesday, and Saturday. Friday is split according to who has done extra work during the week.

5. Babysitters must be called by whoever the sitter is to replace. If no sitter turns up, the parent whose night it is to take responsibility must stay home.

6. Sick Care: this must still be worked out equally, since now wife seems to do it all. (The same goes for the now frequently declared school closings for so-called political protest, whereby the mayor gets credit at the expense of the mothers of young children. The mayor only closes the schools, not the places of business or the government offices.)

7. Weekends: split equally. Husband is free all of Saturday, wife is free all of Sunday, except that the husband does all weekend transportation, breakfasts, and special shopping.

8. Cooking: wife does all dinners except Sunday nights; husband does all weekend breakfasts (including shopping for them and dishes), Sunday dinner, and any other dinners on his nights of responsibility if wife isn't home. Breakfasts are divided week by week. Whoever invites the guests does shopping, cooking, and dishes; if both invite them, split work.

9. Shopping: divide by convenience. Generally, wife does local daily food shopping, husband does special shopping for supplies and children's things.

10. Cleaning: Husband does all the housecleaning, in exchange for wife's extra child care (3:00 to 6:30 daily) and sick care. Dishes: same as 4.

11. Laundry: wife does most home laundry. Husband does all dry cleaning delivery and pick up. Wife strips beds, husband remakes them.

After only four months of strictly following our agreement, our daughter said one day to my husband, "You know, Daddy, I used to love Mommy more than you, but now I love you both the same."

24

WOMEN AS PROPERTY

VERNA TOMASSON

A porno movie house on Eighth Avenue had a film on its bill recently called simply, *Divorcee*. That one word was supposed to call up enough libidinous fantasies to induce customers to pay the $5 entrance fee. Yet, the real obscenity in a divorced woman's life—a brutal and dehumanizing experience—is her encounter with the judicial system, which is stacked in custom and practice against her, and her degrading visits to the house of horrors on East 22nd Street, known as Family Court.

Sitting in the parallel pews of the large antechamber and waiting for your name to be called is the closest experience to Limbo that anyone can imagine. Although all litigants are ordered to appear at 9:30 A.M., those without attorneys must wait until those with attorneys get through, the theory being, one supposes, that the time of a professional is worth something, but the time of a poor person, or a stranded mother, is worth nothing at all.

The worst part of the waiting, though, is the knowing that the outcome of your hearing depends on pure luck—and that in all likelihood you will very soon be back here again. Since there are between thirty and thirty-five cases on each judge's calendar per day, that leaves about ten minutes per case. Ten minutes allotted to each tale of heartbreak, ten minutes to decide the standard of living of a family, or determine who should have custody of a child.

You learn, after your first few visits here, that the patience of the average Family Court judge is extremely thin. He usually asks about four or five questions, which he prefers answered in monosyllables. All other information must be tersely and unemotionally presented, or the judge will become annoyed and do something spiteful. If the matter appears at all complex, your case will be postponed, and the whole grueling procedure will begin again.

A "good" lawyer is not as much help as one might think. First of all, they are almost impossible to get. The lack of any state or federal standards covering questions of alimony and child support makes the courtroom procedure a matter of guesswork resting on the whims of the judge. For this reason and because of the depressing atmosphere of this court—and also because there is very little to be gained in fees from this kind of work—most attorneys are reluctant to take such cases, and women face the ordeal alone.

Even if you do manage to enlist the services of an attorney, he can often do you more harm than good. Too often he is untrained in this particular branch of the law, embarrassed at having to take sides in an acrimonious interpersonal dispute, and unprepared for patterns which present themselves. Most ex-husbands, for example, attempt to mask their actual income and engage in wild accusations as a technique of obfuscation, so skillful detective work is involved. And, in all too many cases, lawyers will sell themselves to the highest bidder and go into collusion with the husband's attorney. Note the pronoun "he" in relation to antecedent "lawyer." There are still too few women lawyers devoted to working for women's rights, and those few are swamped with history-making constitutional decisions and unable to handle individual cases. The Women's Center, which serves as a clearinghouse for services for women, reports floods of frantic phone calls from women desperate for legal help, and some who just want a "sister" to go down to the court with them to offer emotional support.

One woman I spoke to had been in and out of Family Court eight times. She had had eight different judges. Each judge spent most of the time trying to determine what the judge before had decided. This is not unusual. The latest Senate Judiciary Subcommittee report on the Family Court mentioned that "some 30 appearances have been required by one petitioner without achieving finality."

Unfortunately, the probation officer, who is the only person having direct contact with all aspects of a case from the beginning (he or she interviews all parties to a dispute at intake, and in about half the cases, actually settles cases before they come to court), never personally appears in court, so that pertinent facts about a family situation often never find their way to the judge at all.

The infamous Fulmanero case brought to national attention the bureaucracy and insensitivity of one province of the Family Court: child abuse and custody. But the areas of child support and alimony remain hidden because most of the women involved are afraid of endangering what little income they do receive, and risking starvation for themselves and children. So the myth of the "gay divorcee," who supposedly was married for less than a year, did not work, and now lives a life of an extravagant, overdressed spendthrift and promiscuous pleasure-seeker at her ex-husband's expense, remains unchallenged.

Here are some of the actual cases now pending at Family Court. The women have asked that their real names not be used, for fear of prejudicing their cases. "Barbara" has been fighting for nine years for support for her handicapped daughter. Her husband makes $55,000 a year in his own business. He refuses to pay for special care for the handicapped child. The court has thus far upheld him.

"Linda" is the wife of a "successful" physician who kept a succession of mistresses. When she asked for a separation, he threw her and their five-year-old child out of the house, and cleared the apartment of all the belongings, including hers. When she went to see him, he sprayed mace in her face. She requested a protection bond from Family Court. In court, he accused her of being a whore, and of having sexual relations with a fourteen-year-old friend of her son. Despite her excellent character witnesses and glowing reports from her children's schools, the judge ruled "provocation proved."

"Lucille's" former husband has thrown his two children on the ground and stepped on them. When the son cried out, he called him a homosexual. The judge ruled that unless the father molested the children sexually, visiting rights could not be denied.

"Death levels all ranks," said an English poet. So does divorce. "Virginia," a black welfare mother whose husband had skipped off to another state and whose children were confiscated and put into a "shelter," is not much worse off than the suburban woman, "Mary," who was left with a $100,000 house but no income to maintain it. All bills and taxes had to be paid; the lawn had not been mowed in a year. She was also unable to keep up payments for the children's private schools. The court has on record doctors' statements showing that she was hemorrhaging under the severe emotional strain of being stranded in an isolated community without a car and trying to maintain herself and two children at their previous level for two years without funds.

How have these and other atrocities been allowed to take place? Through some very basic flaws in the organization, structure and functioning of this most peculiar court.

The New York State Family Court was set up in 1962, a carry-over from Children's Court and the old Domestic Relations Court. It has jurisdiction over neglect, support, paternity, juvenile delinquency, persons in need of supervision, and family offenses. Questions of divorce, annulment and separations are handled in Supreme Court; custody is not a concern of the court if it primarily arises in connection with matrimonial action; adoptions are still handled in Surrogate's Court; and juvenile offenders over sixteen are tried in Criminal Court. So there's the first problem right there. A multiplicity of agencies (with separate monetary allocations) to deal with similar and overlapping areas.

When the Family Court was established, it was stated by the legislature: "It [the Family Court] must deal with sensitive and difficult areas of life about which reasonable men and women differ. Hence it is necessarily an experimental court . . . and looks to improvements based on experience and observation." Every year, in its annual reports to the legislature, the Senate Judiciary Subcommittee has been reiterating the sorry tidings that the experiment is a failure. The 1968 subcommittee report, for instance, reveals that during the three judicial years 1963–66, the backlog of undisposed cases at the end of these years increased from over 30,000 to 45,000 (about 50 percent), and this despite the steady increase in the number of judges and court personnel.

That report lists three principal areas responsible for the court's ineffectiveness: (a) lack of facilities for placement; (b) lack of qualified auxiliary personnel; and (c) lack of coordination between those implementing services that are available and the judiciary.

"Qualitative probation and allied services," says the report, "are a key to a successful Family Court. Unfortunately, neither probation nor other auxiliary services are capable of meeting the needs of the court or the community." The most recent Senate Judiciary Subcommittee report (March 3, 1970) states: "It is our conclusion that there exists a remoteness and a lack of rapport relative to the day-to-day functioning of the Family Court and the responsible members of the Administrative Board of the Judicial Conference, and of the Appellate Divisions." The new report continues, "This unique situation of a court being assigned to deal with criminal offenses with no penal authority and being dependent upon the cooperation and assistance of other municipal agencies and private social organizations, so often understaffed and ill-equipped to meet even the minimum needs and demands of this court, contributes heavily to its inability to become the social forum it was designed to be."

The main reason for the poor quality of the probationary and other counseling services is insufficient budgetary appropriations. Mrs. Elizabeth Schack at the Community Service Society (one of the private social organizations which attempt to work in conjunction with the Family Court) says that one of the biggest frustrations in trying to implement Family Court decisions is the constant turnover in court personnel, a direct result of low salary levels. Secretaries at Family Court make $5,200 a year, and after training, usually leave for some other place. Probation officers make $9,700 per annum, and there is almost no opportunity for upward promotion.

Many reforms have been suggested for the reorganization of the Family Court. Last year, the Liberal party recommended the unification of the Claims, Surrogates, and Family Court with the Supreme Court, and the League of Women Voters of New York State came out with a pamphlet decrying what they called "fragmented justice." They urged that there be "one court to handle all matters affecting children and families. . . . It is more *economical* to centralize all supporting services in one place; more *effective* to have one court deal with interrelated family problems; more *equitable* to follow uniform practices" in the state.

But more restructuring would not go far enough. That is because the courts are committed to uphold the present marriage and divorce laws, which are based on the antiquated assumption that woman in marriage is the property of the man. The wife, for example, is still required to perform all domestic services, and she must have sexual relations with her husband *on demand* (legalized rape?) unless she is physically ill.

Family Court also perpetuates the oppressive alimony system. Usually thought of as a boon to women and a hardship on men, the concept of alimony is an insult to women. It does not represent payment for household labor done. It represents a concession to the fact that men and women do not have equal opportunities for employment and job training. It is also supposed to make up for the fact that the state does not provide adequate day-care facilities so that the divorced woman can go back to work. Alimony says, "here, you poor, helpless, unqualified and useless person, take this." The woman has to pay taxes on alimony; the ex-husband takes it as a deduction.

Digging one level deeper, the legislation on these matters will probably not be changed unless the societal values and attitudes underlying the laws are changed. Despite the much advertised sexual revolution, a double standard still prevails in the courts. The main manifestation of the double standard is that man's work is respected, and woman's is not. In a case in Nassau County Family Court, the court psychiatrist had judged the husband "emotionally immature and emotionally disturbed," yet when the husband announced he was a physician and listed some of his property holdings, the judge became reverent.

A double standard of morality also prevails in that during the two-year separation period preceding a New York State divorce, if a wife has sex relations once with a man other than her husband, she can be declared an unfit mother and her children taken from her. The only way a father can be declared unfit is if it can be proved he has sexually molested the children. Beatings, drunkenness, drug addiction, adultery are not enough grounds.

Also operative against women at court is an assumption that women should be quiet, passive, pleasant and "warm." If in response to a bald-faced lie or false accusation she cries out or raises her voice, she is usually called a "hysterical woman" or other adjectives such as "vindictive" or "overemotional" and silenced by the judge.

The only area where a double standard is not evident at court is the one area where it should be—that of employment. Many women are told by the court, "If you need more money, go get a better job," without any recognition of the fact that child rearing and housekeeping are full-time occupations in themselves, and furthermore, that the economy does not welcome women in high-paying levels of employment. They forget, too, that over 60 percent of married women age 35–64 do not work outside of the home and are in need of education and job training.

Several women's rights groups are turning their attention to the revision of marriage and divorce laws and the restructuring of the courts. The program of the National Organization of Women (NOW) for last year included some of the following recommendations:

— that a pamphlet setting forth general personal and property rights of each partner in marriage under New York State law he distributed to applicants for marriage licenses, and that the applicants be given a test (the way drivers are) before receiving a license.
— that facilities for the rehabilitation and training of the divorced woman be established, and a guidance counselor be assigned to the court handing down the decree, for the benefit of those who do not have jobs or appropriate ones.
— that the spouse, if financially able, should assume financial responsibility for education of the divorced woman. A special program for divorced persons could be established at state colleges.
— that social security benefits be extended to the divorced women, and that the housewife be insured as an individual, not as her husband's dependent. (Housewife is the only occupation where the social security benefits go to the next occupant of the job rather than being credited to the employee.)

Another group, the League for Women's Rights, is a newly formed band of "victims" who have been subjected to harassing court experiences; and women civil rights lawyers who have committed themselves to supporting the aims and activities of the group, which are: to inform all women of the double standard inherent in the law and promulgated by the courts; to substitute for the word "alimony" a realistic concept of "accrued income" to be based on the recognition of wifehood and motherhood as recompensible employment; to put divorce on an equal footing with the dissolution of a business partnership. Elements to be considered would be the number of years of marriage; whether the woman brought in income or property; number of children involved; was household help provided if the woman was sick or disabled; was there compensation for any physical damage resulting from childbearing or child rearing (workman's compensation); social security, medical insurance, and life insurance coverage; provision for job training for the dependent spouse at the dissolution of marriage; finally to prepare the way for federal standardization of marriage and divorce procedures backed by the constitutional guarantee of equal rights for all.

The answer, these groups agree, is not to appoint a few more women judges to the bench. Society has got to stop seeing women as carefree, one-dimensional sex objects, and then becoming hostile when they exhibit problems and needs. The Family Court must stop sweeping women and children under the rug.

25

DIVORCE AS SURVIVAL: THE BUCK STOPS HERE

CAROL SCOTT and JEAN OKEN

Divorce is more frequently becoming a positive, creative process. As women begin to recognize the degree of oppression inherent in the marriage situation, divorce can be approached like an operation that, while painful and frightening, is absolutely necessary for survival. We can tell you some things we learned about beginning to function on our own that might enable some women to decide whether this is something they can handle.

We found that we didn't have to be very brave or strong or aggressive to get divorced. We just realized that our situation would destroy us if we remained in it. Making radical changes in the way we live thus becomes a simple act of self-preservation. We didn't get much sympathy from the people we had to deal with in the process; the law is an unwieldy relic of medieval times that seems to work against women oftener than it protects our rights. Divorce lawyers are disgusting men by and large, oriented toward establishing innocence on the part of the clients and gouging as much money as possible from the "guilty" party. Unfortunately their technical skill is really required in most situations in order to accomplish the legal and financial arrangements as efficiently and equitably as possible. However, it would be a great mistake to expect a lawyer to act as a source of approval and reinforcement. We feel that the more a woman resists the urge to solicit his protective sympathy, the less time will be wasted that could be better spent in his helping her determine exactly what her legal position is, and the less money he will charge. One divorce lawyer has a bar in his office and while he "sympathetically" commiserates over a relaxing drink, he reveals his true attitudes with statements such as, "Of course the alimony won't really matter—a beautiful young woman like you . . . won't be long before some other poor devil comes along. . . ." We advise you keep your legs crossed and insist that he restrict his expensive time to the business at hand.

Hardly anyone can accept that we could have decided unilaterally, with no ulterior motives (such as splitting with *another* man) that ending our marriages and making it alone is a desirable and responsible goal. It's probably better not to waste energy trying to justify the decision to people who don't instantly understand; just say what is absolutely necessary and let them draw their own conclusions.

Every woman has a well of insecurity that is tapped by accusations of selfishness, immaturity, and neurotic motivations. The resultant guilt can obscure the central fact of her situation: that she is acting to remove herself from the influence of a destructive relationship with a person whose needs preclude the satisfaction of her needs, whose values negate and supersede her values, and whose ego demands the sacrifice of her ego. Being clear about the legitimacy of this act makes it easier to avoid getting hung up with the endless defensive gestures that can divert one from her appointed course.

To the degree that a woman has internalized the passive-dependent role as someone's wife, she will be horrified by the sheer weight of responsibility for children, house, car, appliances, insurance, taxes, etc. that falls on the Head of the Household. Many women are defeated in advance by the fear that they will be unable to cope with these jobs that have always been taken care of by fathers and husbands. We can only say that our helplessness in these areas was unrivaled by any woman we have ever met; when we began doing the things it really was hard; we made lots of hideous, potentially disastrous blunders, but the jobs got done and most of the machinery is still functioning.

It became difficult to relate to most of the people who were a part of our married lives. This is one of the few things in divorce books that we found to be true. They ask all sorts of more or less insulting questions like, "How is it affecting the children?" (any answer sounds defensive); "Are you dating anyone yet?" (still of primary importance in their minds, and how embarrassing if a woman has to say *no!*); "What are you going to *do?*" It's useless to try to answer these questions, since they are asked from a frame of reference which we have rejected, and explanations are only misunderstood.

This alienation is real, and before we can get comfortable in a new environment it is necessary to relinquish our death-grip on the old one whose mechanisms are no longer effective. It's a frightening, ongoing process but we found that in doing the thinking that leads up to the decision to get divorced, we had already made a lot of the changes in our values and priorities.

Learning to live alone, or alone with children, is easier than might be expected. Of course, we feel loneliness, but never again the hopeless loneliness of being stuck for life with a person we couldn't stand. By this time there is little value in having another body in bed when that person's presence makes it impossible to get to sleep. Certainly sexual frustration is unpleasant, but it is quite nice to make love *only* when we really dig it, rather than to make up for the damage we and our husbands had done to each other all day. Not quite enough great sex is infinitely preferable to a surfeit of mechanical, mutual exploitation.

Crises still arise that are no fun to handle without support and relief from another adult. Children still get sick. They still throw up and cry all night with ear infections, just as they always did. Tires get flat, toilets overflow, cats eat gerbils, fuses blow, televisions and washing machines break down just as they always did. The only difference *now* is, instead of calling our husbands only to have them tell us to call a plumber, we simply eliminate that step and call the plumber. It's not hard at all—there will be no lectures on our ineptitude in running a house, no installation of guilt—the plumber is even glad for the business. He doesn't need to be repaid with a slice of our egos—all *he* wants is money. After we had dealt with a few of these bummers by ourselves, we began to expect them and then allowed for them in our planning. And after we had handled one we could have a drink and go to bed without wading through a fresh pile of personal shit about why we didn't feel like a little old roll in the hay.

Women contemplating divorce can reject a lot of the guilt to which we are vulnerable by beginning to question the value of the nuclear family as the *only* environment in which children can flourish. We must be careful not to substitute the structure of the family for the goal of the family: a healthy atmosphere for raising children. The structure (one woman, one man, plus children) is Not an absolute, but an accepted standard in our culture. The same culture, incidentally, which accepts slumlords, imperialism, and organized crime, to name a few, as facts of life.

Before freaking on being other than average in the eyes of the great majority, we should consider these alternatives to the misery we support "for the children's sake." One of the most rewarding and immediate results of a divorce is the advent of peace in the home. The mere absence of those terrifying explosions of hate, not to mention the often more disturbing undercurrent of suppressed anger, does wondrous things for children. (Let's not kid ourselves, even if we saved our grievances for after their bedtime, they *knew*.) Within a few days the tension melts from their faces and they noticeably relax. In addition to these direct results, they reap the rewards of their mother's own increased peace of mind. No one can respond effectively to young children's needs when her energies are being drained in a daily struggle for her very existence as a person.

There is always the fear that the children will be desperately lonesome for their father. But consider the superiority of two solid hours of Father's undivided attention to twenty-four hours of annoyed brush-offs, preoccupied grunts, disinterested stares with a sprinkling of Almighty Approval and ego-powered rage. In addition, the clearly defined "fun" with Dad is a useful tool for giving children the necessary image of Dad as a good guy when you are hard put to find material in support of that image.

There is a potential for a bad trip when we inevitably think, "If only I didn't have these children to worry about . . ." However, if we hadn't gotten divorced we'd have them anyway *plus* their father! Besides, their presence forced us to action when we might have been vulnerable to the seduction of withdrawal. We found ourselves able to enjoy them much more when we weren't preoccupied with the stresses of unhappy marriages.

It's important to be clear about what is wrong with marriage so that we can more easily tune out when people start telling us why we can't fit into it. Women often spend a lot of money and energy trying to justify our dissatisfaction with marriage only to be told with varying degrees of articulateness and assurance by our husbands, their families, our families and our psychiatrists that we are ego deficient, suffering from extreme role confusion and penis envy, and that we *need to be in treatment* for our inability to adjust to reality. Somehow it emerges that all these descriptions are indeed true, but that to assign pathology to the distress we feel, and to seek treatment for it, would be to accept false assessments of us, and to adjust on their terms, which are designed to perpetuate the structure of marriage regardless of its diminishing validity. We are right to feel uncomfortable in a role that requires constant denial of our own needs in deference to others' needs. We are right to experience penis envy if it is defined as a desire to get some of the goodies to which the possessor of a penis has sole access. And perhaps the treatment we need consists of recognizing that our situation is indeed painful and threatening, and that we must take steps to change it.

When we perceive that the difficulties that we encounter with divorce are not insurmountable, the rewards for having accepted the challenges these difficulties represent begin to filter through, and it becomes possible to conceive of new ways to live: relating to men as coworkers, friends, brothers who are part of our lives but not our whole lives. We can cease to think of ourselves as some man's woman because we have assumed concrete responsibilities and developed separate identities. We can learn to love men without possessing or being possessed, without using permanence or exclusiveness as criteria for the worth of a relationship. We can enjoy sex without becoming vulnerable to the competitive game playing that has characterized our marriages. We can try to avoid allowing sexual manipulation to compromise our insistence on equal, human to human interaction.

It would be easier and better to start off with these goals but those of us who have been married and/or are mothers obviously have not always known what we know now, and we have to find ways to grow and change within the framework of lives filled with real, inescapable responsibilities to children. We have to be optimistic because experience proves repeatedly that fear of the unknown is not sufficient reason to endure the shelter (which becomes a prison) of unsatisfactory one-to-one relationships that were once our reason for being.

Possibly the greatest value in a divorce lies in the knowledge that our sins, our failings, our friends, our food, our vibes, our triumphs, our karma, our *life* is our doing and ours alone. All responsibility, all criticism and all praise belong only to us. There is indescribable strength and pride in the knowledge that the buck stops here.

PART FOUR

FAMILY FUNCTIONS AND THE LIFE CYCLE

A
Family Functions
and Structural Alternatives

B
Prospects for Middle Age

A

Family Functions
and Structural Alternatives

In most discourse on the importance of the family institution in American society, both the functions it fulfills and the particular structure believed to perform them best come under consideration. There is still widespread acceptance, by and large, of the functionalist postulation, stated most clearly by G. P. Murdock,[1] that the nuclear family is universal and that it always and everywhere fulfills the four basic functions of sexual regulation, reproduction, economic cooperation, and socialization. The article by Reiss shows ample evidence to refute such a postulation, for one or more of these four functions—as well as additional functions thought by some sociologists to characterize the nuclear family—is performed largely or entirely in some societies by other than nuclear units specifically, if not by other than familial units generally. After considering evidence from cross-cultural data, studies of other primates and studies of effects on children of maternal separation, Reiss himself concludes, tentatively at least, that the family is universally a small kinship-structured group which performs the functional prerequisite of nurturant socialization of the newborn.

From the feminist perspective of family change, the concern to define a universal family form as a functional requisite is seen as a quest for limits which opposes experimentation and innovation. Given the dysfunctionality of modern-day life in nuclear family units[2] and the great probability that structural alternatives which

---

1. George Peter Murdock, *Social Structure* (New York: Macmillan, 1949).

2. For discussions of both functions and dysfunctions of life in nuclear families at the present time see William J. Goode, *World Revolution and Family Patterns* (New York: Free Press of Glencoe, 1963); and Arlene Skolnick and Jerome Skolnick, eds., *Family in Transition: Rethinking Marriage, Sexuality, Childrearing and Family Organization* (Boston: Little, Brown, 1971), pp. 1–32.

---

are more beneficial to women can (and do, to some extent) exist in the United States, feminists are directing their attention to such alternatives to accomplish the important societal functions of sexual regulation, reproduction, economic cooperation, and socialization of children. Partly in response to the strength of the women's movement, social scientists, too, are recognizing increasingly the pluralism of family structures and functions and are focusing more on the marital dyad in contrast to the maternal dyad.[3]

Taking the functions common to the nuclear family one at a time, we shall consider the constraints which this arrangement imposes on women currently and some alternative ways of fulfillment being advanced in the literature. First, female sexuality and the consequences of control of its expression were discussed at length in the general Introduction and in introductions B and C in part 2. We emphasize again here that women are far from free "to control their own bodies" and that for this to occur it is clear that elements of the typical psychosexual development process as well as various structures of society must change. Equality between the sexes, in turn, is necessary for the emergence and survival of alternatives to exclusivity in marriage. As Ramey maintains,

> A woman who is dependent on her husband must grant his requests, including the demand for sexual exclusivity, even though she may know that he is not practicing the same exclusivity. An economically emancipated wife, on the other hand, is in a much better position to insist on equality because of her much enhanced economic self-sufficiency. Thus the stage is set for pair-bonding

---

3. As recently as 1966 Clark Vincent pointed to family sociologists' neglect of the adaptive function of the family institution and of the marital, as opposed to the maternal, dyad. See Clark E. Vincent, "Family Spongia: The Adaptive Function," *Journal of Marriage and the Family* 28, no. 1 (February 1966): 29–36; and idem, "Mental Health and the Family," *Journal of Marriage and the Family* 29, no. 1 (February 1969): 18–39.

In 1971 the Groves Conference on Marriage and the Family in San Juan, Puerto Rico, was organized around the theme of Changing Life Styles and Family Forms. The October 1972 issue of the *Family Coordinator*, edited by Marvin B. Sussman, is also organized around this theme and is comprised, in part, of papers presented at the San Juan Conference. See in this volume the articles by Joy D. and Howard J. Osofsky and James W. Ramey.

between equal partners, each able to sustain a life outside marriage, so that both enter into the relationship voluntarily on the assumption that the anticipated benefits will be greater than would be available in a non-pair-bonded state. Furthermore, survival of the marriage depends on each continuing to place a higher value on maintaining the pair-bond than on reverting to their previous state.[4]

Each partner has an equal number of options for roles outside the marriage and consensual sexual activity outside the pair bond would be among these options. Ramey relates the various marriage alternatives to depth and complexity of commitment individuals are willing to make. In this way he distinguishes free-love activities such as affairs, adultery, and swinging from situations involving commitment such as intimate friendship, evolutionary communes, and group marriage. It is a group-marriage structure that Ramey sees as the next major development for the family, especially among the more affluent classes.

With respect to the childbearing function, it is true at present that only women can have babies and, thereby, bear the bulk of the "burden" of the reproductive function. One element of feminist concern is the nature of the pregnancy and childbirth experience and the elimination of some of its most burdensome aspects. In general the most popular ameliorative for the obstetrical practices typical of the American medical establishment is training in the Lamaze technique of natural childbirth or some variation therein,[5] for, among other things, use of such a technique minimizes pain and promotes awareness and active participation—of both parents—in a truly creative activity.

Although the encouragement of educated childbirth is important, it is ultimately less central a concern for the equality of women than the creation of legitimate alternative activities to childbearing for some, if not all, women in our society. Indeed, in

4. James W. Ramey, "Emerging Patterns of Behavior in Marriage: Deviations or Innovations?" *The Journal of Sex Research* 8, no. 1 (February 1972): 9–10.

5. See, for example, Lindsy Van Gelder, "The Aesthetics of Childbirth," *Ramparts* 9, no. 10 (May 1971): 48–51.

the second selection, Grossman maintains that for as long as human beings are reproduced within the female body, there will remain some truth in Sigmund Freud's epigram that "anatomy is destiny." With the apparently forthcoming development of an artificial womb and the possibility of "test-tube babies," however, sexual intercourse and reproduction can be separated completely and men and women's reproductive roles can be equalized, nearly. Clearly, a number of likely consequences from development of an artificial womb could benefit women as well as society in general. These include elimination for women of the dangers and discomforts of childbirth and elimination of all doubt re paternity; facilitation of "sexing" of the embryo; and improvement of fetal medicine in several ways. It is not at all clear, however, that, as Grossman indicates, there will result certain "inevitable" effects on the relations between the sexes, between the generations and between the state and children thus reproduced. We maintain, rather, that the availability of alternative roles for women and the provision of adequate public child-care facilities will depend on lay and professional interest no less than will the development of an artificial womb.

Apart from the possibility someday of reproduction in an artificial environment, there are now alternative means to minimize women's reproductive roles through the provision and use of various contraceptive techniques.[6] There is national interest (stemming, to be sure, more from concern about environmental pollution and depletion of resources, than about women's rights) in determining the efficacy and adequacy of voluntary public family-planning programs, in comparison with other measures, as a means to further reduce fertility levels. One leading critic argues that whereas family-planning programs permit a narrowing of the gap between couples' desired family size and actual family size, childbearing congruent with current desires would not represent an adequate reduction in population growth.[7] At the individual level, nevertheless, the positive consequences of successful family planning are surely real.

Among the measures which Davis and others advocate to

---

6. See in this volume the section on birth control.

7. Kingsley Davis, "Population Policy: Will Current Programs Succeed?," *Science* 158, no. 3802 (November 1967): 730–39.

---

change family-size desires is the provision of alternative roles for women, including employment roles.[8] Although the cause-effect process is not clear, an inverse correlation between fertility and pursuit of professional careers is certainly indicated in the literature generally and Perrucci's study of women engineers and scientists, specifically. She finds that among married respondents, career women are more likely than noncareer women to be childless; and, if they have a family, career women are more likely than noncareerists to have only one child and to bear the child at a later stage in their work careers.

In professional fields such as engineering and science, however, women are underrepresented, with even less than 1 percent of engineers being women. Within these fields, moreover, Perrucci shows that there is significant "selective patterning" of careers and differential career success by sex of college graduates. Discrepancies between occupational values of women employees in these fields and perceptions of their actual work situation may indicate potential problems in their employment and, consequently, may temper potential effects of orientation to work (outside the home) on fertility and childspacing behavior.

It is possible, of course, for a happily employed career woman to become pregnant, by intent or by accident. For the pregnant woman, several decisions must be made, including whether to abort or not; if not, whether to keep the baby or put it up for adoption; and if keeping it, whether to raise it alone or with a husband. The selection by Harriman is the story of an unwed mother's decision to bear and rear an illegitimate child all on her own. She is rejected repeatedly—by the biological father, her employer, her uncle—for her decision not to abort and later, not to give up the child. Amid all difficulties her sisters—a sibling and a consciousness-raising group—are supportive and the employment of a daytime baby-sitter makes it possible for working mother and child to get along all right.

The unavailability of day-care facilities which Harriman encountered is generally characteristic in the United States today despite (or because of) the potential importance of group child

8. John Scanzoni and Martha McMurry, "Continuities in the Explanation of Fertility Control," *Journal of Marriage and the Family* 34, no. 2 (May 1972): 315–22.

care for the liberation of both women and children. As Gross and MacEwan relate, the dominant orientation toward public child care in this country has been and remains to provide it only in such times of national (wartime) or personal (welfare cases) crisis that mothers are required to work outside the home and away from their children—and then to do so primarily for economic interests rather than to benefit children or their mothers. Day care, however, can be seen legitimately as a healthy alternative to the potentially stifling atmosphere of the nuclear family. In contrast to the isolated family, Gross and MacEwan argue that "Group child care . . . has the potential to provide an environment in which children will have more of an opportunity to develop social sensitivity and responsibility, emotional autonomy and trust, and a wider range of interests."

Among group child care supporters there exist various views regarding the important matters of spatial location of the facilities, composition of users of the facilities, nature of the program, and control of the program and activities.[9] The feminist perspective discussed by Gross and MacEwan is a humanitarian one which emphasizes probable effects against sexism of day-care centers which have non-sex-segregated staff and curricula.

Day-care centers represent one alternative or supplement to the nuclear family to accomplish the important function of child socialization.[10] Another alternative to nuclear family units are "households" as proposed by Firestone in the final selection in this section. In a cybernetic socialist society, Firestone maintains that these limited-term groups could adequately perform the functions of reproduction, economic "support," "regulation" of sexual relations and socialization—and without what Reiss calls "rights of possession" as a basis of motivation. She emphasizes, however, that functional though it may be, such a life style may

---

9. For discussions of the issues on these matters see Bettye M. Caldwell, "A Timid Giant Grows Bolder," *Saturday Review* 54, no. 8 (February 1971): 47–49, 65–66; and Vicki Breitbart, *Day Care, Who Cares?* (Detroit, Mich.: Radical Education Project, n.d.).

10. It is important to note that the first feminist requirement for child care in the future is flexibility; that is, many forms of child care should be acceptable. Among other possible solutions are for: (1) a relative or unrelated hired person to assume or share in child-care responsibilities; (2) the father or mother to take full-time care of the children while they are very young; and (3) both parents to work part-time and take care of young children part-time.

appeal, especially during an initial transition period, to only part of the population for a part of their lives; that "households" are not proposed as final answers to questions about alternatives; and that, finally, the most important characteristic to be maintained in the feminist (as in all others) revolution is that of flexibility, the permission of multiple options.

26

THE UNIVERSALITY OF THE FAMILY: A CONCEPTUAL ANALYSIS *

IRA L. REISS

During the last few decades, a revived interest in the question of the universality of the family has occurred. One key reason for this was the 1949 publication of George Peter Murdock's book *Social Structure*.[1] In that book, Murdock postulated that the nuclear family was universal and that it had four essential functions which it always and everywhere fulfilled. These four functions were: (1) socialization, (2) economic cooperation, (3) reproduction, and (4) sexual relations. Even in polygamous and extended family systems, the nuclear families within these larger family types were viewed as separate entities which each performed these four functions.

The simplicity and specificity of Murdock's position makes it an excellent starting point for an investigation of the universal functions of the human family. Since Murdock's position has gained support in many quarters, it should be examined carefully.[2] Brief comments on

---

* The author is grateful to his colleagues David Andrews, June Helm, and David Plath, all of whom read this article and gave the benefits of their comments.

1. George P. Murdock, *Social Structure* (New York: Macmillan, 1949).

2. Many of the textbooks in the family field fail to really cope with this issue and either ignore the question or accept a position arbitrarily. The Census definition also ignores this issue: "A group of two persons or more related by blood, marriage, or

Murdock's position appear in the literature, and some authors, such as Levy and Fallers, have elaborated their opposition.[3] The present paper attempts to go somewhat further, not only in testing Murdock's notion but in proposing and giving evidence for a substitute position. However, it should be clear that Murdock's position is being used merely as an illustration; our main concern is with delineating what, if anything, is universal about the human family.

The four functions of the nuclear family are "functional prerequisites" of human society, to use David Aberle's term from his classic article on the topic.[4] This means that these functions must somehow occur for human society to exist. If the nuclear family everywhere fulfills these functions, it follows that this family should be a "structural prerequisite" of human society, i.e., a universally necessary part of society.[5] The basic question being investigated is not whether these four functions are functional prerequisites of human society—almost all social scientists would accept this—but whether these four functions are necessarily carried out by the nuclear family. If these functions are not everywhere carried out by the nuclear family, then are there any functional prerequisites of society which the nuclear family or any family form does fulfill? Is the family a universal institution in the sense that it always fulfills some functional prerequisite of society? Also, what, if any, are the universal structural features of the family? These are the ultimate questions of importance that this examination of Murdock's position is moving toward.

Murdock's contention that the nuclear family is a structural prerequisite of human society since it fulfills four functional prerequisites of human society is relatively easy to test. If a structure is essential, then finding one society where the structure does not exist or where one

---

adoption and residing together." The recently published *Dictionary of the Social Sciences*, ed. Julius Gould and William Kolb (Glencoe, Ill.: Free Press, 1964), defines the nuclear family as universal. See pp. 257–59. Parsons, Bales, Bell, and Vogel are among those who also seem to accept Murdock's position. See Talcott Parsons and Robert F. Bales, *Family, Socialization and Interaction Process* (Glencoe, Ill.: Free Press, 1955); Talcott Parsons, "The Incest Taboo in Relation to Social Structure and the Socialization of the Child," *British Journal of Sociology* 5 (January 1954): 101–17; *A Modern Introduction to the Family*, ed. Norman Bell and Ezra Vogel (Glencoe, Ill.: Free Press, 1960).

3. Marion J. Levy, Jr. and L. A. Fallers, "The Family: Some Comparative Considerations," *American Anthropologist* 61 (August 1959): 647–51.

4. David F. Aberle et al., "The Functional Prerequisites of a Society," *Ethics* 60 (January 1950): 100–111.

5. Ibid.

or more of the four functions are not fulfilled by this structure is sufficient to refute the theory. Thus, a crucial test could best be made by focusing on societies with rather atypical family systems to see whether the nuclear family was present and was fulfilling these four functions. The more typical family systems will also be discussed. A proper test can be made by using only groups which are societies. This limitation is necessary so as not to test Murdock unfairly with such subsocietal groups as celibate priests. For purposes of this paper, the author accepts the definition of society developed by Aberle and his associates:

> A society is a group of human beings sharing a self-sufficient system of action which is capable of existing longer than the life-span of an individual, the group being recruited at least in part by the sexual reproduction of the members.[6]

A Test of Murdock's Thesis

One of the cultures chosen for the test of Murdock's thesis is from his own original sample of 250 cultures—the Nayar of the Malabar Coast of India. In his book, Murdock rejected Ralph Linton's view that the Nayar lacked the nuclear family.[7] Since that time, the work of Kathleen Gough has supported Linton's position, and Murdock has accordingly changed his own position.[8] In letters to the author dated April 3, 1963 and January 20, 1964, Murdock took the position that the Nayar are merely the old Warrior Caste of the Kerala Society and thus not a total society and are more comparable to a celibate group of priests. No such doubt about the societal status of the Nayar can be found in his book. Murdock rejects the Nayar only after he is forced to admit that they lack the nuclear family. In terms of the definition of

---

6. Ibid., p. 101.

7. Murdock, *Social Structure*, p. 3.

8. For a brief account of the Nayar, see Kathleen Gough, "Is the Family Universal: The Nayar Case," pp. 76–92 in *A Modern Introduction to the Family*. It is interesting to note that Bell and Vogel, in their preface to Gough's article on the Nayar, contend that she supports Murdock's position on the universality of the nuclear family. In point of fact, Gough on page 84 rejects Murdock and actually deals primarily with the marital and not the family institution. See also *Matrilineal Kinship*, ed. David M. Schneider and Kathleen Gough (Berkeley: University of California Press, 1961), chaps. 6 and 7. A. R. Radcliffe-Brown was one of the first to note that the Nayar lacked the nuclear family. See his *African Systems of Kinship and Marriage* (New York: Oxford University Press, 1959), p. 73.

---

society adopted above, the Nayar seem to be a society even if they, like many other societies, do have close connections with other groups.

The matrilineage is particularly strong among the Nayar, and a mother with the help of her matrilineage brings up her children. Her husband and "lovers" do not assist her in the raising of her children. Her brother typically assists her when male assistance is needed. Assistance from the linked lineages where most of her lovers come from also substitutes for the weak husband role. Since many Nayar women change lovers rather frequently, there may not even be any very stable male-female relation present. The male is frequently away fighting. The male makes it physiologically possible for the female to have offspring, but he is not an essential part of the family unit that will raise his biological children. In this sense, sex and reproduction are somewhat external to the family unit among the Nayar. Very little in the way of economic cooperation between husband and wife occurs. Thus, virtually all of Murdock's functions are outside of the nuclear family. However, it should be noted that the socialization of offspring function is present in the maternal extended family system. Here, then, is a society that seems to lack the nuclear family and, of necessity, therefore, the four functions of this unit. Even if we accept Gough's view that the "lovers" are husbands and that there really is a form of group marriage, it is still apparent that the separate husband-wife-child units formed by such a group marriage do not here comprise separately functioning nuclear families.

One does not have to rely on just the Nayar as a test of Murdock. Harold E. Driver, in his study of North American Indians, concludes that in matrilocal extended family systems with matrilineal descent, the husband role and the nuclear family are often insignificant.[9] It therefore seems that the relative absence of the nuclear family in the Nayar is approached particularly in other similar matrilineal societies. Thus, the Nayar do not seem to be so unique. They apparently demonstrate a type of family system that is common in lesser degree.

A somewhat similar situation seems to occur in many parts of the Caribbean. Judith Blake described a matrifocal family structure in which the husband and father role are quite often absent or seriously modified.[10] Sexual relations are often performed with transitory males

9. Harold H. Driver, *Indians of North America* (Chicago: University of Chicago Press, 1961), pp. 291–92.

10. Judith Blake, *Family Structure in Jamaica* (Glencoe, Ill.: Free Press, 1961). Whether

who have little relation to the raising of the resultant offspring. Thus, in Jamaica one can also question whether the nuclear family exists and performs the four functions Murdock ascribed to it. Socialization of offspring is often performed by the mother's family without any husband, common law or legal, being present. Naturally, if the husband is absent, the economic cooperation between husband and wife cannot occur. Also, if the male involved is not the husband but a short-term partner, sex and reproduction are also occurring outside the nuclear family.

The above societies are all "mother centered" systems. A family system which is not mother centered is the Israeli kibbutz family system as described by Melford Spiro.[11] Here the husband and wife live together in a communal agricultural society. The children are raised communally and do not live with their parents. Although the kibbutzim are only a small part of the total Israeli culture, they have a distinct culture and can be considered a separate society by the Aberle definition cited above. They have been in existence since 1909 and thus have shown that they can survive for several generations and that they have a self-sufficient system of action. The function which is most clearly missing in the kibbutz family is that of economic cooperation between husband and wife. In this communal society, almost all work is done for the total kibbutz, and the rewards are relatively equally distributed regardless of whether one is married or not. There is practically no division of labor between husbands and wives as such. Meals are eaten communally, and residence is in one room which requires little in the way of housekeeping.

Here, too, Murdock denies that this is a real exception and, in the letters to the author referred to above, contends that the kibbutzim could not be considered a society. Murdock's objection notwithstanding, a group which has existed for over half a century and has developed a self-sufficient system of action covering all major aspects of existence indeed seems to be a society by almost all definitions. There is nothing in the experience of the kibbutzim that makes it difficult to conceive of such groups existing in many regions of the world or, for

Jamaicans actually prefer to marry and have a more typical family system is a controversial point.

11. Melford E. Spiro, *Kibbutz: Venture in Utopia* (Cambridge, Mass.: Harvard University Press, 1956); and Melford E. Spiro, *Children of the Kibbutz* (Cambridge, Mass.: Harvard University Press, 1958).

that matter, existing by themselves in a world devoid of other people. They are analogous to some of the Indian groups living in American society in the sense that they have a coherent way of life that differs considerably from the dominant culture. Thus, they are not the same as an average community which is merely a part of the dominant culture.

Melford Spiro concludes that Murdock's nuclear family is not present in the kibbutz he and his wife studied. He suggests several alterations in Murdock's definition which would be required to make it better fit the kibbutz. The alterations are rather drastic and would still not fit the Nayar and other cultures discussed above.[12] There are other societies that are less extreme but which still create some difficulty with Murdock's definition of the nuclear family. Malinowski, in his study of the Trobriand Islanders, reports that except for perhaps nurturant socialization, the mother's brother rather than the father is the male who teaches the offspring much of the necessary way of life of the group.[13] Such a situation is certainly common in a matrilineal society, and it does place limits on the socialization function of the nuclear family per se. Further, one must at least qualify the economic function in the Trobriand case. The mother's brother here takes a large share of the economic burden and supplies his sister's family with half the food they require. The rigidity of Murdock's definition in light of such instances is apparent. These examples also make it reasonable that other societies may well exist which carry a little further such modifications of the nuclear family. For example, we find such more extreme societies when we look at the Nayar and the kibbutz.

Some writers, like Nicholas Timasheff, have argued that the Russian experience with the family evidences the universality of the nuclear family.[14] While it is true that the communists in Russia failed to abolish as much of the old family system as they wanted to, it does not follow

---

12. Spiro suggests that "reference residence" be used in place of actual common residence. The kibbutz children do speak of their parents' room as "home." He suggests further that responsibility for education and economic cooperation be substituted for the actual doing of these functions by the parents. The parents could be viewed as responsible for the education of their children, but since nothing changes in economic terms when one marries, it is difficult to understand just what Spiro means by responsibility for economic cooperation being part of the family. Spiro also would alter Murdock's definition of marriage so as to make emotional intimacy the key element.

13. Bronislaw Malinowski, *The Sexual Life of Savages in North-Western Melanesia* (New York: Harvest Books, 1929).

14. Nicholas S. Timasheff, "The Attempt to Abolish the Family in Russia," pp. 55–63 in Bell and Vogel, *Introduction to the Family.*

that this demonstrates the impossibility of abolishing the family.[15] In point of fact, the family system of the Israeli kibbutz is virtually identical with the system the Russian communists desired, and thus we must admit that it is possible for at least some groups to achieve such a system. Also, the communists did not want to do away with the family in toto. Rather, they wanted to do away with the patriarchal aspects of the family, to have marriage based on love, easy divorce, and communal upbringing of children. They ceased in much of this effort during the 1930s when a falling birth rate, rising delinquency and divorce rates, and the depression caused them to question the wisdom of their endeavors. However, it has never been demonstrated that these symptoms were consequences of the efforts to change the family. They may well have simply been results of a rapidly changing social order that would have occurred regardless of the family program. Therefore, the Russian experience is really not evidence pro or con Murdock's position.

The Chinese society deserves some brief mention here. Marion Levy contends that this is an exception to Murdock's thesis because in the extended Chinese family, the nuclear family was a rather unimportant unit, and it was the patrilineal extended family which performed the key functions of which Murdock speaks.[16] Regarding present-day Communist China, it should be noted that the popular reports to the effect that the Chinese communes either aimed at or actually did do away with the nuclear family are not supported by evidence. The best information indicates that the Chinese communists never intended to do away with the nuclear family as such; rather, what they wanted was the typical communist family system which the Israeli kibbutzim possess.[17] The communists in China did not intend to do away with the

15. Timasheff refers to the family as "that pillar of society." But nothing in the way of convincing evidence is presented to support this view. The argument is largely that since disorganization followed the attempt to do away with the family, it was a result of that attempt. This may well be an example of a *post hoc ergo propter hoc* fallacy. Also, it should be noted that the love-based union of parents that the early communists wanted might well be called a family, and thus that the very title of Timasheff's article implies a rather narrow image of the family. For a recent account of the Soviet family, see David and Vera Mace, *The Soviet Family* (New York: Doubleday, 1963); and Ray Bauer et al., *How the Soviet System Works* (Cambridge, Mass.: Harvard University Press, 1959).

16. Levy and Fallers, "The Family," pp. 649–50.

17. Felix Greene, *Awakened China* (New York: Doubleday, 1961), esp. pp. 142–44. Philip Jones and Thomas Poleman, "Communes and the Agricultural Crises in Communist China," *Food Research Institute Studies* 3 (February 1962): 1–22. Maurice

identification of a child with a particular set of parents or vice versa. If the Israeli kibbutz is any indication, it would seem that a communal upbringing system goes quite well with a strong emphasis on affectionate ties between parent and child.[18] However, it is well to note that the type of communal family system toward which the Chinese are striving and have to some extent already achieved, clashes with Murdock's conception of the nuclear family and its functions in just the same way as the kibbutz family does.

Overall, it appears that a reasonable man looking at the evidence presented above would conclude that Murdock's position is seriously in doubt. As Levy and Fallers have said, Murdock's approach is too simplistic in viewing a particular structure such as the nuclear family as always, in all cultural contexts, having the same four functions.[19] Robert Merton has said that such a view of a very specific structure as indispensable involves the erroneous "postulate of indispensability." [20] Certainly it seems rather rash to say that one very specific social structure such as the nuclear family will always have the same consequences regardless of the context in which it is placed. Surely this is not true of specific structures in other institutions such as the political, religious, or economic. The consequences of a particular social structure vary with the sociocultural context of that structure. Accordingly, a democratic bicameral legislative structure in a new African nation will function differently than in America; the Reform Jewish Denomination has different consequences in Israel than in America; government control of the economy functions differently in England than in Russia.

The remarkable thing about the family institution is that in so many diverse contexts, one can find such similar structures and functions. To this extent, Murdock has made his point and has demonstrated that the nuclear family with these four functions is a surprisingly common social fact. But this is quite different from demonstrating that this is always the case or necessarily the case. It should be perfectly clear that the author feels Murdock's work has contributed greatly to the advancement of our knowledge of the family. Murdock is used here because he

---

Freedman, "The Family in China, Past and Present," *Pacific Affairs* 34 (Winter 1961–62): 323–36

18. Spiro, *Kibbutz*.

19. Levy and Fallers, "The Family."

20. Robert K. Merton, *Social Theory and Social Structure* (Glencoe, Ill.: Free Press, 1957), p. 32.

is the best known proponent of the view being examined, not because he should be particularly criticized.

A safer approach to take toward the family is to look for functional prerequisites of society which the family fulfills and search for the full range of structures which may fulfill these functional prerequisites. At this stage of our knowledge, it seems more valuable to talk of the whole range of family structures and to seek for a common function that is performed and that may be essential to human society. What we need now is a broad, basic, parsimonious definition that would have utility in both single and cross-cultural comparisons.[21] We have a good deal of empirical data on family systems and a variety of definitions—it is time we strove for a universal definition that would clarify the essential features of this institution and help us locate the family in any cultural setting.

Looking over the four functions that Murdock associates with the nuclear family, one sees that three of them can be found to be absent in some cultures. The Nayar perhaps best illustrate the possibility of placing sex and reproduction outside the nuclear family. Also, it certainly seems within the realm of possibility that a "Brave New World" type of society could operate by scientifically mating sperm and egg, and presenting married couples with state-produced offspring of certain types when they desired children.[22] Furthermore, the raising of children by other than their biological parents is widespread in many societies where adoption and rearing by friends and relatives is common.[23] Thus, it seems that sex and reproduction may not be inexorably tied to the nuclear family.[24] The third function of Mur-

---

21. Zelditch attempted to see if the husband-wife roles would be differentiated in the same way in all cultures, with males being instrumental and females expressive. He found general support, but some exceptions were noted, particularly in societies wherein the nuclear family was embedded in a larger kinship system. Morris Zelditch, Jr., "Role Differentiation in the Nuclear Family: A Comparative Study," in Parsons and Bales, *Family*. The kibbutz would represent another exception since both mother and father play expressive roles in relation to their offspring.

22. Aldous Huxley, *Brave New World* (New York: Harper & Bros., 1950).

23. See *Six Cultures: Studies in Child Rearing*, ed. Beatrice B. Whiting (New York: John Wiley, 1963). Margaret Mead reports exchange of children in *Coming of Age in Samoa* (New York: Mentor Books, 1949). Similar customs in Puerto Rico are reported in David Landy, *Tropical Childhood* (Chapel Hill: University of North Carolina Press, 1959).

24. Robert Winch, in his recent textbook, defines the family as a nuclear family with the basic function of "the replacement of dying members." In line with the present author's arguments, it seems that the actual biological production of infants can be removed from the family. In fact, Winch agrees that the Nayar lack the family as he

dock's which seems possible to take out of the nuclear family is that of economic cooperation. The kibbutz is the prime example of this. Furthermore, it seems that many other communal-type societies approximate the situation in the kibbutz.

The fourth function is that of socialization. Many aspects of this function have been taken away from the family in various societies. For example, the kibbutz parents, according to Spiro, are not so heavily involved in the inculcation of values or the disciplinary and care-taking aspects of socialization. Nevertheless, the kibbutz parents are heavily involved in nurturant socialization, i.e., the giving of positive emotional response to infants and young children. A recent book by Stephens also reports a seemingly universal presence of nurturance of infants.[25] It should be emphasized that this paper uses "nurturance" to mean not the physical, but the emotional care of the infant. Clearly, the two are not fully separable. This use of the term nurturant is similar to what is meant by "expressive" role.[26] Interestingly enough, in the kibbutz both the mother and father are equally involved in giving their children nurturant socialization. All of the societies referred to above have a family institution with the function of nurturant socialization of children. This was true even for the extreme case of the Nayar.

The conception of the family institution being developed here has in common with some other family definitions an emphasis on socialization of offspring. The difference is that all other functions have been ruled out as unessential and that only the nurturant type of socialization is the universal function of the family institution. This paper presents empirical evidence to support its contention. It is important to be more specific than were Levy and Fallers regarding the type of socialization the family achieves since all societies have socialization occurring outside the family as well as within. It should be noted that this author, unlike Murdock, is talking of *any* form of family institution and not just the nuclear family.

As far as a universal structure of the family to fulfill the function of nurturant socialization is concerned, it seems possible to set only very

---

defined it because they lack a permanent father role in the nuclear family. See *The Modern Family* (New York: Holt, 1963), pp. 16, 31, and 750.

25. William N. Stephens, *The Family in Cross Cultural Perspective* (New York: Holt, Rinehart & Winston, 1963), p. 357. Stephens discusses the universality of the family in this book but does not take a definite position on the issue. See chapter 1.

26. Zelditch, "Role Differentiation," pp. 307–53.

broad limits, and even these involve some speculation. First, it may be said that the structure of the family will always be that of a primary group. Basically, this position rests on the assumption that nurturant socialization is a process which cannot be adequately carried out in an impersonal setting and which thus requires a primary type of relation.[27] The author would not specify the biological mother as the socializer or even a female, or even more than one person or the age of the person. If one is trying to state what the family must be like in a minimal sense in any society—what its universally required structure and function is—one cannot be too specific. However, we can go one step farther in specifying the structure of the family group we are defining. The family is here viewed as an institution, as an integrated set of norms and relationships which are socially defined and internalized by the members of a society. In every society in the world, the institutional structure which contains the roles related to the nurturant function is a small kinship-structured group.[28] Thus, we can say that the primary group which fulfills the nurturant function is a kinship structure. Kinship refers to descent—it involves rights of possession among those who are kin. It is a genealogical reckoning, and people with real or fictive biological connections are kin.[29]

This specification of structure helps to distinguish from the family institution those nonkin primary groups that may in a few instances perform nurturant functions. For example, a nurse-child relation or a governess-child relation could, if carried far enough, involve the bulk of nurturant socialization for that child. But such a relationship would be a quasi family at best, for it clearly is not part of the kinship structure. There are no rights of "possession" given to the nurse or the child in such cases, and there is no socially accepted, institutionalized, system of child rearing involving nurses and children. In addition, such supervisory help usually assumes more of a caretaking and disciplinary aspect, with the parents themselves still maintaining the nurturant relation.

Talcott Parsons has argued, in agreement with the author's position, that on a societal level, only kinship groups can perform the socialization function.[30] He believes that socialization in a kin group predisposes

27. The key importance of primary groups was long ago pointed out by Charles Horton Cooley, *Social Organization* (New York: Scribners, 1929).

28. The structural definition is similar to Levy and Fallers, "The Family."

29. Radcliffe-Brown, *African Systems of Kinship.*

30. Parsons, "The Incest Taboo."

the child to assume marital and parental roles himself when he matures and affords a needed stable setting for socialization. Clearly other groups may at times perform part of the nurturant function. No institution in human society has an exclusive franchise on its characteristic function. However, no society exists in which any group other than a kinship group performs the dominant share of the nurturant function. Even in the Israeli kibbutz with communal upbringing, it is the parents who dominate in this area.

Should a society develop wherein nonkin primary groups became the predominant means of raising children, the author would argue that these nonkin groups would tend to evolve in the direction of becoming kin groups. The primary quality of the adult-child relation would encourage the notion of descent and possession. Kin groups would evolve as roles and statuses in the nonkin system became defined in terms of accepted male-female and adult-child relationships and thereby became institutionalized. Once these nonkin groups had institutionalized their sex roles and adult-child (descent) roles, we would in effect have a kinship-type system, for kinship results from the recognition of a social relationship between "parents" and children. It seems that there would be much pressure toward institutionalization of roles in any primary group child-rearing system, if for no other reason than clarity and efficiency. The failure of any one generation to supply adequate role models and adequate nurturance means that the next generation will not know these skills, and persistence of such a society is questionable. The importance of this task makes institutionalization quite likely and kinship groups quite essential. To avoid kinship groups, it seems that children would have to be nurtured in a formal secondary group setting. The author will present evidence below for his belief that the raising of children in a secondary group setting is unworkable.

In summation then, following is the universal definition of the family institution: *The family institution is a small kinship-structured group with the key function of nurturant socialization of the newborn.* How many years such nurturant socialization must last is hard to specify. There are numerous societies in which children six or seven years old are given a good deal of responsibility in terms of care of other children and other tasks. It seems that childhood in the West has been greatly extended to older ages in recent centuries.[31] The proposed definition focuses on what are

31. Phillippe Aries, *Centuries of Childhood* (New York: Alfred A. Knopf, 1962).

assumed to be the structural and functional prerequisites of society which the family institution fulfills. The precise structure of the kinship group can vary quite radically among societies, and even within one society it may well be that more than one small kinship group will be involved in nurturant socialization. The definition seeks to avoid the "error" of positing the indispensability of any *particular* family form by this approach. Rather, it says that any type of kinship group can achieve this function and that the limitation is merely that it be a kinship group. This degree of specification helps one delimit and identify the institution which one is describing. Some writers have spelled out more specifically the key structural forms in this area.[32] Adams has posited two key dyads: the maternal dyad and the conjugal dyad. When these two join, a nuclear family is formed, but these dyads are, Adams believes, more fundamental than the nuclear family.

There are always other functions besides nurturant socialization performed by the kinship group. Murdock's four functions are certainly quite frequently performed by some type of family group, although often not by the nuclear family. In addition, there are some linkages between the family kinship group and a larger kinship system. But this is not the place to pursue these interconnections. Instead, an examination follows of evidence relevant to this proposed universal definition of the family institution.

Evidence on Revised Conception

The evidence to be examined here relates to the question of whether the definition proposed actually fits all human family institutions. Three types of evidence are relevant to test the universality of the proposed definition of the family. The first source of evidence comes from a cross-cultural examination such as that of this article. All the cultures that were discussed were fulfilling the proposed functional prerequisite of nurturant socialization, and they all had some sort of small-kinship-group structure to accomplish nurturant socialization. The author also examined numerous reports on other cultures and found no exception to the proposed definition. Of course, other

---

32. Richard N. Adams, "An Inquiry into the Nature of the Family," pp. 30–49 in *Essays in the Science of Culture in Honor of Leslie A. White*, ed. Gertrude E. Dole and Robert L. Carneiro (New York: Thomas Y. Crowell, 1960).

functions of these family groups were present in all instances, but no other specific universally present functions appeared. However, the author hesitates to say that these data confirm his position because it is quite possible that such a cross-cultural examination will reveal some function or structure to be universally *present* but still not universally *required*. Rather, it could merely be universally present by chance or because it is difficult but not impossible to do away with. As an example of this, one may cite the incest taboo. The evidence recently presented by Russell Middleton on incest among commoners in Ptolemaic Egypt throws doubt on the thesis that incest taboos are functional prerequisites of human society.[33] We need some concept of functional "importance," for surely the incest taboo has great functional importance even if it is not a prerequisite of society. The same may be true of the functional importance of Murdock's view of the nuclear family.

If being universally present is but a necessary and not a sufficient condition for a functional prerequisite of society, then it is important to present other evidence. One source of such evidence lies in the studies of rhesus monkeys done by Harry Harlow.[34] Harlow separated monkeys from their natural mothers and raised them with surrogate "cloth" and "wire" mother dolls. In some trials, the wire-mother surrogate was equipped with milk while the cloth mother was not. Even so, the monkeys preferred the cloth mother to the wire mother in several ways. The monkeys showed their preference by running more to the cloth mother when threatened and by exerting themselves more to press a lever to see her. Thus, it seemed that the monkeys "loved" the cloth mother more than the wire mother. This was supposedly due to the softer contact and comfort afforded by the cloth mother. One might speculatively argue that the contact desire of the monkeys is indicative of at least a passive, rudimentary nurturance need. Yerkes has also reported similar "needs" in his study of chimpanzees.[35]

Further investigation of these monkeys revealed some important

33. Russell Middleton, "Brother-Sister and Father-Daughter Marriage in Ancient Egypt," *American Sociological Review* 27 (October 1962): 603–11.

34. See the following articles, all by Harry F. Harlow: "The Nature of Love," *American Psychologist* 13 (December 1958): 673–85; "The Heterosexual Affection System in Monkeys," *American Psychologist* 17 (January 1962): 1–9; (with Margaret K. Harlow), "Social Deprivation in Monkeys," *Scientific American* 206 (November 1962): 1–10.

35. Robert M. Yerkes, *Chimpanzees* (New Haven: Yale University Press, 1943), esp. pp. 43, 68, 257–58; and Robert M. Yerkes and Ada W. Yerkes, *The Great Apes* (New Haven: Yale University Press, 1929), passim.

findings. The monkeys raised by the surrogate mothers became emotionally disturbed and were unable to relate to other monkeys or to have sexual relations. This result was produced irreversibly in about six months. One could interpret this to mean that the surrogate mothers, both cloth and wire, were inadequate in that they gave no emotional response to the infant monkeys. Although contact with the cloth mother seemed important, response seemingly was even more important. Those laboratory-raised females who did become pregnant became very ineffective mothers and were lacking in ability to give nurturance.

Harlow found that when monkeys were raised without mothers but with siblings present, the results were quite different. To date, these monkeys have shown emotional stability and sexual competence. In growing up, they clung to each other just as the other monkeys had clung to the cloth mother, but in addition they were able to obtain the type of emotional response or nurturance from each other which they needed.

Harlow's evidence on monkeys is surely not conclusive evidence for the thesis that nurturant socialization is a fundamental prerequisite of human society. There is need for much more precise testing and evidence on both human and nonhuman groups. Despite the fact that human beings and monkeys are both primates, there is quite a bit of difference in human and monkey infants. For one thing, the human infant is far more helpless and far less aware of its environment during the first few months of its life. Thus, it is doubtful if placing a group of helpless, relatively unaware human infants together would produce the same results as occurred when monkeys were raised with siblings. The human infant requires someone older and more aware of the environment to be present. In a very real sense, it seems that the existence of human society is testimony to the concern of humans for each other. Unless older humans care for the newborn, the society will cease to exist. Every adult member of society is alive only because some other member of society took the time and effort to raise him. One may argue that this care need be only minimal and of a physical nature, e.g., food, clothing, and shelter. The author believes that such minimal care is insufficient for societal survival and will try to present additional evidence here to bear this out.

One type of evidence that is relevant concerns the effect of maternal separation or institutional upbringing on human infants. To afford a precise test, we should look for a situation in which nurturant socialization was quite low or absent. Although the kibbutzim have institutional upbringing, the kibbutz parents and children are very much emotionally attached to each other. In fact, both the mother and father have expressive roles in the kibbutz family, and there is a strong emphasis on parent-child relations of a nurturant sort in the few hours a day the family is together.

A better place to look would be at studies of children who were raised in formal institutions or who were in other ways separated from their mothers. Leon J. Yarrow has recently published an excellent summary of over one hundred such studies.[36] For over fifty years now, there have been reports supporting the view that maternal separation has deleterious effects on the child. The first such reports came from pediatricians pointing out physical and psychological deterioration in hospitalized infants. In 1951, Bowlby reviewed the literature in this area for the World Health Organization and arrived at similar conclusions.[37] More recent and careful studies have made us aware of the importance of distinguishing the effects of maternal separation from the effects of institutionalization. Certainly the type of institutional care afforded the child is quite important. Further, the previous relation of the child with the mother before institutionalization and the age of the child are important variables. In addition, one must look at the length of time separation endured and whether there were reunions with the mother at a later date. Yarrow's view is that while there is this tendency toward disturbance in mother separation, the occurrence can best be understood when we learn more about the precise conditions under which it occurs and cease to think of it as inevitable under any conditions. In this regard, recent evidence shows that children separated from mothers with whom they had poor relationships displayed less disturbance than other children. Further, infants who were provided with adequate mother-substitutes of a personal sort showed much less severe reactions. In line with the findings on the kibbutz, children who were in an all-day nursery gave no evidence of serious disturbance.

Many studies in the area of institutionalization show the importance of the structural characteristics of the institutional environment. When

---

36. Leon J. Yarrow, "Separation from Parents During Early Childhood," pp. 89–136 in *Review of Child Development*, ed. Martin L. Hoffman and Lois W. Hoffman (New York: Russell Sage Foundation, 1964), vol. 1.

37. John Bowlby, *Maternal Care and Mental Health* (Geneva: World Health Organization, 1951).

care is impersonal and inadequate, there is evidence of language retardation, impairment of motor functions, and limited emotional responses toward other people and objects.[38] Interestingly, the same types of characteristics are found among children living in deprived family environments.[39] One of the key factors in avoiding such negative results is the presence of a stable mother-figure in the institution for the child. Individualized care and attention seem to be capable of reversing or preventing the impairments mentioned. Without such care, there is evidence that ability to form close interpersonal relations later in life is greatly weakened.[40] As Yarrow concludes in his review of this area:

> It is clear from the studies on institutionalization that permanent intellectual and personality damage may be avoided if following separation there is a substitute mother-figure who develops a personalized relationship with the child and who responds sensitively to his individualized needs.[41]

The evidence in this area indicates that some sort of emotionally nurturant relationship between the child in the first few years of life and some other individual is rather vital in the child's development. Disease and death rates have been reported to rise sharply in children deprived of nurturance. The author is not rash enough to take this evidence as conclusive support for his contention that nurturant socialization is a functional prerequisite of human society which the family performs. Nevertheless, he does believe that this evidence lends some support to this thesis and throws doubt on the survival of a society that rears its children without nurturance. In addition, it seems to support the position that some sort of kin-type group relationship is the structural prerequisite of the nurturant function. Indeed, it seemed that the closer the institution approximated a stable, personal kinship type of relationship of the child and a nurse, the more successful it was in achieving emotional nurturance and avoiding impairments of functions.

---

38. Yarrow, "Separation from Parents," p. 100.
39. Ibid., pp. 101–2.
40. Ibid., p. 106.
41. Ibid., pp. 124–25.

Summary and Conclusions

A check of several cultures revealed that the four nuclear family functions that Murdock states are universally present were often missing. The nuclear family itself seems either absent or unimportant in some cultures. An alternate definition of the family in terms of one functional prerequisite of human society and in terms of a broad structural prerequisite was put forth. The family was defined as a small kinship structured group with the key function of nurturant socialization of the newborn. The nurturant function directly supports the personality system and enables the individual to become a contributing member of society. Thus, by making adult role performance possible, nurturant socialization becomes a functional prerequisite of society.

Three sources of evidence were examined: (1) cross-cultural data, (2) studies of other primates, and (3) studies of effects on children of maternal separation. Although the evidence did tend to fit with and support the universality of the new definition, it must be noted that much more support is needed before any firm conclusion can be reached.

There is both a structural and a functional part to the definition. It is theoretically possible that a society could bring up its entire newborn population in a formal institutional setting and give them nurturance through mechanical devices that would reassure the child, afford contact, and perhaps even verbally respond to the child. In such a case, the family as defined here would cease to exist, and an alternate structure for fulfilling the functional requirement of nurturant socialization would be established. Although it is dubious whether humans could ever tolerate or achieve such a means of bringing up their children, this logical possibility must be recognized. In fact, since the evidence is not conclusive, one would also have to say that it is possible that a society could bring up its offspring without nurturance, and in such a case also, the family institution as defined here would cease to exist. The author has argued against this possibility by contending that nurturance of the newborn is a functional prerequisite of human society and therefore could never be done away with. However, despite a strong conviction to the contrary, he must also admit that this position may be in error and that it is possible that the family as defined here is not a universally required institution. There are those, like Barrington

Moore, Jr., who feel that it is largely a middle-class sentimentality that makes social scientists believe that the family is universal.[42] It is certainly crucial to test further the universality of both the structural and functional parts of this definition and their interrelation.

The definition proposed seems to fit the existing data somewhat more closely than Murdock's definition. It also has the advantage of simplicity. It affords one a definition that can be used in comparative studies of human society. Further, it helps make one aware of the possibilities of change in a society or an institution if we know which functions and structures can or cannot be done away with. In this way, we come closer to the knowledge of what Goldenweiser called the "limited possibilities" of human society.[43] If nurturance in kin groups is a functional and structural prerequisite of society, we have deepened our knowledge of the nature of human society for we can see how, despite our constant warfare with each other, our conflicts and internal strife, each human society persists only so long as it meets the minimal nurturant requirements of its new members. This is not to deny the functions of social conflict that Coser and others have pointed out, but merely to assert the importance of nurturance.[44]

In terms of substantive theory, such a definition as the one proposed can be of considerable utility. If one views the marital institution, as Malinowski, Gough, Davis, Radcliffe-Brown, and others did, as having the key function of legitimization of offspring, then the tie between the marital and family institution becomes clear.[45] The marital institution affords a social definition of who is eligible to perform the nurturant

42. Barrington Moore, Jr., *Political Power and Social Theory* (Cambridge, Mass.: Harvard University Press, 1958), chap. 5.

43. Alexander A. Goldenweiser, *History, Psychology, and Culture* (New York: Alfred A. Knopf, 1933), esp. pp. 45–49.

44. Lewis Coser, *The Functions of Social Conflict* (Glencoe, Ill.: Free Press, 1956).

45. See Gough, "Is the Family Universal?"; Kingsley Davis, "Illegitimacy and the Social Structure," *American Journal of Sociology* 45 (September 1939): 215–33; Radcliffe-Brown, *African Systems of Kinship*, p. 5. The structure of the marital institution is not specified in terms of number or sex, for there are cultures in which two women may marry and raise a family. See B. E. Evans Pritchard, *Kinship and Marriage Among the Nuer* (London: Oxford University Press, 1951), pp. 108–9. It is well to note here that Murdock stressed a somewhat different view of marriage. He focused on sexual and economic functions, and the woman-woman marriage found in the Nuer would not fit this definition. Morris Zelditch recently has used this legitimacy function as the key aspect of his definition of the family rather than marriage. Such a usage would, it seems, confuse the traditional distinction between these two institutions. See p. 682 in *Handbook of Modern Sociology*, ed. Robert Faris (New York: Rand-McNally, 1964).

function of the family institution. However, it is conceivable that a family system could exist without a marital system. This could be done by the state scientifically producing and distributing infants or, as Blake believes occurs in Jamaica, by the absence of socially acceptable marriage for most people until childbirth is over.[46]

There may be other universally required functions of the family institution. Dorothy Blitsten suggests universal family contributions to the social order.[47] Kingsley Davis posits several universal functions, such as social placement, which are worth investigating further.[48]

One major value of the approach of this paper is that it has the potentiality of contributing to our ability to deal cross-culturally with the family. Surely it is useful to theory building to ascertain the essential or more essential features of an institution. Such work enables us to locate, identify, and compare this institution in various cultural settings and to discover its fundamental characteristics. In this respect, Murdock has contributed to the search for a cross-cultural view of the family by his work in this area, even though the author has taken issue with some of his conclusions. It should be clear that this "universal, cross-cultural" approach is not at all presented as the only approach to an understanding of the family. Rather, it is viewed as but one essential approach. Research dealing with important but not universal functions is just as vital, as is empirical work within one culture.

Also of crucial importance is the relation of the family institution to the general kinship structure. It does seem that every society has other people linked by affinal or consanguineal ties to the nurturant person or persons. It remains for these aspects to be further tested. The family typologies now in existence are adequate to cover the proposed definition of the family, although a new typology built around the nurturant function and the type of kin who perform it could be quite useful.

The interrelations of the marital, family, and courtship institutions with such institution as the political, economic, and religious in terms of

---

46. Blake, *Family Structure in Jamaica.*

47. Dorothy R. Blitsten, *The World of the Family* (New York: Random House, 1963), esp. chap. I.

48. Kingsley Davis, *Human Society* (New York: Macmillan, 1950), p. 395. Davis lists reproduction, maintenance, placement, and socialization of the young as universal family functions. Social placement is the only function that differs from Murdock's list. One could conceive of this function as part of the marital rather than the family institution.

both important and essential functions and structures is another vital avenue of exploration. One way that such exploration can be made is in terms of what, if any, are the functional and structural prerequisites of these institutions and how they interrelate. It is hoped that such comparative research and theory may be aided by a universal definition of the family such as that proposed in this paper.

27

EMERGING PATTERNS OF BEHAVIOR IN MARRIAGE: DEVIATIONS OR INNOVATIONS?

JAMES W. RAMEY

The mass media are replete with sensational stories of free love, swinging, communes, and group marriages, usually implying ruptured standards, moral decay, and threats to the institution of marriage. Moralists point with alarm to one out of four marriages ending in divorce, freely circulating swinger ad magazines, campus orgies, and flourishing communes. Here is their proof that the minions of hell are fast taking over. Fortunately there is another, more positive, explanation for these phenomena. Viewed in the context of diffusion of innovation, we are witnessing the realignment of traditional marital relationship patterns rather than deviations from the norm. As Beigel indicated, this is a supportive development aimed at reforming monogamous marriage.[1]

Diffusion of innovation refers to the process of change and the generally accepted means of determining which of many possible changes is actually taking hold. It has been found that no matter how long a particular practice has been accepted by small groups here and

---

1. Hugo Beigel, "In Defense of Mate Swapping," *Rational Living* 4 (Summer 1969): 15–16.

there, such changes do not move into the main stream of society until approximately 7 to 10 percent of the population adopt them.[2] Once this level of saturation is reached, general acceptance rapidly follows, so that within a few years, the vast majority of people can be expected to accept ideas, or activities, that may have been the norm for a small percentage of the population for decades. As an example of this kind of change, despite social disapproval, some women were smoking cigarettes over a generation ago, but it was not until World War II that this activity was accepted generally as proper behavior. When acceptance did come, it happened almost overnight—in just under a decade.[3]

This paper presents a paradigm, or model, for research in the area of evolutionary sexual behavior in marriage. This model serves three purposes. First, it provides a basis for systematic classification of current research on alternative sexual life styles for pair-bonded couples, particularly free love, swinging, communal living, and group marriage. We shall examine some of this research and shall organize analysis of this material in respect to the paradigm. Second, the paradigm is designed to foster further inquiry, to suggest fruitful lines of endeavor for new research. It should not be conceived as a complete theory of evolutionary marital sexual behavior, but is offered merely as a proposal that ultimately may lead to the development of a useful theory. Third, the model provides marriage partners with a cogent way of conceptualizing their relationship, and hence affords them a guide for analyzing their pair-bond behavior and evaluating their own degree of commitment and effectiveness as partners in a union of equals.

Before introducing our definitions of the behaviors with which this paper is concerned, let us define the scope of the inquiry, the point of view from which we are undertaking it, and the limits we have imposed upon it. We are initially making an attempt to link several types of marital behavior generally considered to be deviant behavior. We will present our reasons for believing that these behaviors are in fact evolutionary, stemming from changes, which we will identify, in our society. We do this for the purpose of trying to clarify and comprehend the growing number of often contradictory statements, many of which claim to be based on actual participant-observer experience, with

2. H. Earl Pemberton, "The Curve of Culture," *American Sociological Review* 1, no. 4 (August 1936): 547–56.

3. James W. Ramey, "Diffusion of a New Technological Innovation," *Health Sciences TV Bulletin* (O.S.) 4 (Spring 1963): 2–3.

regard to swinging, communes, and group marriage. We hope and believe such an attempt to relate these disparate reports will help to focus research in the field on the gaps that would seem to have the highest payoff potential in increasing our understanding of what is happening. We do not expect, within the confines of this single paper to evaluate and/or relate all of the research material we currently have on hand. It is much more important to sketch in the broad picture as we see it, leaving more detailed analysis to later efforts. It would seem appropriate to begin with our own definitions of free love, swinging, commune, and group marriage.

Free love is open-ended sexual seeking and consummating without legal or other commitment of any kind.

Swinging generally involves two or more pair-bonded couples who mutually decide to switch sexual partners or engage in group sex. Singles may be included either through temporary coupling with another individual specifically for the purpose of swinging or as part of a triadic or larger group sexual experience.

When individuals agree to make life commitments as members of one particular group, rather than through many different groups, they may constitute a *commune.* The number of common commitments will vary from commune to commune, the critical number having been reached at the point at which the group sees itself as a commune rather than at some absolute number.

In a *group marriage* each of the three or more participants is pair-bonded with at least two others.

We use the term *pair-bond* to reduce ambiguity. A pair-bond is a reciprocal primary relationship involving sexual intimacy. A pair-bonded couple see themselves as mates. This is not necessarily the case in a "primary relationship" which can be one-sided, and need not necessarily include sexual intimacy. We prefer the term "pair-bond" rather than "married couple" because not all pair-bonded couples are married.

Our four basic definitions deal with a range of behavior that is increasingly complex. They are interrelated and often sequential. Today's world is increasingly inundated with evidence that man tends to increase the complexity of his interactions. So much so, in fact, that Toffler has added a new word to our lexicon—"future shock." [4] Yet

---

4. Alvin Toffler, *Future Shock* (New York: Random House, 1970).

somehow one of our age-old institutions, marriage, has resisted this trend. Why should this be?

There appear to be two interrelated causes. First is the existence of male dominance in our society. Second, in the past (and indeed in many subcultures and in much of the lower-middle- and working-class levels of society today) two married persons in a stable and permanent social context expected little from each other. Psychological and interpersonal needs could be satisfied in a variety of ways through kin, neighbors, and friendship. Husband and wife literally lived in two different worlds.

Marriage did not change much, over the ages, until the pair-bond was composed of peers. As long as the woman was considered chattel, the relationship was not one of equality. Such terms as "doing wifely duty," "Marriage rights," and "exclusivity," literally meant, and for most people still mean, that the pair-bond is male dominated. Little wonder, then, that marriage has so long resisted the universal human urge to intensify the complexity of relationships. Komarovsky and Babchuk and Bates have strongly supported the thesis that both husband and wife maintain close relationships with same-sex peers and that the marital relationship tends to be male dominated in both blue-collar (Komarovsky) and lower-middle-class couples (Babchuk and Bates).[5]

It is possible to point to attempts by some, at various times and places, to free marriage, to some degree, from the restraint of male domination and by thus proclaiming equality of the sexes, to permit the emergence of alternatives to exclusivity in marriage. These efforts always failed or were tolerated only in certain special, small, restricted, and segregated groups, because in the larger society women were not yet peers. Bird shows how, in a patriarchal society, conditions at a physical or economic frontier may, of necessity, produce equality of the sexes, but as soon as the period of consolidation and stability sets in, it becomes a mark of status to keep an idle woman.[6] We also note the emergence of free love in conjunction with revolutionary movements time and again, only to see the return of male-dominated pair-bond

5. Nicholas Babchuk and Alan P. Bates, "The Primary Relations of Middle-Class Couples: A Study in Male Dominance," *American Sociological Review* 23, no. 3 (June 1963): 377–84; Mirra Komarovsky, *Blue-Collar Marriage* (New York: Random House, 1962).

6. Caroline Bird, *Born Female: The High Cost of Keeping Women Down* (New York: Pocket Books, 1970).

exclusivity as soon as the revolution succeeds or fails. Indeed, free love can be considered a revolutionary tool, for it quickly sets apart and isolates the in-group from family and friends, both symbolically and literally.

In this context it is important to understand that "revolutionaries" or dissidents can be political, social, religious, economic, cultural, or a combination of these. Often the combination is called "utopian," "hippie," or "anarchistic" without regard to the actual goals or beliefs involved. A few of these people are regarded as "the lunatic fringe" and are tolerated by the larger society because they are amusing and sometimes even productive, especially the cultural radicals, such as musicians, artists, or theatrical types. Others have been less tolerated, typically driven out or underground, and often persecuted, no matter what the stripe of their dissident bent. The survival factor in such groups appears to be strong patriarchal and/or religious orientation and considerable structure. Almost invariably they have eased away from sexual experimentation in favor of exclusive male-dominated marriage bonds. This happens in spite of the fact that in theory, at least, any alternative to pair-bond exclusivity could be practiced in a closed group, provided the group was willing to accept joint child-rearing and nurturing responsibility.

Nevertheless, until the society as a whole began to accept the right of the female to be a peer, such excursions into marriage alternatives could but fail. A woman who is dependent on her husband must grant his requests, including the demand for sexual exclusivity, even though she may know that he is not practicing the same exclusivity. An economically emancipated wife, on the other hand, is in a much better position to insist on equality because of her much enhanced economic self sufficiency, which may also increase her social self sufficiency. Thus the stage is set for pair-bonding between equal partners, both able to sustain themselves outside marriage, so that both enter the relationship voluntarily on the assumption that the anticipated benefits will be greater than would be available in a non-pair-bonded state. Furthermore, survival of the marriage depends on each continuing to place a higher value on maintaining the pair-bond than on reverting to their previous state. That is to say, maintaining the marriage depends on each continuing to extend to the other the privileges inherent in such a pair-bond. The final touch to this new equal status in the pair-bond is female control over conception, for the first time in history.

In the 1950s the trends toward increased geographic and career mobility and toward greater social and economic freedom for women began to come together to set the stage for the emergence of the new life styles in marriage with which we are concerned. Academic, professional, and managerial people became increasingly mobile. The U.S. Census Bureau pointed out that 20 percent of the population moved to a new location, outside the county in which they had been living. Riesman, Glazer, and Denny pointed out that we were living in an "other directed" society and identified these same types of individuals as typifying the new breed who must be capable of self-restraint while recognizing that groups vary in what they consider desirable and undesirable behavior.[7] The other directed individual must be acutely sensitive and responsive to group norms while recognizing the essential arbitrariness, particularity, and limited relevance of all moral imperatives. Pity the inner directed conformist, therefore, the "throwback" who was programmed from birth to display a limited range of responses in all situations, regardless of environmental variation, which, while possibly heroic, is excessively simple-minded. Slater was the first to rephrase Riesman's definition of the "inner-directed" man in this manner.[8]

As Slater goes on to develop the "temporary systems" theme, following in the footsteps of Komarovsky, and others cited earlier he says:

> Spouses are now asked to be lovers, friends, mutual therapists, in a society which is forcing the marriage bond to become the closest, deepest, most important, and putatively most enduring relationship of one's life. Paradoxically then, it is increasingly likely to fall short of the emotional demands placed upon it and be dissolved.

The endpoint of Slater's argument is that people can and must press toward the full exploitation of all their talents, since in a truly temporary society everyone would have to be a generalist, able to step into any role in the group he happens to belong to at the moment. This

---

7. David Riesman, Nathan Glazer, and Reuel Denny, *The Lonely Crowd* (Garden City, N.Y.: Doubleday, 1955).

8. Philip E. Slater, "Some Social Consequences of Temporary Systems," in W. G. Bennis and Philip E. Slater, *The Temporary Society* (New York: Harper & Row, 1968), pp. 77–96.

is in marked contrast to the present situation in which the upper bohemians tend to specialize in certain roles (which is one of the reasons they are mobile) both on the job and in social situations. Consequently, each time they move to a new geographic location they must search for groups that need "their" roles.

It is for these several reasons that we have begun to see some of the results, in the sexual area, of shifting from ritualistically determined marriages based on rights, to self-determined ones based on privilege. Highly mobile pair-bonds, who are here today and moved tomorrow, must turn to each other and evolve a much more complex relationship to replace kin, neighbor, and friendship relational structure that is no longer available on a long-term basis. They must also develop means of getting informally "plugged-in" quickly whenever they move. When Lynes coined the "Upper Bohemian" label, it was for the purpose of describing just such informal networks, although he did not describe their sexual overtones.[9] It is interesting to find Farson and Stoller advocating various forms of intimate networks as a means of dealing with the interpersonal intimacy impoverishment of the isolated nuclear family.[10]

This temporary systems strata is the group, by and large, in which women are most apt to be treated as peers. This group is augmented by others with sufficient education and exposure to ideas to be strongly influenced by current trends.[11] Now that 40 percent of our college-age population is in college, we can expect that there may soon be a significant rise in their numbers. Already we find in many of these young people the same attitudes toward peer relationships in the pair-bond that exist among some of the better educated upper-middle-class members of the "depression generation."

We see the current forays into sexual alternatives to monogamy as

---

9. Russell Lynes, *A Surfeit of Honey* (New York: Harpers, 1953).

10. Richard Evans Farson, *The Future of the Family* (New York: Family Service Association of America, 1969); Frederick H. Stoller, "The Intimate Network of Families as a New Structure," in *The Family in Search of a Future*, ed. Herbert Otto (New York: Appleton-Century-Crofts, 1970).

11. Marshall McLuhan and George B. Leonard, "The Future of Sex," *Look* 31, no. 15 (25 July 1967): 56–63; George C. O'Neill and Nena O'Neill, "Patterns in Group Sexual Activity," *Journal of Sex Research* 6, no. 2 (May 1970): 101–12; James W. Ramey, "Group Marriage, Communes, and the Upper Middle Class," *Journal of Marriage and the Family* 34, no. 4 (November 1972): 647–55; James R. Smith and Lynn G. Smith, "Co-Marital Sex and the Sexual Freedom Movement," *Journal of Sex Research* 6, no. 2 (May 1970): 131–42.

attempts to build a more complex network of intimate relationships that can absorb some of the impact of the new-found complexity of the pair-bond, by short-circuiting the process of developing ancillary relationships in the usual ritualistic manner. We believe this occurs for two reasons: (1) because there is not time to go through a long, drawn-out process of finding a group that needs the roles the couple can fill, and (2) because using sexual intimacy as an entry role guarantees the couple that, other things being equal, they can fill the role. Particularly if such ties are to take up the slack of the unavailable kin-neighbor-friendship relational systems, as well as relieve some of the pressure on the newly complex pair-bond interaction, they must begin on a much deeper, more intimate basis than the ties they replace. The relationship must cut through the ritual layers quickly in order to be of any help. What better way to ensure that this will happen than to attempt to relate in a "taboo" area? Everyone has had the discouraging experience of pursuing a friendship for many months only to discover suddenly an emotional block to further progress toward meaningful interaction. We usually have no means of discovering what the other fellow's taboos will be until we come up against them. While the assumption that those without sexual taboos will have a minimum of other taboos to intensive interaction on the "gut" level is not necessarily a valid one, it seems to hold up well for many people in many situations, perhaps because sexual inhibitions are among the deepest rooted for many of us.

Entry into swinging relationships typically takes place from this set of circumstances. Entry into communes and group marriage sometimes takes place without going through either of these stages, but often proceeds from them, especially among the over-30 age group.[12]

Although it certainly does not follow that all couples in this situation will react by becoming involved in one of the alternative life styles under discussion, conditions described do foster such behavior on the part of some of these people. And for them it will be a more successful adaptation than for those whose pair-bond is not a relationship of peers. It is evident that this behavior is also emulated by others who are neither in the "temporary systems strata" nor peers in the pair-bond, as well as by a few who may be part of the working class.[13]

---

12. Ramey, "Group Marriage."

13. Ramey, "Group Marriage"; Smith and Smith, "Co-Marital Sex"; Carolyn Symonds, "The Utopian Aspects of Sexual Mate Swapping" (Paper delivered at the

The Model

A major area of confusion in most discussions of swinging, communes, and group marriage has to do with the difference between committed and uncommitted relationships. Kanter distinguishes between three types of commitment: cathectic, or commitment to the individual; cognitive, which involves weighing the value of continuing in a group or leaving it; and evaluative, which involves belief in the perceived moral rightness of group ideology.[14]

This paper proposes the following hypotheses. (1) Nonconsensual adultery and swinging are "free-love" activities which involve no commitment or very minimal commitment. (2) Consensual intimate friendships, evolutionary communes, and group marriage involve considerable individual commitment, and in the case of communes and group marriage, commitment to the group as well. (3) Swinging may constitute a transitional step between lack of individual commitment and growth of such commitment between husband and wife. (4) Once husband and wife have begun to experience the joy and satisfaction of individual growth through joint dialogue and commitment, they may find their newfound responsiveness to one another so satisfying that they drop out of swinging. (5) As the marriage takes on more and more aspects of a peer relationship, the couple may consensually agree to increase the complexity of their relationship through the development of intimate friendships with other individuals or couples, through which the sense of commitment to the individual is extended to these significant others. (6) A significant portion (apparently about 50 percent) of the couples who become candidates for evolutionary communes or group marriage come from among those who have developed intimate friendships.[15] (7) Group marriage, which combines commitment to the group with multiple pair-bonding among the members of the group, is the most complex form of marriage. (8) These various marriage alternatives can be placed on a continuum that ranges from dyadic marriage with minimal commitment (in which there may be nonconsensual individual adultery), to swinging, to peer marriage, to

---

annual meeting, Society for the Study of Social Problems, Washington, D.C., September 1970); Gilbert D. Bartell, "Group Sex Among the Mid-Americans," *Journal of Sex Research* 6, no. 2 (May 1970): 113–30.

14. Rosabeth M. Kanter, "Communes," *Psychology Today* 4, no. 2 (July 1970): 53–78.

15. Ramey, "Group Marriage."

peer marriage with consensual intimate friendships, to the evolutionary commune, to group marriage.

Swinging

Swinging was defined at the beginning of this paper as:

> Generally involving two or more pair-bonded couples who mutually decide to switch sexual partners or engage in group sex. Singles may be included either through temporary coupling with another individual specifically for the purpose of swinging or as part of a triadic or larger group sexual experience.

To say that swinging "generally involves two or more pair-bonded couples" may seem inexact. Actually, swinging may involve adding only one person, of either sex, to the pair-bond. Some couples find it easier to locate one person who is compatible with both than to find another couple in which both the male and the female are compatible with both husband and wife. Singles are thus involved in swinging directly. It is surprising that this point has been disputed by some reporters on the swinging scene especially since many acknowledge that it is the swinging singles who sometimes give the total swinging scene a bad name.[16] Palson points out that:

> To singles, swinging looks more like a long line of sexual encounters with no attempt to form the "proper" kind of personal union, whereas married couples, secure in their own union, can experience friendly sex with others, knowing that they have achieved a permanence with one mate as morality ordains, and that sex with others can actually enhance this relationship.[17]

Many researchers have interviewed threesomes and it would appear that there are more stable threesome relationships than any other

---

16. William Breedlove and Jerrye Breedlove, *Swap Clubs* (Los Angeles: Sherbourne Press, 1964).

17. Chuck Palson and Rebecca Markle Palson, "Swinging: The Minimizing of Jealousy" (Ms., Philadelphia, Pa., 1970), p. 20. Mimeographed.

type.[18] Also, more triads have been found than any type of group marriage.[19] The author recently analyzed ads in four major swinger ad magazines and found that the second-most-looked-for situation, whether the advertiser was a couple, a single male, or a single female, was "couples or single females desired." The third-ranked desire was for "couples or singles, male or female." Bartell reports similar results.[20]

The implied threat to the pair-bond of accepting a single into a sexual union, even on a temporary basis, obviously is a problem for the uncommitted couple only, and not for the committed couple. Far more couples swing with single women than with single men. In a male dominated pair-bond, the male has little to gain from swinging with a single male, and the threat of direct competition in the swinging situation with his wife, unless he happens to enjoy sexual contacts with other men. Even in the latter case, he would be unlikely to expose such inclinations to his wife. Such activity would be much more likely to occur if the couple regarded themselves as equals, free to explore all kinds of multiple sexual relationships.

The swinger magazine ads for single females mentioned above, when placed by a couple, generally specify that a "versatile" female is desired or that the wife is "ac/dc" if participation is expected to be three-way. Many men appear to "recycle" sooner after an orgasm if they can watch lesbian sexual activity. The recent report of the President's Commission on Obscenity and Pornography suggests that women are also stimulated by watching such activity.[21] This may help account for the fact that lesbian contacts are often a part of the swinging scene, although few female swingers consider themselves lesbians, by any stretch of the word. Males do not enjoy the same freedom of same-sex contact because they run the risk of being categorized as homosexuals even though the women do not.

Singles may also form temporary couples for the purpose of swinging with those uncommitted couples who will not swing with a single alone or because the single is a married person whose mate refuses to swing.

18. Smith and Smith, "Co-Marital Sex"; O'Neill and O'Neill, "Patterns in Group Sexual Activity."

19. Larry L. Constantine and Joan M. Constantine, "Where Is Marriage Going?" *The Futurist* 4, no. 2 (April 1970): 44–46; and "How to Make a Group Marriage," *The Modern Utopian* 4 (Summer 1970).

20. Gilbert D. Bartell, *Group Sex* (New York: Wyden, 1971).

21. President's Commission on Obscenity and Pornography, *The Illustrated Presidential Report of the Commission on Obscenity and Pornography* (San Diego: Greenleaf Classics, 1970).

Our definition also emphasized that swinging does not necessarily involve mate switching. It simply may involve participation in group sex. Group sex, as defined by the O'Neills is:

> Three or more persons involved in consensual sexual activity together, including the more common and primarily heterosexual variety among opposite sexes, the mixed heterosexual and homosexual activity among opposite sexes and the rarer exclusively homosexual pattern among same-sex participants. Group sex subsumes some voyeurism and exhibitionism, with partner sharing or exchange occurring in the same place at the same time.[22]

Some swingers who will not swing with a single are quite willing to involve singles in group sex, as at a party. The O'Neill's definition states this well.

We have separated swinging into a beginner's state and an escalated state. Both are of an uncommitted nature and are linked to intimate friendship to which many swingers graduate.

Couples get involved in swinging for many reasons: to "make out"; they seek an alternative to clandestine individual adventures outside the pair-bond; they see other people doing it; or one partner, usually the husband, forces the other into it (often to assuage guilt or to "save the marriage!"). They make an issue of swinging without any emotional involvement, at least at the beginning. "It is just a sex thing."

The committed couple, by contrast, becomes involved in intimate friendship because they wish to expand their already joyous relationship by joint investment in other people at the sociosexual level, in responsive, responsible relationships. In either case, the societal pressures, outlined earlier, will have contributed greatly to developing the climate in which such activity can be expected to flourish.

Many committed couples grow into intimate friendship naturally with friends of long standing. Others are introduced by mutual friends into intimate friendships where the person-to-person interaction is more important than the genital-to-genital interaction and the object is to form relationships that may include sexual involvement as one part of a much larger and more complex level of interaction. The nature of the

---

22. George C. O'Neill and Nena O'Neill, personal communication to the author, 1969.

involvement varies much in the same way the nature of the involvement between mates in a pair-bond varies.

How does one become a swinger? An essential ingredient is to see oneself as a swinger. Many people who switch partners from time to time do not consider themselves swingers, although others might say they are.

Once the decision is made to try swinging, one must find the swingers. If the potential swinger does not have swingers among his friends that he knows about, he may attempt to seduce friends to try it for a lark. This can be risky business, especially in the eyes of the neophyte, who may turn next to public entry points into swinging. Apparently only about 5 percent are forced to do this[23] although Bartell claims it is the most used method.[24] A number of public swinging institutions have parallels in the "singles" world, such as swinging bars, swinging socials, the Sexual Freedom League, swinger ad magazines, and personal columns in underground newspapers.

Some of the uncommitted appear to move comfortably in this public arena. They are willing to advertise themselves as a couple by exhibiting nude photos of the wife in nationally circulated swinger ad magazines. They become long-term supporters of the Sexual Freedom League, where anyone with the price of admission can "make out." They frequent swinger bars and socials, and send "action" pictures through the mail. They are not aware that others believe such behavior is grossly inappropriate. What they find in such places is each other.

The second swinging stage, which we call "Escalated Swinging," is avoided by most swingers. Those who do get there may do so because they make a poor decision. It may take some time for the uncommitted couple to arrive at this decision point. It occurs when satiation sets in. She may begin to feel like a whore. He may begin losing erections. Without relating to people, having sex with them gets stale pretty quickly.

Some people simply drop out at this point. They decide that swinging is not for them after all. Others realize that they must invest in people if swinging is to continue to have meaning for them. These people may graduate to intimate friendship. A few make the third choice—they escalate. Potency can be restored, they find, by "Upping the ante";

23. Breedlove and Breedlove, *Swap Clubs.*
24. Gilbert D. Bartell, "Group Sex Among the Mid-Americans."

experimenting with drugs, bondage, discipline, sadism, witchcraft, or other "way out" intensification of the mechanics of sex. Ultimately this decision must form a closed loop, returning the couple to the initial decision point: to drop out or to begin relating to people as people and not as sex objects.

The uncommitted included the people Symonds identifies as "recreational" swingers:

> Politically conventional, geographically limited, conforming life style except for swinging, reluctant to be identified with their job, conventional child-rearing attitudes, sexual agreements with mates ranging from very loose to rigidly exclusive except for the swinging situation.

We believe many swingers also exhibit some of the attributes Symonds identifies with "Utopian" swingers:

> Broad spectrum libertarians, rejection of the two party political system (!), swinging only one aspect of an experimental life style, mobile, seekers, geographically and otherwise, swinging integrated with total life style, often willing to be identified with specific job, radical attitudes toward child-rearing, flexible and loose sexual arrangements with mates, the limit being that outside ties don't interfere with normal daily living with mate.

As Bartell says, "The chief characteristic all couples in my sample exhibited was their inherent normality. They were average, commonplace, and uncomplicated in almost all respects." [25] Most swingers exhibit *some* of the attributes Symonds identifies with recreational swingers (political conventionality, for example), while few, if any, swingers exhibit all of her utopian attributes and none of her recreational attributes. We believe Symonds may have failed to differentiate between those beginners who constitute the extremist fringe at the lower end of the spectrum and those swingers who are in academic, professional and managerial strata and tend to exhibit more of the attributes of her utopians than of her recreationals.[26] Also there is

25. Gilbert D. Bartell, personal conversation reported by Edward M. Brecher in *The Sex Researchers* (Boston: Little, Brown, 1969).

26. Edward M. Brecher, *The Sex Researchers*; Ramey, "Group Marriage"; O'Neill and O'Neill, "Patterns in Group Sexual Activity."

the possibility that she failed to distinguish between this group and the beginners who are still overwhelmed with the idea of swinging, and even more with relating to people on a more complex level. This could be especially important in California where knowledge of swinging has permeated many layers of society that are not used to complex pair-bond relationships.

A distinguishing characteristic that is essential to understand the modus operandi of the intimate friendship, commune or group marriage, is their ability to relate. Carl Rogers said: "Experience which, if assimilated, would involve a change in the organization of self tends to be resisted through denial or distortion of symbolization." [27]

Thus the uncommitted swinger must either drop out or ritualize the swinging experience. Recognizing this, those who wish to help the uncommitted bridge the gap must relax the situation and reduce the threat. As Rogers goes on to say:

> The structure and organization of self appears to become
> more rigid under threat; to relax its boundaries when
> completely free of threat. Experience which is perceived as
> inconsistent with the self can only be assimilated if the
> current organization of self is relaxed and expanded to
> include it.

The committed instinctively recognize this. Their most striking characteristic is their emphasis on openness, immediacy, feedback, communication at a "feeling level", the here-and-now, and the need to increase their ability to express deeper feelings and accept differences of perception and opinion.[28] The in-group is perceived as peers who share the ability to relate on an open, accepting, helping basis, while there are outsiders who must be taught to relax and relate if they are to be brought into the peer situation.

Observers of the swinging scene have been consistently impressed by the degree to which swingers accept people as they are, let them express their feelings and attitudes freely and nonjudgmentally, and operate in a generally democratic manner, treating males and females as peers.[29]

---

27. Carl Rogers, *Client Centered Therapy* (New York: Houghton Mifflin, 1951).

28. James W. Ramey, "The Relationship of Peer Group Rating to Certain Individual Perceptions of Personality," *Journal of Experimental Education* 27, no. 2 (December 1958): 143–49.

29. Brecher, *The Sex Researchers*; Richard W. Lewis, "The Swingers," *Playboy* 16, no. 2 (April 1969): 149–228; Kanter, "Communes."

The basic rule is to be responsive to the other person's needs and desires; the next most basic: "do your own thing." It is this atmosphere of permissiveness and understanding that provides a situation free of threat in which the beginners can work out their own internal frame of reference and reach responsible interpretations and insights. The resulting self-acceptance generally leads to observable improvement in the individual's interpersonal relations. It also facilitates graduating from swinging to intimate friendship.

Communes

A commune is an expression of the desire to make the dyadic pair-bond a subset of one, rather than many, mediating groups between it and the society at large. Most of us make life commitments through a number of groups; work groups, play groups, special interest groups, hobby groups, health groups, religious groups, economic groups, social groups, political groups, cultural groups. The critical point is that most of us do not make a large percentage of our commitments through one single group. This definition seems more restrictive than necessary. Huxley claimed that:

> All effective communities are founded upon the principle of unlimited liability. In small groups composed of members personally acquainted with one another, unlimited liability provides a liberal education in responsibility, loyalty, and consideration . . . individual members should possess nothing and everything—nothing as individuals and everything as joint owners of communally held property and communally produced income. Property and income should not be so large as to become ends in themselves, not so small that the entire energies of the community have to be directed to procuring tomorrow's dinner.
>
> At all times and in all places communities have been formed for the purpose of making it possible for their members to live more nearly in accord with the currently accepted religious ideals than could be done "in the world." Such communities have devoted a considerable proportion of their time and energy to study, to the performance of ceremonial acts of devotion, and, in some cases at any rate, to the practice of "spiritual exercises."

> From . . . the salient characteristics of past communities
> we can see what future communities ought to be and do. We
> see that they should be composed of carefully selected
> individuals, united in a common belief and by fidelity to a
> shared ideal. We see that property and income should be
> held in common and that every member should assume
> unlimited liability for all other members. We see the
> disciplinary arrangements may be of various kinds, but that
> the most educative form of organization is the democratic.
> We see that it is advisable for communities to undertake
> practical work in addition to study, devotion and spiritual
> exercises; and that this practical work should be of a kind
> which other social agencies, public or private, are either
> unable or unwilling to perform.[30]

Many of the essential elements are pointed out in this lengthy quote from Huxley. In order to encompass all of the groups that claim to be communes today, however, it is necessary to devise a less restrictive definition, such as the one at the beginning of this paper:

> When individuals agree to make life commitments as members
> of one particular group rather than through many different
> groups they may constitute a commune. The number of
> common elements will vary from commune to commune, the
> critical number having been reached at the point at which the
> group sees itself as a commune rather than at some absolute
> number.

Although some communes do share dining and/or sleeping quarters and some espouse joint ownership, income, and function,[31] this is hardly the case for all communes. Quite a few communes have separate quarters, either in a jointly owned apartment building or in separate houses, for example. The type and range of common commitments is such that "being a commune" is almost a state of mind. Some groups, that have many more of the kinds of commitments in common than is the case for some communes, call themselves coops.

Which of the many life commitments are most commonly met throughout a commune? Creating goods and services, worshiping in a

---

30. Aldous Huxley, *Ends and Means* (New York: Greenwood, 1937).

31. Paul J. Marks, *A New Community* (San Diego: Youth Resources, 1969).

specific manner, merchandising, purchasing, property ownership and management, farming, travel, educating and rearing children in a specific manner, study, friendship, social or political action, are some of the common attributes of communes. We have always lived in a world of and functioned through interest groups. The most common of these, through the ages, has been the tribe, and its components, the families. One of the most often cited reasons for the current upsurge of interest in communes is the desire to return to an extended family, or tribal grouping. Indeed, many, many communes refer to themselves not by name, but simply as, "the family."

It is not by accident that the successful communes, i.e., those that have survived, have not been extended families but have instead been groups with a strong unifying and motivating drive and a strong leader. In many cases, especially historically, this unifying factor has been religious. Currently, in addition to the religious drive, there are a substantial number of successful communes built around the desire to optimize coping capacity in a quasi-capitalistic society, i.e., these are people who establish a commune in order to do better what they are already doing well.

There are three major varieties of communes and one trial variety. They can be classified as the religious communes, which have existed in America since 1680, if not earlier; the utopian communes; and the new breed of evolutionary communes mentioned above. What distinguishes this latter group is that they are not about to drop out of or attempt to change the existing society. They simply seek to increase their ability to work effectively within the system. The fourth type of commune is the student commune, which will be handled in a separate section because of its two unique characteristics—it is temporary and it is a learning situation.

Religious communes have enjoyed the highest survival rate among all U.S. communes, but they are not the concern of this paper. Neither are the utopian communes, many of which are unjustifiably called "hippie communes" while others actually fit this designation. The new breed among communes (I shall call them evolutionary communes) are the least known. They are springing up across the metropolitan areas without fanfare, avoid publicity in most cases, realizing that if they attract attention they will be diverted from their goals. We are particularly concerned about evolutionary communes in this paper because they appear to be the most attractive to those academic, professional and managerial people who make up the temporary systems strata, assuming they elect to continue working within the present society.

While there may be those who are enamored with the "back-to-the-land" movement, most of the evolutionary communalists have no intention of abandoning either their careers or their middle-class comforts. The basis for establishing such a commune is the desire of a group of people to cope with our present-day society in a more successful manner than they can manage as couples or individuals. This coping can take many forms; which ones are involved for a particular group depends on the group. The desire to provide better schooling for their children, to pool resources for investment, for shelter, for purchasing, to provide access to luxuries otherwise unavailable, are among the reasons for this movement. One group may be especially concerned about providing the buffer of group security against extended unemployment so that members can be free to stay in a particular geographic area without suffering career setbacks because they refuse to move physically in order to move up the career ladder. A related concern in many groups is the desire to provide educational opportunities for group members or their children that are beyond the resources of a single couple.

The most basic reason for becoming involved in an evolutionary commune, however, is the desire to expand the complexity of interrelationships beyond the possibilities inherent in the pair-bond itself. In the widest sense, the key term is propinquity, for communal living makes possible a person-to-person intimacy, on both sexual and nonsexual levels, that goes far beyond even the most closely knit intimate friendships. We are still talking about a level of interaction that falls short of multiple pair-bonds however. While group marriages have been found embedded in communes, most communalists are not yet ready to go so far as to consider themselves married to several people at once. The size of most communes argues against such intimacy, if the "readiness state" of the members does not, for evolutionary communes range in size from 10 to 130 individuals.

Before discussing evolutionary communes further, two important points about communes in general must be made: first, with respect to how they get established, and second, with regard to how they handle sexual intimacy.

Some communes are started with almost no preplanning or attention to the basic questions that should be thrashed out in order to avoid almost certain failure. This is the case especially with so called "hippie communes," where the word of the day is "Action! Let it all hang loose and it will all come together." This kind of simple faith in miracles is pathetically common and the communes that begin this way are almost certainly doomed to failure. Others engage in talk marathons that may go on for months, without ever discussing the basic questions that must be resolved, or without resolving them. Again, the end result is usually failure. The religious commune groups usually seem to avoid this problem because they are typically led by a strong man who makes all the decisions and will not brook dissension and because they are united in religious fervor, i.e., the strong leader is expressing God's will. The evolutionary communes are most likely to have approached the decision to establish a commune by establishing a consensual process for working through structure and process as the first step in moving from being "talkers" to becoming "doers." [32]

Five distinct types of sexual intimacy prevail in communes, some of which are so destructive that, because of the sexual structure, the commune is still very failure-prone. One of these patterns is celibacy. A commune that practices celibacy can last only one generation unless it is able to attract enough recruits to replace those who die. The Shakers were one such group that didn't make it. Exclusive monogamy is another sexual stance. In most religious communes exclusive monogamy is practiced with extreme prohibitions against the transgressor. Free love is sometimes the sexual mode of the commune, but this is less often the case than is generally imagined. A few communes claim to practice free love on a committed basis, i.e., the group consists of "brothers and sisters" who are all one family and the family takes responsibility jointly for child rearing and nurturing. Since they practice free love only within the group, albeit without pair-bonding, they are enjoying the best of two worlds. Their responsibility is to the group, not to the individual and then to the group, but they are not a group marriage, because no one is pair-bonded. The author knows of at least one such group that has survived for over two years and appears to be getting stronger over time. It is too early to speculate about the long-range effects, however, even though one is strongly tempted to

---

32. James W. Ramey, "Conflict Resolution Through Videotape Simulation" (Paper presented at annual meeting, Amercian Psychiatric Association, Detroit, May 1967).

draw parallels with the early days of the kibbutzim, many of which began this way.

The most generally practiced intimacy pattern is intimate friendship, especially in the evolutionary commune but also in many utopian communes. Group marriages can sometimes be found embedded in a commune, usually involving three to six individuals out of the total population of the commune. A commune that involves both group marriage and intimate friendship is not likely to break up over sexual problems. On the other hand, a commune that includes both exclusive monogamy and any kind of sex outside the pair-bond is a good candidate for trouble. Combinations of exclusive monogamy and free love, exclusive monogamy and group marriage, or celibacy and free love, are very unlikely to occur.

The *evolutionary commune* appears to be a comparatively recent development on the commune scene. It is clearly distinguishable from the utopian commune because its members are not reacting against the system. They come together out of the desire to do better what they are already doing well. In an economic sense, the lesson of the coop movement is not lost on these people. But in general, especially if they have already explored the possibilities inherent in intimate friendships, they are aware that there is a tremendous exhilaration in pushing the limits of interaction potential. They know that involvement at higher levels of complexity is more demanding on the individual than staying within the limits of the pair-bond. Also they are aware that it is more rewarding, the degree of pleasure equalling the amount of investment in these relationships. Some couples develop friendships to a degree of interaction that transcends the usual taboos on "gut level" dialogue and makes possible direct exploration of the possibilities inherent in communal sharing of life commitments. This paper has concentrated on the swinging stage of this development because at this time, more people seem to be at this stage of growing into more complex interrelationships than are possible within the exclusive framework of the pair-bond.

Group Marriage

Group marriage involves an even greater degree of complexity of interaction than communal living. The Constantines have defined this type of union admirably. As they put it: "A multilateral marriage is one in which three or more people each consider themselves to have a primary relationship with at least two other individuals in the group." [33]

The definition at the beginning of this paper is a restatement of the Constantine's definition which simplifies and clarifies the nature of the relationship: "In a group marriage each of the three or more participants is pair-bonded with at least two others." We believe the term "pair-bond" is more explicit than "primary relationship" for the reason stated earlier, i.e., pair-bonded individuals are mates.

Group marriage may involve a couple and a single, two couples, two couples and a single, three couples, or three couples and a single. As far as is known to the author, no group marriage consisting of more than seven individuals has been verified as existing, and the likelihood that such a group might exist is slim. The addition of one individual greatly increases the number of possible pair-bonds in the group. Triads and two-couple group marriages are the most popular type.

Implicit in any serious discussion of group marriage is an examination of reactions to same-sex pair-bonds. Same-sex pair-bonds are quite common among females in group marriages. The Constantines have found same-sex bonds between males both less frequent and much more critical to the success of the marriage. The author also knows of other instances in which incipient development of a male-male relationship broke up the marriage. It would seem relatively safe to say that a group marriage in which everyone is ambisexual will have higher survival potential, all other things being equal, than one involving one or more monosexual individuals.

The complexity of interaction that must be faced upon establishing a commune or group marriage is several orders of magnitude greater than that faced upon moving from pair-bond exclusivity to intimate friendship. The situation is further complicated by the fact that each group must work out its own ground rules. Premarital courting at the dyadic level occurs within an understood structure that is already well defined by society. Each couple makes major and minor decisions in terms of already internalized givens and expectations about marriage, and what is appropriate and permissible within the framework of

---

33. Larry L. Constantine and Joan M. Constantine, "Report on Ongoing Research in Group Marriage" (Presentation to January meeting, Society for the Scientific Study of Sex, New York, January 1971).

marriage. Since society has not proscribed norms, standards, and activities for group marriages or communes, a great deal more preplanning and exploration must be undertaken to work through expectations and structure behavior for these largely uncharted waters than is the case upon entering into dyadic marriage.

A partial list of the types of problems that must be dealt with will indicate the magnitude of the task.

> Decision-making procedures, group goals, ground rules, prohibitions, intra- and extra-group sexual relationships, privacy, division of labor, role relationships, careers, relationship with outsiders, degree of visibility, legal jeopardy, dissolution of the group, personal responsibilities outside the group (such as parent support), urban or rural setting, type of shelter, geographic location, children, child-rearing practices, taxes, pooling assets, income, legal structure, education, trial period, etc.

Many decisions can be put off until after the group embarks upon their new adventure, but most of those listed above must be worked out in the planning stage.

Age appears to be a prominent earmark of success in both communes and group marriages. The complexities to be faced are such that personal hangups, pair-bond hangups, and career hangups should have been solved before a couple takes this step, since a tremendous investment of time, effort, and emotional energy will be required to achieve success in the new undertaking. It follows that one would expect to find people over thirty most often involved in successful groups and indeed, this is the case. In fact, the Constantines have not found a group marriage with participants under this age level still extant, while we have knowledge of only one tetrad in which one individual is twenty-eight and another is twenty-five.

The two areas of concern that most frequently pop up in discussions of group marriage, money and the division of labor, turn out to be the two least worrisome in actual practice. Developing a viable decision-making pattern is much more involved, because consensus takes an inordinate amount of time. Once sufficient trust has developed to assign functional responsibility, the group will only have to consider major or policy decisions, just as in a dyadic marriage or any other organization.

Although a set of ground rules will probably be established initially, these will become less and less important as the marriage develops informal norms, standards, and activities. It has been suggested that a rough measure of the current stability of a group marriage is the degree to which they persist in clinging to the formal rules and contracts set up at the beginning of the marriage.

A trial period of some sort is essential to the success of dyadic marriage, in the eyes of many people. This is an even more important factor in working through the developmental stages of a group marriage, and many would maintain, of a commune as well. Of course this can get out of hand if it isn't handled on a reasonable basis. A recent advertisement in the *Village Voice* placed by a group of would-be communalists revealed an interesting problem. These people wished to start the commune with ten couples and made it a prerequisite for all the individuals in the group to live with each other for one week in pairs first. A quick count reveals that 190 pairs are involved here, so that for 19 weeks every individual would be separated from his own mate while living with all the others. Yet these people were surprised when the impracticality of this plan was pointed out to them. Nevertheless, however it is arranged, some kind of physical sharing is an important step in the planning stage. Many people handle this trial stage by planning a joint vacation or renting a summer place together. Others join one of the communal work brigades that are becoming an important part of the utopian rural commune scene.

Perhaps the most deep-rooted difference that can develop in a group marriage has to do with child rearing. Deciding about parentage is easy, and agreement on having children and on what to do about the children if the marriage breaks up can be settled beforehand. Groups that start with babies or no children find it much easier to work out joint child-rearing agreement than those who come into the marriage with older children. Not only must the parents work out a mutually agreeable program that is also agreeable to the nonparents, there is also the problem of compatibility and adjustment among the children themselves. Finally, there is the incipient problem that many swingers avoid, of deciding how developing children should fit into the sexual interrelationship of the marriage.

Uncommitted swingers almost universally hide their swinging activities from their children, whereas many individuals involved in intimate friendships are as open with their children about their interfamily relationships as they are about all other aspects of life. Historically, some of the successful communes (Oneida, for example) initiated the children into full sexual participation in the life of the commune at puberty. There are, however, little or no data available about current practices. Some swinging groups include unmarried teen-agers and/or married children and their spouses. The author has heard of at least one group involving a three-generation swinging family. How widespread such practices might be, nobody knows, since it is only very recently that anybody has been willing to talk. The author has knowledge of one group marriage that consisted of a widow, her son and daughter, and their spouses. This group broke up over an incipient sexual relationship between the two males because one was unable to handle the possible implication that he would be deemed homosexual if he allowed the union to develop.

The New Generation

The quasi-courtship behavior patterns that middle-class youth learn from their elders (which are not a part of the growth pattern of lower-class youth) tend to combine romantic love with active sexuality.[34] Today, the great bulk of these middle-class youth attend college. By the time they reach college age, 42 percent of the males and 29 percent of the females say they have had sexual intercourse.[35] The books many cite as most influential in their lives are Heinlein's *Stranger in a Strange Land* and Rimmer's *Harrad Experiment*, and *Proposition 31*, all of which proclaim the message of sexual equality and the pleasure and merit to be derived from sexual complexity within a group larger than a dyad but with the sanctity and attributes of dyadic marriage.[36]

Thus, it is not surprising to find student communes flourishing wherever colleges and universities are found. Rossi's sample, which included 8,000 freshmen and juniors attending 48 four-year colleges

34. Albert E. Scheflen, *Quasi-Courtship Behavior in Psychotherapy* (William Alanson White Psychiatric Foundation, Monograph 28, 1965).

35. Peter H. Rossi, W. Eugene Groves, and David Grafstein, *Life Styles and Campus Communities* (Baltimore, Md.: Johns Hopkins Press, 1971).

36. Robert Heinlein, *Stranger in a Strange Land* (New York: Avon Books, 1967); Robert H. Rimmer, *The Harrad Experiment* (New York: Bantam Books, 1967); and *Proposition 31* (New York: Signet Books, 1968).

and universities, revealed that 17 percent favored communal living and an additional 48 percent approved it for others although they were not personally interested in joining. A significant point is that 40 percent of college-age youth are attending college today.

Whether students call their shared living quarters a crash pad, a coop, a "nest," a commune, or simply a shared apartment, all these loosely organized coed living arrangements afford the students an opportunity to experiment with a number of living modes, of varying complexity, with the tacit understanding that they are not making permanent commitments. Under these circumstances, free love, serial monogamy, and group sex can be fully explored without the pressure of value judgments with respect to "success." Casual nudity, brother-sister type nonsexual intimacy, and celibacy all find acceptance in such a setting. Changes in the personnel of the group often lead to dramatic shifts in sexual practices, and the Pill makes all of this investigation safe, within a loving, sharing, nonjudgmental setting that permits much freer expression and exploration of relationship potentials than is possible in the more highly structured adult society.

Although this is almost always uncommitted behavior, with respect to the individual, it is most decidedly committed behavior with respect to the group search for a satisfying life style, in terms of equality of the sexes and critical examination of accepted societal marriage standards. These young people can be counted on to form pair-bonds based on equality. With their trial experience in more complex relationships they can be expected to swell the ranks of evolutionary communes and group marriages, assuming they decide to cast their lot with existing society and work within existing social structures. Those who decide on a more utopian stance, will, along with the evolutionary communalists and group marriages, cause a dramatic upsurge in these complex marital structures which can be expected to have a major impact on restructuring marriage in the direction of societal sanction of intimate friendship, communes, and group marriage.

28

THE OBSOLESCENT MOTHER:
A SCENARIO

EDWARD GROSSMAN

For almost as long as Man has been human, birth has been a big event, a disturbance, and more or less a shock, so much so that at least one mythology has accounted for the pain of it as punishment for an original sin against Almighty God. Considering how long Man has been human—defined biologically or mythologically—it is just yesterday that childbirth began to be mitigated. . . .

While women couldn't have begun to be liberated from the special pains and dangers of their biology without the help of certain men, there have always been, at each "critical juncture," other men opposing this liberation, or at least the technical means of achieving it. . . .

Innovators, great benefactors of women like Simpson, have generally had complicated feelings, their sympathy being sharpened by ambition. Only women, once they have realized the meaning for themselves of these innovations, have displayed uncomplicated enthusiasm, which finally proves more effective than anything else in overcoming tradition. . . .

Other men made further advances: antisepsis in surgery, antibiotics, refinements in diagnosis and delivery. Because of this accumulation of knowledge, to have a child in an industrial country today is no longer dangerous. The process may be bothersome and uncomfortable for many, but very few women die in childbirth anymore. However, despite this, it is still not possible to say that we take birth as casually as animals do. . . .

The process of childbearing, with its final event as if something were coming to inexorable term, still has about it a sense of prehistory, savage and elemental, even though it is surrounded by rubber gloves and stainless steel. It is a spectacle that impresses the civilized no less than the savage mind as awesome, and together with the other striking biological events associated with a woman's body, may lead a man like Sigmund Freud to write, "Anatomy is destiny." However, this epigram, with its numerous social, sexual, economic, and political implications, has had its portion of incontrovertible truth reduced in the years since it was written, and again, this has been thanks to men. The female's circular, periodic, excitable, "destined" biology has been brought closer to the linear biology of the male as a result of new knowledge of the chemistry of sexual differentiation and functioning, and the technology that this knowledge has made possible—above all, the Pill. . . .

To gain knowledge which would lead to new and better technology and social programs in these areas of daily concern, embryologists have needed to observe, measure, and experiment with the first phases of human reproduction. Now, these first phases, including culturing of the human egg, its fertilization by sperm, and development as an embryo, have been carried out under the microscope, or in the scientific terminology, *in vitro*, "under glass." . . .

According to the published reports, all the genetic work has been done on embryos which spontaneously stopped growing. In fact, officially, the problem of deciding to take the next step is postponed and somewhat eased by the report that none of the embryos has survived in vitro past the sixteen-cell stage, while only an embryo developed well past that stage can successfully implant itself or be implanted into the uterus. However, when the Edwards group does succeed in culturing embryos to the implantation stage, the decision to implant a given embryo will have to be based on statistical evidence, and on hope—it will not be possible to karyotype the embryo itself. As Edwards' colleague, Dr. Steptoe, says, it will call for a "brave decision."

Toward the other end of the process of childbearing, or gestation (Latin, *gestare*, "to bear," "to carry"), other researchers, quite independent of the sort of in vitro embryological work being done by Edwards, have been devising ways to save babies when a woman's natural machinery fails and the fetus is born too soon. This new branch of medicine is called "fetology." The fetus, its umbilical cord to the natural placenta having been cut, is placed in an incubator which supplies heat and oxygen. There it is fed intravenously, and its breathing is forcibly assisted by an iron lung. By such means, doctors are now able to save most seven-month-old premature babies (average weight two pounds), some six-and-a-quarter- to seven-month-old "premies," and a very few under six and a quarter months. Incubators, which have been in use for a long time, substitute for many of the functions of the womb or placenta in order to permit the premature baby to gain size and weight. However, the baby is indeed a baby, and not a fetus anymore, because the umbilicus has been cut and the lungs are working. Some fetuses are expelled from the mother's body even earlier in gestation, and they die in an incubator. The challenge is to build an environment that duplicates the ordinary environment of a fetus, in which it will not have to do things for which its body is unready. Fetologists are trying various approaches. . . .

The editorialist of the *New Scientist* has said, ". . . the development of the 'perfect' artificial placenta can only be a matter of time." . . .

The *New York Times*, under the headline, "Test Tube Babies Ahead?" published an editorial about the Edwards' experiments praising the hope they hold out for childless couples. Then the *Times* said:

> Ultimately the prospect looms of human babies engendered by fertilization and development completely outside any woman's body—test tube babies, in the most literal sense. . . . Abuses are easy to envisage, but it is encouraging that so far at least there is no evidence of such abuses in the use of artificial insemination to help women conceive. The real question even now is whether—and how—people can develop the sense of social responsibility that will be required if, by the year 2000 or earlier, women are able to have children without any of the morning sickness, special diets and other discomforts and dangers pregnancy now entails.

The *Times* mentions artificial insemination. At least twenty thousand babies are conceived by mechanical means in the United States each year, and there may be a million Americans now alive who were so conceived. This indicates a widespread acceptance of the technique, though a recent Harris poll on "New Methods of Reproduction" had only 5 percent of the sample knowing what artificial insemination is. However, once it was explained to them, 49 percent of men and 62 percent of women approved insemination with the husband's sperm in cases of infertility; 24 percent of men and 28 percent of women approved insemination with anonymous donor sperm. The poll takers also explained other techniques still not in existence, and got opinions on these. Thirty-two percent of men, 39 percent of women would approve of embryo implants of the sort planned by Edwards—37 percent of men, 48 percent of women said they "would feel love" for a baby of their own conceived in this way. The poll takers then asked about "test-tube babies," babies who at no time would be inside the mother's body. Thirty percent of men, 35 percent of women were of the opinion that "this would be justified if wife might die or be crippled from childbirth." However, if "a woman just wanted to skip pregnancy and have a baby too," more than 90 percent of men and women would disapprove. Forty-seven percent of men, 53 percent of women said they "would feel love" toward such a "test-tube baby" of their own (for some reason, the percentage here, for both men and women, was higher than in the case of the embryo implant). Fifty-five percent of men, 61 percent of women said they believed a "test-tube baby would feel love for [its] family." A striking aspect of the results of this poll is that women invariably display a greater readiness to consider "new methods of reproduction" than men. This readiness is enhanced when the responses are broken down by age group: for example, of the women under thirty, fully 57 percent approved embryo implants. And yet, there was confusion too. Many of the men and women who approved of the new methods, including "test-tube babies," said they saw in them a way to bolster the ideal of monogamous marriage by ensuring that no couple need be childless; yet it was admitted that the new methods might have exactly the opposite effect—that is, of undermining further the ideal of the family.

The *Times* editorial and the Harris poll seem to show that there is important "public" enthusiasm for the goals, both official and possible, of the embryological research now under way, even if this enthusiasm is qualified by some doubts and fears. . . .

Leaving aside for the moment the question whether such a method is desirable—is it feasible? The answer would have to do with technology, with whether ways could be devised to transfer the embryo fertilized in vitro to an artificial placenta which would duplicate for eight and a half months the environment of the natural placenta. . . . It would be, at the least, a delicate, painstaking, and drawn-out task of plotting the career of a human embryo and fetus in the placenta from minute to minute, and then fabricating the machinery to duplicate the placenta and a computer to monitor and direct it and oversee the piping-in of nutrients and carrying-off of wastes. The technological problems here are formidable, as fetologists working on the margins already know; but are they more formidable than those involved in, say, Apollo 11? Probably not, and using Apollo as a hackneyed but serviceable example, it might be said that for the United States, there is no technological project that is not assured of success provided the decision is made to invest whatever talent and money are necessary; provided also that there is a strong enough sense of national priority so that any misfortune (such as the death by fire of three astronauts on the pad at Cape Kennedy) does not endanger the life of the project itself. It would be too much to expect an artificial womb to "work" the first time, and people would have to be ready to accept the death of a fetus, even though, in contrast with Gus Grissom, the fetus never volunteered.

What reason would there be to make the development of an artificial womb a national priority? Once they are compiled, the specific and predictable benefits of an efficient artificial womb make an impressive list:

1. Fetal medicine would be much improved. By being able to monitor growth and development continuously, fetologists would be able to catch, and perhaps treat, sickness that occurs in the natural womb but does not show up until after birth.

2. Likewise, fetologists would be able to immunize a child for the diseases it would be likely to contract in the world, but while it is still in the sterile safety of the womb.

3. Tissue samples could be taken from the fetus, cultured, and frozen for storage, which would resist the rejection phenomenon should the human born ever require organ transplants.

4. An efficient artificial womb, far from increasing the incidence of birth defects, would reduce them by keeping the fetus in an absolutely safe and regular environment; safe, for example, from infection by German measles or drugs taken by the mother. There are now thousands of babies born in the United States each year with defects, ranging from relatively minor ones like harelip, to deformed limbs and congenital diseases of the nervous system. Whatever the magnitude of the defect, it is disastrous: doctors say that the immediate and overwhelming response of the parents is not love or pity, but anger; they are angry at the doctor, and angry at their deformed child for choosing them as its parents. This behavior is evident on the part of both parents alike: there is no special redemptive mother-love. Some

parents will reject the child, or, after a guilty reaction, some will gird themselves for the job of lifelong sacrifice, of being "noble."

5. The same new conditions that would allow fetologists to prevent birth defects would allow geneticists eventually to be able to program a fetus' development for some superior trait on which society could agree: larger brain capacity, for example. This would seem to be the direction that is being taken anyway now, with genetic counseling. The artificial womb would lift such work out of the realm of the haphazard.

6. An artificial womb would make "sexing" (choosing the sex of the embryo) a simple matter.

7. That part of the population which would use the artificial womb would not have to worry about illegitimacy or doubtful paternity. For the first time it will be possible to prove beyond a shadow of a doubt that a man is the father of his children.

8. Women who are prone to miscarry, or who because of body structure or constitution run a danger of injury in childbirth, would be spared the unhappiness, disappointment, and danger. Other women would be spared the discomfort.

9. Women who decided to have children by the artificial womb might choose to undergo the operation in which the fallopian tubes are tied. This would not affect fertility, but it would be an instant, guaranteed, and permanent barrier to conception from sexual intercourse. No other "birth control" would have to be exercised, and the Pill, together with its harmful and unknown side effects, could be dispensed with. Of course, these women would never have to have abortions, either.

It would seem that from the development and use of an artificial womb, all of society would benefit, but women would stand to gain the most. The artificial womb would set about breaking to pieces the stubborn remnant of biological fact and cultural myth that makes all women pay. The invidious question whether women are different from men in some ultimate and irreducible metaphysical way, whether as a result they should be set and should set for themselves different goals and different styles of life, would be removed from the context of biological difference, which has so far complicated its resolution with gratuitous factors, and would be set in a context of biological equity. Culturally, if the artificial womb "catches on," it will mean that the awfulness associated with pregnancy and childbirth will have nothing to feed on, and motherhood, if it continues to excite any awe at all, will not do so more than fatherhood. This will have its inevitable effect on the relation of women to men, women to their children, and the society or state to children. Once a woman has no more difficult or lengthy role in reproduction than a man (or not much more difficult or lengthy: she will still have to undergo laparoscopy once, when several dozen eggs will be collected and put into cold storage), she will find that society does not expect her to have a special relation to her offspring that takes up years of her life, and also she will not expect it of herself. Too, a society that can grow fetuses in a laboratory will be more disposed to have meaningful day- and night-care centers and communal nurseries on a large scale, for the state, being a third parent, will wish to provide for the maintenance and upbringing of its children.

Natural pregnancy may become an anachronism. The two tiny laparoscopy scars, exposed by a bikini on the beach, will be as ordinary as our smallpox vaccination, but women will no longer have lost their figures in childbearing. The uterus will become appendixlike, though the ovaries will be as crucial as before. At the age of twenty, each girl will be able to choose to be superovulated and her eggs collected and frozen, as it is known that babies conceived by young women are less likely to suffer from mongolism and other birth defects. If there are advances in prenatal care, it may not be necessary to prohibit natural childbearing in the interest of public health and eugenics. In that case, the women who wish to put up with the old style and all that it implies will be free to do so. But it will be a throwback and increasingly rare as the manifest advantages of the artificial womb make it likely to win the competition.

Most, if not all, of its *disadvantages* might be more apparent to us than real to the next generations. We bear it in mind that a man-made mutation like this, finishing what the Pill started, unprecedented in evolution perhaps since sea creatures grew lungs and came out on land or apes developed the ability to touch thumb to forefinger, must have its effect on the body and mind of everyone in society, men not much less than women. Might not everyone, and particularly women, also *suffer* from the artificial womb? The myth of the beatific Madonna has, after all, among its various sources the fact that some women do experience unusual well-being when they have a baby. A more recent myth is that women on the Pill for a long time, who have much sex but never a baby, suffer the opposite of the bodily and psychic happiness of the

Madonna. Does this mean the body has its own wisdom and that for women to be given access to an artificial womb would be to go against the deepest instincts provided by nature?

Again, the question may be invidious. In the first place, as a matter of fact, for every beatific mother in our society there is at least another with "postpartum blues." To propose a "fundamental nature" for women (or men) to which it is immoral or unwise to offer an alternative may be to support a fallacy which is really old-fashioned. The well-being of the Madonna, her rosy complexion, may have as simple an explanation as that during pregnancy and lactation, her body's production of estrogen has shot up: maybe a woman having a baby by the artificial womb might take estrogen orally.

But won't women be "alienated," as we say, from their children, causing further distance to be put between all of us from the crucial beginning, which is not what we need? Again, perhaps an invidious question. In the 1840s, opponents of Dr. Simpson asked whether (actually they claimed that) anesthesia during labor would make children "strangers" to their mothers. Has this proven true? Maternal love does not seem to be connected with the pain of childbirth, or even with childbirth; we know that some women beat the children they have borne, while others love the children they have adopted.

However, by "creating life" won't we be raising ultimate questions that we are not prepared to answer, such as "What is a human being?" The effect may well be to raise such questions. As for "creating life," that is to misunderstand what the artificial womb will do. It will not "create" life, for the materials which contain all the factors for differentiation, growth, and genetic coding—the egg and sperm—will not be created or fabricated: they will only be given another environment in which to work out their process. Sexual reproduction will be preserved; only intercourse and reproduction will be separated, once and for all.

The "ultimate" questions will be harder to ignore, perhaps. But this has been predicted. Jean Rostand, the French biologist and Nobel Prize winner, has considered what life will be like and what questions people will have to face up to when the artificial womb and other "inevitable" technologies become a reality:

> People will live for two hundred years, or even more.
> There will be no more failure, no more fear, no more
> tragedy. Life will be safer, easier, longer. But will it still be

worth living? . . . How shall we contrive to exercise the
formidable powers allotted to us . . . ? How . . . shall we
avoid finding ourselves on the perilous slope and yielding to
the abuses of a Promethean intoxication?

Well, Rostand says, "our task will be to improvise the solution, taking
account of the collective mentality, of the social and moral situation [and
remembering Bacon's warning], 'Knowledge, if it be taken without the
true corrective [charity] hath in it some nature of venom or malignity.'"

Rostand assumes the artificial womb and other such innovations are
"inevitable": that seems a peculiar idea. He also predicts that when the
womb arrives it must have a universal effect. Here he is evidently right.
If there is a single prototype artificial womb made and successfully
tested, it is unlikely that it will turn out—as the Apollo missions
might—an exorbitant stunt without consequence for "the man in the
street." Because it will literally be down to earth, an artificial womb
will have the potential to change the life of every person. But is the
artificial womb "inevitable," as Rostand says? "Inevitable" seems to
imply that something will come to pass without our doing anything or
despite our intervention, which in the case of an artificial womb is
nonsense. And yet there is a meaning of "inevitable" which, in this
context, is not ridiculous. This is the meaning which in effect asks to
what extent human beings exercise free will, and to what extent they
are determined by forces forever beyond them. A very ancient question.
Yet is it conceivable that if Dr. Simpson, in 1842, had not decided to
give anesthesia to a woman in labor, anesthesia would not be routinely
used in labor today? It is not conceivable. If he had not done it, some
other doctor would, driven by the combination of curiosity, sympathy,
and ambition which many men, not just a single indispensable man, are
endowed with. The picture of the solitary scientist breaking ground
may be excessively romantic. Without denying the medical scientist in
particular his glory, his Nobel Prize, and the gratitude of the people
whose suffering he has eased, it may be said that the scientist is far from
being on his own, that he is, as we all are, an agent of something,
determined by a force, a momentum which blurs distinctions between
"it has become possible to do it," "it should be done," "it must be
done," and is resolved in the inevitable: "it will be done."

Looked at in this light, it would not seem to make much difference
(except, obviously, to the volunteer childless couples at Cambridge)
whether Dr. Edwards decides to implant an embryo: the operation is

going to take place pretty soon whatever he decides or does. Likewise the question whether what is about to be done in embryology, and what is about to be done in fetology, will ever come together in its logical consummation. If it becomes a national priority, it will be achieved sooner; if unlimited money and support are not forthcoming, it will be achieved later. But it is hard to imagine it not being achieved at all.

Certainly it would take more exertion, over the long run, to prevent it than to achieve it, and why prevent it? Who is to say that Monsignor Vallainc, the Vatican press officer who branded the Edwards experiments "immoral acts and absolutely illicit," is not the hapless spokesman of cruelty and stupidity, our contemporary version of the ministers who damned Simpson? In any case, it is not the thirteenth century anymore, and the centers of research happen not to be in Russia or in Roman Catholic theocracies. There is no forbidding most things and no arresting Dr. Edwards and charging him with murder. More than this: the research is conducted quietly, indoors; it does not require the vast hardware of an Apollo project, and there are no thunderous blasts and clouds of smoke. The expunging of perhaps our foremost Myth, with its ancient, numberless effects of inspiration and practice, habit and suffering, may be accomplished both inevitably and quietly—which leads to the ironic part, that whether anyone, or any movement, comes out for the artificial womb, or not, will make little difference in the end. The only difference it might make—and perhaps this is no small thing for the race—is that at least we will be able to say that our liberation did not catch us by surprise.

29

MINORITY STATUS AND THE PURSUIT OF PROFESSIONAL CAREERS: WOMEN IN SCIENCE AND ENGINEERING[1]

CAROLYN CUMMINGS PERRUCCI

Minority status, whether based on sex, race, ethnicity, or religion, is an important influence upon occupational placement, even in high-

1. Revision of a paper presented at the Tenth International Seminar on Family

status professional occupations.[2] With respect to sex, it is found that many professions are sex typed,[3] resulting by and large in the continuation of either male or female predominance among the practitioners therein.[4] Consistent with the minority status of women, female-dominated professions tend to be of lower status than those dominated by men.[5]

Investigation of the relative integration of minorities into the world of work reveals variations by minority group and by specific profession and work place.[6] In general such integration appears to be occurring most slowly, if at all, for those whose minority status is most visible and at the same time irrevocable, including race and sex distinctions.[7] When it occurs, sexual integration of traditionally female-dominated professions appears to involve a form of intraprofessional stratification whereby men assume the supervisory or otherwise more prestigious

Research, Teheran, Iran, March 1968. The author is indebted to the American Council of Learned Societies for making her participation at this Seminar possible.

Research reported in this paper is part of a larger study of women in science and engineering supported by the Manpower Administration, U.S. Department of Labor, Grant No. 91-16-67-43.

Gratitude is expressed to Robert Perrucci for his critical reading of an earlier version of this paper, and to Edward Barboni, Karen D. Tate, and Michael Spinelli for assistance in data analysis.

2. Oswald Hall, "The Informal Organization of the Medical Profession," *Canadian Journal of Economics and Political Science* 12, no. 1 (February 1946): 30–44; Oswald Hall, "Stages of a Medical Career," *American Journal of Sociology* 53, no. 5 (March 1948): 327–36; Jerome Carlin, *Lawyers on Their Own* (New Brunswick, N.J.: Rutgers University Press, 1962); Jerome Carlin, *Lawyers' Ethics* (New York: Russell Sage Foundation, 1966); Jack Ladinsky, "Careers of Lawyers, Law Practice, and Legal Institutions," *American Sociological Review* 28, no. 1 (February 1963): 47–54; Erwin O. Smigel, *The Wall Street Lawyer* (New York: Free Press, 1964); E. Wilbur Bock, "The Female Clergy: A Case Professional Marginality," *American Journal of Sociology* 72, no. 5 (March 1967): 531–39.

3. Cynthia F. Epstein, "Woman's Place: The Salience of Sex Status in the Professional Setting" (ms., Columbia University, 1967). Mimeographed.

4. Edward Gross, "Plus Ca Change . . . ? The Sexual Structure of Occupations Over Time," *Social Problems* 16, no. 2 (Fall 1968): 198–208.

5. Epstein, "Woman's Place."

6. Harold L. Wilensky and Jack Ladinsky, "From Religious Community to Occupational Group: Structural Assimilation Among Professors, Lawyers and Engineers," *American Sociological Review* 32, no. 4 (August 1967): 541–61.

7. Daniel O. Price, "Changes in Occupational Distribution of the Negro Population" (ms., 1964), cited in Wilensky and Ladinsky, "From Religious Community to Occupational Group," p. 561; John B. Parish and Jean S. Block, "The Future for Women in Science and Engineering," *Bulletin of the Atomic Scientists* 24, no. 5 (May 1968): 46–49.

forms of the occupation[8] or, in effect, take control of the occupation.[9]

Similarly, there is evidence that women who work in traditional male professions are overrepresented in the lower-prestige specialties within the profession and are more likely than men to serve only minority-status clients.[10] They are also more likely than not to have work functions which reflect an extension of their sex role in the society in question. It is suggested that possession of a "deviant" sex status by women professionals may pose distinctive problems coming from the confusion of sex roles with occupational roles or from attitudes about the priorities of sex roles over occupational roles.[11] With respect to the latter concern, however, studies which focus on the dynamic aspects of timing of marital and fertility behavior (seen here as the most relevant aspects of women's sex roles) in relation to stages in women's professional training and career are rare indeed. Also lacking are attempts to assess career-family patterns of cohorts or generations of women professionals with the noteworthy exception of a longitudinal study of a sample of college graduates—class of 1961—for which preliminary analysis of data indicates a relationship between career goals at graduation and marital and work behavior three years later.[12]

Variation in minority-group integration into specific occupations is considered in Blalock's developing theory of minority-group relations.[13] It is postulated that, given constancy of job prestige level and general labor market conditions, integration of visible minorities into professions is most likely for work having several specified characteristics, including that in which it is difficult to prevent the minority from acquiring the necessary skills; individual performance is positively related to the productivity of the work group (which is preferably a

---

8. Gross, "Plus Ca Change."

9. Harold L. Wilensky, "Women's Work: Economic Growth, Ideology, Structure," *Industrial Relations* 7, no. 3 (May 1968): 235–48.

10. Everett Hughes, *Men and Their Work* (New York: Free Press, 1958); Epstein, "Women's Place."

11. Epstein, "Woman's Place."

12. Alice S. Rossi, "Barriers to the Career Choice of Engineering, Medicine, or Science Among American Women," in *Women and the Scientific Professions*, ed. Jacqueline A. Mattfeld and Carol Van Aken (Cambridge, Mass.: MIT Press, 1965), pp. 51–127.

13. Hubert M. Blalock, "Occupational Discrimination: Some Theoretical Propositions," *Social Problems* 9, no. 3 (Winter 1962): 240–47; and Hubert M. Blalock, *Toward A Theory of Minority-Group Relations* (New York: Wiley, 1967).

team of various specialists), all of whom share in the productivity rewards; individual performance level is relatively independent of skill in interpersonal relations; high individual performance does not lead to power over other members of the work group; individual performance is readily evaluated; total productivity is not markedly limited by consumer demand; and there is extensive competition among employers for outstanding personnel. Although the above characteristics are acknowledged to be typical of few areas of work in the American occupational structure, save professional baseball and some other entertainment fields, it is suggested that science-based professions fit the model fairly closely. This is largely an untested assumption for, to date, little detailed information concerning sex (or race) differences in scientific work experiences has been published. A beginning has been made by Rossi who shows sex differences in income, type of employer, and work hours for scientists and engineers employed at the time of the 1960 Census.[14]

The present study attempts to broaden understanding of the integration of minorities into the world of work by focusing on sexual integration of professions, specifically, the place of women in science and engineering. This objective is approached in two ways: (1) by presenting for the first time, detailed description of some salient features of women scientists' labor force participation in comparison to work experiences of men in the same fields; and (2) by analyzing the education–work–family temporal patterns for two age groups of women science and engineering graduates. Comparative analysis of employment experiences of men and women graduates permits documentation of the existence or absence, as well as the nature of sex differences in utilization. An examination of work profiles for initial and current employment determines trends in sex-based patterns over time. Finally, analysis of work-family temporal patterns will indicate whether the successful pursuit of a career by minority-status holders requires adaptations aimed at offsetting the "deviant" status. In the case of sex as the minority status, it is expected that the negatively valued aspect of female status consists primarily of the possible intrusion of marital and maternal roles into the occupational role, to the presumed detriment of the latter.[15] The general hypothesis here is that "careerist" women will

---

14. Rossi, "Barriers to the Career Choice."
15. Josephine J. Williams, "The Woman Physician's Dilemma," *Journal of Social Issues*

adjust their marital and maternal roles in order to minimize the difficulties of their minority sex status.

Method and Procedure

Data analyzed in this paper were collected as part of a larger study of postwar engineering and science graduates of a large midwestern university.[16] Seven populations were selected for study: (1) recipients of the Bachelor of Science degree in engineering of the classes of 1947 through 1964; (2) recipients of the Master of Science degree in engineering, 1950 through 1964; (3) recipients of the Doctor of Philosophy degree in engineering, 1950 through 1964; (4) all other living women engineering graduates; (5) recipients of the Bachelor of Science degree in science of the classes of 1947 through 1964; (6) recipients of the Master of Science degree in science, 1950 through 1964; and (7) recipients of the Doctor of Philosophy degree in science, 1950 through 1964.

For the bachelor's degree engineering and science samples, equal numbers were selected by major field by year of graduation. The fields within engineering which were included were aeronautical, agricultural, air transportation, industrial, chemical, civil, electrical, engineering mechanics, engineering science, mechanical, and metallurgical. Four science fields were included: biological science, chemistry, physics, and mathematical sciences. For the four advanced degree samples, equal numbers were selected by year of graduation only. A questionnaire containing items about precollege backgrounds, college, and postcollege experiences was mailed to all who were sampled. The percent returns ranged from a low of 64.2 percent for the doctorate scientists to a high of 78.5 percent for the doctorate engineers, with an overall percent return of 69.5, representing 3,589 respondents, 3,289 of whom are male and 300 of whom are female graduates.

With respect to the objective of examining selected work experiences

6, no. 3 (Winter 1950): 38–44; Fred Davis and Virginia Olesen, "Initiation into a Women's Profession: Identity Problems in the Status Transition of Co-ed to Student Nurse," *Sociometry* 26, no. 1 (March 1963): 89–101.

16. Carolyn C. Perrucci and William K. LeBold, "The Engineer and Scientist: Student, Professional, Citizen," *Engineering Extension Series Bulletin*, No. 125 (Lafayette, Ind.: Purdue University, 1967).

by sex of graduates, comparability of educational level among respondents is necessary. Owing to the small number of women having graduate degrees, career aspects are documented for bachelor's degree recipients only; 75 percent of the women ($N = 225$) and 45 percent of the men ($N = 1,480$) are classified thusly. Initial employment characteristics are contrasted for *noncareerist* and *careerist* women in order to ascertain possible clues which anticipate the eventual dropping out of the *noncareerist* women. Regarding current employment characteristics of women graduates, data obtained from the *young* and *old careerists* only are utilized for they alone have sufficient experience in the labor market to be contrasted with men graduates' current employment as well as women *careerists'* initial employment (from the point of view of determining long-range career patterns). Ninety-eight of the 225 women bachelor's degree recipients (43 percent) are *careerists*.[17]

For analysis of education–work–family temporal patterns of women engineers and scientists, women graduates are classified into four groups on the basis of length of time, in years, since highest degree and proportion of that time actually spent in full-time occupational employment. With median years since highest degree for all women as the cutting point, those with ten or fewer years from graduation to time of data collection (1965) are labeled "young" while women with eleven or more years since graduation are labeled "old." The *young* group of women is actually younger in age as well; median age is twenty-nine, with three-fourths being twenty-seven or older. Median age is forty for the *old* women, with three-fourths being thirty-six years of age or older. Each of these two groups is dichotomized into those who have worked less than a majority of the years since graduation (*noncareerists*) versus those who have worked a majority (or all) of the years since college graduation (*careerists*). Of the total group of female engineering and science graduates, 18.3 percent (55) are *young noncareerists;* 32.7 percent (98) are *young careerists;* 33 percent (99) are *old noncareerists;* and 16 percent (48) are *old careerists.*

17. The decision to compare current employment characteristics of the 98 *career* women only (rather than all currently working women) to work characteristics of men involves loss of less data than might at first be supposed. Of the total sample of 300 women graduates, only 28 percent are currently employed on a full-time basis. It should be pointed out that of the group of *career* women, two-thirds have worked continuously since receipt of the B.S. degree and the remaining one-third have worked full time at least a majority of the years from date of college graduation to the present study date (1965).

For the very recent graduates of both sexes, initial job after bachelor's degree and current job are one and the same.

Table 29.1. Work Place of Initial and Current (1965) Job for B.S. Degree Recipients by Sex and Career Pattern (in percent)

	Initial Job					Current Job		
	Non-careerist Women (1a)	Careerist Women (2a)	Total Women (3a)	Men (4a)	Total	Careerist Women* (1b)	Men (2b)	Total
Agriculture, transportation, communication, engineering services, construction, mining	08	07	07	15	14	03	14	13
Durable manufactured product industry	20	22	21	47	43	24	46	45
Nondurable manufactured product industry	21	14	18	15	15	13	14	14
Miscellaneous business, consulting, research lab	16	12	14	04	06	11	05	06
Educational institution	12	19	15	02	04	28	04	05
Government	13	16	14	15	15	13	14	14
Other	10	10	10	02	03	08	03	03
N	93	83	176	1,245	1,421	71	1,356	1,427

* Includes *young careerists* and *old careerists* only.
Column Comparisons
(1a)–(2a) *NS*
(2a)–(4a) $\chi^2 = 118.17\ df = 8\ p \le .01$
(3a)–(4a) $\chi^2 = 153.16\ df = 6\ p < .001$

(2a)–(1b) *NS*
(4a)–(2b) $\chi^2 = 13.89\ df = 6\ p \le .05$
(1b)–(2b) $\chi^2 = 38.96\ df = 6\ p \le .001$

Results

Male and Female Work Profiles

Almost all the graduates who do not immediately pursue advanced degree studies embark on their initial job directly after college graduation. Selected aspects of the initial employment of graduates, including place of employment, level of technical and supervisory responsibility, principal function and average monthly salary are considered and compared with identical aspects of their current (1965) employment for *noncareer* and *career* women and men.

Beginning with type of work place, there are pronounced differences by sex of employee observable from data in table 29.1. Although industry and business (first four categories) employ about three-quarters of all engineering and science graduates, they account for a larger proportion of men than women as sites for initial and current employment. Men, for example, are twice as likely as women to work in durable manufactured product industry. Regarding nonindustrial employers, educational institutions employ a larger percent of women than men at both times. Moreover, a comparison of the distribution of *career* women graduates across the various work places for initial and current jobs indicates a larger percent of *careerists* now working in educational institutions compared with the percent of all women graduates working initially therein (28 percent vs. 19 percent), although this shift is not statistically significant.

Principal function at work varies significantly according to career pattern of women as well as sex of graduates. It can be seen from data in table 29.2 that *noncareerists* are more likely than *careerists* to work

Table 29.2. Principal Function for Initial and Current (1965) Job for B.S. Degree Recipients by Sex and Career Pattern (in percent)

	Initial Job					Current Job		
	Non-careerist Women (1a)	Career-ist Women (2a)	Total Women (3a)	Men (4a)	Total	Careerist Women* (1b)	Men (2b)	Total
1. Preprofessional	29	21	25	18	19	10	02	02
2. Research	19	16	18	07	08	13	07	07
3. Development	07	14	10	18	17	13	16	16
4. Design	04	06	05	14	13	08	12	12
5. Operations and production	04	06	05	14	12	08	15	15
6. Testing, construction, sales and service	16	05	11	17	16	03	19	18
7. Teaching	04	17	10	02	03	22	02	03
8. Management and consulting	02	01	02	04	04	11	20	19
9. Others	15	14	14	06	07	12	07	07
N	93	86	179	1,266	1,445	74	1,352	1,426

* Includes *young careerists* and *old careerists* only.
Column Comparisons
(1a)–(2a) $\chi^2 = 14.88$ $df = 6$ $p \leq .05$ categories   (3a)–(4a) $\chi^2 = 161.55$ $p \leq .001$ $df = 8$
    4 & 5 collapsed; categories 7 & 8 collapsed   (2a)–(1b) *NS*
(2a)–(4a) $\chi^2 = 52.32$ $df = 6$ $p < .01$ categories   (4a)–(2b) $\chi^2 = 314.25$ $df = 8$ $p < .01$
    4 & 5 collapsed; categories 7 & 8 collapsed   (1b)–(2b) $\chi^2 = 117.16$ $df = 8$ $p \leq .001$

initially in a preprofessional capacity; in development; testing, construction, and sales; and are less likely to teach. In comparison with men, *career* women are more likely to perform initially in a research or teaching capacity and are less likely to be in testing, construction, sales and service. Comparison of current and initial functions of employees indicates that *career* women are less likely to be involved now than previously in work of a preprofessional nature and are more likely to be in teaching and management. Men, also, are less likely to work currently than previously in a preprofessional capacity, and more likely to function in an administrative capacity, but the shifts in these functions over time are more pronounced for men than for women employees.

Table 29.3. Supervisory Responsibility for Initial and Current (1965) Job for B.S. Degree Recipients by Sex and Career Pattern (in percent)

	Initial Job					Current Job		
	Non-careerist Women (1a)	Career-ist Women (2a)	Total Women (3a)	Men (4a)	Total	Careerist Women* (1b)	Men (2b)	Total
1. No supervisory responsibility	65	76	70	70	70	51	28	29
2. Supervision of nontechnical personnel	19	13	16	14	14	12	13	13
3. Supervision of technical personnel only (except professional)	02	05	03	07	06	08	08	08
4. Supervision of technical and nontechnical personnel (except professional)	06	03	05	06	06	06	14	14
5. Supervision of professionals	04	01	03	01	02	12	17	17
6. Supervision of management	04	02	03	02	02	11	20	19
N	94	87	181	1,268	1,449	74	1,375	1,449

* Includes *young careerists* and *old careerists* only.
Column Comparisons
(1a)–(2a) NS categories 3–6 collapsed   (2a)–(1b) $\chi^2 = 14.59\ df = 4\ p < .01$ categories 3–6 collapsed
(2a)–(4a) NS   (4a)–(2b) $\chi^2 = 654.22\ df = 5\ p < .01$
(3a)–(4a) NS categories 5 & 6 collapsed   (1b)–(2b) $\chi^2 = 255.26\ df = 3\ p < .001$ categories 2–4 collapsed

Involvement in supervisory positions is an especially important aspect of women's careers in the high-prestige professions since such positions are likely to give women authority over male colleagues. Data in table 29.3 show that only 30 percent of all graduates say that they have any supervisory responsibility in their initial job after college. The minority who supervise, moreover, do so for nonprofessional personnel, usually nontechnical employees. Over the years, however, there appears

Table 29.4. Technical Responsibility for Initial and Current (1965) Job for B.S. Degree Recipients by Sex and Career Pattern (in percent)

	Initial Job				Current Job		
	Non-careerist Women (1a)	Career-ist Women (2a)	Total Women (3a)	Men (4a)	Careerist Women* (1b)	Men (2b)	Total
1. Simple operations; no knowledge of principles	08	07	07	11	00	02	01
2. Sequence of standardized operations; limited knowledge of principles	14	09	12	14	07	02	02
3. Applies basic principles; general knowledge of them	18	22	20	24	07	03	03
4. Selects alternatives using prescribed methods; working knowledge of principles	29	30	30	25	22	08	09
5. Devises alternate methods of standardized analysis; good knowledge of methods	11	13	12	12	07	15	15
6. Complex tasks; thorough knowledge of methods	18	18	18	12	43	50	50
7. Plans and conducts pioneering work	01	01	01	02	14	19	19
8. Nationally recognized scholar in specialized field	01	00	01	†	00	01	01
N	93	86	179	1,428	72	1,330	1,402

* Includes *young careerists* and *old careerists* only.

† Less than .05 percent.

Column Comparisons
(1a)–(2a) *NS* categories 6–8 collapsed   (2a)–(1b) $\chi^2 = 27.00$ *df = 4 p < .01* categories 6–8 collapsed
(2a)–(4a) *NS*   (4a)–(2b) $\chi^2 = 1078.59$ *df = 6 p < .01* categories 7 & 8 collapsed
(3a)–(4a) *NS*   (1b)–(2b) $\chi^2 = 7.48$ *df = 3 p < .10* categories 1–3; 4 & 5 collapsed

to be a significant difference in the career line of *career* women and men. In their current work positions, 72 percent of men compared with only 49 percent of women assume some supervisory duties. This sex differential in supervisory responsibility concerns primarily the supervi-

Table 29.5. Median Monthly Salary for Initial and Current (1965) Job by Sex, Career Pattern, Type of Employment, and Field

	Noncareerist Women	Careerist Women	Total Women	Men
Initial Job				
All B.S. graduates	$284*	$402*	$341*	$432†
(N)	(81)	(83)	(164)	(1,230)
Graduates (excluding those *not in* industry and government, and those *in* preprofessional, teaching, unspecified functions)				
All fields	$270†	$435†	$407†	$436†
(N)	(25)	(26)	(51)	(751)
Engineering only	$412†	$358†	$371†	$438†
(N)	(11)	(11)	(22)	(632)
Science only	$350†	$491†	$438†	$431†
(N)	(14)	(15)	(29)	(119)
Current Job				
All B.S. graduates			$622‡§	$902†
(N)			(73)	(1,333)
Graduates (excluding those *not in* industry and government, and those *in* preprofessional, teaching, and unspecified functions)				
All fields			$720§	$812‖
(N)			(20)	(600)
Engineering only			$700§	$817‖
(N)			(10)	(504)
Science only			$724§	$775‖
(N)			(10)	(96)

* Median year of college graduation is 1954.
† Median year of college graduation is 1956.
‡ Includes *young* and *old careerists* only.
§ Median year of college graduation is 1958.
‖ Median year of college graduation is 1960.

sion of relatively higher levels of personnel in the work place, that is, professionals and management.

Engineers and scientists also engage in work which varies considerably in terms of the level of technical expertise required. Technical responsibility for initial and current job, categorized by the nature of work that is done and the knowledge required for the job, is shown for men and women graduates in table 29.4. The distributions of graduates according to technical responsibility in initial jobs are similar; that is, tasks tend to be relatively simple and standardized (first five categories) for at least 80 percent of both sexes regardless of career pattern. Career advancement of women tends to fall short of that experienced by men, however, when initial and current positions are compared; specifically, 57 percent of the women and 70 of the men perform complex and pioneering tasks in their current work.

A final characteristic of graduates' work to be considered is remuneration (see table 29.5). Despite comparable levels of technical and supervisory responsibility in initial jobs after college,[18] women engineers and scientists earn lower salaries than men ($341 vs. $432 respectively).[19] It is probable that two factors mentioned earlier account at least in part for this initial income differential by sex of employee; that is, variation in place of employment and principal function. It is known, for example, that salaries in educational institutions tend to be lower than those in industry; and women are more likely than men to work in the former. A third factor which may be contributing to lower salaries for women is the smaller proportion of women (32 percent) than men (75 percent) who initially work in an engineering rather than a science field. It is shown elsewhere that at each college-degree level, the median salaries of engineers exceed those of scientists in the study sample.[20]

---

18. Rossi presents previously unpublished data from a postcensal survey of professional and technical occupations which are being analyzed by Seymour Warkov, National Opinion Research Center, University of Chicago. At each level of education, median salary of women is considerably lower than that for men employed in engineering, physics, biology, and mathematics-statistics. Differences between men and women besides educational level which are suggested to explain income differentials are type of employer, work activity, and length of work week, although salary data are not presented by sex while controlling for these additional variables. See Rossi, "Barriers to the Career Choice," p. 67.

19. It should be noted that ability, as indexed by college grades, does not differ for women and men in either science or engineering (data not shown).

20. Carolyn C. Perrucci, "Engineers and Scientists: A Comparative Analysis of Professional Values and Behavior" (research report to the U.S. Department of Labor,

In order to make better male–female comparisons, the base of cells is confined to include only those graduates who are comparable in terms of work place and principal function and field, as is shown in table 29.5. First is the exclusion from analysis of the data from graduates whose initial place of employment is *other than* industry and government and whose initial function involves teaching and any unspecified activity. With these groups excluded, a discrepancy in salary between the sexes remains but it is diminished in magnitude ($407 for women versus $436 for men) and pertains only to *noncareer* women versus men. A second effort to improve sex comparisons is made by controlling for field of initial employment. The data then show that it is among engineers only that women earn a lower salary for initial job than men. Although the number of cases becomes quite small, a comparison of initial salary according to career pattern within field shows that among scientists, *noncareerists* only earn less than men. Among engineers, however, both *noncareerists* and *careerists* earn less, on the average, than men, with *careerists* earning the least of all three engineering groups.

The salary differential by sex is markedly larger for current job than for initial job after college graduation, as shown in the lower half of table 29.5. It is no doubt related to different trends in employment on the part of women and men, particularly the increased proportion of *career* women who work in educational institutions (most of whom teach), contrasted with the increased proportion of men who move into management. In addition, field of current employment is more likely to be engineering for men than for women graduates (70 percent versus 30 percent respectively). When the base of cells is confined to provide comparability in terms of work place, function and field, it is found that current, as well as initial, salary differential by sex of employee is greater among engineers than among scientists. On the average, men's annual salaries exceed those of *career* women by $1,400 in engineering and by $600 in science.[21]

Grant No. 91-16-66-28, Purdue University, 1967); Perrucci and LeBold, "The Engineer and Scientist."

21. There are two variables mentioned in the literature as possible causes of such large current salary differences between men and women which are not examined above but for which some limited data are available. One factor is the alleged immobility of female professionals, especially married ones. The latter are often viewed as more exploitable since their ability to seek better positions is presumably limited by husbands' career needs. See Jerome Hull, "Opportunities for Advancement of Women in Professional Engineering Employment" in *Proceedings of the National Conference on Women in Engineering* (Los

Differential utilization of women and men in science-based fields and the correlated income differential by sex may negatively influence retention of women employees; data concerning work values of our sample of graduates, discussed in detail elsewhere support this interpretation.[22] Briefly, men and women are compared for a total of thirty-four work values dealing with the nature of work, career advancement, colleague relationships, and professional activities. Sex differences are found for only 6 of the 34 values. It is concluded that, in general, values are relatively similar for working women and men of comparable education, yet women are less likely to hold positions which enable them to realize their goals.

Temporal Patterns in Marriage and Childbearing

The second objective of this paper is to examine family and career sequences among women scientists and engineers in order to determine possible adaptations to mitigate the effects of "deviant" sex status in the professional context.[23] Marital status is generally assumed to be a key

---

Angeles: University of Southern California, 1963), pp. 27–31. A comparison of number of employers during the career for both men and women in this study provides no support for the immobility-exploitation hypothesis. Since receiving the bachelor's degree, 80 percent of the women and 86 percent of the men report having three or fewer employers. This may suggest that career women are no less mobile than men in science and engineering. It is not known, however, what motivated members of either sex to change employers.

The second factor to be considered is length of workweek, especially overtime work, which could result directly in greater earnings. Census data for 1960 show that men work overtime to a much greater extent than women. Women engineering and science graduates in this study, however, are no less likely than their colleagues to "spend time at home on work-related matters." Work at home is generally not extensive for these graduates, for 90 percent of the women and 83 percent of the men report that they work six or fewer hours per week at home. Moreover, marital status of men and women makes no significant difference in their work hours. See Rossi, "Barriers to the Career Choice," p. 69.

22. Carolyn C. Perrucci, "The Female Engineer and Scientist: Factors Associated with the Pursuit of a Professional Career" (research report to the U.S. Department of Labor, Grant No. 91-16-67-43, Purdue University, 1968).

23. It is known that, apart from the selective process leading to marriage, marriage and childbearing tend to have conservative effects on women's participation in the labor force. Rossi suggests that another process may operate such that advances in formal education and experience in the work place affect women scientists' self-concept and expectations regarding the place of marriage and career in their lives. See Rossi, "Barriers to the Career Choice." Although the measure of careerism used in the current paper is behavioral, it is assumed to reflect a careerist orientation and is used as an independent

---

variable in the work lives of women but not especially so for men.[24] Indeed, work and marriage are considered to have once been mutually exclusive alternatives for women professionals.[25] An examination of census data for 1960 indicates that marriage is still more problematic[26] for employed women than for men; four out of five men are married and living with their wives, but an average of only two out of five women in engineering and science are married and living with their husbands.

Of our sample of women scientists and engineers, 82 percent are currently married or have been married at some time in their lives.[27] Marital status varies with career pattern of women in that *careerists,* in general, are less likely to ever marry than are *noncareerists.* This pattern persists, moreover, when level of education is controlled (B.S. degree vs. advanced degree recipients, data not shown).[28] More specifically, among the *old* group of women, one-quarter of the *careerists* are single; whereas, none of the *noncareerists* is single. Among the *young* women, 32

---

variable in tables 29.6 through 29.9. It is believed that some justification of this procedure lies in the fact that work experience precedes in time sequence both marriage and childbearing for a majority of the engineers and scientists in this study.

24. For focus on marital-career patterns among male engineers see Carolyn C. Perrucci, "Social Origins, Mobility Patterns and Fertility," *American Sociological Review* 32, no. 4 (August 1967): 615–25; Vincent J. Salvo, "Familial and Occupational Roles in a Technical Society," in *The Engineers and the Social System,* ed. Robert Perrucci and Joel Gerstl (New York: Wiley, 1969), pp. 311–34.

25. Viola Klein, *Britain's Married Women Workers* (London: Routledge & Kegan Paul, 1965).

26. Marriage may be less likely for educated career women of today because they find fewer men desirable to them as well as because fewer men may find them, as intelligent career women, desirable as a wife.

27. Of the married women engineers and scientists, 93 percent have husbands with bachelor's degrees or higher education; specifically, 48 percent have husbands with the B.S., 21 percent with the M.S., and 24 percent have husbands with the Ph.D. degree. Census data indicate that a much greater proportion of all married women college graduates have husbands with only some college or less education. Among older women this is as high as 60 percent. Even among married women college graduates under age thirty-five, a full one-third are married to men with less education than themselves. Why the women in our sample are different then becomes an interesting, albeit unanswerable question. One speculation is that as a consequence of attending a largely male institution, indeed, one which emphasizes science and engineering, they had a greater opportunity to meet that minority of men who would be attracted to a woman scientist and/or to whom women scientists would be attracted.

28. Postcensal survey data of engineers and scientists indicate that among women the proportion married declines with each degree beyond the bachelor's degree, but among men educational attainment bears no relationship to marital status. See Rossi, "Barriers to the Career Choice," p. 73.

---

percent of the *careerists* compared with 18 percent of the *noncareerists* are unmarried. The greater proportion of single women among the *young* than *old* groups, irrespective of career pattern, partially reflects differences in age; it will be remembered that median age is twenty-nine for the former and forty years for the latter group.

Table 29.6. Time Interval Between College Graduation (B.S.) and Marriage by Career Pattern (in percent)

	Young Non-careerists (1)	Young Careerists (2)	Old Non-careerists (3)	Old Careerists (4)	Total Women (5)
Marriage preceded graduation	23	16	11	13	15
Marriage and graduation same year	33	23	25	19	25
Marriage followed graduation:	44	61	63	68	60
By one year	17	16	28	19	21
Two–three	20	23	26	13	23
Four–five	07	16	05	16	08
Six or more	00	06	04	20	08
N	30	51	79	31	191

Column Comparisons
Marriage preceding and same year as graduation categories collapsed for *chi*-square analysis.
(1)–(2) $p \leq .05$ $x^2 = 4.18$ $df = 1$ (1)–(3) $p \leq .10$ $x^2 = 3.55$ $df = 1$
(3)–(4) *NS*
(2)–(4) *NS*
Marriage preceding, same year as or following graduation *3* years or less collapsed for *chi*-square analysis.
(1)–(2) *NS*   (2)–(4) *NS*
(3)–(4) $p \leq .01$ $x^2 = 9.67$ $df = 1$ (1)–(3) *NS*

For the married women only, timing of marriage in relation to college graduation and initial employment is examined in tables 29.6 and 29.7, respectively. It can be seen from data in table 29.6 that three-fifths of all women engineers and scientists marry after or very near the close of their college work rather than prior to completion of this basic professional training. The college graduation-marriage time interval varies directly by career duration for women; for instance, 36 percent of the *old careerists* compared with 9 percent of the *old noncareerists* marry as late as four or more years after leaving college. There also appears to be a secular trend of decreasing age at marriage, especially when *young* and *old noncareerists* are compared; that is, 56 percent of the *young noncareerists* marry prior to or during year of graduation, whereas, only 36 percent of the *old noncareerists* marry this soon. Despite such a trend, among the most recent graduates (i.e., *young* groups) *careerists* are more likely than *noncareerists* to complete their basic college studies before marrying.

In examining timing of marriage in relation to initial employment, one can see that 55 percent of all the married women embark upon a career prior to marriage (table 29.7). Marked variation in length of time interval between first job and marriage (if not the basic work–marriage sequence itself) according to career pattern occurs for the *old* women especially. Thirty-five percent of the *old careerists* work four or more years prior to marriage, compared with 9 percent of the *old noncareerists* who do so. Again, there is a time trend evident in that the *young* groups of women engineers and scientists (*careerists* and *noncareerists*) are less likely than *old* groups to become employed prior to marriage.

A common aspect of marriage which may inhibit women's work in science-based fields is childbearing and rearing. *Career* women in our sample are more likely than *noncareerists* to be childless. Among the *old*

Table 29.7. Time Interval Between Initial Job After College Graduation (B.S.) and Marriage by Career Pattern (in percent)

	Young Non-careerists (1)	Young Careerists (2)	Old Non-careerists (3)	Old Careerists (4)	Total Women (5)
Marriage preceded initial job	33	22	16	19	21
Marriage and job same year	33	23	23	16	24
Marriage followed job	34	55	61	64	55
By one year	10	14	27	19	19
Two–three	21	21	25	10	21
Four–five	3	16	5	16	9
Six or more	0	4	4	19	6
N	30	51	79	31	191

Column Comparisons
Marriage preceding and same year as job categories collapsed.
(1)–(2) $p \leq .10$ $\chi^2 = 3.53$ $df = 1$ (1)–(3) $p \leq .001$ $\chi^2 = 34.79$ $df = 1$
(3)–(4) *NS*
(2)–(4) $p \leq .02$ $\chi^2 = 7.56$ $df = 1$
Marriage preceding, same year as, or following job by three or fewer years collapsed.
Column Comparisons
(1)–(2) $p \leq .10$ $\chi^2 = 2.99$ $df = 1$ (1)–(3) *NS*
(3)–(4) $p \leq .01$ $\chi^2 = 9.67$ $df = 1$
(2)–(4) *NS*

Table 29.8. Time Interval Between Marriage and Birth of First Child by Career Pattern (in percent)

	Young Non-careerists (1)	Young Careerists (2)	Old Non-careerists (3)	Old Careerists (4)	Total Women (5)
Marriage and first child same year	05	06	01	03	03
First child followed marriage	95	94	99	97	97
By one year	38	32	33	43	35
Two years	24	29	23	10	23
Three years	26	15	17	07	17
Four or more years	07	18	26	37	22
N	42	34	99	30	205

Column Comparisons
Child born same year as and following marriage by three or fewer years categories collapsed for *chi*-square analysis.
(1)–(2) *NS*　　　　　　　　　　(2)–(4) $p \leq .10$ $\chi^2 = 2.89$ $df = 1$
(3)–(4) *NS*　　　　　　　　　　(1)–(3) $p \leq .02$ $\chi^2 = 7.34$ $df = 1$

female engineers and scientists, for example, 17 percent of the *careerists* are childless, whereas none of the *noncareerists* is without children. In addition, another 14 percent of the *old careerists* have only one child while 2 percent of the *old noncareerists* have so small a family. A majority of the *young careerists* (51 percent) has no children; but only 7 percent of the *young noncareerists* are childless at this stage in their lives.[29]

For respondents who are mothers, data regarding time interval between marriage and initial childbirth are presented in table 29.8. Over half of these women become parents prior to the completion of three years of married life. The data suggest that a somewhat greater length of time elapses between onset of marriage and initiation of a family among *career* women; that is, within each age grouping of women, a larger percent of *careerists* than *noncareerists* bear their first child four or more years subsequent to marriage. The *young* appear less

29. Total marginals regarding number of children for married women engineers and scientists($N = 246$) are as follows: 18 percent, childless; 15 percent, one child; 26 percent, two children; 29 percent, three children; and 13 percent, four or more children. When the base for percentages is all 300 women in the sample, not married women only, percents regarding number of children are as follows: 18 percent single, no children; 14 percent married, no children; 12 percent married, one child; 21 percent married, two children; 24 percent married, three children; and 11 percent married, four or more children.

likely than the *old* scientists and engineers to remain childless for so long a time.

One factor which may influence the extent to which childbearing inhibits women professionals' work outside the home is the stage in their career at which this event occurs. For married women who are mothers, data concerning the timing of the firstborn child in relation to initial employment are presented in table 29.9. It is obvious that families are seldom begun prior to initial employment of graduates. The data suggest patterns in child spacing after college for *career* vs. *noncareer* women; the former tend to begin their families at a later point in the career. For example, almost twice the percent of *old careerists* as *old noncareerists* work six or more years prior to bearing their first child (44 percent and 22 percent respectively). Also, it can be seen that *young careerists* tend to have less work experience before starting their families than do *old careerists*.

Summary and Implications

The integration of a visible minority group into the occupational structure, specifically the sexual integration of science and engineering is investigated in the current study by comparing selected social characteristics of *career* with *noncareer* women and men trained in these fields.

Deviation of science, and especially engineering, from the ideal-typical model of rational professions (with regard to integration of minorities) is indicated in the finding of significant "selective patterning" of careers by sex of engineer and scientist, which is evident to some extent when graduates first enter the labor market and which becomes more pronounced during the course of their careers. Specifically, male and female graduates' initial employment positions are relatively similar in the levels of technical and supervisory responsibility which they entail, but dissimilar in terms of remuneration. The initial salary differential (which favors male employees, in engineering at least) is largely accounted for by the greater proportion of women than men who work in nonindustrial settings, especially educational institutions; who perform in a preprofessional, research, or teaching capacity; and who work in science rather than engineering fields. Differential sex

Table 29.9. Time Interval Between Initial Job After College Graduation (B.S.) and Birth of First Child by Career Pattern (in percent)

	Young Non-careerists (1)	Young Careerists (2)	Old Non-careerists (3)	Old Careerists (4)	Total Women (5)
First child preceded initial job	11	12	06	04	08
Child and job same year	00	08	00	08	02
First child followed job	89	80	94	88	90
By one year	15	04	10	12	10
Two	30	12	11	08	14
Three	15	16	19	12	17
Four	11	12	20	04	15
Five	11	16	12	08	12
Six or more	07	20	22	44	22
N	27	25	79	25	156

Column Comparisons
Child preceded and same year as job categories collapsed.
(1)–(2) *NS*   (1)–(3) *NS*
(3)–(4) *NS*
(2)–(4) *NS*
Child preceded, same year as, or followed job by five years or less categories collapsed.
(1)–(2) *NS*   (1)–(3) *NS*
(3)–(4) *NS*
(2)–(4) $p \leq .05$ $\chi^2 = 4.25$ $df = 1$

concentration by current field reflects sex differences in college major field which are more pronounced in engineering than in science.[30] Sex segregation of work function pertains primarily to *noncareerist* women vs. men with respect to preprofessional-level work. That *careerists* are more likely than men to be teaching (in educational institutions) is consistent with the hypothesis that work functions often reflect an extension of the sex role for women.[31] Most importantly, perhaps, as an indication of future trends, is the relatively large proportion of women compared to men in research. Women's opportunities may increase with the possibility of increased government research contracts[32] and, presuma-

30. Rossi, "Barriers to the Career Choice"; Epstein, "Woman's Place."
31. Epstein, "Woman's Place."
32. Robert F. Mello, "Government Interest in the Employment of Women," in *Women and the Scientific Professions,* ed. Jacqueline A. Mattfeld and Carol Van Aken (Cambridge, Mass.: MIT Press, 1965), pp. 206–13.

bly, nondiscriminatory hiring and promotion practices in government and industry.[33] It should be recognized, of course, that the latter puts all minorities, not only women, into competition for the new positions.

A comparison of current job of *career* women with that of men indicates some advancement over the years for all, but an even greater disparity in career paths between the sexes for current than initial job. This disparity is consistent with the hypothesis of intraprofessional stratification[34] in that men are more likely than women to have higher levels of responsibility and to earn a higher salary.[35] Even when amount of work experience, place of employment and principal job function are comparable, *career* women currently earn less than men; this salary differential by sex is twice as great among engineers as among scientists.

The significance of increasing disparity in career paths and career success between the sexes for women's participation in engineering and science cannot be ascertained easily with the data at hand. It is sometimes posited in the literature, for instance, that even for women in the high-prestige masculine fields, other factors such as lack of financial "need" characterize women compared to men and serve to offset possible negative influences of differential success. That is to say that single women presumably have no need for as high an income as men who, by and large, have family responsibilities, so that motivation for comfortable living is more readily satisfied at a lower salary for unmarried women scientists than their married men colleagues. It is further suggested that a high proportion of the married women who work in science-based fields have college-educated, employed husbands, so they do not need the income and responsibility that goes with it that men scientists do. For our sample of graduates, however, work values are relatively similar for working women and men of comparable education, yet women are less likely to hold positions which enable them to realize their goals. It is suggested, therefore, that discrepancies between what women employees themselves value and their perceptions of their actual work situation may indicate potential problems in their employment.

---

33. Price, "Changes in Occupational Distribution of the Negro Population."

34. Bock, "The Female Clergy"; Epstein, "Woman's Place."

35. In a study of recent male and female doctorate recipients, Simon and colleagues also find salary discrepancies by sex, especially at the associate professor level. There is a steady decrease in size of salary discrepancy, however, from 1959 to 1963. See Rita J. Simon, Shirley M. Clark, and Kathleen Galway, "The Woman Ph.D.: A Recent Profile," *Social Problems* 15, no. 2 (Fall 1967): 221–36.

The second major finding of this paper concerns possible adaptations to mitigate the effects of "deviant" sex status in the professional context; specifically, for two age groups of women pursuit of a fulltime career in science and engineering is related to a temporal ordering of the events of college graduation, employment, marriage, and childbearing. *Career* women are more likely than *noncareerists* to be unmarried. Among the married women, *careerists* are more likely than *noncareerists* to complete college work and embark upon a career prior to marriage. *Careerists* are more likely than *noncareer* women to be childless. If they have a family, *careerists* are more likely than *noncareerists* to have only one child and to bear the child at a later stage in their work careers. It is also found that *young careerists,* compared to *old careerists,* are less involved in marriage and childbearing. This may merely reflect the fact that the former are in an earlier stage of the family life cycle. On the other hand, *young careerists* in engineering and science may be tending toward complete avoidance of marital and especially maternal roles rather than making a temporal adaptation to career demands (i.e., postponing marriage and childbearing). In any event, it is known that *young careerists* are no less likely than *old careerists* to pursue advanced degree work; some indication of commitment to their field. Over half of the *young* married *careerists* wait until after the completion of basic college training (B.S. degree) to marry.[36] Also important is the fact that most *careerists* work prior to marriage, which is correlated with work after marriage.[37] and work several years prior to starting families. Given these indicators of the greater importance of the career role over marriage and the maternal roles during early adulthood, it is quite possible, but not yet undisputable, that the marital and maternal status of *career* women are consequences of values they hold and the most acceptable balance they can strike between work and family under current circumstances.

---

36. Given a continuation of the recent secular trend of rising age at first marriage for women, apart from career planning, a follow-up of the *young* groups of women might reveal that a high percent do marry and bear children, only at a somewhat later age. See Robert Parke and Paul C. Glick, "Prospective Changes in Marriage and the Family," *Journal of Marriage and the Family* 29, no. 2 (May 1967): 249–56.

37. Mildred Weil, "An Analysis of Factors Influencing Married Women's Actual or Planned Work Participation," *American Sociological Review* 26, no. 1 (February 1961): 91–96.

30

"IN TROUBLE"

JANE HARRIMAN

There was a cold heaviness reeling inside me. If it was an illness, it would be fatal because it was stronger and more powerful than I could ever be. When sleep was less urgent, I would face it. Two weeks later, it was worse. I could no longer eat. The floor was bubbling, sometimes buckling dangerously. And I was scared, terribly scared, until one morning I dreamed a formless sort of warmth, a love without fear or sadness. When I awoke, I was reassured enough to go to a doctor. On the way to his office I prepared a list of symptoms. However, when I began to speak to him and stared at the desk-top photograph of his pig-tailed daughters, I diagnosed what I was only simultaneously ready to face: "I'm pregnant."

He questioned and considered: "Nonsense. Highly unlikely." He prodded and peered: "Possible." He tested: "Yes, about nine weeks. Where's the father? No chance of marriage? What are you going to do?"

"Have a baby. Become a mother, I suppose."

"You should think about abortion, adoption. There are alternatives."

But actually, there were no alternatives for me. After years of thinking that I believed in abortion, I was mortally afraid when it was more than a word to me. I felt that what was inside me was not an embryo or a fetus but the essence of life itself. The spark of human existence was demanding that my body clothe it in tissue that it might be born. If I fought that spark, or allowed anyone to put it out, I would be destroyed in a most complete and terrifying way.

So I was going to become an unwed mother. But surely not in the traditional sense of the young, helpless girl cast away in the blizzard, "in trouble." I was twenty-seven years old, and had worked for a metropolitan newspaper for six years. Although my father was dead and there was no money in the immediate family, I was earning $10,000 a year and was dependent on no one. Of course, it would be embarrassing, and it would perhaps be emotionally difficult, but I was too well schooled in the Christian ethic—all worthwhile things are difficult, you must stand up to life's challenges—to let that faze me.

Gradually, I became more and more excited about the idea of having a baby. As I thought about it I realized it was the one thing I'd always wanted. My reservations had been about marriage. And unless I came to view marriage with less fear, my child would have only one parent. This was a handicap, but a fairly common one. I had always had lots of men in my life, and there was no reason to expect this to change. The child would have male role models.

The child would be illegitimate (the father was neither available, nor on the evidence, likely to be), but what did that mean? It meant the parents had done something illegal, not the child. I would say to it: "Most women are married when they have a baby, most, but not all. I was not married when I had you. And I had to decide whether to give you away to a married couple or to keep you myself. Some people thought it would be better for you if I gave you away so you could have a mother *and* a father. But I just loved you too much. I wanted you to live with me, your real mother, and I hoped we would have a good life together until you grew up."

At the end of my fourth month, the only people who knew I was pregnant were the baby's father, my physician, my obstetrician, my sister, and a psychiatrist I had consulted to make sure I was doing the right thing. Soon I would look pregnant, and so when opportunities arose, I would begin to tell people. I was confident and optimistic. And naive. I had no idea of how vulnerable I had made myself by following the course I had to.

A great many people assumed that I hoped they would refer me to an abortionist. "But I'm four months' pregnant!" "OK. Good-bye." An hour later the telephone would ring and yet another name and modus operandi would be presented: a doctor in San Juan; a chiropractor in New Jersey; a med school dropout who made house calls in Cambridge.

I began to think of going away to a place where I could gestate in peace, a place where there would be no negative vibrations toward the baby, where I would be free to work things out inside myself without embarrassing or endangering anyone. If I could get a leave of absence from my job, I would go to England on my vacation and stay on for a while. When I came back with a giant belly or a baby, no one could nag me about abortion.

I asked one of the executives if I could have a leave of absence, saying

I wanted to do some freelance work from England and I would need the money. I wanted very much to come back to work in four or five months. He thought this was possible, although they'd regret losing me for that long a time. Yes, of course. What was I planning to do?

"Have a baby, actually."

This, he said, changed the picture somewhat. He would have to talk it over with one of the other executives.

That night he telephoned me at home. I was not going to get married? Would I consider having an abortion?—a friend of theirs had gone to Sweden. Would I consider giving the baby up for adoption? No? In that case, he was sorry but I was fired. I could have my vacation pay, and I could probably collect unemployment insurance. I offered to announce a phony marriage to a Vietnam serviceman. No. I was still fired.

Unfortunately, there was no newspaper guild to which I could appeal. White-collar employees were covered by an employees' association whose principal function was to sponsor annual picnics and bowling leagues. The contract it had agreed to allowed employees to be fired without cause and specified that severance pay did not have to be given in the case of "gross personal misconduct" (that was me). Apparently, I had been too quick to laugh when people had said, "You won't be able to support a baby without a husband."

When I hired a lawyer, the newspaper agreed to let me resign and to give me about as much severance pay as I would have received from several months of unemployment compensation. It also arranged a partial compensation for the medical expenses I found would not be covered by my health insurance plan. (I'd have been protected if injured robbing a bank, or driving while drunk, but unwed mothers, manifestly, fall into a forbidden category.)

The State Division of Employment Security suggested that I try temporary office work until my seventh month, when, as I recall, I could no longer work legally. With my two-fingered typing, I was unlikely to realize a financial windfall through that, so I set about relearning to type. But it was ridiculous. I could not possibly earn enough money to stay in my apartment, or even pay for another one in the Boston area. Life in England was less costly. I would certainly earn enough money there to support myself. My severance pay would cover the time between delivery and reemployment.

Before I risked the cost of a round-trip ticket to England, however, I thought I should protect myself against unforeseen disaster. My only male relative was an uncle to whom I had felt very close before he had retired to live in the Caribbean. When he flew into town for a week, I told him about my pregnancy and asked if he would, in the case of an emergency, be willing to lend me some money. He was amazingly supportive. He was proud of the way I was handling a difficult situation. Of course he'd help. He was a man of considerable means. He wanted to write me a check then and there.

"No, thank you," I said, "I'm taking on a responsibility, and I think I should prove myself capable of it."

The next day he had changed his mind. He'd talked it over with his wife and the best course for me was to have a Caesarean abortion. Their old friend, a Boston gynecologist, had agreed, patient unseen, to perform it.

I refused.

"Well, I think you're making a mistake, but that doesn't change anything. I'll still help you in any way you want," he said.

The day I was to leave the country, he telephoned long distance. I hadn't been to see his friend, the gynecologist.

"You won't take the mature and reasonable course. I am afraid I have nothing more to say to you, and you can forget about asking me for help, ever."

"Tell her you won't support the baby, either," his wife urged in the background.

I hung up, and my mind snapped off. I was tired down to my bone marrow. The new tenants and their furniture would fill my empty apartment at any minute. I was going thousands of miles away to a strange land, where I knew two people. But I was leaving nothing, as it had turned out. I pressed my hands into the dusty linoleum of the floor until I was very quiet, and then I called the baby's father.

"You're being very weak, chickening out," he said. "I think going is the best thing for you. I'll write to you; I've already arranged to send you money."

I believed him. For the first time in two years, I trusted him completely. He was good and strong and he'd never abandon me. I felt quite happy as I dragged my suitcase down the subway steps toward the airport.

Eight months later he stood up in a crowded courtroom, glanced nervously in my direction, and pleaded "not guilty" in my paternity suit.

I came back six weeks before the baby was due. London had been humane but grim. Earning 5 shillings an hour as a typist, I had just enough money to cover my living expenses. There would be a few weeks following the baby's birth when I could not go out to work every day, and it seemed best to find a way to live for free then.

My sister had a one-room apartment, and I shared her single bed while I looked for a situation where I could earn my room and board. No employment agency could help, and the Massachusetts Bay United Fund referred me to the Florence Crittenton League's shelter for "girls in trouble."

The Crittenton assured me that it encouraged girls to make their own decisions about what they would do with their babies. But that decision is almost always to give them up for adoption. In fact, girls who are fairly sure they will keep their babies are discouraged from entering the home. They are judged to be too emotionally disturbed, or too much of a threat to the smooth group processes.

A social worker spent several hours telling me why I could not keep my baby. I would never find a baby-sitter. I was being selfish: I wanted the baby to make up for my lonely, empty life (no husband). If I had normal, healthy maternal feelings, I would come to want what was best for the baby—adoption. She then got down to practicalities: the Crittenton rate was $100 a week (as I recall), plus $500 for the delivery. No matter what I claimed, the health insurance policy would not cover the medical expenses, she said, and she would have to have the $500 in advance. She figured, I guess, that the type of client she attracted might flee while the sheets were still warm.

A stay in the Crittenton would not leave me penniless; it would leave me in debt, and out of work, with an infant to support.

"Well," she said, "you may decide that the responsible thing to do is to give up your baby. It takes some courage, but most of our girls find it."

When I decided not to enter the Crittenton, its social worker referred me to a nurse who would give me room and board in exchange for helping her get dressed and bathed. She had a broken leg.

In addition to helping her, the invalid explained, I would be expected to keep the seven-room house clean, attend to her husband's laundry, and prepare three meals a day. I didn't have to wear a maid's uniform, a plain, dark dress and apron would be enough, and I would please wear a hairnet (over my Joan of Arc hairdo). She understood, she told me, that girls like me weren't bad, they had made a bad mistake. And usually, she found, it didn't show in the children. Her son and his wife had been forced to adopt "two of them," infant girls, and honestly, to look at them today you'd never suspect there was anything wrong or unusual about them.

I next visited a university professor who was looking for a cook-typist. Just supper, and four or five hours of typing a day. A nice room for me, with a desk and books. I was leaving to get my suitcase, when he grabbed me: "Why not? You are already pregnant."

I finally found much more acceptable arrangements, which were generous enough to leave my days pretty much free. A minister also got me a typing job in an office in Boston, and I worked until the day the baby was born.

But I was not yet through with the Crittenton social worker. She gave me the name of a community service organization in Cambridge which would make day-care arrangements for me. The social worker there sang the old adoption song. A slightly new ending was that she'd take care of everything to do with the adoption for only $125.

When she was apparently convinced that I was going to keep my baby, she discussed my psychological responsibilities. It would be very harmful to the baby to go home from the hospital with me and stay with me for several weeks before beginning a day-care routine. Trust would be established and then broken at the tender age of one month. It would be much better for me not to see the baby until I was completely settled in a new job, and could send for it, if I still wanted to. (Apparently the trust which would be established between the "wonderfully warm" foster-home mother and my baby could be broken with no ill effects, or with less harm than would be caused by the disruption of *my* full-time presence.)

For an hour or so I answered questions about my family, life, and health record. When I could not tell her a great deal about the baby's paternal grandparents, she asked to interview the father. I really thought that was unnecessary. It seems amazing that I did not wonder why such detailed information was necessary to find good day care. But I did not. I suppose I still believed that helping agencies were in business only to help those in need.

A week later she telephoned me to say she was sorry, but she'd "forgotten"—her agency had not been making any day-care arrangements for years; in fact, it was philosophically opposed to the idea. She didn't want to leave me in the lurch, though. She had found an excellent adoptive home, if I'd reconsider. I hung up, and fortunately my fury and panic were soon interrupted by the sudden onset of labor.

My baby was born at the Boston Lying-In. I watched in overhead mirrors as the intern (who had told me I was too whimsical to be a mother) guided a tiny head, bleating like a lamb, into the world. It was healthy. It was a boy. It was really all right. It squinted its dark eyes and glared at me. What was it? Where had it come from? That wasn't the thing that had been tapping out messages inside me for so long. Where was my baby? I hoped I didn't have to hold that thing, I was too tired.

About seventy-two hours later, a nurse woke me up, as usual, at one in the morning. She had the shrieking, thrashing, furious red lizard in her arms. "He's really hungry this morning," she said.

I took hold of it, and it sunk its gums ravenously into my breast. I screamed, and then burst into tears of joy. He was a separate human being, strong, savage, completely untamed. He was ruthlessly taking what he had to have to survive. He was unafraid and unawed by me or anyone. Oh, little baby, how glad I am to meet you.

In the fall, I accepted a writing job at a research and consulting firm which prides itself on its liberalism. I made no mention of marital status or child when I applied for work, and when the company discovered, after several months, that I had a child, the question seemed academic.

While the unwed mother has to assume almost complete responsibility for her child, society does not really consider her a responsible adult. To give an example, in order to get life insurance, I was told by the salesman that I had to lie and call myself "divorced." Also, the first diaper service I called asked my husband's name, and then, after I said "unmarried," would not accept me as a customer. When I called a second service, I said, with a catch in my voice, "Wid-dowed." The diapers were delivered that day.

Contrary to the social workers' predictions, I had no trouble whatsoever finding a marvelous, intelligent, affectionate baby-sitter who genuinely loves and respects children. She is part of a large, closely knit, happy family. David spends his days in her house with grandparents, parents, aunts, uncles, brothers, and sisters. He gets sunshine and fresh air and home-grown fruits and vegetables. He also has a natural mother who is very happy to be with him every morning and evening.

This day-care situation is expensive, however. It costs a quarter of my income, and I am always just making ends meet. I cannot remember the last time I bought red meat or owned more than one pair of shoes.

When I first began to look for child care, I called the state and was transferred from one agency to another. Finally a man in the Welfare Department explained to me that there was no day care available in Massachusetts for children under two. In fact, until very recently, it had been illegal. The General Court had finally seen its way to legalizing it, and calling for the establishment of licensing procedures. In its wisdom, however, the legislature had consistently failed to appropriate even the minimal funds required to inspect privately financed centers. In this situation, it was illegal for a woman to take in a baby for the day without having a license, and a license was unobtainable. He suggested that I come on the welfare rolls.

I had hoped that when I went back to work as a writer, when summer was over and David was settled down, my social life would improve. It grew worse. There is not much room in society for a single woman, particularly one with a child.

Before, I had had lots of friends, but they were men. A few men seemed willing to accept me, but I did not want them. I had a full-time job, a small household to run, and a baby to care for. David and I continually traded respiratory infections. I was simply too tired to play games with men, to sit, drink in hand, eyelashes fluttering, listening, far into the night. I needed friendship and exchange, not an additional demand. I had, in conventional terms, nothing to give a man.

I absorbed everyone's feelings and reactions toward unmarried mothers. At best, these feelings were ones of curiosity and timid identification: "What was it like, all alone? Dreadful? You know my husband never really shared . . ."

The more liberal and the more compassionate reacted, after reflection, "You're so brave." Such comments did not in any way boost my spirits; rather they affirmed the existence of the opposition and condemnation I already felt. I didn't want to be brave. I simply wanted to be—without comment or judgment.

When I began to suffer crying fits of unknown origin, I sought professional help. Because I could not afford psychotherapy, I went to a Family Service agency. I was referred to a social worker who specialized in unmarried mothers. Her orientation was strongly toward adoption (I couldn't believe it—my baby was more than a year old!). Yes, she did counsel a few women who kept their babies. I asked if her agency would sponsor a group of unmarried mothers in therapy or at least regular discussions. I felt we could lend one another support and begin to work out solutions to mutual problems. She discussed the idea with her supervisors: no, the agency did not think it was a good idea.

But I did. I wrote an advertisement: "*Unwed Mothers*. Same wants to meet you. Object, mutual support and aid." None of the aboveground newspapers would carry it.

Parents Without Partners mailed me material which asked if the recipient were divorced, widowed, or separated. I telephoned and asked if unmarried parents were eligible. "I wouldn't think so, would you?" a woman said. I didn't pursue the question any further because the organization was so blatantly dedicated to remarriage. (Its pamphlet was decorated with a waltzing couple. Several dozen events were listed for the month, only one of which was of a nonsocial nature—a lecture on "Your Teen-ager," or something along that line. The first meeting I could have attended was a "happy hour" in the cocktail lounge of Sammy White's Brighton Bowl.) I note, with interest, that PWP's current literature welcomes as members parents who have "never married."

My needs—to talk about my experiences with someone who would listen, to regain a sense of self-respect and a sense of my worthiness as a human being, to feel myself an accepted member of some segment of society—would not be met by any kind of mating game with which I was familiar.

A friend gave me some literature on Women's Liberation. I read a few paragraphs and tossed it aside: "lesbian anarchists." Several hours later, I fished it out of the trash. The language was extreme, but the message was true and not entirely new to me.

(I had read *The Golden Notebook* and *The Second Sex* and *A Room of One's Own*. I had searched for five years to find a psychiatrist who would not urge me to get married at the end of the initial interview, but would yell at me, "You're a woman, sure, but goddamnit, you're a human being. Why don't you act like one?")

I went to a Women's Liberation meeting. It was run along the lines of Alcoholics Anonymous—everyone told something about her own life. After I spoke, a woman next to me murmured, "You kept the baby! Good for you." But that was the only reaction I perceived.

I joined a group of a dozen women, and for almost a year we have met once a week to discuss our lives, past and present, and our future role as women in the world, as well as in the home. None of us hates men, none of us wants to live a life without men. We feel that we have been oppressed by society and by our own attitudes. We recognize that men are often as oppressed as women, if not more so. And children are the most oppressed of all. In a technological society, there is no need for strongly defined sexual roles—in fact, to say that a man must be aggressive and competitive, and a woman must stay at home and cook frozen foods, is more than arbitrary, it is barbarous.

I hope that someday I will meet a man who is sure enough of his own identity and his own sex to love me as an equal human being, and participate in all facets of the life we build within the community. I hope to find a man who feels, as I do, that children are not extensions of your body and soul, but individual human beings lent you for a few years to cherish and enjoy, while you are guiding them toward an early liberation.

I think of David and the delight people take in him: "I've never seen such a happy child, so loving and outgoing. I can't get over it; he has some strange power."

I look at him, and of course he wears a halo because he and I have shared much laughter and love and anger and tears.

But why does he look special to other people? Do they expect a "bastard" to be ugly and miserable? Perhaps. I like to think, however, that they unconsciously expect something unusual of a child born in ancient symbolism, outside of wed*lock*, a happy, healthy child, conceived and carried and born in independence and freedom from the constraints of society. A child whose existence and whose nature have today—as at all times—the power to begin to change the world once more.

31

ON DAY CARE

LOUISE GROSS and PHYLLIS MACEWAN

[Day care has become one of the central issues of the Women's
Liberation Movement. It is quite clear that free and public day-care
centers would be an important means for liberating women from the
traditional tasks of child rearing. It has been suggested—and in some
places carried out—that women should demand day-care services from
the institutions in which they work or study and from the large
corporations which profit from and expand into the communities in
which they live.

The authors of this discussion paper think it is a mistake to view day
care solely as an issue of Women's Liberation. We would like to assert
that day-care centers in which children are raised in groups by men
and women could be as important for the liberation of children as it
would be for the liberation of women. Group child care—if well
conceived—has a radical potential through the impact it could have on
children's early development. It is therefore necessary that people in the
movement gain a deeper understanding of the day-care center as an
environment for child rearing.

We consider this paper to be an introduction to the problems of
existing day care centers and the possibilities for future centers.
Although we have pointed out some specific areas for radicalizing a
day-care center, we certainly have not developed a comprehensive
model describing what an ideal day-care program would look like.

We hope to develop this paper into a more thorough pamphlet and
we welcome groups that are presently organizing day-care centers or
teachers who are working in centers to send us their ideas and
suggestions.

Why Day Care Has Existed in the United States

Historically in the United States full-day care programs, as contrasted to half-day nursery schools, have been provided in periods of

---

economic stress—during World War II and the depression—when women were required in the work force.[1] These programs were created primarily as a service to the corporations which needed womanpower, not as an educational and social opportunity for children. Although wartime day-care centers often became educational opportunities for children, their rapid closing following World War II was a clear indication that these centers had not been organized primarily to benefit children or even to liberate women. Rather they had been organized to facilitate the carrying out of needed production.

In the past few years there has been an upsurge of state and national government interest in developing day-care facilities for welfare mothers. This current interest parallels the expansion of day care during earlier periods of economic crisis. Today the main impetus behind the new drive for day care is the goal of lowering welfare costs by channeling welfare recipients into "desirable" occupations (like key-punch operating). In both periods the official drive for day care has been motivated by the "needs" of the economy rather than by a concern for the welfare of either women or children.

Why Day Care Has Not Developed in the United States

The underlying reason for the failure of day-care programs to develop in this country exists in the traditional ideology that young children and their mothers belong in the home. Even today a strong bias exists against the concept that day care is potentially good for children and mothers. That women should *have* to work and therefore *have* to put their children in day care centers are circumstances which are generally considered to be necessary evils in this society.[2]

1. For example, the Kaiser Child Service Centers in Portland, Oregon, which served more than 4,000 children from November 8, 1943, to September 1, 1945.

2. Today in the United States there are 4 million working women who have children under the age of 6 years, out of a total of 30 million working women. There presently are enough day-care facilities to take care of 500,000 children. Compared to a number of other Western industrialized countries, the United States is backward in the field of day care. (Figures from *New York Times*, 16 October 1969.)

The Demand for Day Care

The current demand for day care by the Women's Liberation Movement springs from a rejection of the ideology which says that women belong in the home. Yet the movement's present demand parallels the historical attitude toward day care in its nonchild-centered approach. The primary reason for demanding day care is the liberation of women. While recognizing that day care is essential for women's liberation, the authors want the movement to further recognize that day care is essential for the liberation of children. Group child care, in contrast to the more isolating private home environment, has the potential of providing an environment in which children will have more opportunity to develop social sensitivity and responsibility, emotional autonomy and trust, and a wider range of intellectual interests.

The struggle for day-care centers must be considered a people's liberation issue, not just a women's issue, because children are people. Both men and women who are concerned with children's development must demand day care.

What Is a Day-Care Center Like Today?

The majority of existing U.S. day-care centers, which are run as profit-making enterprises, are glorified baby-sitting services—dumping grounds—where children are bored most of the time. In these centers children are emotionally brutalized; they learn the values of obedience and passivity. They are programmed through a daily routine in which opportunities for personal choice and meaningful social relationships with adults and other children are minimal. Eating and naptime are managed in a mass production style which values efficiency over dignity. The adults as well as the children become routinized and enslaved to the daily schedule.

In contrast, there are a few day-care centers where children have meaningful social and educational experiences, and where they participate in nonalienating play/work activities. In these centers self-directed learning and discovery are valued, and curriculum is developed in terms of the children's interests. Social cooperation is based on a rational group-problem-solving approach, rather than on rules impersonally established. Eating and resting activities are designed to be responsive to children's individual and group needs, rather than to meet the efficiency goals of the day-care operation.

Why We Must Demand Space and Money and Not the Day-Care Centers Themselves

We feel that differences among existing day-care centers reflect a conflict in values and attitudes toward human development. This conflict in the care and education of young children is directly related to conflicting values and attitudes expressed in the economic and political behavior of adults. Values in competitive enterprise and individual rather than social achievement, respect for private property, adoration of the nuclear family—are attitudes that are nurtured in childhood and expressed in adult society.

As radicals we must understand that *our* goals for children are in conflict with those of the institutions—corporations and universities— from whom we will be demanding day-care services. This implies that when we make demands for day care they should be solely in terms of money and space. The corporations and universities should have no control.

The Hidden Curriculum

In organizing day-care centers, we need to become aware of how values and attitudes are translated into programs for young children. We need to be aware of the existence of the day-care center curriculum—hidden or explicit—and how it affects children's development.

It is well documented that attitudes toward work, race, sex (including male/female roles), initiative, and cooperation are being formed during the first five years of life. It follows that as radicals, concerned with developing a radical consciousness on these issues, we need to be seriously concerned with what happens inside the day-care center.

The kind of interaction that takes place between the child and the human and physical environment (be it a home or a day-care center) affects the kind of capacities that the child will have as an adult. The capacity to feel deeply and be sensitive toward other people, the capacity to trust oneself and use one's initiative, the capacity to solve problems in a creative and collective way—these are all capacities that can be given their foundation or stifled in the first five years.

By the age of four, children are assimilating the idea that a woman's place is in the home. Three- and four-year-old children are already learning that it's better to be white. They are learning to follow directions and rules without asking why. They are learning how to deny their own feelings and needs in order to win approval from adults.

These are examples of learnings that most commonly result from early childhood experiences. These are elements of the hidden curriculum that usually characterize the child's environment in our society.

The Child's Perspective

To a young child, curriculum in a day-care center is everything that he or she experiences: painting a picture, having to take a nap, experimenting with sand and water, wetting your pants or making it there on time, listening to an interesting story, eating lunch, riding a trike, being socked in the nose and having it bleed, observing one teacher being bossed by the other teacher, being told that blue is called blue, figuring out a hard puzzle, being hugged by the teacher, watching a building be demolished, seeing the mother guinea pig give birth, having everyone sing happy birthday to you, hammering a nail hard, and waiting to be picked up.

Although as adults we can place these events into categories of social, intellectual, emotional, and physical experiences, for the young child each event is experienced in a total way. That is, the experience of painting a picture simultaneously involves emotional, intellectual, physical, and even social capacities. Emotionally a child may be using paint to express feelings of anger, loneliness, contentment, or boredom. Intellectually a child may be using the paint to discover what happens when different colors are mixed or learning how to write different letters. Physically, the child uses the paint brush to explore her/his own coordination, movement, and rhythm. Socially, painting can give the child an opportunity to be alone, with a friend, or in a group—depending on how the teacher has structured the painting experience.

The adult can seldom know the value that a particular experience has for a particular child. The same experience (e.g., painting a picture) will have a different value for different children, a different value to the same child at different times.

The Teacher's Ideology

The teacher's values and attitudes form the base from which the structure and therefore the style of the group are formed. A single activity such as "juice time" illustrates how a teacher's goals and attitudes affect the way the situation is structured. One teacher might have three-year-olds pour her/his own juice from a pitcher, whereas another would have the children take already filled cups from a tray. What underlies the difference? Presumably both teachers know that three-year-olds are in the process of developing muscle as well as eye-hand coordination. Also, three-year-olds are usually concerned with becoming independent and self-sufficient. By letting children pour their own juice the teacher is structuring the situation to allow for growth—however groping—in the areas of self reliance and manual dexterity. By filling cups for the children, the other teacher is structuring the situation for maximum efficiency and neatness: to keep the routine running smoothly. One teacher uses juice time as an opportunity for children to gain some control over their activity, while the other teacher uses juice time to take control. In the first case the child gets to act upon the environment, while in the second case the child is treated as a passive recipient.

The traditional "housekeeping corner" of the nursery school and day-care center is another dramatic illustration of how the teacher's values expressed in actions can have impact.

Let us take two teachers who have undergone similar training in early childhood education and have learned that the housekeeping corner provides an opportunity for children to "act out" adult roles thus contributing to their "ego growth" and "sex identification." One of the teachers sets up a housekeeping corner which encourages girls to be Mommy, the Housewife, and boys to be Daddy, the Worker. The other teacher sets up an area in the classroom in which both boys and girls are given opportunities to cook, play with dolls and trucks, sew, hammer, build with blocks, wash clothes and dishes, dress up as doctors, firemen and firewomen, construction workers, and other interesting occupations. In other words, one teacher uses the housekeeping corner to promote the learning of traditional stereotyped roles, while the other transforms the housekeeping corner into an area where children can explore and test out various adult activities.

Men in the Day-care Center/ Work in the Day-care Center

Another way that children learn the traditional stereotyped roles is through observing that almost all day-care teachers are women. The children quickly comprehend the concept that there is "women's work" and "men's work." This in itself would be sufficient argument for us to insist that men be included at all levels in the day-care staff.

Furthermore, without including men in the day-care program, the demand for day care runs the risk of contradicting the goals of women's liberation. Women should not demand simply that there be special institutions for child care, but also that men take an equal role in child care.

There is another good reason that *both* men and women should be involved in the day-care center. Teaching/working/playing with children can be an extraordinarily creative and nonalienating job. What often makes the caretakers of young children—teachers and mothers—feel apologetic about their occupation and what deprives men the opportunity of working with children is the fact that our society considers child care "women's work"—a low-status/cheap labor occupation biologically relegated to the weaker, "sensitive" sex.

A day-care program which had a sexually integrated staff—and salaries in keeping with the value of this work—would make child rearing a desirable and rewarding occupation. Finally, it seems self-evident that it's best for children—emotionally, socially, and politically—that they be cared for equally by both men and women.

Some Conclusions

Day care is a people's liberation issue. Women, of course, will gain from a good day-care program, but in the final analysis women's liberation depends on an entire transformation of society, not just on one institution. However, that one institution, if radically structured, can help obtain that transformation of society. The way children develop is part of that transformation.

In order to develop a radically structured day-care program we must not allow any control to be in the hands of the universities and corporations. Our demand to these institutions for day care must be a demand solely for space and money. Control must rest with those who struggle for and use the day-care center.

One of our prime tasks in that struggle is to develop an awareness of what a good day-care program can be. We have simply attempted to make clear in this paper that day care is a complex issue.[3] The self-education which the movement must undergo on day care should be as thorough as on more obviously political issues.

Suggested Readings and Sources of Literature Related to Day Care

Boguslawski, Dorothy. *Guide for Establishing and Operating Day Care Centers for Young Children*. Child Welfare League of America, Inc., New York: 1968.

Burgess, Evangeline. *Values in Early Childhood Education*. Department of Elementary-Kindergarten-Nursery Education, National Education Association, 1965.

Dittman, Laura, ed. *Early Child Care: The New Perspective*. New York: Atherton Press, 1968.

Federal Panel on Early Childhood. *Good References on Day Care*. U.S. Department of Health, Education, and Welfare, Social and Rehabilitation Service, Children's Bureau, July 1968.

Hartley, Ruth, et al. *Understanding Children's Play*. New York: Columbia University Press, 1952.

Hunt, J. McV. *Intelligence and Experience*. New York: Ronald Publishing Company, 1961.

Hymes, J. L. *Teaching the Child Under 6*. New York: Prentice-Hall, 1963.

Jones, Betty, and Prescott, Elizabeth. *Group Day Care as a Child-Rearing Environment: An Observational Study of Day Care Program*. Pasadena,

---

3. There are numerous implications of day-care organizing which we have not included in this paper such as the questions of developing the day-care center as a base for community political action, the day-care center as a place to organize parents around their children's rights in the public school system, and the whole issue of day care for infants and collective child rearing.

Calif.: Children's Bureau, Social Security Administration, U.S. Department of Health, Education, and Welfare, 1967.

Kritchevsky, Sybil, and Prescott, Elizabeth. *Planning Environments for Young Children*. Washington, D.C.: National Association for the Education of Young Children, 1969.

Moustakas, Clark. *The Authentic Teacher*. Cambridge, Mass.: Doyle Publishing Company, 1966.

Piaget, Jean. *The Language and Thought of the Child*. New York: Meridian Books, 1955.

U.S. Department of Labor, Women's Bureau. *Report of a Consultation on Working Women and Day Care Needs*, 1968 (free), and *Working Mothers and the Need for Day Care Services*, 1968 (free).

Warner, Sylvia Ashton. *Teacher*. New York: Bantam Books, 1963.

32

THE ULTIMATE REVOLUTION

SHULAMITH FIRESTONE

Households

I shall now outline a system that I believe will satisfy any remaining needs for children after ego concerns are no longer part of our motivations. Suppose a person or a couple at some point in their lives desires to live around children in a family-size unit. While we will no longer have reproduction as the life goal of the normal individual—we have seen how single and group nonreproductive life styles could be enlarged to become satisfactory for many people for their whole lifetimes and for others, for good portions of their lifetime—certain people may still prefer community-style group living permanently, and other people may want to experience it at some time in their lives, especially during early childhood.

Thus at any given time a proportion of the population will want to live in reproductive social structures. Correspondingly, the society in general will still need reproduction, though reduced, if only to create a new generation.

The proportion of the population will be automatically a select group with a predictably higher rate of stability, because they will have had a freedom of choice now generally unavailable. Today those who do not marry and have children by a certain age are penalized: they find themselves alone, excluded, and miserable, on the margins of a society in which everyone else is compartmentalized into lifetime generational families, chauvinism and exclusiveness their chief characteristic. (Only in Manhattan is single living even tolerable, and that can be debated.) Most people are still forced into marriage by family pressure, the "shotgun," economic considerations, and other reasons that have nothing to do with choice of life style. In our new reproductive unit, however, with the limited contract (see below), child rearing so diffused as to be practically eliminated, economic considerations nonexistent, and all participating members having entered only on the basis of personal preference, "unstable" reproductive social structures will have disappeared.

This unit I shall call a *household* rather than an extended family. The distinction is important: The word *family* implies biological reproduction and some degree of division of labor by sex, and thus the traditional dependencies and resulting power relations, extended over generations; though the size of the family—in this case, the larger numbers of the "extended" family—may affect the strength of this hierarchy, it does not change its structural definition. "Household," however, connotes only a large grouping of people living together for an unspecified time, and with no specified set of interpersonal relations. How would a "household" operate?

Limited Contract

If the household replaced marriage perhaps we would at first legalize it in the same way—if this is necessary at all. A group of ten or so consenting adults of varying ages[1] could apply for a license as a group in much the same way as a young couple today applies for a marriage

---

1. An added advantage of the household is that it allows older people past their fertile years to share fully in parenthood when they so desire.

license, perhaps even undergoing some form of ritual ceremony, and then might proceed in the same way to set up house. The household license would, however, apply only for a given period, perhaps seven to ten years, or whatever was decided on as the minimal time in which children needed a stable structure in which to grow up—but probably a much shorter period than we now imagine. If at the end of this period the group decided to stay together, it could always get a renewal. However, no single individual would be contracted to stay after this period, and perhaps some members of the unit might transfer out, or new members come in. Or, the unit could disband altogether.

There are many advantages to short-term households, stable compositional units lasting for only ten-year periods: the end of family chauvinism, built up over generations, of prejudices passed down from one generation to the next, the inclusion of people of all ages in the child-rearing process, the integration of many age groups into one social unit, the breadth of personality that comes from exposure to many rather than to (the idiosyncrasies of) a few, and so on.

Children

A regulated percentage of each household—say one-third—would be children. But whether, at first, genetic children created by couples within the household, or at some future time—after a few generations of household living had severed the special connection of adults with "their" children—children were produced artificially, or adopted, would not matter: (minimal) responsibility for the early physical dependence of children would be evenly diffused among all members of the household.

But though it would still be structurally sound, we must be aware that as long as we use natural childbirth methods, the "household" could never be a totally liberating social form. A mother who undergoes a nine-month pregnancy is likely to feel that the product of all that pain and discomfort "belongs" to her ("To think of what I went through to have you!"). But we want to destroy this possessiveness along with its cultural reinforcements so that no one child will be a priori favored over another, so that children will be loved for their own sake.

But what if there is an instinct for pregnancy? I doubt it. Once we have sloughed off cultural superstructures, we may uncover a sex instinct, the normal consequences of which *lead* to pregnancy. And perhaps there is also an instinct to care for the young once they arrive. But an instinct for pregnancy itself would be superfluous—could nature anticipate man's mastery of reproduction? And what if, once the false motivations for pregnancy had been shed, women no longer wanted to "have" children at all? Might this not be a disaster, given that artificial reproduction is not yet perfected? But women have no special reproductive *obligation* to the species. If they are no longer willing, then artificial methods will have to be developed hurriedly, or, at the very least, satisfactory compensations—other than destructive ego investments—would have to be supplied to make it worth their while.

Adults and older children would take care of babies for as long as they needed it, but since there would be many adults and older children sharing the responsibility—as in the extended family—no one person would ever be involuntarily stuck with it.

Adult/child relationships would develop just as do the best relationships today: some adults might prefer certain children over others, just as some children might prefer certain adults over others—these might become lifelong attachments in which the individuals concerned mutually agreed to stay together, perhaps to form some kind of nonreproductive unit. Thus all relationships would be based on love alone, uncorrupted by objective dependencies and the resulting class inequalities. Enduring relationships between people of widely divergent ages would become common.

Legal Rights and Transfers

With the weakening and severerance of the blood ties, the power hierarchy of the family would break down. The legal structure—as long as it is still necessary—would reflect this democracy at the roots of our society. Women would be identical under the law with men. Children would no longer be "minors," under the patronage of "parents"—they would have full rights. Remaining physical inequalities could be legally compensated for: for example, if a child were beaten, perhaps he could report it to a special simplified "household" court where he would be granted instant legal redress.

Another special right of children would be the right of immediate transfer: if the child for any reason did not like the household into which he had been born so arbitrarily, he would be helped to transfer out. An adult on the other hand—one who had lived one span in a household (seven to ten years)—might have to present his case to the court, which would then decide, as do divorce courts today, whether he had adequate grounds for breaking his contract. A certain number of transfers within the seven-year period might be necessary for the smooth functioning of the household, and would not be injurious to its stability as a unit so long as a core remained. (In fact, new people now and then might be a refreshing change.) However, the unit, for its own best economy, might have to place a ceiling on the number of transfers in or out, to avoid depletion, excessive growth, and/or friction.

Chores

As for housework: The larger family-sized group (probably about fifteen people) would be more practical—the waste and repetition of the duplicate nuclear family unit would be avoided, e.g., as in shopping or cooking for a small family, without the loss of intimacy of the larger communal experiment. In the interim, any housework would have to be rotated equitably; but eventually cybernation could automate out almost all domestic chores.

City Planning

City planning, architecture, furnishings, all would be altered to reflect the new social structure. The trend toward mass-produced housing would probably continue, but the housing might be designed and even built (perhaps out of prefabricated components) by the people living there to suit their own needs and tastes. Privacy could be built in: either through private rooms in every household, or with "retreats" within the larger city to be shared by people of other households, or both. The whole might form a complex the size of a small town or a large campus. Perhaps campus is the clearer image: we could have small units of self-determined housing—prefabricated component parts set up or dismantled easily and quickly to suit the needs of the limited contract—as well as central permanent buildings to fill the needs of the community as a whole, i.e., perhaps the equivalent of a "student union" for socializing, restaurants, a large computer bank, a modern communications center, a computerized library and film center, "learning centers" devoted to various specialized interests, and whatever else might be necessary in a cybernetic community.

The Economy

The end of the family structure would necessitate simultaneous changes in the larger economy. Not only would reproduction be qualitatively different, so would production: just as we have had to purify relations with children of all external considerations we would first have to have, to be entirely successful in our goals, the socialism of a cybernetic industrial state, aiming not just to redistribute drudgery equitably, but, eventually, to eliminate it altogether. With the further development and wise use of machines, people could be freed from toil, "work" divorced from wages and redefined: Now both adults and children could indulge in serious "play" as much as they wanted.

In the transition, as long as we still had a money economy, people might receive a guaranteed annual income from the state to take care of basic physical needs. These incomes, distributed equitably to men, women, and children, regardless of age, work, prestige, birth, would in themselves equalize in one blow the economic class system.

Activity

What would people do in this utopia? I think that will not be a problem. If we truly had abolished all unpleasant work, people would have the time and the energy to develop healthy interests of their own. What is now found only among the elite, the pursuit of specialized interests for their own sake, would probably become the norm.

As for our educational institutions: the inadequacy of the public school system practically guarantees its breakdown in the near future. Perhaps we could replace it with noncompulsory "learning centers," which would combine both the present functions of our lower educational institutions, the teaching of rudimentary skills, with those of the higher, the expansion of knowledge, including everyone of any age or level, children and adults.

Yes, but what about basic skills? How, for example, could a child with no formal sequential training enter an advanced curriculum like architecture? But traditional book learning, the memorizing of facts, which forms the most substantial portion of the curriculum of our elementary schools, will be radically altered under the impact of cybernation—a qualitative difference, to the apparatus of culture at least as significant a change as was the printing press, even as important as the alphabet. McLuhan pointed out the beginning of a reversal from literary to visual means of absorbing knowledge. We can expect the escalation of this and other effects in the development of modern media for the rapid transmittal of information. And the *amount* of rote knowledge necessary either for children or adults will itself be vastly reduced, for we shall have computer banks within easy reach. After all, why store facts in one's head when computer banks could supply quicker and broader information instantaneously? (Already today children wonder why they must learn multiplication tables rather than the operation of an adding machine.) Whatever mental storing of basic facts is still necessary can be quickly accomplished through new mechanical methods, teaching machines, records and tapes, and so on, which, when they become readily available, would allow the abolition of compulsory schooling for basic skills. Like foreign students in the pursuit of a specialized profession, the child can pick up any necessary basic "language" on the side, through these supplementary machine methods. But it is more likely that the fundamental skills and knowledge necessary will be the same for adults as for children: skill in operating new machines. Programming skills may become universally required, but rather than through years of nine-to-five schooling, it would have to be learned (rapidly) only in conjunction with the requirements of mastering a specific discipline.

As for "career indecision": those people today whose initial "hobby" has survived intact from childhood to become their adult "profession" will most often tell you they developed it before the age of nine.[2] As long as specialized professions still existed, they could be changed as often as adults change majors or professions today. But if choice of profession had no superimposed motives, if they were based only on interest in the subject itself, switches in mid-course would probably be far fewer. Inability to develop strong interest is today mostly the result of the corruption of culture and its institutions.

Thus our conception of work and education would be much closer to the medieval first-hand apprenticeship to a discipline, people of all ages participating at all levels. As in academia today, the internal dynamics of the various disciplines would foster their own social organization, providing a means for meeting other people of like interests, and of

2. If children today were given a realistic idea of the professions available—not just fireman/nurse—they might arrive at a special interest even sooner.

sharing the intellectual and aesthetic pursuits now available only to a select few, the intelligentsia. The kind of social environment now found only in the best departments of the best colleges might become the life style of the masses, freed to develop their potential from the start: Whereas now only the lucky or persevering ones ever arrive at (usually only professing to) "doing their thing," then everyone would have the opportunity to develop to his full potential.

Or not develop if he so chose—but this seems unlikely, since every child at first exhibits curiosity about people, things, the world in general and what makes it tick. It is only because unpleasant reality *dampens* his curiosity that the child learns to scale down his interests, thus becoming the average bland adult. But if we should remove these obstructions, then all people would develop as fully as only the greatest and wealthiest classes, and a few isolated "geniuses," have been able to. Each individual would contribute to the society as a whole, not for wages or other incentives of prestige and power, but because the work he chose to do interested him in itself, and perhaps only incidentally because it had a social value for others (as healthily selfish as is only Art today). Work that had only social value and no personal value would have been eliminated by the machine.

Thus, in the larger context of a cybernetic socialism, the establishment of the household as the alternative to the family for reproduction of children, combined with every imaginable life style for those who chose to live singly or in nonreproductive units, would resolve all the basic dilemmas that now arise from the family to obstruct human happiness. Let us go over our four minimal demands to see how our imaginary construction would fare.

1. *The freeing of women from the tyranny of their biology by any means available, and the diffusion of the childbearing and child-rearing role to the society as a whole, to men and other children as well as women.* This has been corrected. *Childbearing* could be taken over by technology, and if this proved too much against our past tradition and psychic structure (which it certainly would at first) then adequate incentives and compensations would have to be developed—other than the ego rewards of possessing the child—to reward women for their special social contribution of pregnancy and childbirth. Most of *child rearing*, as we have seen, has to do with the maintaining of power relations, forced internalization of family traditions, and many other ego concerns that

war with the happiness of the individual child. This repressive socialization process would now be unnecessary in a society in which the interests of the individual coincided with those of the larger society. Any child-rearing responsibility left would be diffused to include men and other children equally with women. In addition, new methods of instant communication would lessen the child's reliance on even this egalitarian primary unit.

2. *The economic independence and self-determination of all.* Under socialism, even if still a money economy, work would be divorced from wages, the ownership of the means of production in the hands of all the people, and wealth distributed on the basis of need, independent of the social value of the individual's contribution to society. We would aim to eliminate the dependence of women and children on the labor of men, as well as all other types of labor exploitation. Each person could choose his life style at will, changing it to suit his tastes without seriously inconveniencing anyone else; no one would be bound into any social structure against his will, for each person would be totally self-governing as soon as he was physically able.

3. *The total integration of women and children into the larger society.* This has been fulfilled: The concept of childhood has been abolished, children having full legal, sexual, and economic rights, their educational/work activities no different from those of adults. During the few years of their infancy we have replaced the psychologically destructive genetic "parenthood" of one or two arbitrary adults with a diffusion of the responsibility for physical welfare over a larger number of people. The child would still form intimate love relationships, but instead of developing close ties with a decreed "mother" and "father," the child might now form those ties with people of his own choosing, of whatever age or sex. Thus all adult–child relationships will have been mutually chosen—equal, intimate relationships free of material dependencies. Correspondingly, though children would be fewer, they would not be monopolized, but would mingle freely throughout the society to the benefit of all, thus satisfying that legitimate desire to be around the young which is often called the reproductive "instinct."

4. *Sexual freedom, love, etc.* So far we have not said much of love and sexual freedom because there is no reason for it to present a problem: there would be nothing obstructing it. With full license human relationships eventually would be redefined for the better. If a child does not know his own mother, or at least does not attach a special

value to her over others, it is unlikely that he would choose her as his first love object, only to have to develop inhibitions on this love. It is possible that the child might form his first close physical relationships with people his own size out of sheer physical convenience, just as men and women, all else being equal, might prefer each other over those of the same sex for sheer physical fit. But if not, if he should choose to relate sexually to adults, even if he should happen to pick his own genetic mother, there would be no a priori reasons for her to reject his sexual advances, because the incest taboo would have lost its function. The "household," a transient social form, would not be subject to the dangers of inbreeding.

Thus, without the incest taboo, adults might return within a few generations to a more natural "polymorphously perverse" sexuality, the concentration on genital sex and orgasmic pleasure giving way to total physical/emotional relationships that *included* that. Relations with children would include as much genital sex as the child was capable of—probably considerably more than we now believe—but because genital sex would no longer be the central focus of the relationship, lack of orgasm would not present a serious problem. Adult/child and homosexual sex taboos would disappear, as well as nonsexual friendship (Freud's aim-inhibited love). All close relationships would include the physical, our concept of exclusive physical partnerships (monogamy) disappearing from our psychic structure, as well as the construct of a Partner Ideal. But how long it would take for these changes to occur, and in what forms they would appear, remains conjecture. The specific need not concern us here. We need only set up the preconditions for a free sexuality: whatever forms it took would be assuredly an improvement on what we have now, "natural" in the truest sense.

In the transitional phase, adult genital sex and the exclusiveness of couples within the household might have to be maintained in order for the unit to be able to function smoothly, with a minimum of internal tension caused by sexual frictions. It is unrealistic to impose theories of what *ought* to be on a psyche already fundamentally organized around specific emotional needs. And this is why individual attempts to eliminate sexual possessiveness are now always inauthentic. We would do much better to concentrate on altering the social structures that have produced this psychical organization, allowing for the eventual— if not in our lifetime—fundamental restructuring (or should I say destructuring?) of our psychosexuality.

Above, I have drawn up only a very rough plan in order to make the general direction of a feminist revolution more vivid: Production and reproduction of the species would both be, simultaneously, reorganized in a nonrepressive way. The birth of children to a unit which disbanded or recomposed as soon as children were physically able to be independent, one that was meant to serve immediate needs rather than to pass on power and privilege (the basis of patriarchy is the inheritance of property gained through labor) would eliminate the power psychology, sexual repression, and cultural sublimation. Family chauvinism, class privilege based on birth, would be eliminated. The blood tie of the mother to the child would eventually be severed—if male jealousy of "creative" childbirth actually exists, we will soon have the means to create life independently of sex—so that pregnancy, now freely acknowledged as clumsy, inefficient, and painful, would be indulged in, if at all, only as a tongue-in-cheek archaism, just as already women today wear virginal white to their weddings. A cybernetic socialism would abolish economic classes, and all forms of labor exploitation, by granting all people a livelihood based only on material needs. Eventually drudge work (jobs) would be eliminated in favor of (complex) play, activity done for its own sake, by both adults and children. Love and sexuality would be reintegrated, flowing unimpeded.

The revolt against the biological family could bring on the first successful revolution, or what was thought of by the ancients as the Messianic Age. Humanity's double curse when it ate the Apple of Knowledge (the growing knowledge of the laws of the environment creating repressive civilization), that man would toil by the sweat of his brow in order to live, and woman would bear children in pain and travail, can now be undone through man's very efforts in toil. We now have the knowledge to create a paradise on earth anew. The alternative is our own suicide through that knowledge, the creation of a hell on earth, followed by oblivion.

B

Prospects for Middle Age Women who have
followed societal prescriptions, deriving their entire sense of
self-worth from the roles of wife and mother, are likely to
experience crisis when they reach middle age. At this time, the
bases of prestige for the two primary feminine roles become
visibly eroded. In order to attract a husband, and thus enter the
role of wife, a woman in our culture is expected to be young and
beautiful. According to the myth of romantic love, a man selects a
woman for marriage because of his love for her—a love based on
an idealization of her qualities, especially her physical qualities.
Beauty and youth in America are inextricably intertwined, and no
matter how desperately she tries, no woman can become younger.
As long as the wife's contribution to the marriage is supposed to
be her physical attractiveness, she is bound to become uneasy
with increasing awareness of aging.[1] In addition, romantic love
inevitably loses its qualities of obsession and idealization after
several years of marriage, if not sooner. Real and fictionalized
accounts of middle-aged women whose husbands have left them
contribute further to cases of the "forty-year-old jitters." At the
same time, a pervasive societal emphasis on youth does, in fact,
drive many husbands to seek reassurance of their vitality from
younger women.

Even if a woman is secure in her role as wife, this role cannot
be enlarged to compensate for the constriction of the mother role,
because middle-aged men are still involved in their work. Even if
her marriage is stable and a woman can learn to cope with the
realization of aging, the basis of prestige for the housewife-mother
role is almost certain to disappear. Henry attributes the early

---

1. For a discussion of the difference between the awareness of mortality that afflicts
everyone and the anxious awareness of aging that pains women, see Susan Sontag, "The
Double Standard of Aging," *Saturday Review: The Society* 52, no. 39 (October 1972): 29–38.

decline in the prestige of the mother role to two phenomena: (1) American women are still quite young when they stop bearing children; (2) these children are expected to be relatively free from supervision during the teen years. We have noted earlier that throughout American society the role of housewife-mother has a relatively low or negative evaluation. The housewife-mother gains prestige within her immediate circle, however, when a large number of people benefit from her activities, when the people she serves are obviously dependent on her, and when she performs her role obligations well. Much of the meaning is removed from the housewife-mother role as children gradually withdraw (the "shrinking circle" stage) and finally leave the home (the "empty nest" stage).[2]

Women are socialized not to seek accomplishments outside the home. Instead they are admonished to live vicariously through their husbands and children. A person whose identity is derived entirely from other people is vulnerable to depression when those people leave.[3] If a woman's sense of self is based on her own achievements as well as on the achievements and dependence of other people, middle age may still be a difficult time, but it certainly will be less likely to destroy her. While all roles are based on interaction with others, the mother role of each individual woman involves a set of specific, dependent others, who, if the mother performs her job well, inevitably become independent and leave the home. At this time, although intergenerational interaction continues to take place, patterns of visitation may not meet parental expectations.[4]

The loss that many women experience in varying degrees as their children become less dependent is not only a private trouble but a public, societal problem as well. It is those women who have followed the traditional expectations and derived their entire sense of self-esteem from the roles of wife and mother who suffer

2. Helen Znaniecki Lopata, "The Life Cycle of the Social Role of Housewife," *Sociology and Social Research* 51, no. 1 (October 1966): 12–14.

3. Pauline Bart, "Mother Portnoy's Complaints," *Trans-action* 8, nos. 1 and 2 (November/December 1970): 74.

4. Gordon F. Streib, "Intergenerational Relations: Perspectives of the Two Generations on the Older Parent," *Journal of Marriage and the Family* 27, no. 4 (November 1965): 469–76.

most. For various reasons, including early marriage and longer life expectancy, increasing numbers of women are experiencing the "shrinking circle" and "empty nest" stages of the role of housewife.[5] Despite the fact that middle age is therefore a problematic time for a substantial proportion of women, there are no positive guidelines for the postparental housewife. Henry suggests that women be continuously educated and continuously aware of the work contingency so they will be able to work when their children withdraw from the home.

Middle-aged women, however, face difficulties in various areas of their lives when they try to locate sources of satisfaction outside the home.[6] In the employment area, these women are at a disadvantage because of lack of skills or decay of skills, because of general pay discrimination, and because of the requirement of many jobs that women employees be young and attractive. If they return to school to increase specific job skills or for general knowledge, these older students may find a heavy workload and much required material that is irrelevant to their current interests. In addition, the woman who returns to work or to school is likely to experience conflict between the expectations of her family and the obligations of the worker or student role. It is not unusual, for example, for a husband to continue to expect his wife to cook, clean, and take care of the children in addition to working or studying. The middle-aged woman may find herself with a diploma in one hand and a divorce decree in the other.[7]

Rossi suggests that, at present, one way to avoid potentially severe problems in middle age is for women (even those with young children) to return to school or reenter the job market as soon as possible. She suggests elsewhere that the sooner a woman reenters the job market, the less rigid her family's expectations of her housewife duties will be.[8] Rossi accentuates the positive

5. For a discussion of the relative newness of the postparental phase as a stage in the life cycle, see, for example, Harold T. Christensen and Kathryn P. Johnsen, *Marriage and the Family* (New York: Ronald Press, 1971), pp. 448–49.

6. Rose Gladstone, "Planned Obsolescence: The Middle-Aged Woman," *Up From Under* 1, no. 1 (May/June 1970): 29–30.

7. For a perceptive fictional account of the impact on her marriage of one woman's return to school, see Dorothy Bryant, *Ella Price's Journal* (New York: J. B. Lippincott, 1972).

8. Alice S. Rossi, "Barriers to the Career Choice of Engineering, Medicine, or Science

effects of employment for women, for their children, and for their marriages when women deliberately choose to work. Children benefit from independence training and from seeing women as both housewives and as workers. In the nuclear family the competitive drive which surfaces all too often as competition between a woman and her husband for the allegiance of their children will be reduced when wives return to work and no longer feel that their sole source of success lies with their children. Since husbands and wives usually work in separate areas or at differing levels occupationally, occupational competition will not endanger the marriage. Rossi thus alludes to the alleged dangers of husband and wife working within the same area and at the same level.[9] If her description is apt, it points in part to the rigidity of sexual stratification wherein marriage cannot contain a reversal of society's description of women as the inferior sex. If the woman is not considered a competitor, she states, "The active involvement of a wife, even in the same field as her husband, is more apt to add spice and zest to the marriage than it is to create competitive feelings and marital difficulties."

Rossi also advises women who are returning to work to reject jobs that are beneath their skills or talents. The closer a job is to the worker's abilities, the greater will be both the intrinsic rewards and the paycheck. An additional benefit from such rejection is that when a woman feels her work is worthwhile, she is less likely to feel cross-pressured by requests for time commitments from outside organizations or by domestic duties. Finally, the higher the level of work, the greater the flexibility in working hours. Those who choose to work, then, can more likely afford to insist on a job equal to their capabilities and such insistence by women generally is necessary to end discrimination.[10]

Returning to work, nevertheless, can be an intermediate solution only for most women—even for those who can afford to

Among American Women," in *Women and the Scientific Professions*, ed. Jacquelyn A. Mattfeld and Carol G. Van Aken (Cambridge, Mass.: MIT Press, 1965), p. 107.

9. Talcott Parsons, "The Kinship System of the Contemporary United States," in *Essays in Sociological Theory*, ed. Talcott Parsons (New York: Free Press, 1954), pp. 177–96.

10. See, for example, Dean D. Knudsen, "The Declining Status of Women: Popular Myths and the Failure of Functionalist Thought," *Social Forces* 48, no. 2 (December 1969): 190–92.

choose to work. Rossi herself describes elsewhere the dependence of the present economic system on the retention of most women at home.[11] All wives are expected to take care of domestic details and to create a warm home atmosphere. Furthermore, the very women who can choose to work are the ones who are expected to be social assets to their husbands' careers. In addition, many educated women assist their husbands in their careers per se; for example, by providing knowledge or research assistance.[12] Although it is rewarding, then, it is very difficult for two people to maintain careers while sharing household responsibilities.[13] The situation is often described by members of dual-career families in the following manner: "When the alarm goes off in the morning it's like the horses off at the races." [14]

The difficulties involved in the coordination of two careers point to the general difficulty with attempts to create change at the individual family level in the absence of other changes in society. All of the societal arrangements—school, work, household, and child care are now coordinated in terms of the married male having full-time occupational commitment and his wife remaining at home. There has been some limited institutional change as evidenced by the increasing proportion of mothers among women workers.[15] However, changes in other areas have not kept pace with the emerging reality of mothers at work and a new vision of marital and work roles has certainly not come.[16]

Henry offers some suggestions toward a general change in the world of work directed toward providing both men and women

---

11. Alice S. Rossi, "Sex Equality: The Beginnings of Ideology," *Humanist* 29, no. 5 (September–October 1969): 3–6, 16.

12. For a discussion of the two-person career, see Hanna Papanek, "Men, Women, and Work: Reflections on the Two-Person Career," *American Journal of Sociology* 78, no. 4 (January 1973): 852–72.

13. For a discussion of the positive aspects as well as the difficulties involved in the dual career family, see Rhona Rapoport and Robert N. Rapoport, "The Dual-Career Family: A Variant Pattern and Social Change," *Human Relations* 22, no. 1 (February 1969): 3–30.

14. Lynda Lytle Holmstrom, *The Two-Career Family* (Cambridge, Mass.: Schenkman Publishing, 1972), p. 88.

15. Valerie K. Oppenheimer, *The Female Labor Force in the United States,* Population Monograph Series, No. 5, University of California, Berkeley, 1970.

16. The government of Sweden has proposed society-wide change in the work and family roles of both men and women. See Maj-Britt Sandlund, *The Status of Women in Sweden: Report to the United Nations,* 1968 (Stockholm: The Swedish Institute, 1968), p. 4.

with a more satisfying quality of life. First, women should share in the occupational world. Automation should be used to expand the job market for women rather than to create unemployment and deadening jobs. Work in the public service sector, now either low-paid or volunteer, should be adequately rewarded. If necessary, government should subsidize labor, perhaps in the form of a guaranteed annual wage. Henry notes that the concept of work has shifted from survival to satisfaction, but the realities of work do not yet measure up to that concept. Spokeswomen for the women's movement are also raising issues about the general quality of contemporary work roles. For relatively privileged women the goal is not to give up a subordinate role in an "expressive" realm for a superordinate role in a ruthless, competitive economic system. For underprivileged women, moreover, life in a factory today cannot be seen as liberation.

We return, therefore, to the importance of public solutions in the elimination of private troubles. In order to solve the individual trouble experienced by women as the "forty-year-old jitters," a collective solution is required ultimately. Toward such a solution, Pauline Bart outlines succinctly the ways in which the women's movement is organized toward a re-definition of sex roles for both men and women:

> The Women's Liberation Movement, by pointing out alternative life styles, by providing the emotional support necessary for deviating from the ascribed sex roles and by emphasizing the importance of women actualizing their own selves, fulfilling their own potentials can help in the development of personhood for both men and women.[17]

Individually and in groups, women have begun to question the traditionally accepted definition of their lives. Individually, women have begun to change their own lives, to solve private troubles. In groups, women are striving to change the lives of others, to restructure society, to solve public problems. The feminist goal for men and women of all ages is the creation of a combination of personal relationships and work arrangements which fosters human development.

17. Bart, "Mother Portnoy's Complaints," p. 74.

33

FORTY-YEAR-OLD JITTERS
IN MARRIED URBAN WOMEN

JULES HENRY

It seems to me that I learned about a disease called involutional melancholia when I began to attend grand rounds at a psychiatric hospital in the mid-1930s. At that time, I learned that involutional melancholia was a psychotic depression afflicting aging women, that it came upon them like cancer; that it was organically determined, and that it was just as difficult to cure as cancer. Involutional melancholia, I learned, was a function of organic decay, somehow related to the female reproductive system; nothing could be done about the onset, though there might be some hope of recovery—just as there was for cancer. As we have learned more about emotional illness, however, we have dropped the notions of inevitability and incurability; and our assurance about physical determinants has decreased proportionally as our sensitivity to environmental factors and our capacity to discriminate among patterns of illness have increased. The so-called involutional melancholia, the deep depression that sometimes afflicts aging women, can no longer be viewed as a simple consequence of a physiological aging that has, in certain cases, merely reached an extreme; it must be seen as a disease in which the environment is important, and which is an extreme expression of a widespread disturbance present in most women as a consequence of aging in our culture.

Emotional illness, we know, is a phenomenon of vulnerability; and we express this conviction by saying that people become emotionally ill when their defenses either break down or are too rigid. Society defends most of us against attacks from within and without by giving us a role and a reasonably good opinion of ourselves, by surrounding us with friends, and so on. In the woman of forty or so, many of these culturally determined defenses are crumbling, so that the feeling of vulnerability grows and sometimes becomes acute to the point of serious impairment of function—involutional, in other words; it is therefore important to review what a woman's culturally determined defenses are, and how, one by one, they may be swept away, leaving her standing alone and unprotected.

Just as a physician looks at the functioning of the body when he deals with illness, so the social scientist must look at society. For example, the causes of venereal disease, tuberculosis, cholera, typhoid, and even measles and most other diseases are obviously social as well as physiological; the social scientist, asked to discuss the misery of aging women, must just as surely look for the causes of it in the culture as the physician must look for them in the body. In this case, as in most cases of emotional upset, the social scientist is probably closer to the truth than the ordinary physician. I shall therefore outline what I consider to be the cultural sources of the female misery called forty-year-old jitters. I begin with some general features of our social organization.

While some people may be driven mad by those around them, most of mankind is not, but rather finds a personal community a necessary condition of existence. Yet, societies around the world vary enormously in the degree to which they guarantee everyone a personal community —a group of people on whom one can rely for approval and support.[1] For example, the families of traditional China and contemporary India are extended so that one can always count on a group of people related to one through one's father. Beyond that, in traditional China, was the wider reach of the lineage or clan—the even more extended group of paternal relatives. India extends the network even further, to the caste—the people united through similar occupations and religious observances. One of the most astonishing facts of social life is that almost the entire population of both China and India lived for uncountable ages under this family type, which anthropologists call the joint family. Evidently, it has given such shelter, security, and comfort that, with all its internal stresses, it has survived for thousands of years. The joint family is only one example of the variety of forms of permanent and sheltering kinship structures that have protected mankind against starvation, loneliness, and discard.

When we turn to the societies of the contemporary West and to many of the Soviet Union and its allies, we discover radically different conditions, for in industrialized nations, one is not born, as the Chinese were and as most peasant Indians are today, to a permanent supporting

---

1. Jules Henry, "The Personal Community and Its Invariant Properties," *American Anthropologist* 60 (1960): 827–31.

personal community that can never turn its face away.[2] In our societies, extended obligatory, mutual involvements are rare, and we are not even obliged by law to support our parents—a monstrous condition when viewed from the perspective of India or traditional China or, indeed, in the historic perspective of mankind. Thus, in our culture, there is no guarantee that we will never stand alone. Only the ringing of the telephone tells the urban dweller that a friend is calling, reminding the family that they are not alone.

Nevertheless, there is always the danger that the phone will cease to ring. People die, particularly as we grow older or move away, and there is scarcely a writer on American life who has not commented on our enormous historic mobility in space. And now we know that it is not only spacial mobility that disunites people, but movement up or down in the social scale, so that people who mixed with us yesterday no longer call us because they have become too important. The same is true of our own behavior—too often, we value people not so much because they are loyal, but because they are somebody.

Finally, we are separated from one another by *middle-class intangibles* —the trivia of personality that make us say, with a shrug or a grimace, "I don't know—there is something about Mary. . . . I can't put my finger on it, but I can't stand her any more. We used to be good friends, but she has a way. . . . I don't know whether it's what she says or the way she says it. . . . And then her husband . . . I remember when they were first married, he seemed such a nice man but now. . . . Maybe it's because of her. . . ." And so it goes; the reason for the break is never quite known, either to the person who breaks off or to the one who is dropped. We are a people committed to evanescence; it makes it easier to separate. But this impermanence of relationships also isolates us from one another. On the other hand, however, the ills that life brings are easier to bear when we are not alone—and thus, it comes about that so many women have so few people they can rely on, that when the phantasms of aging begin to gather, they must fight them alone, without an extended and protecting personal community.

I have mentioned the family structures of China and India, but I have only begun to discuss the advantages for adults in such families. China and India are parent-centered societies, while ours is child-cen-

2. I am aware that there are still some relatively stable enclaves even in industrial centers nowadays. Even these, however, lack the stability of tribal and most peasant societies.

tered. This difference is expressed beautifully in the *Twenty-Four Examples of Filial Piety*,[3] a book of lessons about family life studied by children in traditional China.

For example:

Tale IV
Resigns Post (to)[4] Seek Mother

When Chu Shou-chang . . . was seven years of age, his mother left the family and remarried because of the jealousy of her husband's other wife. Thereafter mother and son did not see each other for fifty years. At last . . . Chu Shou-chang gave up his official post . . . having sworn to his own family that he would not return unless he found his mother. (His) travels took him to the prefecture of Tungchou, and there he met his mother, who was then more than seventy years old.

Tale VII
Weeps (among) Bamboos (and) Sprouts Grow

In the kingdom of Wu lived Meng Tsung. His father had died when he was young, and his mother was aged and very sick. During the winter months she longed for soup made of bamboo sprouts, but Tsung found no way to obtain them. Then he went to a grove, where he embraced the bamboos and wept. His filial piety moved Heaven and Earth, and all of a sudden the ground burst open and a few sprouts sprang up. Bringing them home, he cooked a soup for his mother; and when she had eaten it she found herself *well*.

Tale XV
For Mother's Sake, (He) Buried (His) Son

Ko Chü . . . who was very poor, had a son three years of age. Ko Chü's mother (used to) cut down on her own food in order to provide more for her grandson. (At last Ko Chü) said to his wife: "We are so poor that we cannot (properly) support our mother. Furthermore, our son shares mother's

---

3. Mischa Titiev and Hsing-Chih Tien, eds., "A Primer of Filial Piety," *Papers of the Michigan Academy of Sciences, Arts and Letters* 33 (1947).

4. Elements in parentheses are not present in a literal translation from the Chinese and have been added by the editors to make good English.

---

food. Why not bury this son? We can have sons again, but never (another) mother." His wife did not dare to disobey.

One day Chü dug a hole more than three feet deep. Suddenly he saw a piece of yellow gold on which were inscribed characters reading: "Heaven sent this yellow gold to th filial son, Ko Chü. Let no official confiscate it, and let no citizen take it away from him."

It is clear that in the culture portrayed in these stories a mother did not suffer, as do many among us, from the loss of her mature children. Though these are but tales and represent unattainable ideals, they do express much of the essence of family life in old China—a parent-centered society.

Along with parent-centeredness went ancestor-centeredness, a devout and conforming attitude toward ancestors that so anchored the culture in the past that new generations differed little from old ones, and children, parents, grandparents, and departed ancestors had so much in common that the domestic cleavage and communication block we find between generations in our culture—a blockage that isolates parents from children and causes conflict—could not arise to separate the generations and make a mother feel lonely and cast aside. It is true that the parent-ancestor-centered society changed with great difficulty and that the personalities of family members were submerged by adherence to the family ideal, but we pay a toll in loneliness and conflict for our own individualistic type of family.

The emphasis on youth, beauty, and romantic love is a sustaining force in our economy. While it is ancient—having roots in the Judeo-Christian and Greek traditions[5]—this emphasis, amounting to an implied metaphysic, has reached unparalleled expansive significance in our economy, which must monetize everything in order to remain viable. Without the pecuniary exploitation of romantic love and female youth and beauty, the women's wear, cosmetics, and beauty-parlor industries would largely disappear and the movie, television, and phonograph-record businesses would, on the whole, cease to be economically functional, degenerating, perhaps, to the relative economic insignificance of education. It is true that women would still

---

5. While Abraham became a hero as an older man, subsequent heroes and heroines were mostly young: Jacob, Deborah, Benjamin, David, Moses, etc. Christ was yet a child when he confounded the priests; His disciples were young, and Christ was still young when He died on the cross. Only the miserable role of prophet seems to have been reserved for older men. The role of young and beautiful men in Plato is familiar.

need clothes to protect themselves from the elements and that civilization demands that they cover their bodies even in hot weather, but the billions spent on women's wear these days is more in the interest of making women attractive than in protecting them from the cold. Furthermore, without the erotic effects of the metaphysic of youth, beauty, and romantic love, cigarettes, hard and soft drinks, beer, automobiles, and so on, would not sell nearly so well. As a matter of fact, even men's wear and toiletries could not be marketed so efficiently without an adoring, pretty woman (well under thirty-five years of age) looking at a man wearing a stylish shirt or sniffing at a man wearing a deodorant.

While the saturation of the pecuniary media with the metaphysic of youth, beauty, and romantic love should not be attacked, lest the economy collapse—just as if we suddenly attacked the profit motive—and while the metaphysic speeds up courtship and the birth rate, thus adding further to expenditures and to the gross national product, obsession with youth, beauty, and romantic love punishes the woman who, having reached thirty-five, begins to see in the mirror the fact that the metaphysic and its implied defenses no longer exist for her. We have a metaphysic for beauty and youth but none for the years when these are gone. In this sense, the West is probably unique; for while throughout history, culture has provided a set of principles for guidance through every stage of life, in the contemporary West, aging hangs in nothingness. For many a woman of thirty-five and beyond, therefore, it is as if the universe had physically withdrawn and left her hurtling into nothingness. And thus, deprived of the youth, beauty, and romantic love which once made them feel safe, many women feel they have no place to go but down.

Since a metaphysic is a system of first principles underlying a subject of inquiry, since our subject of inquiry is urban woman, and since she is without a metaphysic after forty, we are bound to state what the metaphysic was in the first place. It should be mentioned, in passing, that it is not necessary that a metaphysic be "true," for it can just as well be a system of principles supporting a false position—and the history of thought has shown that this is usually the case.

The metaphysic of which I speak embodies the following principles: (1) A man validates himself by working and supporting, a woman validates herself by getting a man. (2) A man does, a woman is. Man performs, woman attracts. Behind this principle lies the fact that urban woman has lost most of her productive economic functions; and even when she does productive labor, the money she earns is used largely to expand the family's life style, rather than to create fundamental conditions for living. (3) Existence must be made aesthetically pleasing. (4) Since man's province is that of action, it is up to the woman to make life aesthetically attractive to him and to display his masculinity by being attractive. (5) From all this it follows that women must be beautiful. (6) Since beauty is by definition physical and since the body loses its freshness even before the end of the childbearing years, a woman is in danger of losing her husband in this period. To these principles, deriving from the metaphysic of youth and beauty, add the following from romantic love: (7) Since in our culture, marriage is not arranged by parents and the spouse is not determined by highly specific social rules, every woman must find and attract a husband for herself. Often, in traditional peasant China, a girl did not even see her husband before the wedding day, for the marriage was arranged by the parents. In many tribal cultures, on the other hand, a girl's husband is selected for her even before birth, because she has to marry a specific person according to rules prescribed by tradition. (8) Romantic love is based on obsession with the beloved to the exclusion of all others, and it requires the idealization of the object. It is clear, meanwhile, that grand obsession and idealization can rarely withstand the rigors of marriage. It follows from principles (7) and (8) that, as youth and beauty wane and as the realities of marriage erode obsession and idealization, urban woman in our culture is bound to become uneasy, for what once seemed to protect her from nothingness seems to be going away.

To summarize, in a somewhat oversimplified way: as long as a woman has little to offer other than her physical person, love as obsession and idealization will fade as she gets old and as the daily collisions of marriage make living together difficult or merely routine.

Since in our urban culture, marriage is not consolidated through cooperative work but through a complicated hallucination of intangibles based on obsession and idealization, the loss of youth and beauty may appear to threaten a woman whose youth and beauty are passing. Meanwhile, since she probably knows many cases in which an older man has deserted his wife for a younger and more attractive woman, a wife cannot but ask, "When will it happen to me?"

I have pointed out that historically, society has swung between two extreme types of parent-child relations—parent-centered and child-centered. It may seem a paradox that in parent-centered societies children are more valued than in child-centered ones, but a moment's reflection shows that, far from being a paradox, such a high valuation of children is a necessary consequence of a parent-centered society. In parent-centered societies, the child is bound to support his parents—never to desert them; and this bond is partly a rigid economic one, for children, especially sons, must provide for parents. Hence, it would be folly, besides being shameful, for a father to desert his children. The economic obligation, however, is reinforced by the requirement that the sons perform the ceremonies necessary for the tranquil and comfortable existence of the father's soul in the next world—double reason for never deserting the children. In a child-centered culture, the only thing binding parents and children is the vulnerable love relationship. If a father who wants a new love affair decides he does not need his children's love, there is nothing other than legalities to keep him home. Thus, when the youth and beauty of his wife have faded, the attractions of a new and younger love may overwhelm a man's attachment to his children, because they are not a necessary condition of his existence here and in the hereafter.

This brings us to the problems of the husband.

So far, I have considered only the woman's vulnerability; but her vulnerability has to be considered in relation to her husband's. There are many factors in a man's life at the age of forty that make him anxious and may cause him to turn to a young and pretty woman for comfort and reassurance; so that just as the vulnerability system is making his wife fearful, it is pressing her husband so hard that the very circumstance she fears may indeed hasten upon her. We know, for example, that in the man's occupational world, emphasis is on the young and "coming," so that a man of forty may be looking anxiously over his shoulder at the wolf pack yapping and slobbering at his heels as he slips along over competitive business ice. At forty, the status of many a man, whether in business or on the assembly line, is frozen, so he feels stuck and fearful. So also, especially if he is in one of the "creative" professions, he may feel that his powers are lessening. Hence, driven by anxieties, he may turn to a young and pretty woman for reassurance; and she, in turn, gives him a feeling that he is not lost after all, he is not as weak as he thinks. She will, he feels, give him new creative powers, because her sex interest proves that he is not dead wood. It is a commonplace that sex narcotizes anxiety; and when numerous illusions dress it up, it can seem to be *the* solution to all a man's problems.

There is also the special illusion that appears under the slogan, "Life is to be lived." For the man who does not find satisfaction in his work, who has done what he had to do, rather than what he wanted to do, or whose life work has turned out to be not quite what he thought it was, or whose inherent feelings of nothingness are too great for any work to defeat—for any such man, the cure to his lifelong disorder may seem to be the young and beautiful woman. The tragedy is that just when his wife needs him most, a man's own tragedy may leave him with less and less to give her.

Yet, even the successful man may intensify his wife's anxiety, for as he drives himself in his business and career and as these continue to make enormous demands on his time and energy, his absorption may seem to confirm his wife's worst anxieties. Interpreting his preoccupation as a turning away from her, she may become a nag or importune him when he is involved in other things, and this starts a vicious cycle—for the more she protests that he does not love her and the more she importunes when his mind is on his affairs, the more irritated he may become, with consequent mutual withdrawal and an increase in the wife's anxiety.

As the children grow up, they not only don't need their mother as much as they used to, they may positively resent her intervention in their lives—except, of course, when she intervenes on their side to persuade the father to consent to something.[6] Recently, I saw the following on television: Mrs. Jones has bought Dotty a low-cut formal as a present for her thirteenth birthday, and Dotty has gotten a date with a boy who is going to take her dancing to a really swank hotel. High heels and lipstick enhance the formal. Then Daddy, who has been away on a trip, comes home and is outraged by the whole idea—low-cut dress, lipstick, heels—and the swank hotel. He is defeated in the ensuing argument because his wife sides with Dotty. Just before I turned out, Daddy had fallen asleep in the living room and had a dream in which Dotty is a call girl and he is beaten up by her pimp. This skit expresses a great deal about American family life, but what is particularly important for our present interest is Mrs. Jones's "late

6. Some of the problems raised here have been anticipated and discussed by Betty Friedan in *The Feminine Mystique* (New York: Norton, 1963), especially in chapter 14.

maternal function"—for she now attempts to bind her daughter to her by taking sides with her against the father. Obviously, Mrs. Jones, who is clearly at the dangerous age, can only intensify her problems with her husband as she tries to find a new way of establishing herself with a daughter who no longer needs her the way she did five years ago.

Our contemporary small families no longer require long-range exercise of simple maternal functions, for the few children soon learn to take care of themselves. This leaves the mother with nothing to do in the family but meddle in her children's lives. This, in turn, is related to two things. In the first place, it is no longer chic to continue having children after you have passed thirty-five. Such fertility may make the neighbors wonder whether Mrs. So-and-so "doesn't know when to stop." The notion of "meddling" in children's lives is, in turn, related to permissive attitudes toward children, to the freeing of the sexual impulses, to the increase in allowances for fun expenditures, to the idea that parents and children are equals—so that mother and father are now more like older sister and brother—and to the children's discovery that they can undermine parental authority by ganging up under the slogan, "Mary Smith's mother lets her do it, why don't you let me do it?" In this way, children have snatched power from parental hands; and instead of children fearing loss of parental love, urban American parents fear loss of their children's. Children can gang up on parents simply because they are united in the peer group while parents are disunited—among neighbors and within families.

What drives the message home is the fact that the mobilization of the adolescent cohorts occurs just when the mother is worried that, because she is past her peak, her husband won't love her. What makes her anxiety worse is her knowledge that giving in because she fears the anger of her adolescent children may alienate her husband—if she lets the children have their way over her husband's objections, he may not forgive her—especially if the consequences are serious. The fundamental issue is that just as the urban woman becomes more dependent on her husband, she is beginning to collide with her adolescent children. At the present time, we are, perhaps, witnessing an intensification of these problems, because early marriage and the early cessation of childbearing leave a woman without maternal functions even sooner than before.

I am under the impression that, even nowadays, menopause may symbolize to many women that they have somehow ceased to be women. When I was a child involutional melancholia was viewed by the medical profession as a predictable consequence of the physiology of menopause. Surely, if such depression is related to menopause, it must be largely in a symbolic sense, rather than a hormonal one. Menopause must mean to such women that, since they are no longer good for children, they are good for nothing; and surely, to them, menopause must be more of a symbolic than a physiologic decline. A central issue is the overvaluation of fertility—so many women have not been trained for anything else, they have been given no other goal than home and children. Of equal importance is their feeling that, having reached menopause, they will go rapidly downhill, losing all attractiveness.

The process through which a woman gives up early ambitions for marriage has been mentioned by Betty Friedan in *The Feminine Mystique*. Duty to her womanhood, a real desire for a home and children, fear that she will never be able to realize career dreams, and even a desire to be taken care of because, fundamentally, she fears life—all make their contribution to that complex sensation of love, guilt, yearning, and anxiety with which many women enter marriage. At any rate, however complex her feelings may be, many a woman gets married with the idea that some day, after her children no longer need her, she will return to her original hopes for herself. As the years pass, however, and as one child follows upon another, with all the hardship that raising a family and coping with her husband involve, it becomes ever clearer to her that the early ambition will never be realized. This loss of hope contributes to her misery.

Everything is made worse by the fact that women are given no training in keeping the Self alive. Quite the contrary, woman in our culture is trained in renunciation; it is her destiny to give up—to give up for her husband and to give up for her children. All the lovingly acquired knowledge of the French Renaissance poets disappears easily in fifteen years, and the hands that held a violin bow or paint brush may have lost their elasticity in the endless round of household chores. The deadliest influence of all is to have married a troglodyte, for however loving he may be, a dull husband is poison to the intellect. Thus, the woman wakes up one day to discover that she has made no preparation for later life, she has not kept her gifts alive—and nobody has insisted that she ought to. All of this is happening while her children grow up and no longer need her and her husband is having his own forty-year-old jitters.

Betty Friedan's examination of the lives and hopes of college-educated women over forty is heavily weighted in favor of the women with special talents and job desires, and thus overlooks the mass of women who lack both, but who find, during the later years, that simply taking care of the house and engaging in voluntary work—the most easily available work after thirty-five—is not satisfying.

Much of the work a homemaker can do outside the home is voluntary and unpaid, and this is precisely the work that women interviewed by Friedan end up despising. There are two kinds of work: egoistic work, which one enjoys because it gives deep satisfaction or because one gets paid; and work oriented toward others and motivated by the desire to help them. Activities available to untrained women, even though they be college graduates, are mostly of the latter kind. Friedan's women—and perhaps most women—belittle work on local committees, on the PTA, and so on, while yearning for careers in egoistic activities. The problem here is that, except for top-level jobs, our culture has never valued public-oriented work. Just as we readily spend on egoistic consumption—on things that contribute directly to pleasure and comfort—and are stingy about spending for public benefits, so we are contemptuous of work not immediately gratifying to the self-image, even though the gratification is merely in being paid. So it is that a trivial job for which a woman is paid, even though she does not need the money, seems more rewarding than a public-oriented job for which she receives no pay. Since industry needs paid labor and people who will spend their pay on what industry produces, we have been taught that significant work is egoistic work and that public service is, on the whole, contemptible and is mostly for people who could not make it any other way; and all our lives we have been told that what counts is money income. It is absurd to expect women to derive a sense of fulfillment from a job that is public oriented and unpaid.

One possible solution to the problem is to emphasize public service in college courses and to make some public service obligatory for all students. An even better answer would be to pay people for doing the jobs that are now voluntary. This, however, requires greater public willingness to spend on public services. In a large hospital in my town, the coffee shop is run largely by upper-middle-class women volunteers. It is true that this saves the hospital money, but it is also true that if people were not so stingy with money that might go to the hospital, the women would be paid. But this, in turn, would deprive those who really need the jobs. The solution is, expanded federal subsidies to hospitals.

The predicament of the woman over forty is the product of a culture that provides her with no defenses as she grows older. Or put another way, the illusions and the realities that stabilized her through earlier years are swept away. Such a state of affairs owes its existence to the economy and to the flight of philosophy from life. Throughout history, philosophy has not examined the nature of folk metaphysics because philosophy has rejected "the many." The analytical capabilities of philosophy must be brought to bear on folk metaphysics.

"Forty-year-old jitters" are the result of the imposition of the primordial image of the big-bellied, heavy-breasted, fat-hipped figure of the Palaeolithic caves on contemporary life. This image, basically unchanged, except for slimming and uplifting features introduced by modern cosmetic technology, still dominates thinking about women. Nowadays, however, there is much more for her to do than those activities represented by the caves, and even her vast reproductive capabilities are obsolescent. In the Old Stone Age, when the race needed women who could reproduce frequently in order to overcome the high death rate of infants; when it was multiply or perish, when survival of species and tribe was determined by the fact that, when two biological forms live in the same habitat and use the environment in the same way, the form that reproduces faster will win; when a man lost the next world as well as this one if he had no children—when man existed under these conditions, high fertility was important, as were other primordial maternal functions. This past has been preserved in altered form in the folk ideology that binds the modern housewife, making her vulnerable to forty-year-old jitters—the disease of modernity and urbanism.

When children meant hands to work the field, sons to track and kill animals, destroy the enemy, and carry on the ancestor cult; when daughters were for house and field and to sell off to buy wives for sons; and when all was threatened by a high infant mortality, reproductive capability was vital. And when occupations were few, it made sense to keep woman bound to her functions in house and field. But nowadays, occupational possibilities for women have increased more than a thousand-fold [7] and the necessary qualifications are diverse enough to suit every woman.

7. The latest census gives 296 occupations, each divided into so many subsidiary ones

It is useless to attack this position on the grounds that, since our society is running out of jobs for men because of automation, anything that gets women out of traditional roles will contribute to a masculine employment crisis. In the first place, in this country we misuse automation, for instead of using the increased productivity resulting from it to lower prices and expand consumption, and hence production and employment, it is being employed to displace workers, while much of the savings made possible by the new techniques are distributed in profits. This has always been the case when new technology has been invented, and it usually takes a century and terrifying depressions to alter the situation. In the second place, government does not adequately subsidize labor. Since the government subsidizes the armaments industry, air transportation, agriculture, and shipping, among other industries; since it has given great subsidies to the railroads through land grants; since it subsidizes oil through generous depletion allowances, and so on, government subsidy for labor is long overdue. For over a century, government subsidy to industry has been a commonplace, but labor has been subsidized only in times of dire need—when, indeed, it was absolutely necessary in order to renew purchasing power, as an indirect subsidy to industry. Subsidies to labor must become as much a matter of course as subsidies to industry. Thus, we must not be bamboozled by "the specter of automation," for it becomes manageable when viewed against the background of all economic possibilities, including the gigantic powers of government.

The simple fact is that an exclusively private-enterprise economy is no longer able to use all of our human potentialities. The paradox inheres in the fact that private enterprise, while liberating many creative powers in man and woman, often leaves them unused, because unilateral adherence to the profit motive creates unemployment and dead-end jobs. Meanwhile, again paradoxically, as Friedan points out, the unused potential of women is ploughed back into industrial profits through advertising's plugging "creative housekeeping."

Nowadays, the woman of forty is a casualty of the metaphysics of youth, beauty, and romantic love, and of a conception of woman's functions having roots in the Stone Age. Until the beginning of the

---

that there are thousands; see the 1960 *Census of Population, Alphabetical Index of Occupations and Industries* (revised), U.S. Department of Commerce, Bureau of the Census.

---

twentieth century, we were filling up a vast country, and children and mothers died early because of poor sanitation, ignorance, and hard work. Meanwhile, however, industry has pumped humanity out of all of Europe to man our new industrial machine—even sending recruiters abroad and combining with steamship companies to stimulate the poor of Europe to come to America, land of promise. We do not need fast increase of population any more. Furthermore, the concept of work has shifted from survival through work to satisfaction in work. Along with this change must go the question about woman's role in the home: is it necessary for the survival of the family, or is it necessary for her satisfaction as a woman? Such considerations, examined by Betty Friedan, are inseparable from the problem of forty-year-old jitters.

Why does psychoanalysis cling to the idea that housewifely dissatisfaction is an expression of "rejection of the feminine role"? In the first place, most psychoanalysts are like everybody else—they are nice people trying to get along. Why should they question outworn ideas they learned in school? In the second place, the woman who is miserable because her family role no longer gives her satisfaction looks to them like a kind of delinquent, for she has stepped out of line, just like a kid who smokes marijuana. Furthermore, every dissatisfied and jittery wife could be the analyst's wife: how would *he* feel if when *he* came home, everything was not shipshape—as must often be the case when a wife has outside interests? Fighting the housewife patient who wants to get out of the house, therefore, has a certain virtuous puritanism about it; but the psychoanalytic belief in the metaphysical necessity of the stereotypic feminine role inevitably collides with the destructive consequences for the woman of forty of the metaphysic of youth, beauty, and romantic love and with the real opportunities of urban life, particularly for college women. Yet, on the other hand, what would happen to our economy if the metaphysic of youth, beauty, and romantic love were to vanish? Building airships to carry two thousand people or even crisscrossing all of Central America with canals would not save us. Thus has psychoanalysts' conservatism become a bulwark of the economy. In their own way, they are as necessary to it as the engineers.

To avoid forty-year-old jitters, middle-class women must be trained for later life—for the time when their children no longer need them; and they must not be permitted to forget that, as children grow to puberty in contemporary America, the maternal function has little reward and that guidance is resented by the children they have liberated by their permissiveness. At all stages, suitable educational materials must be provided women so their minds will not go to pot. It is striking that, while even the cereal-and-toy-vending television programs for little children are interlarded here and there with educational bits, daytime programs for housewives are strictly at the visceral level. Educational daytime shows for those soon to become victims of the youth-beauty-romantic-love-metaphysic, however, would sell more hair spray, bath oil, cake mixes, bacon, shortening, refrigerators, and so on, than a dozen *Peyton Places*, because they would not be nearly so depressing. Women ought to be acquainted with their predicament and coached on how to get out of it. Back-to-school programs for women are very good, but as a college teacher, I know that some who come back at forty do not have much of a brain anymore. On the other hand, how many thousands who might like to come back do we never see at all, because their minds have lost elasticity during twenty years of marriage?

The forty-year-old wife of the blue-collar worker is probably no different.[8]

In closing, I return to involutional melancholia. It is not biology, but the lifelong cumulative effects of a punitive and uncomprehending environment impinging on the vulnerabilities of aging that cause this disease. Yet, the victims themselves are part of its causation, because so many of them believe that all they should have to offer is youth, beauty, romantic love, and children, and because many of them have entered marriage as an escape from taking responsibility for themselves.

---

8. Claude C. Bowman, "Mental Health in the Worker's World," in *Blue Collar World*, ed. Arthur B. Shostak and William Gomberg (New York: Prentice-Hall, 1964), p. 374.

34

A GOOD WOMAN IS HARD TO FIND

ALICE S. ROSSI

In the 1960s the word "reentry" has very special connotations. It evokes an image of the critical stage during space flight when a capsule reestablishes contact with the earth's atmosphere. Reentry is a stage of considerable tension, with some unforeseeable problems, and the astronaut can breathe more easily once it is accomplished.

American women, too, have a period of reentry in their lives. Some women leave the job market when they marry, and most women leave when they start to raise a family; their reentry period is the time when they are taking the first steps toward rejoining the occupational world. For them, too, this period is filled with tensions and unpredictable problems.

I have experienced a "woman's reentry" twice: once when I returned to college after a four-year absence during World War II, and a second time, when I returned to teach sociology on a part-time basis after several years of childbearing and rearing. What I have to say here is drawn predominantly from social science research on sex roles, tempered by the experiences I have had before and since my most recent reentry. I am concerned here with the effects of employment on women who deliberately choose to work. The impact of employment which is forced on women by economic pressure is probably quite different. A number of the studies I shall cite on the effects of employment on women and on their families demonstrate that this factor of choice is crucial.

Because for most women it is at the very heart of the matter, I want to begin by considering the effect on children when mother returns to work. There is a widespread belief in our society that children suffer when they are not cared for, full time, by their own mothers. Social science research does *not* support this belief. Much of the research on maternal employment and its effects on marriage, children, and working mothers themselves has been gathered together in *The Employed*

Mother in America, published by Rand, McNally and Co. in 1963. The authors, F. Ivan Nye and Lois Wladis Hoffman, are both sociologists particularly interested in the study of family life. The essential finding of all the studies on children they report is that the children of working mothers are not different, in any significant way, from the children of mothers who stay at home.

My husband has coined the phrase, the "fire-department ideology of child rearing" to describe this quality of contemporary middle-class motherhood—the view that a mother should be available to her children ten hours a day, on the chance that the child may need or want her help for one of the ten hours. With the shrinking and simplification of home maintenance tasks, many American women have expanded and elaborated the maternal role to make it a full-time job. The result is not good mothering, but a kind of smothering that can develop excessive dependency between mother and child. The results of this process can be seen in a variety of ways. No society has as widespread a tendency toward adolescent rebellion as the United States. Young people *have* to rebel because there are so many strings to sever, and it is painful for both the parent and the child. Counselors report that a major task in helping college students is the loosening of excessively dependent ties to their parents, particularly their mothers. Girls are not ready to live independent lives when they complete their education, but plunge into ever-younger marriages, seeking to live through their husbands, and later through their children, and thus perpetuating the cycle from one generation to the next.

If we truly believe that the adult is what the child was, and if we consider self-assertion, independence, and responsibility to be desirable traits in adults, then children should be reared to facilitate the development of these qualities. One of the best ways of doing this is for the mother to be a living model of these qualities herself. When mothers add the role of student or employed woman to their roster of social roles, they enrich the conception their children have of an adult woman's role. As "fire-department mothering" is curtailed the child's opportunities for privacy and experience in doing, thinking, and worrying through things for himself will increase.

There is support in social research for the idea that a mother's employment creates a model of active, independent womanhood for her children. Social psychologist Elizabeth Douvan, working from interview data drawn on a nationwide sample, has shown that the teen-age daughters of women who work because they choose to are active in many groups, well adjusted to their families, relatively autonomous in decision making. These girls feel close to their families, but are not emotionally dependent on them. They choose their mothers as models of the women they would like to be. Several other researchers have replicated Douvan's finding that children are more likely to choose their mothers as models when mother works. Several studies of styles of child rearing have shown that professionally active mothers stress independence training, while stay-at-home mothers emphasize protection and emotional security as the important elements of mothering.

In this view, the question of "how old should my child be before I return to school or work" receives a new answer. I would say "the younger the better." For one thing, it is much easier to *establish* a pattern consistent with the goal of the kind of adult one wishes the child to become than it is to *change* a pattern once established. Second, children develop an idea of what is "appropriate" for each sex at a very early age. For a young boy or girl, seeing their mother not only cooking, cleaning, chatting with neighbors, sewing, or gardening, but also studying, keeping appointments, being excited by ideas, holding down a job, provides an invaluable background upon which to build their own lives. This experience could free them from many of the doubts and conflicts we in our generation have experienced and are surmounting only with considerable pain.

So much of the negative has been stressed in the literature on women and sex roles, that I want to counteract it by placing a strong emphasis on the positive side. I believe that marriage can be strengthened and enriched by a wife's return to study and work.

Many sociologists and counselors have claimed that the American marital relationship is so fragile a thing that it cannot withstand the added strain of occupational competition between husband and wife. Able young women students with high abilities and genuine interests have restricted their occupational choices while they were in college, believing that a professional career would restrict their chances to make a good marriage. This notion persists, despite several studies which found *no* difference in marital satisfaction between marriage where the wife works and marriage where the wife stays home.

Competing for the Children

Professional competition between spouses can be avoided by goal restrictions, but it may be replaced by a quite invidious competition of another sort entirely. An able and alert woman must have some scope for the development and expression of a sense of her own self-worth. When she does not have an occupational outlet for this she may seek it in the management of her home and in the lives of her children. Since home and the children constitute her major sphere, she is often under psychological pressure to keep her husband out of these spheres, or prevent his being an equal partner in the more creative aspects of home management and child rearing. He may do the dirty work in the house and garden, or bring his wife the thermometer for her to minister to a sick child at night, but be excluded from the opportunity to become a child's intimate comforter. The husband-father is thus subtly urged into a subordinate role as mother's helper, the father who does *not* know best. When a woman warns her children to "behave when Daddy gets home" because he will be "tired," what appears on the surface to be solicitude for her husband's comfort and relaxation may communicate to the child an image of father as a fragile person who needs rest and care the same way the child does. The father is symbolically relegated to the subordinate position of the child in the family structure, and the mother reigns supreme in the socioemotional atmosphere of the home. If a woman's job provides her with a sense of self-worth away from home, both she and her husband may find a subtle shift in the balance of feeling in the family, a shift which is quite surely a gain from the point of view of her family.

Many American men and women begin married life as companionable equals but soon begin to go their separate ways, with less and less real conversation between them. Once parental roles are assumed, their daily lives become sharply different in content and style. A wife's return to work can bring a return at a more mature level of the kind of interchange experienced early in marriage. Competition need not be a problem for several reasons:

— If your view of marriage is a partnership of two people looking outward to a wide and exciting world in which a lot of jobs need doing well, the working wife and her husband can feel they are both participating in this exciting venture of contributing to the larger society.

— It takes two to compete, and many if not most working wives find such primary gratification in their marital and maternal roles that competition does not loom very large in the motivational complex they bring to bear upon their work situation.

— Competition implies a seeking for the same rewards or positions sought by another; it is rarely the case that a husband and wife seek the same rewards in the same part of the occupational world. In this sense they may be far more competitive for the love of their children than they are for the rewards of the job world.

Even when, as in my own personal case, the professional wife is working in the same field as her husband, a "field" of work is big enough to include many dissimilar career paths, making assessment of relative success a difficult thing. In addition, an important consequence of a woman's withdrawal from her career field for child-rearing purposes is that she reenters her field at a stage in which comparison is more appropriate with younger men than her husband, again reducing the objective grounds for considering her husband a competitor. As a result, the active involvement of a wife even in the same field as her husband, is more apt to add spice and zest to the marriage than it is to create competitive feelings and marital difficulties.

Satisfaction in Moving Up

A woman returning to work should not set as her goal a job or occupation which is beneath her talents. The more a woman works toward a position that really challenges and utilizes her growing skills, the greater will be the intrinsic satisfactions she derives from the work itself, and the larger will be her paycheck. This is not customary advice in many quarters. One article in a Chicago paper recently urged older women to stay away from the labor force unless they were willing to work for *less* money than men doing the same job, unless they were sure they did *not* want to be supervisors or bosses, and were willing to be the first ones laid off when and if economic conditions required. Most of us today would be shocked to read the same kind of advice openly offered to Negroes seeking employment, for there is an ideology which presses for fuller and more equal participation of Negroes in our occupational system. But most readers of the Chicago article probably reacted to these words of advice to women as a "realistic" statement of the "hard fact" that women have been expendable Girl Fridays in the job world.

There is evidence to support my contention that a mother's employment will be most successful if her job is a *high-level* one. The Douvan study cited earlier and a study by Lois Hoffman on the effects of maternal employment on children both indicate that women who like their work have a better relationship with their children than women who work from economic necessity. Ivan Nye's study of two thousand working mothers showed that employed women were generally more satisfied with life than nonemployed women, and that this relationship was strongest for the best-educated women. Although his study had shown some evidence that marital discord is associated with wives working, these differences almost disappeared in the higher educational and occupational categories. Nye interprets this finding as showing that the increased satisfactions of high level work compensate for any disruptive effects that working has on marriage. Nye's finding that *older* employed women were *less* satisfied with life is also traceable to educational factors. The older employed women in his sample had less education and worked at lower status jobs than the young women.

I stress seeking a high-level job because a woman who is truly absorbed in her work is less likely to feel in conflict about the cross-pressures of job and home. A woman with a deep commitment to the worth and significance of her job is less likely to feel she must attend personally to every small domestic crisis. She finds it easier to say no to requests to participate in organizations which would spread her energies too thin. To the extent that her individual performance as an employed married woman is of a high order of competence, she will contribute in the most meaningful way to easing the acceptance of her daughter's generation at all occupational levels.

Furthermore, the higher the job level, the greater is the flexibility possible in the allocation of time. This is something of very special importance to women who carry home *and* work responsibilities: there *are* emergencies at home, and there may be other community obligations and interests to continue along with paid employment. A secretary working full- or even part-time must work steadily through a day of rather rigidly set hours; if she leaves to attend a meeting or care for a convalescent child, she is apt to be docked for the time away from the job. In many organizations, however, her boss may take a whole afternoon to speak to a local business or professional club, spend two or more hours over lunch with a client, shop for a new suit, or work out at the gym, with no loss to the salary he takes home. The criteria that are important to his success, and to the salary he brings home each month, are geared to the quality of the work he produces, and only secondarily to his presence during set hours of a day. His most productive hours may be between nine and eleven at night, or five and seven in the morning, and nobody could care less, so long as he is doing the job well. To be able to manipulate her working hours freely is a very great asset to a woman holding a job, rearing children, and homemaking.

The Dirty-work Stereotype

A second point I would like to discuss concerning the choice of an occupational goal is the actual content of a possible job, as opposed to its stereotypic images. A very good illustration of what I mean can be seen in the case of engineering. An outsider's image of an engineer is often of a rough-and-ready, highly masculine individual working amid noise and dirt, supervising a crew of workmen. That many women have this image, I know from preliminary findings of research on why women do not choose engineering as a career field: they consider it "unfeminine" and "dirty." In our time, however, the engineer is far more apt to be found in a pleasant air-conditioned office, and his job is no more physically taxing than such familiar women's jobs as a teacher of physical education or physical therapist. I think all American women would be eternally grateful to the women who, hopefully, would train for and hold down industrial design jobs in companies manufacturing the things we use in our everyday life. It may await a woman, for example, to design a refrigerator that not only defrosts automatically, but that is easy to *clean* inside.

Women's education is generally a "pay-as-you-go" proposition. Young women of college age do not take out loans for their schooling as young men often do. If by working, and with her father's help, a girl can't pay for her education, she doesn't get it. Both she and her father

---

are hesitant to saddle some future "unknown" husband with repayment of such a loan. Women are not considered to have "futures" as men have in this regard.

But where education at a later age is concerned, it seems to me to be highly inappropriate to apply the same reasoning. For married women with homes, husbands, and families, the odds are extremely high that any education completed will be followed by employment. We don't hesitate to spend now what we will earn later in the case of a home purchase, and the same may apply to women's education during their adult years.

I have left to the last the question of social opinion toward women's return to school and work. I say "social opinion" rather than "public opinion," because I believe women are attuned to the opinion of others in their immediate social world much more than they are to an impersonal public "out there" in the community.

Research on sex differences has repeatedly shown that women are more sensitive and responsive to the groups within which they move than men are. One has only to look at the differences in the way boys and girls are reared to see some of the seeds of this sex difference. Girls are expected and encouraged to spend more time with their families than boys are. Independence and exploration are encouraged in boys to a greater extent than in girls.

This also means it is generally more difficult for a woman than a man to depart from a group norm. A published book, a significant painting, a scientific breakthrough, a diagnosis of a family in trouble, are all the products of many lonely hours of thought. Since creativity in any field is a lonely endeavor, it may be that this is why women have tended to create less than men do. In a university, for example, women professors are tempted to give great quantities of their time to students instead of closing themselves in their studies and creating something new in their field. Creativity takes time, *uninterrupted time,* and it is precisely this which girls in our society are seldom socialized to have, and as adult women, seldom able to secure. Look at the very design of a modern house, and you can see how little privacy a woman is assumed to want. Her territory of the kitchen has been invaded by making it an extension of a family room. Her desk is highly visible in a kitchen corner or is a decorative living room piece, though there is often a den or study for the husband. As mother, wife, and friend, a woman is expected to be instantly available.

HQ
535
P47

19,844

CAMROSE LUTHERAN COLLEGE
LIBRARY

Because most women are not the major breadwinner, they are in a far more luxurious position than most men when it comes to seeking employment. Women can afford to wait, to say no to a job offer, to hold out for one which is closer to their abilities and expectations. Women *can* do this if they curb the tendency to be grateful for any job offer, an easy temptation for an older woman who has not been employed for some years. This may take some courage and self-assertion, but if more personnel offices had the experience of being rejected by older women there is a chance that women's salaries would spiral upward and approximate those of men doing comparable work.